The Red and the Black

MANCHESTER
1824

Manchester University Press

Racism, Resistance and Social Change

The Red and the Black

The Russian Revolution and the Black Atlantic

Edited by

David Featherstone and
Christian Høgsbjerg

MANCHESTER UNIVERSITY PRESS

Published by Manchester University Press
Oxford Road, Manchester M1 9PL

www.manchesteruniversitypress.co.uk

British Library Cataloguing-in-Publication Data
A catalogue record for this book is available from the British Library

ISBN 978 1 5261 4430 0 hardback
ISBN 978 1 5261 6698 2 paperback

First published 2021
Paperback published 2022

The publisher has no responsibility for the persistence or accuracy of URLs for any external or third-party internet websites referred to in this book, and does not guarantee that any content on such websites is, or will remain, accurate or appropriate.

Typeset by
Servis Filmsetting Ltd, Stockport, Cheshire

Series editors' foreword

Series editors: John Solomos, Satnam Virdee, Aaron Winter

The study of race, racism and ethnicity has expanded greatly since the end of the twentieth century. This expansion has coincided with a growing awareness of the continuing role that these issues play in contemporary societies all over the globe. *Racism, Resistance and Social Change* is a new series of books that seeks to make a substantial contribution to this flourishing field of scholarship and research. We are committed to providing a forum for the publication of the highest quality scholarship on race, racism, anti-racism and ethnic relations. As editors of this series we would like to publish both theoretically driven books and texts with an empirical frame that seek to further develop our understanding of the origins, development and contemporary forms of racisms, racial inequalities and racial and ethnic relations. We welcome work from a range of theoretical and political perspectives, and as the series develops we ideally want to encourage a conversation that goes beyond specific national or geopolitical environments. While we are aware that there are important differences between national and regional research traditions, we hope that scholars from a variety of disciplines and multidisciplinary frames will take the opportunity to include their research work in the series.

As the title of the series highlights, we also welcome texts that can address issues about resistance and anti-racism as well as the role of political and policy interventions in this rapidly evolving discipline. The changing forms of racist mobilisation and expression that have come to the fore in recent years have highlighted the need for more reflection and research on the role of political and civil society mobilisations in this field.

We are committed to building on theoretical advances by providing an arena for new and challenging theoretical and empirical studies on the changing morphology of race and racism in contemporary societies.

Contents

Part III Africa, the Soviet Union and the Cold War

Figures

Contributors

Cathy Bergin lectures in the Humanities Programme at the University of Brighton. She has published on the relationship between African Americans and Communism in the US between the wars, in *'Bitter with the Past, But Sweet with the Dream': Communism in the African American Imaginary* (Brill, 2015). In collaboration with Anita Rupprecht, she has edited a special issue of *Race & Class* on the theme of Reparative History published in January 2016. Her current research focuses on African American anti-colonial thought and traces the complex formations of internationalism which proliferate in the black radical press of the 1920s and 1930s. Her book *African American Anti-Colonial Thought 1917–1937* (Edinburgh University Press, 2016) republishes key texts produced by African American anti-colonial activists.

Matheus Cardoso-da-Silva (PhD, University of São Paulo), is a postdoctoral fellow in the Department of History, State University of São Paulo and Fundação de Amparo à Pesquisa do Estado de São Paulo (FAPESP). He is currently working on a book about the coverage of Left Book Clubs on imperialism and anti-colonialism and their influence on the circulation of ideas inside the British Empire.

David Featherstone is Reader in Human Geography at the University of Glasgow. He is the author of *Resistance, Space and Political Identities: The Making of Counter-Global Networks* (Wiley-Blackwell, 2008) and *Solidarity: Hidden Histories and Geographies of Internationalism* (Zed Books, 2012). He is currently working on a monograph with the provisional title of *Politicising Race and Labour: Seafarers' Struggles for Equality and the Anti-Colonial Left, 1919–1953*. He is a member of the editorial collectives of *Antipode: A Radical Journal of Geography* and *Soundings: A Journal of Politics and Culture*.

Christian Høgsbjerg is a lecturer in Critical History and Politics in the School of Humanities at the University of Brighton. He is the author of

C.L.R. James in Imperial Britain (Duke University Press, 2014) and *Chris Braithwaite: Mariner, Renegade and Castaway* (Redwords, 2014), and has also edited and co-edited several volumes for the C.L.R. James Archives series with Duke University Press, including *The Black Jacobins Reader* (2017) and a special edition of James's 1937 work *World Revolution, 1917–1936: The Rise and Fall of the Communist International* (2017).

Winston James is Professor of History at the University of California, Irvine. His publications include *Inside Babylon: The Caribbean Diaspora in Britain* (Verso Books, 1993, edited with Clive Harris), *Holding Aloft the Banner of Ethiopia: Caribbean Radicalism in Early Twentieth-Century America* (Verso Books, 1998), which won the Gordon K. Lewis Memorial Award for Caribbean Scholarship of the Caribbean Studies Association, *A Fierce Hatred of Injustice: Claude McKay's Jamaica and his Poetry of Rebellion* (Verso Books, 2000), and *The Struggles of John Brown Russwurm: The Life and Writings of a Pan-Africanist Pioneer, 1799–1851* (New York University Press, 2010). His current projects include a two-volume study of Claude McKay, the first of which, *Claude McKay: The Making of a Black Bolshevik*, was published by Columbia University Press in July 2022.

Maxim Matusevich is Professor of History at Seton Hall University, where he also directs the Russian and East European Studies Program. Matusevich has published extensively on the history of the encounters between Russia/Soviet Union and Africa, and on the history of race in the Cold War. He is the author of *No Easy Row for a Russian Hoe: Ideology and Pragmatism in Nigerian–Soviet Relations, 1960–1991* (Africa World Press, 2003) and editor of *Africa in Russia, Russia in Africa: Three Centuries of Encounters* (Africa World Press, 2007).

Olga Panova is a professor at the Department of Foreign Literature, Faculty of Philology, Lomonosov Moscow State University and lead researcher at the Sector of Modern European and American Literature, A.M. Gorky Institute of World Literature of the Russian Academy of Sciences. She is editor-in-chief of the scholarly journal on the New World literary history, *Literature of the Americas*. She is the author of *The Worlds of Color: The Quest for the National Identity in American Literature* (Moscow State University Press, 2014). Her current research includes African-American literary history, American Modernism and Russian/Soviet–American literary and cultural contacts.

Sandra Pujals is Professor of History at the University of Puerto Rico. She has an MA in Russian Area Studies and a PhD in Russian History, both from Georgetown University in Washington, DC. Her main research interests include Soviet revolutionary culture and Soviet Russia's cultural relationship with Latin America and the Caribbean (1920s–1940s). Her book *Un Caribe soviético: el comunismo internacional en Puerto Rico y el Caribe* will be published in 2021. She is currently working on her second monograph titled *Su Casa Es Mi Casa: The Caribbean Bureau of the Comintern and the Forging of a Soviet Caribbean, 1930–1936*.

Matthieu Renault is Associate Professor in Philosophy at the Université Paris 8 Vincennes-Saint-Denis, and a member of the Laboratoire d'étude et de recherche sur les logiques contemporaines de la philosophie (LLCP). He has authored *Frantz Fanon: De l'anticolonialisme à la critique postcoloniale* (Editions Amsterdam, 2011), *L'Amérique de John Locke: L'expansion coloniale de la philosophie européenne* (Editions Amsterdam, 2014), *C.L.R. James: La vie révolutionnaire d'un 'Platon noir'* (Editions La Découverte, 2016) and *L'Empire de la révolution: Lénine et les musulmans de Russie* (Editions Syllepse, 2017).

Rachel Lee Rubin is Professor of American Studies at the University of Massachusetts Boston, where she is Director of the Center for the Study of Humanities, Culture, and Society. She received her PhD from Yale University (in 1995) in both American Studies and Slavic Languages and Literatures. She has published widely on international currents in cultural history.

Marika Sherwood was born in Hungary and emigrated to Australia, from there to the UK, and has also lived in New Guinea, New York and Sicily. In 1991 she was one of the founders of the Black and Asian Studies Association. She has written many articles and books on aspects of the history of peoples of African/Indian origins/descent in the UK. Some of the most recent are: *After Abolition* (IB Tauris, 2007); *The Origins of Pan-Africanism: Henry Sylvester Williams and the African Diaspora* (Routledge, 2010); *Malcolm X: Visits Abroad April 1964–February 1965* (Savannah Press, 2010); *World War II: Colonies & Colonials* (Savannah Press, 2013); 'An information "black hole": World War I in Africa', in László Z. Karvalics (ed.), *Information History of the First World War* (UNESCO/L'Harmattan Publishing, 2016); *Kwame Nkrumah and the Dawn of the Cold War: The West African National Secretariat, 1945–48* (Pluto Press, 2019; Sub-Saharan Publishers, 2019).

Harold D. Weaver, Jr is Alumni Fellow at the Hutchins Center for African and African American Research and Associate at the Davis Center for Russian and Eurasian Studies, Harvard University. Dr Weaver was the Founding Chair of the Department of Africana Studies at Rutgers

University, and has founded three related projects – The BlackFilm Project, The China–Africa–Russia Project and The BlackQuaker Project – in order to contribute to cross-cultural and international understanding and peace through transnational cultural relations. He has been an active participant and researcher in people-to-people, transnational cultural diplomacy since 1959, focusing on Paul Robeson, Ousmane Sembène, Bayard Rustin and African students in the USSR. He is in the process of reworking his 1985 dissertation in international education into a book in transnational history, *Decolonization and the Cold War: African Student Elites in the Early 1960s*, and writing his memoirs as an African-American Quaker scholar-activist.

Holger Weiss (PhD 1997) is Professor of General History at Abo Akademi University, Finland. His research focuses on global and Atlantic history, West African environmental history, and Islamic Studies (with a special focus on Islam in Ghana). His previous monographs include *Framing a Radical African Atlantic: African American Agency, West African Intellectuals and the International Trade Union of Negro Workers* (Brill, 2014), *Slavhandel och slaveri under svensk flagg: Koloniala drömmar och verklighet i Afrika och Karibien 1770–1847* (Svenska litteratursällskapet i Finland, 2016), and *För kampen internationellt!: Transportarbetarnas globala kampinternational och dess verksamhet i Nordeuropa under 1930-talet* (Työväen perinteen ja historian tutkimuksen seura, 2019).

Nigel Westmaas is Associate Professor of Africana Studies at Hamilton College (New York). He earned his master's and PhD from SUNY Binghamton and BA (Hons) from the University of Guyana. He has published articles in journals and magazines, including *Against the Current, Small Axe, Emancipation Magazine, Caribbean Studies, Guyana Art Forum* and *An Introductory Reader for Women's Studies in Guyana*. He is the co-editor of a UNESCO-assisted booklet *Guyanese Periodicals: 1796–1996*. Westmaas also contributes guest articles to the *Stabroek News*, one of the national newspapers of Guyana. His research work for and contributing introduction to the Marcus Garvey Universal Negro Improvement Association Papers, Caribbean series project (University of California) was published in 2011. He published a chapter titled 'An Organic Activist: Eusi Kwayana, Guyana and Global Pan-Africanism' in the text *Black Power in the Caribbean* (University Press of Florida, 2014). He has also published mini-biographies of eight prominent historical and contemporary Guyanese figures in the *Dictionary of Caribbean and Afro-Latin American Biography*, edited by Franklin Knight and Henry Louis Gates, Jr (Oxford University Press, 2016). Westmaas is a long-time political activist of Guyana's Working People's Alliance (WPA), the organisation in which the late Walter Rodney was a leading member.

Acknowledgements

This volume – and the linked second edited collection on *Revolutionary lives of the Red and Black Atlantic since 1917* – originated at an international conference, 'The Red and the Black: The Russian Revolution and the Black Atlantic', held at the Institute for Black Atlantic Research (IBAR), University of Central Lancashire in Preston in the United Kingdom, in October 2017. Held to mark the centenary of the Russian Revolution, it was a remarkable event which was in many ways very different from a standard academic conference, featuring as it did special performances from Tayo Aluko and David Rovics and readings from Linton Kwesi Johnson. We are grateful to these artists and performers, and also to the British Association for American Studies, the Lipman-Miliband Trust and the US Embassy in London for their generous support. We would like to thank all of those who attended, presented and in so many various ways contributed towards making it the memorable and successful event it was, often travelling from far and wide to do so.[1] In particular, we would like to give special thanks to Professor Alan Rice and Olga Tabachnikova for helping us co-organise the conference, and the wider organising team at IBAR including Izabella Penier, Yvonne Reddick and Raphael Hoermann for their work in helping make the conference happen and run smoothly. The title of the conference back in 2017, and this edited collection, also owes something for its inspiration to both Stendhal and Iron Maiden, and this debt should also be acknowledged.

For this volume in particular we would also like to thank the editors of the series on 'Racism, Resistance and Social Change', particularly the encouragement and support of Satnam Virdee, and Tom Dark, Lucy Burns and the wider editorial team at Manchester University Press for their work, support and patience with this project. We would also like to thank the editors of *Comparative American Studies: An International Journal* for their help with facilitating our inclusion of Winston James's chapter 'Claude McKay's Bolshevisation in London' in this volume. This chapter draws on material previously published as 'In the Nest of Extreme

Radicalism: Radical Networks and the Bolshevization of Claude McKay in London', *Comparative American Studies*, 15:3–4 (2017), 174–203. The editors would like to acknowledge Taylor & Francis for granting the relevant permissions. For making possible the translation of Matthieu Renault's chapter for this volume we would also like to thank the translator Alexis Pernsteiner, as well as the Centre for Memory, Narrative and Histories Research Support Fund at the University of Brighton. There are many others deserving of our thanks including Talat Ahmed, Ian Birchall, A.D. Gladush, Ben Gowland, Mo Hume, Deborah Madden, Brendan McGeever and Jacob Zumoff.

Finally, we would like to thank those who have contributed to this volume for their patience, assistance and support for the project, not least as its appearance has been in one sense a long time coming. Matters were inevitably further delayed in the final stages by the COVID-19 pandemic. Here it might be appropriate to remind ourselves that grappling with a pandemic was also an issue for the black radicals inspired by the Bolsheviks and Russian Revolution in the aftermath of 1917, given the devastating influenza in the aftermath of the First World War, a crisis that it seems clear the Bolsheviks handled much better than the advanced capitalist nations of the day. To end on a positive note, it might seem fitting to quote from an editorial from the black American socialist publication, *The Messenger*, edited by A. Philip Randolph and Chandler Owen, from December 1919 entitled 'Strike Influenza':

A year ago, the influenza was raging, and claiming thousands of lives per day in its toll. This year influenza is not so pandemic, but the strike influenza has taken its place. Nearly every country of the world is seething with strikes, the strikes being directly proportional to the intelligence and class consciousness of labor. Strikes are fewest where labor is most ignorant. There are less strikes in the South of the United States than any other part of the world, because the school system and the economic conditions there have kept both white and colored workers ignorant. In the North and West the steel workers, miners, dockmen, laundry workers, milliners, printers, actors, railroad men and in fact the workers in nearly every industry are on strike or have been on strike. England has just ended a railroad and miners strike. France has just settled a subway, street car, munitions and theatre strike. The rice strikes have shaken the musty autocracy of Japan. In South America, the workers of Argentine [sic], Brazil, and Chile are threatening revolution and making uneasy the investments of American, English and French capital … This striking habit has touched every race and national group and we are happy to see the dusky sons of toil lined up in every strike in the United States. We want to see Negroes thoroughly imbibe the strike influenza, ranging their power invariably on the side of their class interests – on the side of labor. The strike influenza is wholesome. It differs from the Spanish influenza in that one gives life and gives it more abundantly, while the other destroys life. One scatters death and destruction while the other exacts high wages, shorter hours and better working conditions, making the human body more able to resist the deadly attack of the germ disease. On with the strike influenza! More power to labor through its genial influence.[2]

Notes

1 For some photos and footage from the event, please see: https://theredandthe black.wordpress.com/ [accessed 1 February 2021].
2 'Strike Influenza', *The Messenger*, 2:11 (1919), 5–6.

Introduction:
Red October and the Black Atlantic

David Featherstone and Christian Høgsbjerg

The Russian Revolution of 1917 was not only one of the most critical events of the twentieth century in its own right, but it also struck powerful blows against racism and imperialism on both a practical and theoretical level which reverberated globally.[1] As the poet, novelist and revolutionary Victor Serge – one of the great humanist witnesses of twentieth-century Communism – reflected in his Mexican *Notebooks* on 1 July 1946:

> the socialist movement, first, then later the Russian Revolution (incompletely) succeeded in healing the oppressed and exploited masses (and the intelligentsia that rallied to these masses) of an age-old inferiority complex of the perpetually defeated ... In this sense the fertile role of the socialist movement is inestimable ... socialism modified the modern notion of man and his rights. (Internationalism broke the circle of the humanism of the white man.)[2]

Yet if Serge is right that socialist internationalism 'broke the circle of the humanism of the white man', the impact of 'Red October' on key black radicals was uneven – something that emerges from the contemporaneous writings of the US-based Jamaican black socialist Wilfred A. Domingo. Writing in July 1919, in *The Messenger*, the US-based 'black revolutionary socialist magazine', Domingo lamented that:

> It is a regrettable and disconcerting anomaly that, despite their situation as the economic, political and social door mat of the world, Negroes do not embrace the philosophy of socialism ... every oppressed group of the world is today turning from Clemenceau, Lloyd George and Wilson to the citadel of Socialism, Moscow. In this they are all in advance of Western Negroes with the exception of little groups in the United States and a relatively organised group in the Island of Trinidad, British West Indies.[3]

Domingo himself, however, went on to passionately make the case why 'Socialism' was 'the Negro's Hope'. He argued that:

> The foremost exponents of Socialism ... are characterised by the broadness of their vision towards all oppressed humanity. It was the Socialist Vandevelde of

Belgium, who protested against the Congo atrocities practiced upon Negroes; it was the late Keir Hardie and Philip Snowden of England, who condemned British rule in Egypt ... today it is the revolutionary Socialist, Lenin, who analysed the infamous League of Nations and exposed its true character; it is he as leader of the Communist Congress at Moscow, who sent out the proclamation: 'Slaves of the colonies in Africa and Asia! The hour of the proletarian dictatorship will be the hour of your release!'[4]

Domingo's reflections on the implications of the Russian Revolution and the Communist International (Comintern) for 'oppressed humanity', and in particular black and colonial liberation struggles, at a time when the League of Nations only paid lip service to the idea of 'national self-determination', speak to the key themes of this book.

Since the rise of the civil rights and Black Power movements in the 1950s and 1960s – and the corresponding development of Black Studies and African Studies, and Caribbean Studies more broadly – there has been a slow but steady rise in scholarship in the neglected field around 'the Red and the Black'. This volume represents a substantial contribution to that developing archive. In 1967, Philip Foner's anthology to mark the fiftieth anniversary of the Russian Revolution, *The Bolshevik Revolution: Its Impact on American Radicals, Liberals, and Labor*, was path-breaking in that it reproduced at least a few of the responses from the black radical and socialist press in the United States, such as *The Messenger*.[5] Since the 1960s, important historical work has been done by many scholars, including Robert A. Hill, Gerald Horne, Marika Sherwood, Winston James, Robin D.G. Kelley, Cedric J. Robinson, Mark Solomon, Joy Gleason Carew, Hakim Adi, Cathy Bergin, Susan Campbell, Mark Naison, Minkah Makalani, Carole Boyce Davies, Holger Weiss, Kate A. Baldwin, Maxim Matusevich, Margaret Stevens, Michael O. West and Jacob Zumoff. This wide-ranging scholarship has focused on important figures, movements and organisations such as Marcus Garvey's Universal Negro Improvement Association (UNIA), the African Blood Brotherhood (ABB), the International Trade Union Committee of Negro Workers (ITUCNW) and the wider relationship between Communism and black liberation struggles.[6] This volume both builds on and dialogues with this rich body of work.

The collection (and the companion volume, *Revolutionary lives of the Red and Black Atlantic since 1917*) brings together contributions from a range of leading and emerging scholars in the field of 'the Red and the Black' who engage with the inspiring international reverberations of the Russian Revolution across the Black Atlantic world as a means to understand the contested articulations of different struggles against racism and colonialism. Through so doing the volume makes a significant contribution to contemporary debates around race, class, anti-colonialism and revolutionary history. In particular, it challenges European-centred under-standings of both the Russian Revolution and the global left who took inspiration from it. The substantive focus of the book enables us to offer new insights on the relations between Communism, various lefts and anti-colonialisms across the Black Atlantic – including Garveyism and various other strands of Pan-Africanism. This introduction charts the rich and multilayered histories of race, class and resistance in which the chapters are contextualised, and also suggests important links to contemporary politics of race and class.

The first section of our introduction explores the relations between black politics and the Russian Revolution. The second section locates the book in relation to debates around the Black Atlantic and on black international-ism, and the final section considers the broader contemporary relevance of intersections between 'the Red and the Black'. This work sheds new light on the emergence of understandings of the intersection of race and class, on the emergence of politicised forms of anti-racism, in particular those arising out of a revolutionary struggle, and on racialised forms of internationalism and agency.

In terms of the structure of the volume itself, Part I 'Racism, resist-ance and revolution' explores how the Russian Revolution and the birth of Soviet power began to transform thinking around race and resistance. In particular, as we shall see in Winston James's chapter, the Bolsheviks' anti-racist and anti-imperialist politics was particularly critical here in inspiring such emblematic figures as the black Jamaican poet and writer Claude McKay to become organised revolutionary socialists – in a sense 'black Bolsheviks'.[7] Matthieu Renault and Olga Panova's chapters explore some of the rich wider theoretical and literary relationships and dynamics around race and the revolutionary process in Russia, particularly in relation to black America.

Part II of the volume, 'Spreading the revolution across the Black Atlantic', examines the formation of organisational relations between Communism (above all the Communist International) and left-wing and anti-colonialist activists in Africa, the Caribbean and in black America and the Atlantic world more broadly. As Cathy Bergin notes in her study of black activists in North America, 'Bolshevism' became spoken of as 'a model of politi-cal identity which can speak to issues of race and anti-colonialism as well as questions of class'. Holger Weiss discusses the ITUCNW – arguably in many ways the most important organisational form to emerge from this early 'Red and Black' conjuncture – and related groups such as the International of Seamen and Harbour Workers.[8] Sandra Pujals looks at the role of the Caribbean Bureau of the Communist International in the early 1930s, Matheus Cardoso-da-Silva explores the Atlantic and transnational dimensions of the Left Book Club and Nigel Westmaas examines the roots of the anti-colonial shock election of 1953 in British Guiana (now Guyana), which saw a left-wing political party briefly come to power in the British Empire.

Finally in Part III, 'Africa, the Soviet Union and the Cold War', Marika Sherwood examines the rise of 'Pan-African socialism' in Ghana under Kwame Nkrumah, exploring the ways in which Nkrumah was influenced by Communism, but also how anti-Communism emerged as a weapon in the context of the Cold War to undermine the potential radicalism of decolonisation. After 'Africa's lost leader', Patrice Lumumba, was assassinated by forces backed by Western imperialism in 1961, a university in Moscow was named in honour of him.[9] Harold D. Weaver, in Moscow himself from 1963–64, writes on how the Patrice Lumumba Friendship University for the Peoples of Africa, Asia and Latin America aimed to further the process of intellectual and political decolonisation, while Rachel Lee Rubin examines how it became demonised in the West during the Cold War. Finally, Maxim Matusevich, a leading Russian historian of the intersection between the Russian Revolution and the Black Atlantic, offers us an afterword exploring the 'longue durée' of black encounters with the Soviet Union. Importantly, Matusevich argues that these encounters were not a 'one-way street' but had consequences for Soviet understandings of black and anti-colonial liberation. He also emphasises that these encounters could be fraught and involved important challenges and tensions alongside forms of solidarity.

Black politics and the Russian Revolution

The Tsarist empire under the Romanovs was described by Lenin as 'the prison house of nations' and was a multinational state where, according to the census of 1897, Great Russians only constituted 43 per cent of the total population of the empire. Tsarist Russia was not just a critical (and as it happened fatally weak) link in the imperialist chain; it also witnessed horrendous levels of state-sponsored racism against Jewish people, from repressive legislation to vicious and bloody pogroms – orchestrated mob violence by 'Black Hundreds' (who also organised the first publication of the notorious anti-Semitic conspiracy theory *The Protocols of the Elders of Zion*). During the late nineteenth century and early twentieth century, Tsarist Russia had the deepest level of anti-Semitism in any country before the rise of Adolf Hitler's Nazis in Germany, and between 1881 and the outbreak of the First World War an estimated 2.5 million Jews had fled or left, one of the largest migrations in history.[10] Yet during the 1905 revolution in Russia, the St Petersburg Soviet (Council) of Workers' Deputies elected a

Jewish revolutionary socialist – Leon Trotsky – to be their chair. They also organised armed detachments of workers which successfully foiled any attempt to trigger a pogrom in the city, testament to the change in mass consciousness under way during that revolutionary year.[11] After the February Revolution in 1917, repressive Tsarist legislation against Jewish people began to be repealed; again the reborn Soviets came to the fore in campaigning and organising against anti-Semitism. In October 1917, Trotsky was again elected chair of the Petrograd Soviet of Workers' and Soldiers' Deputies and the Bolsheviks – a party whose central committee contained six Jews out of twenty-one members – won a majority in the All-Russian Congress of Soviets. Alongside Trotsky, who after organising the October insurrection became Commissar for Foreign Affairs, and then founder of the Red Army as War Commissar, other leading figures of Jewish heritage in the early years of Soviet Russia included Yakov Sverdlov (president of the Soviet Republic until his death in 1919), Grigory Zinoviev (who would become head of the Communist International), Karl Radek, Maxim Litvinov and Lev Kamenev. Moreover, Liliana Riga has analysed the biographical profiles of the ninety-three members (full or candidate) of the Russian Social Democratic Workers' Party (Bolshevik)/Russian Communist Party (RSDRP[b]/RKP) central committees (CCs) in the key revolutionary years 1917–23, inclusive. Riga found that 'ethnic Russians were a substantial minority, but Jews, Latvians, Ukrainians, Georgians, Armenians, Poles, and others made up nearly two-thirds of Russia's revolutionary elite'.[12]

The realities of Bolshevism's transformational and systematic challenge to racism on the ground in Soviet Russia itself amid these early years was clearly a fraught and complicated matter, as the recent important work of Brendan McGeever has registered.[13] Nonetheless, the impact that news of the Russian Revolution and its anti-racist (and indeed anti-imperialist) dynamics made on at least a militant minority among the African diaspora was significant. Soviet Russia, for this minority, appeared as a beacon of hope at a time in the early twentieth century when Africans and people of African descent were suffering under the state racism of European colonial dictatorships and in the Jim Crow United States. The latter had lynch-mob 'pogroms' of its own, such as that which took place in Illinois during the East St Louis race riot of 1917 and across over thirty cities during the 'Red Summer' of 1919.[14] Yet this impact has been somewhat long occluded in Western scholarship on both the Russian Revolution itself and within Black Studies.[15] Much of the classic and contemporary literature on the Russian Revolution tends to still remain within a national lens, though the importance of understanding the crisis of the Russian Empire and the revolutionary process in a transnational framework is increasingly being understood.[16] Even historians of the Russian Revolution who were as alive to questions of 'the international' as E.H. Carr, writing his multi-volume classic history of 'the Bolshevik Revolution' in the 1950s, still focused in his section on 'Soviet Russia and the World' on the 'Revolution over Europe' and the 'Revolution over Asia'.[17] This lack of attention to the African diaspora (with the partial exception of South Africa) has even been true of many histories of the Communist International, though John Riddell's work on editing the proceedings of the congresses is slowly helping to shift the narrative here.[18]

In a sense this neglect reflected two important realities. Firstly, spreading the revolution on Soviet Russia's borders into Asia was strategically a more urgent and critical task than in far-off Africa and the Caribbean. Secondly, in general terms 'the wretched of the earth' most inspired by the Russian Revolution at the time tended to be either from the Jewish diaspora, or those colonial subjects living in the Far East (such as the young Nguyễn Ái Quốc, better known by his later name Ho Chi Minh) or South Asia (for example M.N. Roy).[19] The inspirational impact of a socialist revolution – and one in a country that, unlike many others in Europe, had never pursued colonial ambitions in Africa – on the African diaspora and the Black Atlantic was in many ways at first weaker and slower to materialise than one might have expected. The small number of 'Afro-Russians' aside, the number of black people who found themselves in Russia during the tumultuous year of 1917 was tiny.[20] Some of these – such as the black American Philip Jordan, valet to David Rowland Francis, the American ambassador in Russia – seem to have retained their loyalties to the old order.[21] However there were other African Americans whose relationship to revolution was more enthusiastic.

Frederick Bruce Thomas, born in 1872 in Mississippi to former enslaved black Americans who became prosperous farmers, moved to Moscow at the turn of the twentieth century where he renamed himself Fyodor Fyodorovich Tomas and, through his charm and guile, became the city's richest and most famous owner of variety theatres and the renowned restaurant Maxim. Thomas would later shock a white 'Southern woman from America' by explaining 'there was no colour line drawn' in Russia. In 1917, Thomas initially tried to adapt to the new developing revolutionary situation by helping sponsor a 'soldiers' theatre' for the Moscow Soviet, but after October 1917 his theatres were nationalised, and by 1918 he had fallen foul of the new regime and so by 1919 he had fled with his family to Turkey.[22]

Emma Harris, a black American born in 1875 and originally from Kentucky, decided to stay after touring Russia in the early 1900s, establishing her reputation as a singer and actress and becoming 'Russia's first black film star'. Harris reluctantly adapted to the revolution of 1917, serving with the Soviet Red Cross during the Russian Civil War and staying in the Soviet Union for twenty years before returning to the United States in 1933 shortly before her death in 1937. In March 1918, Harris had attended a huge rally in Red Square in Moscow being addressed by Lenin. According to the journalist Theodore Postan,

> Lenin was explaining the meaning of the Bolshevik cause when he spied a smiling, middle-aged Negro woman in the forefront of the huge gathering. Extending his right hand in a characteristic gesture, he spoke directly to her: 'The ideal of Communism' he said, 'is to open the road for all the downtrodden races of the world. For you, comrade, especially, as we regard your race the most downtrodden in the world. We want you to feel when you come to Russia that you are a human being. The Red Army is ready to give its life at any time for all downtrodden races.' Her neighbors hoisted Emma Harris to their shoulders and bore her triumphantly through the cheering throng …[23]

Equally if not more remarkable still was Coretti Arle-Titz, born Coretté Elizabeth Hardy in 1881 in New York, who had been performing as a singer and dancer in Russia since 1904. She already had some links to the Bolsheviks earlier, and embraced the revolution, touring the Red Army with the 'Concert Brigade of the South-Western Front' in the Ukraine during the Civil War and becoming 'Black Concert Star of the USSR' and a Soviet citizen until her death in 1951.[24]

During the Russian Civil War, several hundred French colonial troops, including Africans from Algeria, Morocco and Senegal – who had been treated appallingly during the First World War, some dying of cold because they didn't have proper uniforms – found themselves sent to Odessa in Russia in late 1918 to contribute to the counter-revolutionary White armies encircling the new Soviet state. Yet it seems very few of these actually participated in any effective counter-revolutionary activity, and indeed the whole experience proved a radicalising one for these Africans, not least as there was shortly a wave of naval mutinies on French ships in the Black Sea in 1919. As J. Kim Munholland noted, 'the French command observed that the refusal of Algerian troops to embark at Constanza for Sebastapol provided dramatic evidence of widespread disenchantment among French units. Over half of the French troops in Sebastapol were colonial soldiers, including Algerian and Senegalese … their discipline was uncertain.'[25] According to one Soviet account, there were 'cases of Moroccans and Algerians joining the Red Army near Odessa and Sevastopol in 1919' and 'evidence that Bolshevik leaflets were distributed in occupied Odessa among the colonial soldiers, particularly among those from Algeria, Morocco and Senegal. Some of these soldiers, together with French soldiers and sailors, took part in distributing revolutionary leaflets. Hadji Omar, a sailor from Oran [Algeria], participated in the revolt of the French fleet in the Black Sea.'[26] Though again corroborating evidence remains hard to come by, according to Vijay Prashad, 'some Senegalese soldiers, fighting under the flag of the French empire, decamped for the Soviet Red Army when they heard of its arrival into world history. Boris Kornilov, the Soviet poet, would later sing in his *Moia Afrika* of a Senegalese soldier who died leading the Reds against the Whites near Voronezh "in order to deal a blow to the African capitalists and the bourgeoisie".'[27]

The significance of October for black activists outside Russia took longer to become apparent. For example it was not until Lenin and the Bolsheviks had put 'world revolution' onto the agenda through forming the Third (Communist) International in March 1919 to replace the Second International, which had so miserably all but collapsed with the outbreak of the First World War, and publishing their Manifesto, that the Jamaican Pan-Africanist Marcus Garvey first commented in public on the Bolshevik revolution. In late March 1919, Garvey referred to the fact that the founding Manifesto of the Communist International advocated self-determination for oppressed peoples, and so thought 'the nightmare of Bolshevism' was 'going to spread until it finds a haven in the breasts of all oppressed peoples, and then there shall be a universal rule of the masses'. Garvey's general interest in and even enthusiasm for the Russian Revolution is striking, even though he ultimately concluded that 'Bolshevism, it would appear, is a thing of the white man's making' and so 'we are not concerned partakers in these revolutions'. Garvey thought that for black people the best that could be hoped for in the short term was that 'the destruction that will come out of the bloody conflict between capital and labour … will give us a breathing space to declare our freedom from the tyrannical rule of the oppressive overlords'.[28]

As Marcus Garvey's comments – and Wilfred Domingo's remarks from July 1919 in *The Messenger* quoted above – suggest, there were significant if uneven exchanges between Communist, socialist and anti-colonial ideas. Both Garvey and Domingo give particular credence to the Bolsheviks' critical engagements with the question of imperialism and national liberation. Lenin had developed his theory of imperialism, building on the work of his fellow Bolshevik Nikolai Bukharin during the First World War, and the Russian Revolution helped to bring the slaughter of that war to an end. Lenin challenged 'Great Russian chauvinism' and championed the rights of nations to self-determination, and the Bolsheviks transformed the old Tsarist empire into a 'Union of Soviet Socialist Republics'. Working in conjunction with others – including M.N. Roy as well as figures like Zinoviev and Trotsky – Lenin played a leading role in ensuring that national liberation movements in the colonies were seen as of central strategic importance by the Communist International. As well as M.N. Roy, other anti-colonialist activists such as Ho Chi Minh, Hadj-Ali Abdelkader and Lamine Senghor critically helped to shape the Communist International's direction. As Timothy Brennan notes, in 1920 the First Congress of the Peoples of the East in Baku, with its slogan 'Workers of the world and oppressed peoples unite!', was 'the first non-Western congress with the explicit purpose of denouncing Western imperial expansion, and of uniting peoples of vastly different languages and religious affinities'. Brennan insists that the Russian Revolution, 'to put it plainly, was an anticolonial revolution; its sponsorship of anticolonial rhetoric and practice was self-definitional'.[29]

Whether or not we wish to follow Brennan in declaring the Russian Revolution itself 'an anticolonial revolution', it is important to register the way in which the majority of the Russian people who made the revolution were regarded by many as non-European 'dark masses'. The impact and influence of the Russian Revolution, especially given the creation of the new Communist International, on a generation of radical black intellectuals, both in North America and those who were colonial subjects of the British and French empires, was manifest and undeniable. As Claude McKay famously put it in September 1919, in Marcus Garvey's *Negro World*:

> Every Negro who lays claim to leadership should make a study of Bolshevism and explain its meaning to the colored masses. It is the greatest and most scientific idea afloat in the world today that can be easily put into practice by the proletariat to better its material and spiritual life. Bolshevism ... has made Russia safe for the Jew. It has liberated the Slav peasant from priest and bureaucrat who can no longer egg him on to murder Jews to bolster up their rotten institutions. It might make these United States safe for the Negro.[30]

The hopes and dreams of October 1917 inspired many to not only identify with revolutionary politics, but also now bring their own narratives and histories of black struggle into established Marxist narratives of revolutionary history in an unprecedented fashion. For example, with respect to the Caribbean, the Haitian Revolution of 1791–1804 now began to be registered in Communist literature and discourse in a way it had never been adequately before. Led by figures like Toussaint Louverture and Jean-Jacques Dessalines, the Haitian Revolution was the only successful slave revolt in history, created one of the world's first post-colonial nations and was part of the world-historic age of 'bourgeois-democratic' revolution. Karl Marx referred to 'the insurgent Negroes of Haiti' in the third part of *The German Ideology* (1845).[31] He noted that Polish troops were sent by Napoleon to try and crush the Haitian Revolution in 1802, and 'threatened by the fire of artillery, they were embarked at Genoa and Livorno to find their graves in St Domingo'. Not mentioned by Marx, but significant for anti-racist politics is the fact that some Polish troops (and for that matter some German troops too) defected across to join the black army fighting for independence, earning the undying respect and gratitude of Dessalines in the process.[32] Haiti was not at the forefront of Lenin's mind in August 1918, as he missed an opportunity to pay tribute to black or anti-colonial leaders when he wrote and signed a decree listing thirty-one revolutionaries and public figures to be honoured with individual monuments in Soviet Russia, ranging from Spartacus to Plekhanov.[33]

The relative neglect of the Haitian Revolution in the international socialist movement would however soon be overcome. By the 1920s a critical mass of black revolutionary socialist intellectuals and activists had formed themselves in the United States around the African Blood Brotherhood (ABB), an organisation of several thousand members at its height, and with an appeal across the African diaspora. Cyril V. Briggs, a black Caribbean activist born in colonial Nevis, was part of the ABB leadership, alongside other founders such as Grace P. Campbell, Wilfred A. Domingo and Richard B. Moore.[34] The organisation coalesced in 1919, in particular in Harlem, around a number of impressive Caribbean intellectuals inspired by the Bolshevik revolution, and critical of the failings of the Socialist Party of America to take race and black self-organisation seriously. Briggs and many ABB members like Campbell and Harry Haywood later joined the Communist Party in the United States. Briggs paid due respect to the heroism of the Haitian revolutionaries, declaring in *The Communist* in 1929 that Toussaint Louverture 'takes his place with the revolutionary heroes and martyrs of the world proletariat ... to the black and white revolutionary workers belong the tradition of Toussaint ... We must see to it that his memory is not wrapped in spices in the vaults of the bourgeoisie but is kept green and fresh as a tradition of struggle and an inspiration for the present struggle against the master class.'[35] Inspired by the Russian Revolution and Marxist theory, some of the most critical, classic and pathbreaking works of 'black history' were now written, such as W.E.B. Du Bois's *Black Reconstruction in America, 1860–1880* (1935) and C.L.R. James's history of the Haitian Revolution, *The Black Jacobins* (1938). The inspiration of Leon Trotsky's *History of the Russian Revolution* (1930) for James in particular was clear, but both *Black Reconstruction in America* and *The Black Jacobins* represented pioneering works of Marxist historiography relating to the African diaspora, which revolutionised historical understanding of the experience of slavery and its abolition.[36]

One high point in the conjuncture between black radicalism and Bolshevism came in 1922 at the Fourth Congress of the Communist International, which was famously attended by Claude McKay. 'Those Russian days remain the most memorable of my life', he would later recall.[37] McKay created a vibrant picture of his Russian experience. 'Whenever I appeared in the street I was greeted by all of the people with enthusiasm ... a spontaneous upsurging of folk feeling.' The complete inverse of his previous experiences in America and Europe, he declared that 'Never in my life did I feel prouder of being an African, a black.'[38] A leading poet of the Harlem Renaissance and a member of the African Blood Brotherhood, McKay helped draft the Comintern's resolution on 'the black question' on 30 November 1922. This hailed the rising black resistance to the attacks of their exploiters and called for the organisation of an international black movement in Africa and across the western hemisphere, for 'the black question has become an essential part of the world revolution'.[39] McKay was also inspired to publish in Russia two little-known volumes about race and resistance in the United States, *Negroes in America* (1923) and *Trial by Lynching: Stories of American Life* (1925).[40]

Black liberation was also a subject McKay passionately and eloquently addressed the Congress on:

> The situation in America today is terrible and fraught with grave dangers. It is much uglier and more terrible than was the condition of the peasants and Jews of Russia under the Tsar. It is so ugly and terrible that very few people in America are willing to face it ... the Socialists and Communists have fought very shy of it because there is a great element of prejudice among the Socialists and Communists of America. They are not willing to face the Negro question ... this is the greatest difficulty that the Communists of America have got to overcome – the fact that they first have got to emancipate themselves from the ideas they entertain towards the Negroes before they can be able to reach the Negroes with any kind of radical propaganda.

McKay closed his speech by declaring that 'I hope that as a symbol that the Negroes of the world will not be used by the international bourgeoisie in the final conflicts against the World Revolution, that as a challenge to the international bourgeoisie, who have an understanding of the Negro question, we shall soon see a few Negro soldiers in the finest, bravest, and cleanest fighting forces in the world – the Red Army and Navy of Russia – fighting not only for their own emancipation, but also for the emancipation of all the working class of the whole world.'[41] While in Moscow, McKay was not able to meet with Lenin (who was too ill) but did meet with such leading Bolsheviks as Zinoviev, Radek, Bukharin and above all Trotsky. Stalin didn't bother to reply to McKay's request for a meeting. However, as McKay remembered in his 1937 autobiography *A Long Way from Home*, the request for a meeting with Stalin 'vanished from my thoughts when I came in contact with the magnetic personality of Trotsky', then Commissar for War.[42]

> Trotsky asked me some straight and sharp questions about American Negroes, their group organisations, their political position, their schooling,

their religion, their grievances and social aspirations and, finally, what kind of sentiment existed between American and African Negroes. I replied with the best knowledge and information at my command. Then Trotsky expressed his own opinion about Negroes, which was more intelligent than that of any of the other Russian leaders ... he was not quick to make deductions about the causes of white prejudice against black. Indeed, he made no conclusions at all, and, happily, expressed no mawkish sentimentality about black-and-white brotherhood. What he said was very practical ... he urged that Negroes should be educated about the labour movement ... he said he would like to set a practical example in his own department and proposed the training of a group of Negroes as officers in the Red army.[43]

McKay's account of his experiences in Moscow in *A Long Way From Home*, however, also speaks to more fraught and troubling aspects of these relations. He describes the discomfort caused by his encounters with Grigory Zinoviev, the president of the Third International, recounting Zinoviev's anger when he told him that he 'came to Russia as a writer and not an agitator'. The passage of *A Long Way From Home* that discusses Zinoviev also draws attention to his feelings that 'Bolshevik leaders' were 'using me for entertainment' to 'satisfy the desires of the people'.[44] Partly as a result of this, McKay's political trajectories became progressively critical of the USSR and the terms on which it envisioned articulations between Red and Black politics.[45] Such animosity was reciprocated. As mentioned below, Olga Panova's chapter notes that Soviet critics became progressively hostile to and dismissive of McKay and his work.

If the socialist McKay had nonetheless been impressed by meeting Trotsky, even the far from socialist Marcus Garvey – amidst the rising militancy and radicalism of the 'New Negro Movement' in the United States – paid tribute to Lenin after his death. In a speech in New York on 27 January 1924, Garvey described Lenin as

One of Russia's greatest men, one of the world's greatest characters, and probably the greatest man in the world between 1917 and 1924, when he breathed his last and took his flight from this world ... We as Negroes mourn for Lenin because Russia promised great hope not only for Negroes but to the weaker people of the world.[46]

While the ABB was short-lived, a younger generation of black radicals now came to the fore. Malcolm Evan Meredith Nurse, a young black Trinidadian Communist (writing under his adopted pseudonym 'George Padmore'), articulated in characteristically fiery words the tasks as he saw it for the 'New Negro' amidst the Harlem Renaissance in 1928 for the *Negro Champion*, paper of the American Negro Labour Congress:

The time has come for Negro youth, students and workers ... to take a more definite and active interest in world problems ... we have seen our brothers massacred on foreign battlefields in defence of the very imperialist social order that today crushes them to earth ... let us join with the masses of the rising colonial peoples and militant class conscious workers to struggle for the establishment of a free and equitable world order. The New Negro has to realise that the salvation and emancipation of any oppressed group can only be achieved by those who in the face of great odds have the courage to raise the standard of revolt. For he who dares to be free, must himself strike the first blow.[47]

Over the next thirty years, few black radicals would emerge to fight with more dedication for black and colonial liberation than George Padmore. After briefly leading the Communist International 'Negro Bureau' and editing its paper, the *Negro Worker*, Padmore worked with his boyhood friend and compatriot, the Trotskyist C.L.R. James, and figures like the Kenyan nationalist Jomo Kenyatta to form militant Pan-Africanist organisations in Britain during the 1930s such as the International African Friends of Ethiopia and International African Service Bureau.[48] By the 1930s, for many black radicals like Padmore the turn to the Popular Front under Stalin's leadership of the Soviet Union and the resultant sidelining of the anti-colonial struggle represented a betrayal. James would later describe in his 1937 history *World Revolution* how the Communist International was thrown into chaos by this 'about turn', and, 'following Stalin, missed the greatest opportunity in years of at best striking a powerful blow against the colonial policy of imperialism, and at worst rallying round itself the vanguard of the working-class movement in preparation for the coming war'.[49] The abandonment of Ethiopia by the Soviet Union in 1935, when it put its own national interests first and sold oil to help Fascist Italy's war machine invade and occupy one of the last independent countries in Africa, marked a serious deviation from the early Comintern's commitment to anti-colonialism.[50] This decision by the Soviet Union threw many black Communists who had previously looked to Moscow as an 'anti-imperial metropolis' into a state of confusion and disbelief.[51]

Yet despite the disaster of Ethiopia for black radicals, the revolution itself continued to matter. In late 1939, in an article marking the twenty-second anniversary of the Russian Revolution, C.L.R. James highlighted how October 1917 could still represent a living inspiration for black Americans:

No Southern capitalist or plantation owner celebrates the anniversary of the Russian Revolution. Should a Negro in the South walk down a public street carrying a banner marked 'Long Live the Russian Revolution', he might be lynched before he had gone fifty yards. And why? Because it stands for the destruction of the rotting capitalist system, with its unnecessary poverty and

degradation, its imperialist war and its fascist dictatorships, its class domination and racial persecution. Every Negro with an ounce of political understanding or a spark of revolt against oppression will recognise the significance
and celebrate the anniversary of the October revolution in Russia.[52]

As James's text emphasises, there were continuing reverberations of the
Russian Revolution for radicals across the Black Atlantic. This raises key
questions about how to conceptualise the connections and trajectories
which were articulated in relation to these reverberations; the next section
seeks to explore different ways of conceptualising these relations, and also
positions the volume in relation to recent debates on black internationalism.

Black internationalism, political trajectories and articulations of solidarity

The preceding section drew attention to the diverse, and often under-
acknowledged, geographies of connection between the Russian Revolution
and the Black Atlantic. Through doing so it signals an important set of
questions about how these connections, relations and trajectories are
understood. In this respect this volume clearly draws on Paul Gilroy's
framing of the Black Atlantic, which sought to move 'discussion of black
political culture beyond the binary opposition between national and
diaspora perspectives'. By locating 'the black Atlantic world in a webbed
network, between the local and the global', Gilroy sought to challenge 'the
coherence of all narrow nationalist perspectives and points to the spuri-
ous invocation of ethnic particularity to enforce them and to ensure the
tidy flow of cultural output into neat symmetrical units'.[53] This challenge
to what he termed the 'narrow nationalism of so much English historiography' drew in part on the pioneering work of historians such as Peter
Linebaugh and Marcus Rediker, whose work on the revolutionary or 'Red'
Atlantic sought to reconfigure the nation-centred character that hitherto
dominated histories from below.[54] Thus Gilroy engaged with Linebaugh's
discussion of the seafaring experience of radical figures such as Robert
Wedderburn and William Davidson, who had been 'sailors moving to
and fro between nations, crossing borders in modern machines that were
themselves micro-systems of linguistic and political hybridity'.[55] This
engagement with Linebaugh and Rediker's work emphasises that notions
of the Red and Black Atlantic can be thought of as co-constituted and
overlapping, rather than as neatly separate political and theoretical projects. While such Atlantic framings have foregrounded histories and geographies of connections in important ways, they have also been unsettled

and challenged. Indeed, Gilroy's conceptualisation of the Black Atlantic arguably tends to ignore the impact and exchanges of the African diaspora on events outside of the 'Atlantic region'. This becomes of particular importance for thinking about the diverse relations between black radicals and the Russian Revolution, but also for their intersections with South and East Asia including anti-colonial movements such as Indian nationalism and figures such as Gandhi; other revolutionary upheavals such as the Chinese Revolution and figures like Mao; or other anti-imperialist struggles such as the Vietnamese against French and American imperialism.

Such connections have, however, been brought to the fore more explicitly in recent work and debates on black internationalism, and it is in relation to such work that this book is most directly positioned. These literatures, which partly emerged in the aftermath of Gilroy's work, have emphasised the extent to which various black radicals in the early to mid-twentieth century were at the forefront of diverse forms of internationalist politics, and include engagements with Pan-Africanism, Communism, Garveyism and black left feminisms.[56] One of the central contributions of these literatures has been to position the coeval forms of political identities and multiple political trajectories that shaped emergent forms of black internationalism. Thus Brent Hayes Edwards has argued that to analyse the dynamic relations between black print cultures in Paris and Harlem in the interwar period it is useful to think about the importance of 'ensuring coevalness in the very structure of any black internationalist discourse'.[57]

Through this approach Edwards foregrounds the 'unruly pattern of follows and alliances' shaped through different articulations of black internationalism. This renders the formation of black internationalist politics as generative, but it is also important in drawing attention to the different and contested forms of such politics. As Kate Baldwin's study of the different engagements shaped by Claude McKay, W.E.B. Du Bois, Langston Hughes and Paul Robeson through their travels in Russia has emphasised, relations between Red and Black Atlantics shaped, and were shaped by, different connections, political trajectories and articulations.[58]

A central theme of recent work on black internationalism has been the productive, inventive and diverse ways in which black radicals engaged with Communism. Such work has demonstrated the complexities and the diverse ways in which these relations were articulated and have usefully unsettled earlier framings of polarities such as George Padmore's famous 1956 opposition of Pan-Africanism and Communism.[59] Recent historiography has thus emphasised the different forms of political agency and identity shaped through connections and relations between forms of left politics such as Communism and diverse forms of black radicalism in different contexts. This has complicated earlier understandings of black radicals as subordinate to the logics of Comintern organising which informed the writings of figures such as Harold Cruse.[60]

Such work has certainly not evaded the important unequal relations of power and racialised articulations of solidarity which structured Communist internationalism.[61] This is clearly important, not least given some of the historic failings of many Western Communist parties to take questions of race and empire as seriously as was demanded. One depressing sign of this was the repression of dissident black activists and anti-colonial militants within the Stalinised Soviet Union itself, such as Lovett Fort-Whiteman – an early black member of the American Communist Workers' Party and one of its delegates to the Fifth Congress of the Comintern, who died in a Soviet gulag in 1939.[62] Another victim of Stalinist terror, for example, was the one-time ITUCNW vice-chair, Sandalio Junco, a black Cuban Communist once responsible for work in Latin America and parts of the Caribbean. After breaking with the Communist International and becoming one of the leaders of Trotskyism in Cuba, Junco was killed by Stalin's agents in 1942.[63]

Recent scholarship has offered a much more nuanced engagement with the forms of political agency, identities and solidarities that black radicals shaped in their interactions with the Russian Revolution and Communism in the early to mid-twentieth century. It is in this spirit that this volume provides a diverse set of perspectives on the Atlantic circulations, trajectories and reverberations of the Russian Revolution. In order to develop a fine-grained sense of the diverse and generative connections between the Russian Revolution and the Black Atlantic world, and the different kinds of international connections and exchanges they generated and shaped, it is useful to consider the terms on which such connections and trajectories were shaped. By approaching these concerns as interrelated and thinking about the diverse political trajectories shaped through such connections and relations, this book contributes to the burgeoning work on black transnationalism. The remainder of this section maps out some of the key interventions through which the volume adds to these debates in distinctive ways.

Firstly, the volume is part of a body of a work that challenges a sense of Communism as an export which sprang fully formed from Europe and/or Russia. Rather, in line with a whole swathe of recent scholarship, we seek to be alive to the ways in which there were ongoing connections and engagements with movements, intellectuals and political figures beyond Europe which shaped these relations. Rather than position Bolshevism and Communism as something that simply impacted on political activism and imaginaries elsewhere, this enables an approach which can also trace the impact of anti-colonial movements on Communist practices and ideas. This also speaks to the strong tensions that existed within the European left in the early twentieth century in relation to imperialism. As Peter Linebaugh has noted, among 'the many things' that Rosa Luxemburg and Lenin agreed on in 1916 was the 'denunciation of the Social Democrats for refusing to intercede on behalf of a comrade in the Cameroons who faced a death sentence for organising an uprising against the war'.[64]

In this regard the transnational impact of the Russian Revolution intersected with different political formations and histories in different contexts. A good example here is the trajectory of the ABB, which as noted above was established in the US in September 1919.[65] Most of the members of the ABB moved *en masse* into the Communist Party of the United States (CPUSA) in the early 1920s, an event which, as Minkah Makalani suggests, 'lies in a history outside the white Left'. He contends that the ABB had operated 'mainly within the New Negro movement' and 'had put forward a program and undertaken political activities based on its sense of the circumstances facing black people around the world'. The problems the organisation had sustaining itself 'led Briggs, Grace Campbell, Richard Moore and others in the ABB to contemplate entering the communist movement'.[66] This was however to be a fraught and contested process with significant tensions both over resources and over the relations between race and class, as Lydia Lindsey shows, for example, in her chapter on Grace Campbell in the companion volume in this series on the Red and the Black.[67]

Makalani emphasises, however, that this encounter between the ABB and Communism was a dynamic set of encounters and engagements. Thus he argues that radicals such as Briggs, Campbell and Moore 'came to the communist movement' as 'they came into the Socialist Party – as activist-intellectuals willing to stretch the boundaries of a political theory so that it might address racial oppression and colonialism'.[68] Makalani's contention that intellectuals like Briggs, Campbell and Moore actively 'stretched' and reconfigured the terms of Communist ideas and theorising is important as it stresses the role of black agency in the formation of Communist ideas and left political cultures. It is important to recognise the plurality of left political cultures in different contexts too. Otto Huiswoud, a leftist from Suriname, for example, attended and addressed the Fourth Congress of the Communist International in Moscow alongside McKay, and was one of the founding members of the CPUSA.[69] This black presence was formed through struggles against dominant left political cultures and effected important forms of political agency. As Sharad Chari and Katherine Verdery note, 'the Comintern created space for anti-imperialists from a variety of regions to rethink concepts and connections'.[70] These were interventions that had significant consequences for the internationalist political imaginaries shaped by Communism in the 1920s. They also resulted in significant challenges to the outlooks of white-dominated left movements, and so had an important impact on the broader perspectives associated with the global left. Thus Winston James has argued that for 'black comrades, the Comintern represented the purest ideals of socialism, untarnished by racism and colonial ambition'.[71]

Indeed, as Jeremy Krikler has noted, 'socialism would only be definitively separated from racism through the actions of the international Communist movement: this is one of the enduring (but largely unnoted) contributions of Communism to socialism more generally'. This was, as Krikler makes clear in terms of the South African context, an uneven and fragmentary process. By 1922, at the time of the uprising of white workers during the Rand Revolt, he notes that 'the task had only just begun, which left South African Communists somewhat confused in their arguments and even saw some in their party compromising with racism'.[72] Krikler's arguments here underline the depth of the articulations between the left, racism and colonialism in the early to mid-twentieth century which form an important context for the emergence of the leftist politics associated with the Russian Revolution.

Secondly, the volume considers the intensely racialised political terrain on which the Russian Revolution impacted, and signals the importance of this in understanding the reactions and engagement of the black left. Thus the global context was decisively shaped by the political legacies of what Hubert Harrison dubbed the 'white world war' with its entrenchment of various forms of discrimination, the ferocious wave of racialised violence in 1919 and the deep investment of much of the organised left in different situations in colonialism and race.[73] The resistances that were forged in this conjuncture were strongly influenced by the global reach and influence of Garveyism. Thus Adam Ewing contends that Garveyism had particular consequences in shaping the way that 'black workers viewed their struggle for economic justice through a prism of racial solidarity'.[74]

In this regard there were both intersections and key differences between Garveyism and emergent black left politics. As Cathy Bergin notes in her chapter in this volume, Wilfred Domingo's defence of Bolshevism in *The Messenger* insisted that 'there is a great connection between the future of the Negro race the world over and the success of the theories – now under trial in Russia – which are collectively known as Bolshevism'.[75] These arguments, Bergin emphasises, were made during a period 'of vicious reaction for African Americans in relation to the "red summer" of 1919 and its aftermath'. In this context, figures such as Domingo viewed Bolshevism as 'a rallying call for racialised subjects in an environment where worker's revolution seems tangential indeed to the daily humiliations of living as a racialised subject in the US. The Bolshevik revolution is reported as a world-changing event in the black radical press precisely because it is represented as an event which has a particular vanguard role for black workers in the lexicon of class politics.'

These emergent articulations between Bolshevism and black radicalisms were constituted, however, through uneven and contested geographies of connection. 'Africa', for example, was represented at the Third Congress of the Communist International in 1921 by David Ivon Jones, a white Welshman from Aberystwyth who had become a leading figure in the Communist Party of South Africa.[76] Further, while Jones had some anti-racist credentials, his report on 'Communism in South Africa', which appeared in the newspaper *Moscow* in June 1921, argued that 'The African revolution will be led by white workers', stressing the uneven forms of representation which structured these connections.[77] The Sixth Congress of the Communist International in 1928 and the following 'Third Period' or 'Class against class' turn saw a noticeable shift towards anti-racism and anti-imperialist activism. This period witnessed some of the most concerted involvement of Communists in black and colonial liberation struggles, such as the International Labour Defence agitation around the Scottsboro Boys case and the League Against Imperialism's agitation around the Meerut Conspiracy Case in India.[78] The relations between black agency and Communist internationalism nonetheless continued to be fraught and contested in the later 1920s and 1930s. Thus Brent Hayes Edwards, for example, draws attention to the 'uneasy, shifting, articulations with the Comintern' shaped by the collaboration between the Trinidadian George Padmore and Garan Kouyaté, from the French Sudan.[79] That both Kouyaté and Padmore eventually broke with or were expelled from the Comintern demonstrates the increasing tensions surrounding attempts to forge spaces for black political organising within the terrain of Communist internationalism.

As Bergin's chapter notes, the relations between gender, race and Communism were also fraught and contested. Thus she observes, based on her reading of the US black left press, that the terms on which race and class were envisioned in such publications were profoundly gendered. She contends that central to such gendering is the 'active assertion of the raced classed subject as a black man' and the ways in which 'the concept of liberation is usually imagined in relation to black men reclaiming traditional masculinity denied them by the pathologically fixated gendered racism of white supremacism'.

In this regard, constructions of race and class intersected with what Lisa Kirschenbaum has described as Communism's 'Man Question'. Observing that 'communist conceptions of men and revolutionary masculinity were at least as ambiguous, fraught and contradictory as communist understandings of women, and feminism', she notes that 'representations of the ideal male communist appear "fixed and unchanging": he was a muscular, tough and disciplined fighter'.[80] The limits of such articulations between race, class and masculinity were, however, refused by black women Communist activists, who articulated powerful versions of what has been subsequently termed 'black left feminism'. Thus Erik McDuffie suggests how key figures who were part of what he terms a 'black women's international' such as Claudia Jones and Louise Thompson 'practiced a radical internationalist, feminist politics within the US and global Communist Left that was committed to building transnational political alliances with women of color and politically progressive white women from around the world'.[81]

The tensions between differently placed black radicals and the broader circuits of Communist internationalism is also a significant theme of various contributions here. Thus in her chapter on the Caribbean Bureau of the Comintern which was established in New York in 1931, Sandra Pujals draws attention to key ways in which Communist engagements with the politics of 'race' failed to translate effectively into Caribbean contexts. Pujals argues that despite the insights of the Caribbean Bureau 'on the potential revolutionary component of race in the region', it had little impact on Spanish Caribbean Communist parties, and observes that 'local communist organisations did very little to integrate Black workers into their groups or to actively engage in activity among them'.

Thirdly, the volume contributes to work on black internationalism by providing detailed engagements with the diverse practices and terms in which black radicals engaged with the Soviet Union. It also traces some of the key and shifting ways in which the work and ideas of key black radicals were understood in Soviet Russia, allowing a dynamic sense of these relations and exchanges. Thus Olga Panova's chapter discusses some of the key ways in which critical black radicals such as Claude McKay and W.E.B. Du Bois were read and received in the Soviet Union in the interwar period, giving us a fascinating sense, for example, of the shifting reception of McKay's work. Panova notes that while earlier in the 1920s McKay was 'lionised', his novels *Home to Harlem* and *Banjo* received a much more hostile reception from Soviet critics. *Banjo* was 'unanimously regarded as ideologically harmful and a complete failure artistically' and McKay was stigmatised as a 'Bohemian lumpen-intellectual' and a 'petty bourgeois Black nationalist'.

The position of racialised minorities in Soviet Russia and the symbolic importance of their treatment, or at least official presentations of that treatment, had a significant impact on black radicals in different contexts. This can be demonstrated by the way that the Soviet Union's nationalities policy was an enduring inspiration for some black radicals (such as George Padmore, whose *How Russia Transformed Her Colonial Empire: A Challenge to the Imperialist Powers* was published in 1946), even after they had formally long broken with orthodox Communism.[82] Such claims to the anti-imperial and anti-racist character of the Soviet Union, however, are complicated by, and need to be situated within, what Ronald Grigor Suny has described as the rapid shift of 'the radically democratic, anti-imperial and anti-nationalist revolution of 1917' into 'an authoritarian imperial state, formally federal but hyper-centralized, and committed to the formation of nations within its borders'.[83]

In this regard, Matthieu Renault's chapter usefully develops a close reading of Lenin's writings on the 'process of *internal colonization* of the Russian Empire's "free" borderlands'. By examining the disappearance of references to internal colonisation after 1916 he traces significant shifts in Lenin's analysis and engagement with ideas of Russian imperialism. He argues that the resulting tensions between 'two discursive strains' that existed 'simultaneously in his work' presaged 'the contradictions the Bolsheviks would face in the borderlands when performing the dual task of promoting the socialist revolution and decolonizing the Russian empire'. Renault's discussion of Langston Hughes's account of his journeys to Soviet Central Asia also focuses on some of the ways different black radicals' experiences were shaped by engaging with different parts and on different terms with the Soviet Union.[84]

As the chapters by Hal Weaver and Rachel Lee Rubin on the Patrice Lumumba University emphasise, Moscow, and Soviet Russia more generally, also proved to be important hubs of connection of different anti-imperial activists and trajectories. In Hal Weaver's case this engagement draws on his own personal experience of working and researching in Moscow during the early 1960s, yet of course there were much earlier histories of such connections and exchanges. In his autobiography *Black Bolshevik*, the black American Communist Harry Haywood – a critical figure whose work is discussed in Holger Weiss's chapter – recalls meeting a range of other radicals committed to anti-imperial politics during his time studying in Moscow in the late 1920s. He describes being particularly influenced by meeting Irish radicals such as 'Sean Murray and James Larkin, Jr (Big Jim's son)', noting that 'as members of oppressed nations, we had a lot in common'. He was to credit discussions with them as having a major impact on his enthusiasm for the 'Black Belt thesis' – one of the central, if controversial, tenets of US Communism in relation to black politics.[85] Maia Ramnath's work has suggested that similar dynamics existed in terms of Indian anti-colonial activists involved in the Ghadar movement on the US West Coast who travelled to Moscow and studied at the Communist University of the Toilers of the East.[86]

Engagements between black radicals and Russia and the other radicals they met in Russia were generative. Yet, while for figures such as Claude McKay, W.E.B. Du Bois and Paul Robeson the experience of visiting the

Soviet Union – a society apparently without racism – was to prove life-changing, it is important to note, however, that for others the experience was more equivocal.[87] Indeed, for some, encounters with some of the realities of the Soviet Union could also swiftly lead to disillusionment with, and foster opposition to Communism. Ted Bryce, a black seafarer from Cardiff who was of Caribbean heritage, explained to St Clair Drake in the late 1940s that his personal hostility to Communism was based on his experience of seeing forms of what he described as 'slave labour' in Archangelsk while working on the North Atlantic convoys during the Second World War.[88]

Histories of Red and Black linkages and contemporary articulations of racism and resistance

With the collapse of the Soviet Union bringing to a close what Eric Hobsbawm called 'the short twentieth century', in a sense this volume is less about recovering the history of a 'Red and Black Atlantic' which remains some kind of living tradition in the twenty-first century, than about diving down in search of what might be called – to evoke the work of J. Hoberman – a lost 'Red and Black Atlantis'.[89] Some of the difficulties presented by trying to recover a 'lost past' such as this have been theorised in the late Richard Iton's work, *In Search of the Black Fantastic*. Iton observes that 'it is noticeable that there is little mention of how the transition was made' from the political struggles associated with Paul Robeson to the 'later civil rights era'. He contends that this rearrangement of 'the visceral scaffolding of black progressive politics is generally cloaked in silence, with the effect of marginalizing the intensity and significance of the earlier commitments to such an extent that, in many instances, they have simply been forgotten, and rendered unremarkable and for all intents and purposes irretrievable.'[90] He goes on to argue that 'the maps that might help us trace the connections between the pre- and post-Robeson moments do not exist, leaving the rather overpowering silence – the unpublished retraction – that has marked the borders and boundaries of the Popular Front era and classic, southern-based civil rights era politics'.[91] We argue here that tracing *connections and disconnections* across the Red and Black Atlantic can redraw some of the maps of connection and articulation that Iton contends have been erased. By so doing the section draws attention to the relevance some of these connections and lineages for contemporary political debates and engagements around racism and resistance.

The intensifying circuits of repression and anti-Communism which impacted on the articulations between black, left and anti-colonial politics after the Second World War are a significant factor in relation to the erasures referred to by Iton.[92] A key strategy which was used to sunder such connections was the concerted harassment of prominent figures associated with the black Left, particularly in the United States. The treatment of Paul Robeson is well known in this regard, with his passport revoked between 1950 and 1958.[93] Other figures, including prominent radicals of Caribbean backgrounds in the US, were imprisoned or exiled, such as the Jamaican-born Communist Ferdinand Smith who as vice president of the National Maritime Union had been a major figure in the American labour movement.[94] The impact of such repression on maps of connection was particularly significant in relation to the black Trinidadian Claudia Jones – one of the leading Communists in the US – who developed pioneering analyses of the relation between class, race and gender in essays such as 'An end to the Neglect of the Problems of Negro Women'.[95] Jones was imprisoned in Alderson prison, and as a British colonial subject was deported to Britain in 1955 where she did significant organising work among Caribbean migrants, but was largely cold-shouldered by British Communists.[96] The repression meted out to these figures contributed to a significant intergenerational rupture in the transmission of radical ideas on the black left in the US and beyond. While Angela Davis continued the tradition of Claudia Jones by joining the CPUSA and developing an analysis which brought together race, class and gender, Malcolm X for example had to find his way to revolutionary politics independently, only developing a relationship with the revolutionary left at the end of his life.[97]

Marika Sherwood and Nigel Westmaas's respective chapters on Ghana and Guyana demonstrate how different attempts to forge states with independent anti-colonial futures were quickly deposed, often with the help of either British or US intelligence. The political projects of such anti-colonial movements shaped different orientations in relation to Communism, at least to its official variety. Thus in Ghana, Kwame Nkrumah's first post-independence government was influenced by Nkrumah's mentor George Padmore, who increasingly tried to forge a new Pan-African socialist vision independent of Stalinism, allied to the broader Non-Aligned Movement.[98] Other black radicals such as Robeson continued to find inspiration in the Soviet Union, despite (or even in some cases because of) Stalin's regime, due to its stated official anti-racism and anti-colonialism.[99]

As Westmaas indicates, while figures like Cheddi and Janet Jagan were certainly influenced by Communism and Marxism had a broader influence on the left in British Guiana, the reforms introduced by the People's Progressive Party after their landslide election in 1953 had much more in common with moderate social democratic regimes.[100] The British government's 'suspension of the constitution' in British Guiana in 1953 was part of a broader use of anti-Communist repression to depose moderate left governments, including the US-supported coup against Jacobo Arbenz in Guatemala in 1954, rather than being based on any realistic assessment that they represented a significant turn to Communism.[101] Anti-Communism was entrenched on the political right but it also had a significant impact on the left. Thus union confederations like the TUC and the UK Labour Party, marshalled by the Fabian Colonial Bureau, supported the suspension of the constitution in British Guiana and, as Westmaas notes, so did post-independence Caribbean leaders such as Grantley Adams, Alexander Bustamante and Norman Manley.[102]

While Sherwood and Westmaas's chapters speak in large part to the negotiation of relations between Red and Black politics and left-wing and Pan-African political parties, they also indicate that it is useful to engage more broadly with the dynamics of left political cultures in the post-war period. Doing so can foreground the diverse forms of agency shaped by black intellectuals and activists as they reworked and reshaped ideas associated with Communism. Robin D.G. Kelley and Jesse J. Benjamin, for example, in their introduction to Walter Rodney's lectures on 'The Russian Revolution', which were originally given while he was lecturing at Dar es Salaam University in Tanzania in the early 1970s, draw attention to the way Rodney's account does more than 'simply re-narrate well-known events' in the course of the revolution. Rather, they argue that Rodney 'took up the more challenging task of interrogating the meaning, representation, and significance of the Russian Revolution as a world-historical event whose reverberations profoundly shaped Marxist thought, Third World liberation movements, and theories of socialist transformation'.[103] They also indicate the importance of situating Rodney's interventions in relation to Julius Nyerere's experiments with 'African Socialism' in Tanzania.[104]

There were also more subaltern articulations and appropriations of such black left ideas. In line with Makalani's arguments, which were noted earlier, about how left politics articulated with diverse black political formations, Robert A. Hill talks of the politicisation of the Unemployed Workers' Council in 1950s and 1960s Jamaica. He argues that this was 'a fascinating formation' made up 'of the working class'. 'They were Marxists and black militants and Rastafarians, all at the same time and in different degrees', and had their own tradition of political activism going back to the 1920s.

> They developed this kind of oral understanding of Marxism as a dread philosophy. Those men used to debate and talk about – I've learnt this from talking over the years with George Myers – those men used to talk about Soviet polit-buro figures like Kaganovich and Suslov and all dem dread man. At the time, Stalin for the militants of the Unemployed Workers' Council was a character of dread, and that explains to some extent the appeal that Russian communism

had for them. They saw it as a doctrine that would tear down the capitalist Babylonian establishment, root and branch. Many of their parents came from the black artisan class of the 1920s, thirties and forties ... they see something that they can incorporate into [their own political tradition], because it is anti-capitalist. It is anti-oppression. Now, it doesn't mean that they are Stalinist, it just means that the Stalinist philosophy has a symbolic meaning, and it gave them a language that allowed them to translate their own dread experiences into an anti-imperialist rhetoric.[105]

This extract indicates how particular racialised forms of internationalism and agency can shape distinctive left political cultures in different geographical contexts. Thus Hill draws attention to the ways in which Marxism was reconfigured as a 'dread philosophy', speaking to the ways in which it was appropriated and re-articulated in different forms, shaping different forms of political agency in the process.[106]

This has significant relevance for thinking about how the terms on which Red and Black politics were articulated in different formations has important legacies in different contemporary contexts. As Westmaas notes, David Scott's critique of conventional narratives of the colonial historiography of the modern state in the Caribbean is relevant here. Scott challenges what he suggests is an '*entire* paradigm' through which decolonisation and the formation of modern post-colonial states have been established – 'with its distinctive organization of chronologies and personalities and events'.[107] Drawing attention to the different connections that stretch beyond particular nations – a key contribution of many of the chapters in this volume – can offer different perspectives on the left political cultures, which might help in Scott's terms to denormalise or unsettle such familiar chronologies. Revisiting these connections can offer alternatives to singular accounts of the trajectories of national lefts, drawing attention to different ruptures and highlighting different and contested articulations of left politics. This can help to foreground neglected forms of political agency and highlight the coexistence of different ways of envisioning political futures from the left, alongside the parties which in most cases led processes of decolonisation.

This is significant, not in terms of seeing such political cultures as secondary to those international connections, but because, as the example Hill gives shows, it permits a focus on the dynamic ways in which elements of transnational left internationalisms get taken up and reworked in different contexts. This has important resonances for ongoing debates in terms of the left in various places. Such a historicisation of questions of racialised politics and the left is necessary for any genealogy of the emergence of politicised forms of anti-racist politics. In this respect, reasserting such lineages and political trajectories is a necessary move to reassert the missing and erased connections identified by Richard Iton.

Reasserting these lineages of resistance also enables an engagement with the different terms on which blackness has been articulated and constructed politically, in part through solidarities and dialogues with others struggling against oppression. It can also usefully dislocate constructions of blackness as either fixed or transcending time or space. As David Austin has argued, 'the tendency to think of identity as a fixed and immutable essence is problematic in so far as it fails to consider the dynamic of being and becoming that essentially defines what it means to be a healthy human living an "authentic" life; an existence that takes it for granted that freedom does not imply abandoning one's self in a sea of universality'.[108] Further, he suggests that a context defined by 'the wholesale incarceration of a now economically redundant surplus black population', and the cumulative effects of what Ruth Wilson Gilmore describes as 'nearly forty years of life-shortening mass criminalization', emphasises the ongoing character of racialised oppression.[109]

Austin notes that in such a contemporary context, 'retreats into pessimism, futurism, or fictitious kingdoms in which royalty rules, however benignly, over its subjects; or reductionist conceptions of identity that falsely separate blacks from the global realities of modern crisis-ridden capitalism, and how the crisis impacts blacks and other oppressed peoples across the globe, are counterproductive'.[110] In this regard a particularly crucial contribution of work at the intersections of the Red and Black Atlantic to left political discourses and thinking is in terms of powerful ways of understanding the mutually constitutive character of race and class, and in more uneven terms through engagement with their articulations with gender and sexuality. Such contributions continue to be necessary in terms of engagements with the broader left.

Thus, in timely interventions in recent debates around race and class in US politics, historian David Roediger has challenged 'the view of David Harvey and many others that race sits outside the logic of capital'.[111] In related terms, Roediger has observed the unhelpful effects of the continued mobilisation of an 'iron distinction between antiracist and anti-capitalist', and has drawn attention to the importance of figures like Walter Rodney in making these arguments.[112] As this indicates, the political thinking and organising articulated at intersections of the Red and Black Atlantic offers important perspectives for transcending such unhelpful oppositions. These perspectives are also necessary for shaping strategies to counter the ascendant form of racialised right-wing populism. This has in part been produced through particular narratives of a dispossessed 'white working class', which are articulated with the reproduction of colonial imaginaries and relations and have been shaped by entrenched whitening of ideas of class in both political and popular discourses.[113] Kirill Medvedev observes that such moves resonate with the silencing of progressive aspects of the histories of the Soviet Union such as anti-racism, feminism and the decriminalisation of homosexuality, noting that when 'the Russian state today appeals to our heroic past, this progressive history is certainly not what it has in mind'.[114]

The chapters collected here emphasise that the important histories of interracial political and labour organising, while fraught and often problematic, have sought to construct political formations and internationalisms which have offered alternatives to the destructive logics of racial capitalisms. As Cathy Bergin and Anita Rupprecht have argued, the 'liberal narratives, which would monumentalise and domesticate histories of slavery and colonialism, struggle with acknowledging the presence of black radicalism, black rebellion, anti-colonial struggle and the alternative cultural memories' that have been integral to movements such as Black Lives Matter.[115] Reinserting the fraught, always uneven and contested articulations between the histories of Communism and the Russian Revolution and the dynamic left and radical political movements of the Black Atlantic into contemporary discourses of racism and resistance cannot offer a neat story with which to challenge such persistent liberal narratives. They can, however, draw attention to forms of political agency, solidarity and connection that have shaped powerful alternatives to forms of white supremacy and colourblind leftisms, and affirmed alternative logics of equality and freedom. They can therefore perhaps also serve as inspiration for those trying to remake a new revolutionary tradition of 'Red and Black Atlantic' organising among the multiracial working class – now developing in renewed forms and intensity – in its struggles against capital and empire today.

Notes

1 Our thanks to Cathy Bergin, Ben Gowland and Winston James for their comments on a draft of this chapter, which has also benefited from assistance from Ian Birchall, Maxim Matusevich and Jacob Zumoff.

2 Victor Serge, *Notebooks, 1936–1947* (New York: New York Review of Books, 2019), 548. For more on Serge, see Victor Serge, *Memoirs of a Revolutionary* (New York: New York Review of Books, 2012).

3 Wilfred A. Domingo, 'Socialism the Negro's Hope', quoted in Cathy Bergin (ed.), *African American Anti-Colonial Thought, 1917–1937* (Edinburgh: Edinburgh University Press, 2016), 28, 30. It seems likely the group in Trinidad Domingo was thinking of was the Trinidad Workingmen's Association, which was very far from being a revolutionary organisation but it was moving left during 1919 amid rising class struggle on the island. The description of *The Messenger* comes from Winston James, *Holding Aloft the Banner of Ethiopia: Caribbean Radicalism in Early Twentieth-Century America* (London: Verso, 1998), 2.

4 Quoted in Cathy Bergin, *African American Anti-Colonial Thought, 1917–1937* (Edinburgh: Edinburgh University Press, 2016), 30.
5 Philip Foner (ed.), *The Bolshevik Revolution: Its Impact on American Radicals, Liberals, and Labor* (New York: International Publishers, 1967). For a more recent relevant collection of contemporary material for this period relating to the United States, see Paul Heideman (ed.), *Class Struggle and the Color Line: American Socialism and the Race Question, 1900–1930* (Chicago: Haymarket, 2018).
6 See for example the work of Robert A. Hill and the team around him in editing the *Marcus Garvey and Universal Negro Improvement Association Papers*, and also Robert A. Hill, 'Racial and Radical: Cyril V. Briggs, *The Crusader* Magazine and the African Blood Brotherhood 1918–1922' in Cyril V. Briggs (ed.), *The Crusader* (New York: Garland, 1987). Gerald Horne has written numerous works on themes around the Red and the Black, including *Black Liberation/Red Scare: Ben Davis and the Communist Party* (Newark, DE: University of Delaware Press, 1994). See also Marika Sherwood, *Claudia Jones: A Life in Exile* (London: Lawrence & Wishart, 2000); James, *Holding Aloft the Banner of Ethiopia*; Robin D.G. Kelley, *Hammer and Hoe: Alabama Communists during the Great Depression* (Chapel Hill, NC: University of North Carolina Press, 1990); Cedric J. Robinson, *Black Marxism: The Making of the Black Radical Tradition* (Chapel Hill, NC: University of North Carolina Press, 2000); Mark I. Solomon, *The Cry Was Unity: Communists and African Americans, 1917–36* (Jackson, MI: University Press of Mississippi, 1998); Joy Gleason Carew, *Blacks, Reds, and Russians: Sojourners in Search of the Soviet Promise* (New Brunswick, NJ: Rutgers University Press, 2008); Hakim Adi, *Pan-Africanism and Communism: The Communist International, Africa and Diaspora, 1919–1939* (Trenton, J: Africa World Press, 2013); Cathy Bergin, 'Race/Class Politics: The *Liberator*, 1929–1934', *Race & Class*, 47:4 (2006) and '"Unrest among the Negroes": The African Blood Brotherhood and the Politics of Resistance', *Race & Class*, 57:3 (2016); Susan Campbell, '"Black Bolsheviks" and Self-Determination', *Science and Society*, 58:4 (1994–95); Mark Naison, *Communists in Harlem During the Depression* (Chicago, IL: University of Illinois Press, 2005); Minkah Makalani, *In the Cause of Freedom: Radical Black Internationalism from Harlem to London, 1917–1939* (Chapel Hill, NC: University of North Carolina Press, 2013); Carole Boyce Davies, *Left of Karl Marx: The Political Life of Black Communist Claudia Jones* (Durham, NC: Duke University Press, 2008); Holger Weiss, *Framing a Radical African Atlantic: African American Agency, West African Intellectuals and the International Trade Union Committee of Negro Workers* (Leiden: Brill, 2013); Kate A. Baldwin, *Beyond the Color Line and the Iron Curtain: Reading Encounters Between Black and Red, 1922–1963* (Durham, NC: Duke University Press, 2002); Maxim Matusevich (ed.), *Africa in Russia, Russia in Africa: Three Centuries of Encounters* (Trenton, NJ: Africa World Press, 2007); Margaret Stevens, *Red International and Black Caribbean: Communists in New York City, Mexico and the West Indies, 1919–1939*

(London: Pluto, 2017); Michael O. West (with William G. Martin), 'Contours of the Black International' in Michael O. West, William G. Martin and Fanon Che Wilkins (eds), *From Toussaint to Tupac: The Black International since the Age of Revolution* (Chapel Hill, NC: University of North Carolina Press, 2009); Jacob A. Zumoff, *The Communist International and US Communism 1919–1929* (Chicago, IL: Haymarket, 2015).

7 See Winston James, *Claude McKay: The Making of a Black Bolshevik, 1889–1921* (New York: Columbia University Press, 2022).

8 For more on these organisations, see Adi, *Pan-Africanism and Communism* and Weiss, *Framing a Radical African Atlantic*.

9 On Lumumba, see Leo Zeilig, *Lumumba: Africa's Lost Leader* (London: Haus, 2014).

10 Edward Acton, *Russia: The Tsarist and Soviet Legacy* (London: Longman, 1995), 106–107.

11 Leon Trotsky, *My Life: An Attempt at an Autobiography* (Harmondsworth: Penguin, 1979), 185, 187; Sarah Lovell (ed.), *Leon Trotsky Speaks* (New York: Pathfinder Press, 1972), 31; Tony Cliff, *Trotsky: Towards October, 1879–1917* (London: Bookmarks, 1989), 97–99. More research is arguably needed on the impact of the 1905 Revolution among black radicals internationally. For how it inspired Gandhi, see Vijay Prashad, *Red Star Over the Third World* (New Delhi: LeftWord, 2017), 35–36.

12 Liliana Riga, 'The Ethnic Roots of Class Universalism: Rethinking the "Russian" Revolutionary Elite', *American Journal of Sociology*, 114:3 (November 2008), 649–650.

13 Brendan McGeever, *Antisemitism and the Russian Revolution* (Cambridge: Cambridge University Press, 2019).

14 On East St Louis 1917, see James, *Holding Aloft the Banner of Ethiopia*, 94–95.

15 In terms of Black Studies and Russia in general, an important early contribution was Allison Blakely, *Russia and the Negro: Blacks in Russian History and Thought* (Washington, DC: Howard University Press, 1986). The importance of the Russian Revolution was recognised on its centenary. See, for example, Jennifer Wilson and Jennifer Suchland, 'Black October: An Introduction', *Black Perspectives* website, 30 October 2017: www.aaihs.org/black-october-an-introduction/ [accessed 1 February 2021]. During the Cold War, as Africa became a site of struggle, having some sense of the impact of the Russian Revolution on Africa became important in Western scholarship for ideological purposes, leading to the appearance of works such as Robert Legvold, *Soviet Policy in West Africa* (Cambridge, MA: Harvard University Press, 1970) and Edward T. Wilson, *Russia and Black Africa before World War II* (New York: Holmes and Meier, 1974).

16 See for example S.A. Smith, *Russia in Revolution: An Empire in Crisis, 1890 to 1928* (Oxford: Oxford University Press, 2017).

17 E.H. Carr, *The Bolshevik Revolution, 1917–1923*, Vol. 3 (Harmondsworth: Penguin, 1984).

18 See for example John Riddell, Nazeef Mollah and Vijay Prashad (eds), *Liberate the Colonies!: Communism and Colonial Freedom 1917–1924* (New Delhi: LeftWord, 2019). See also the recent collection, Oleksa Drachewych and Ian McKay (eds), *Left Transnationalism: The Communist International and the National, Colonial, and Racial Questions* (London: McGill-Queen's University Press, 2020) and the special issue of the journal *Twentieth Century Communism*, 18 (2020) on 'Transnational Communism and Anti-Colonialism'. For discussions of Africa (including South Africa) see for example Allison Drew, 'Communism in Africa' in Stephen A. Smith (ed.), *The Oxford Handbook of the History of Communism* (Oxford: Oxford University Press, 2014); Matt Swagler, 'Did the Russian Revolution Matter for Africa?' *Review of African Political Economy* website, 30 August 2017: http://roape.net/2017/08/30/rus sian-revolution-matter-africa-part/ [accessed 1 February 2021]; Pete Dwyer and Leo Zeilig, 'Marxism, Class and Revolution in Africa: The Legacy of the 1917 Russian Revolution', *International Socialism*, 157 (2018); Oleksa Drachewych (ed.), *The Communist International, Anti-Imperialism and Racial Equality in British Dominions* (Routledge: Abingdon, 2019); David Johnson, *Dreaming of Freedom in South Africa: Literature between Critique and Utopia* (Edinburgh/Cape Town: Edinburgh University Press/UCT Press, 2020).

19 For a recent introduction to the inspiration of the Russian Revolution for colonial subjects in general, see Prashad, *Red Star Over the Third World*. For a sense of the impact of the Russian Revolution on the Indian left in the 1920s, see Kali Ghosh, *The Autobiography of a Revolutionary in British India* (New Delhi: Social Science Press, 2015), esp. 96–99, and Ali Raza, *Revolutionary Pasts: Communist Internationalism in Colonial India* (Cambridge: Cambridge University Press, 2020).

20 Vladimir Alexandrov estimates that there were about a dozen permanent black residents in Moscow in the early twentieth century amid a population of over a million. Vladimir Alexandrov, *The Black Russian* (London: Head of Zeus, 2013), 59.

21 For the experiences of Philip Jordan, see Clinton A. Bliss, 'Philip Jordan's Letters from Russia, 1917–19: The Russian Revolution as Seen by the American Ambassador's Valet', *Bulletin of the Missouri Historical Society*, 14 (1958), 139–166. Jordon himself mentions a 'negro cook who is very black, a West India negro named Green' also working at the US Embassy in Petrograd, but apart from that there were 'few negroes', and 'none like our negroes'. Helen Rappaport notes that one gets 'fleeting sightings of other African Americans' such as Jim Hercules, 'one of the possibly four black American "Nubian guards" at the Alexander Palace, who served Nicolas and Alexandra and their family right up until the revolution, and who may well have been stranded in Russia for some time afterwards'. See Helen Rappaport, *Caught in the Revolution: Petrograd 1917* (London: Windmill Books, 2016), 13, 334.

22 Alexandrov, *The Black Russian*, 60, 140, 150.

23 Theodore Postan, 'Emma Harris: She Was There When', Black New Yorkers website of the Schomburg Center for Research in Black Culture: https://black

newyorkers-nypl.org/wp-content/uploads/2016/06/harris_emma.pdf [accessed 1 February 2021]. For confirmation of her being singled out by Lenin, see 'Old Brooklyn Friends Hold Reception for Emma Harris After 32-Year European Odyssey', *New York Amsterdam News*, 8 November 1933, 9. On Harris, see 'Emma E. Harris "The Mammy of Moscow"', Notable Kentucky African Americans Database: https://nkaa.uky.edu/nkaa/items/show/1930 [accessed 1 February 2021], and also the memorable portrait of her in Langston Hughes, *I Wonder as I Wander* (New York: Hill and Wang, 1993), 82–86; Julia L. Mickenberg, *American Girls in Red Russia: Chasing the Soviet Dream* (Chicago, IL: University of Chicago Press, 2017), 248.

24 On Arle-Titz, see Mickenberg, *American Girls in Red Russia*, 248–249; and for a 1939 photo of Arle-Titz rehearsing with her pianist husband Boris Titz, see the *Chicago Defender*, 10 June 1939, 13.

25 J. Kim Munholland, 'The French Army and Intervention in Southern Russia, 1918–1919', *Cahiers du Monde Russe Année*, 22:1 (1981), 60. See also Alexandrov, *The Black Russian*, 159. On the Black Sea Mutinies, which were unlikely to have involved many Africans directly, see Ian Birchall, 'From Slaughter to Mutiny' in David Morgan (ed.), *'Stop the First World War': Movements Opposed to the First World War in Britain, France and Germany* (London: Socialist History Society, 2016), 35–48.

26 References to A.N. Gromyko (ed.), *The October Revolution and Africa* (Moscow: Progress, 1983) and Larbi Bouhali, *The October Socialist Revolution and the National Movement in Algeria* (Moscow, 1957), quoted in Jonathan Derrick, *Africa's 'Agitators': Militant Anti-Colonialism in Africa and the West, 1918–1939* (London: Hurst, 2008), 115–116.

27 Prashad, *Red Star Over the Third World*, 39. As Paul Dukes notes of the French West African troops in Russia, they 'took back home with them something of the message of October, including revolutionary songs'. See Paul Dukes, *October and the World: Perspectives on the Russian Revolution* (London: Macmillan, 1979), 146.

28 Robert A. Hill (ed.), *The Marcus Garvey and Universal Negro Improvement Association Papers*, Vol. 1 (Berkeley, CA: University of California Press, 1983), 391. See also Daniel Hanglberger, 'Marcus Garvey and his Relation to (Black) Socialism and Communism', *American Communist History*, 17:2 (2018), 205.

29 Timothy Brennan, 'Postcolonial Studies between the European Wars: An Intellectual History', in Crystal Bartolovich and Neil Lazarus (eds), *Marxism, Modernity and Postcolonial Studies* (Cambridge: Cambridge University Press, 2002), 192–194. See also John Molyneux, *Lenin for Today* (London: Bookmarks, 2017), 76.

30 *Negro World*, 20 September 1919.

31 Karl Marx, *The German Ideology*, Chapter 3, Part 4 (1845), online at: www.marxists.org/archive/marx/works/1845/german-ideology/ch03h.htm [accessed 1 February 2021].

32 Kevin Anderson, *Marx at the Margins: On Nationalism, Ethnicity, and Non-Western Societies* (Chicago and London: University of Chicago Press), 69. On

the Polish and German troops' defection during Haiti's war of independence, see C.L.R. James, *The Black Jacobins: Toussaint L'Ouverture and the San Domingo Revolution* (London: Penguin, 2001), 258.

33 As Tariq Ali notes, Lenin's list was 'eclectic' in its choices and 'the old man was clearly in a hurry' for 'he missed, among others, the Europeans James Connolly, John Maclean and Thomas Müntzer, and the non-Europeans Simon Bolivar, the Rani of Jhansi and Toussaint Louverture'. Tariq Ali, *The Dilemmas of Lenin: Terrorism, War, Empire, Love, Revolution* (London: Verso, 2017), 253. Lenin's list did include the Cuban-born Paul Lafargue, son-in-law of Karl Marx, who was the grandson of a 'mulatto' [mixed-heritage] refugee from Haiti and always proud of his African heritage.

34 On the ABB, see for example the works of Winston James and Minkah Makalani already cited, but also Jacob Zumoff, 'The African Blood Brotherhood: From Caribbean Nationalism to Communism', *Journal of Caribbean History*, 41:1 (2007), 200–226. For the international support of the ABB and particularly its appeal among striking West Indian workers in the Panama Canal Zone in 1920, see Jacob A. Zumoff, 'Black Caribbean Labor Radicalism in Panama, 1914–1921', *Journal of Social History*, 47:2 (2013), 429–457.

35 Cyril Briggs, 'Negro Revolutionary Hero – Toussaint L'Ouverture', *The Communist*, 8:5 (May 1929). Toussaint Louverture, described as 'the Black Napoleon', featured on the cover of the *Negro Worker*, 4:8–9 (August–September 1933).

36 On *Black Reconstruction*, see Brian Kelly, 'Slave Self-Activity and the Bourgeois Revolution in the United States: Jubilee and the Boundaries of Black Freedom', *Historical Materialism*, 27:3 (2019). On *The Black Jacobins*, see Charles Forsdick and Christian Høgsbjerg (eds), *The Black Jacobins Reader* (Durham, NC: Duke University Press, 2017) and Rachel Douglas, *Making The Black Jacobins: C.L.R. James and the Drama of History* (Durham, NC: Duke University Press, 2019).

37 James, *Holding Aloft the Banner of Ethiopia*, 180. See also Claude McKay, 'Soviet Russia and the Negro', *Crisis* (December 1923), 61–65.

38 Claude McKay, *A Long Way from Home* (New York: Arno, 1969), 167–168.

39 John Riddell (ed.), *Towards the United Front: Proceedings of the Fourth Congress of the Communist International, 1922* (Leiden: Brill, 2011), 950.

40 For discussion of these, see Baldwin, *Beyond the Color Line and the Iron Curtain*, chapter 1, and also Jacob A. Zumoff, 'Mulattoes, Reds, and the Fight for Black Liberation in Claude McKay's *Trial By Lynching* and *Negroes in America*', *Journal of West Indian Literature*, 19:1 (2010).

41 Claude McKay, 'Report on the Negro Question: Speech to the Fourth Congress of the Comintern', *International Press Correspondence*, 3 (5 January 1923), 16–17.

42 McKay, *A Long Way from Home*, 206–207. For more on Trotsky and black liberation, see Leon Trotsky, *On Black Nationalism and Self-Determination* (New York: Pathfinder, 1972); Christian Høgsbjerg, 'The Prophet and Black Power: Trotsky on Race in the US', *International Socialism*, 121 (2009).

43 McKay, *A Long Way from Home*, 208. Sadly the scheme was blocked by others in the Red Army and Trotsky himself would shortly be sidelined by the rise of Stalin. Nonetheless, as Winston James notes, some black people in Russia, mainly descendants of Africans who had settled several generations before along the Black Sea, did fight for the Soviet Union. 'They fought, distinguished themselves and rose in Trotsky's Red Army, moistened the Russian soil with their blood during the Civil War, and at least one served in the Soviet of Tblisi, the capital of Georgia in the 1920s' (James, *Holding Aloft the Banner of Ethiopia*, 167).

44 McKay, *A Long Way from Home*, 173.

45 See also Gary Edward Holcomb, *Claude McKay, Code Name Sasha: Queer Black Marxism and the Harlem Renaissance* (Gainesville, FL: University Press of Florida, 2007).

46 Robert A. Hill (ed.), *The Marcus Garvey and Universal Negro Improvement Association Papers*, Vol. 5 (Berkeley, CA: University of California Press, 1987), 549, 551, quoted in Zumoff, 'The African Blood Brotherhood', 217.

47 Quoted in Leslie James, *George Padmore and Decolonization from Below: Pan-Africanism, the Cold War and the End of Empire* (Basingstoke: Palgrave Macmillan, 2015), 74.

48 For some recent work in this area, see for example Carol Polsgrove, *Ending British Rule in Africa: Writers in a Common Cause* (Manchester: Manchester University Press, 2012); Christian Høgsbjerg, *C.L.R. James in Imperial Britain* (Durham, NC: Duke University Press, 2014); Marc Matera, *Black London: The Imperial Metropolis and Decolonization in the Twentieth Century* (Berkeley, CA: University of California Press, 2015).

49 C.L.R. James, *World Revolution, 1917–1937: The Rise and Fall of the Communist International* (Durham, NC: Duke University Press, 2017), 372.

50 It is perhaps interesting here to also note that Tsarist Russia had provided military assistance to the Ethiopian army against Italy during the Battle of Adwa in 1896.

51 Bernhard H. Bayerlin, 'Addis Ababa, Rio de Janeiro and Moscow 1935: The Double Failure of Comintern Anti-Fascism and Anti-Colonialism' in Kasper Braskén, Nigel Copsey and David Featherstone (eds), *Antifascism in a Global Perspective: Transnational Networks, Exile Communities and Radical Internationalism* (London: Routledge, 2020), 218–233. Claude McKay's recently discovered novel *Amiable with Big Teeth: A Novel of the Love Affair Between the Communists and the Poor Black Sheep of Harlem* (published in 2018) is evocative of the atmosphere in the late 1930s period in Harlem in the aftermath of this betrayal by the Soviet Union.

52 C.L.R. James, 'The Greatest Event in History', *Socialist Appeal*, 3:87 (14 November 1939): www.marxists.org/archive/james-clr/works/1939/11/greatest.html [accessed 1 February 2021].

53 Paul Gilroy, *The Black Atlantic: Modernity and Double Consciousness* (London: Verso, 1993), 29.

54 *Ibid.*, drawing in particular on Peter Linebaugh and Marcus Rediker's 'The Many-Headed Hydra: Sailors, Slaves and the Atlantic Working Class in the

Eighteenth Century', *Journal of Historical Sociology*, 3:3 (1990), 225–252, which set out the core arguments of their hugely influential book *The Many-Headed Hydra: Sailors, Slaves and Commoners and the Hidden History of the Revolutionary Atlantic* (London: Verso, 2001). See also David Armitage, 'The Red Atlantic', *Reviews in American History*, 29:4 (2001).

55 Gilroy, *The Black Atlantic*, 12–13.

56 Key reference points here include West, Martin and Wilkins, *From Toussaint to Tupac*; Lisa Brock, Robin D.G. Kelley and Karen Sotiropoulos (eds), special issue on 'Transnational Black Studies', *Radical History Review*, 87 (2003); Brent Hayes Edwards, *The Practice of Diaspora: Literature, Translation and the Rise of Black Internationalism* (Cambridge, MA: Harvard University Press, 2003); Erik S. McDuffie, *Sojourning for Freedom: Black Women, American Communism and the Making of Black Left Feminism* (Durham, NC: Duke University Press, 2011); Makalani, *In the Cause of Freedom*; Davies, *Left of Karl Marx*.

57 Edwards, *The Practice of Diaspora*, 117.

58 Baldwin, *Beyond the Color Line and the Iron Curtain*. For a useful overview of Du Bois's response to the Russian Revolution, see Bill V. Mullen, *W.E.B. Du Bois: Revolutionary Across the Color Line* (London: Pluto, 2016), 57–72.

59 George Padmore, *Pan-Africanism or Communism?: The Coming Struggle for Africa* (London: Dennis Dobson, 1956) and notably Adi, *Pan-Africanism and Communism*.

60 Harold Cruse, *The Crisis of the Negro Intellectual* (New York: Morrow, 1967). For a detailed critical engagement with Cruse, see 'Harold Cruse and the West Indians: Critical Remarks on *The Crisis of the Negro Intellectual*' in Winston James's *Holding Aloft the Banner of Ethiopia*, 262–291.

61 See for example Kelley, *Hammer and Hoe*, 92–116, and Naison, *Communists in Harlem During the Depression*.

62 Dick J. Reavis, 'The Life and Death of Lovett Fort-Whiteman, the Communist Party's First African American Member', *Jacobin*, 7 April 2020: www.jacobinmag.com/2020/04/lovett-fort-whiteman-black-communist-party [accessed 1 February 2021].

63 For more on Junco, see Anne Garland Mahler, 'The Red and the Black in Latin America: Sandalio Junco and the "Negro Question" from an Afro-Latin American Perspective', *American Communist History*, 17:1 (2018).

64 Peter Linebaugh, *The Incomplete, True, Authentic and Wonderful History of May Day* (Oakland, CA: PM Press, 2016), 56. On one later leading black Communist from Cameroon, see Robbie Aitken, 'From Cameroon to Germany and back via Moscow and Paris: The Political Career of Joseph Bilé (1892–1959), performer, "Negerarbeiter" and Comintern activist', *Journal of Contemporary History*, 43:4 (2008), 597–616.

65 James, *Holding Aloft the Banner of Ethiopia*, 156.

66 Makalani, *In the Cause of Freedom*, 73.

67 See Lydia Lindsey, 'Gendering the Black Radical Tradition: Grace P. Campbell's Role in the Formation of a Radical Feminist Tradition in African American

Intellectual Culture' in David Featherstone, Christian Høgsbjerg and Alan Rice (eds), *Revolutionary lives of the Red and Black Atlantic since 1917* (Manchester: Manchester University Press, 2022).

68 Makalani, *In the Cause of Freedom*, 73.

69 Joyce Moore Turner with W. Burghardt Turner, *Caribbean Crusaders and the Harlem Renaissance* (Chicago, IL: University of Illinois Press, 2005).

70 Sharad Chari and Katherine Verdery, 'Thinking Between the Posts: Postcolonialism, Postsocialism, and Ethnography after the Cold War', *Comparative Studies in Society and History*, 51:1 (2009), 6–34, quote on 7.

71 James, *Holding Aloft the Banner of Ethiopia*, 181.

72 Jeremy Krikler, *White Rising: The 1922 Insurrection and Racial Killing in South Africa* (Manchester: Manchester University Press, 2005), 110. See also James, *Holding Aloft the Banner of Ethiopia*, 181–182.

73 Hubert Harrison cited in Brian Kwoba, 'Hubert Henry Harrison: Black Radicalism and the Colored International' in David Featherstone, Christian Høgsbjerg and Alan Rice (eds), *Revolutionary lives of the Red and Black Atlantic since 1917* (Manchester: Manchester University Press, 2022). On different aspects of the racist violence in 1919, see Harry Haywood, *Black Bolshevik: Autobiography of an Afro-American Communist* (Chicago, IL: Lake View Press, 1978), 81–92; James, *Holding Aloft the Banner of Ethiopia*, 72, 76; Jacqueline Jenkinson, *Black 1919: Riots, Racism and Resistance in Imperial Britain* (Liverpool: Liverpool University Press, 2008). See also Jonathan Hyslop, 'The Imperial Working Class Makes Itself "White": White Labourism in Britain, Australia, and South Africa Before the First World War', *Journal of Historical Sociology*, 12:4 (1999), 398–421; Satnam Virdee, *Racism, Class and the Racialised Outsider* (London: Palgrave, 2014).

74 Adam Ewing, 'Caribbean Labour Politics in the Age of Garvey, 1918–1938', *Race & Class*, 55:1 (2013), 24.

75 See Bergin's chapter in this volume.

76 Baruch Hirson and Gwyn A. Williams, *The Delegate For Africa: David Ivon Jones, 1883–1924* (London: Core Publications, 1995), 207–220.

77 Cited by Hirson and Williams, *The Delegate For Africa*, 210. For more on the South African left in the first half of the twentieth century, see Allison Drew, *Discordant Comrades: Identities and Loyalties on the South African Left* (Aldershot: Ashgate, 2000) and Johnson, *Dreaming of Freedom in South Africa*.

78 See, for example, James A. Miller, Susan D. Pennybacker and Eve Rosenhaft, 'Mother Ada Wright and the International Campaign to Free the Scottsboro Boys, 1931–1934', *American Historical Review*, 106:2 (2001). See also James A. Miller, *Remembering Scottsboro: The Legacy of an Infamous Trial* (Princeton, NJ: Princeton University Press, 2009).

79 Edwards, *The Practice of Diaspora*, 244.

80 Lisa A. Kirschenbaum, 'The Man Question: How Bolshevik Masculinity Shaped International Communism', *Socialist History*, 52 (2017), 77. See also Michelle Stephens, *Black Empire: The Masculine Global Imaginary of*

Caribbean Intellectuals in the United States, 1914–1961 (Durham, NC: Duke University Press, 2005).

81 McDuffie, *Sojourning For Freedom*, 17–18.

82 George Padmore and Dorothy Pizer, *How Russia Transformed Her Colonial Empire: A Challenge to the Imperialist Powers* (London: Dennis Dobson, 1946). For more on this book, see Theo Williams, 'George Padmore and the Soviet Model of the British Commonwealth', *Modern Intellectual History*, 16:2 (2019), 531–559.

83 Ronald Grigor Suny, 'An Empire to End Imperialism', *Socialist History*, 52 (2017), 95–102.

84 For more on some of the issues around the experience of Muslims in the Soviet Union raised by Renault's chapter, see Dave Crouch, 'The Bolsheviks and Islam', *International Socialism*, 110 (2006): http://isj.org.uk/the-bolsheviks-and-islam/ [accessed 1 February 2021].

85 Haywood, *Black Bolshevik*, 206. For a useful discussion of the Black Belt thesis and its limitations, see Christopher Phelps, 'Introduction – Race and Revolution: A Lost Chapter in American Radicalism', in Max Shachtman, *Race and Revolution* (London: Verso, 2003).

86 Maia Ramnath, *Haj to Utopia: How the Ghadar Movement Charted Global Radicalism and Attempted to Overthrow the British Empire* (Berkeley, CA: University of California Press, 2011), 140–145.

87 Rachel Lee Rubin's chapter includes evidence of continuing undercurrents of racism towards black students at Patrice Lumumba University in Moscow, for example.

88 Schomburg Center for Research in Black Culture, New York, St Clair Drake Papers, 13/6.

89 J. Hoberman, *The Red Atlantis: Communist Culture in the Absence of Communism* (Philadelphia, PA: Temple University Press, 2000).

90 Richard Iton, *In Search of the Black Fantastic: Politics and Popular Culture in the Post-Civil Rights Era* (Oxford: Oxford University Press, 2008), 61. For more on this, see for example Horne, *Black Liberation/Red Scare*; Carol Anderson, *Eyes Off the Prize: The United Nations and the African American Struggle for Human Rights, 1944–1955* (Cambridge: Cambridge University Press, 2003); Carol Anderson, *Bourgeois Radicals: The NAACP and the Struggle for Colonial Liberation, 1941–1960* (Cambridge: Cambridge University Press, 2014).

91 Iton, *In Search of the Black Fantastic*, 61.

92 For more on this see Penny M. Von Eschen, *Race against Empire: Black Americans and Anticolonialism* (Ithaca, NY: Cornell University Press, 1997); Richard Seymour, 'The Cold War, American Anticommunism and the Global "Colour Line"' in Alexander Anievas, Nivi Manchanda and Robbie Shilliam (eds), *Race and Racism in International Relations: Confronting the Global Colour Line* (London: Routledge, 2014).

93 Martin Duberman, *Paul Robeson: A Biography* (New York: The New Press, 1989), esp. 381–428.

94 Gerald Horne, *Red Seas: Ferdinand Smith and Radical Black Sailors in the United States and Jamaica* (New York: New York University Press, 2005).

95 Claudia Jones, 'An End to the Neglect of the Problems of Negro Women' in Carole Boyce Davies (ed.), *Claudia Jones: Beyond Containment* (Banbury: Ayebia Clarke Publishing, 2011), 74–86.

96 Boyce Davies, *Left of Karl Marx* and Denise Lynn, 'Deporting Black Radicalism: Claudia Jones' Deportation and Policing Blackness in the Cold War', *Twentieth Century Communism*, 18 (2020).

97 Angela Davis, *Women, Race and Class* (London: The Women's Press, 1982) and Angela Davis, *An Autobiography* (New York: International Publishers, 1988). Malcolm X was deeply impressed by C.L.R. James's 1948 'The Revolutionary Answer to the Negro Problem in the United States', which he read in the 1960s as a Socialist Workers' Party (SWP) pamphlet. See Paul Buhle and Lawrence Ware, 'Malcolm X, C.L.R. James and Political Choices Today', *Counterpunch*, 12 August 2015. Malcolm X went on to develop a relationship with Trotskyists in the American SWP. For more on Malcolm X's last year, see George Breitman, *Last Year of Malcolm X: Evolution of a Revolutionary* (New York: Pathfinder, 1970) and Marika Sherwood, *Malcolm X: Visits Abroad, April 1964–February 1965* (Oare, Kent: Savannah Press, 2011).

98 James, *George Padmore and Decolonisation from Below*. See also Hakeem Ibikunle Tijani, *Union Education in Nigeria: Labor, Empire and Decolonization Since 1945* (New York: Palgrave Macmillan, 2012).

99 In the US Harry Haywood was probably one of the most significant figures in this regard and was involved in splinter groups from the CPUSA which were based on a Stalinist resolution of the national question such as the Provisional Organising Committee for a Communist Party which was founded in August 1958 and according to Haywood 'consisted mainly of Black and Puerto Rican working class cadres'. See Haywood, *Black Bolshevik*, 622.

100 Cheddi Jagan, *Forbidden Freedom: The Story of British Guiana* (London: Lawrence & Wishart, 1954), esp. 73–77.

101 Vijay Prashad, *The Darker Nations: A People's History of the Third World* (New York: New School Press, 2007); Mark Curtis, *Web of Deceit: Britain's Real Role in the World* (London: Vintage, 2003).

102 See P.S. Gupta, *Imperialism and the British Labour Movement, 1914–1964* (Basingstoke: MacMillan Press, 1975), 359–362. The discussion around the suspension of the constitution in British Guiana at the 1954 congress of the Scottish Trades Union Congress (STUC) gives a strong sense of some of these debates, and also indicates the ways in which the mainstream Labour and TUC position was challenged by a minority within the labour movement, in this case delegates from the Communist-dominated National Union of Mineworkers Scottish Area. See *Fifty Seventh Annual Report of the Scottish Trades Union Congress* (Glasgow: STUC, 1954), 290–291. There was a similar process internally in Jamaica, as Norman Manley's People's National Party moved to the right, in 1952 expelling the 'Four H's' who were leading figures of the party's Marxist left: Richard Hart, Arthur Henry, Frank Hill and Ken Hill.

103 Jesse J. Benjamin and Robin D.G. Kelley, 'Introduction: An "African Perspective" on the Russian Revolution' in Walter Rodney, *The Russian Revolution: A View From the Third World* (London: Verso, 2018), xx. See also Yousuf Al-Bulushi, 'Thinking Racial Capitalism and Black Radicalism from Africa: An Intellectual Geography of Cedric Robinson's World-System', *Geoforum* (2020, online early view).

104 See Matthew Quest, 'The Historical Retrieval and Controversy of Walter Rodney's Russian Revolution', *New Politics*, 68 (2020). For a defence of Ujamaa, see Ralph Ibbott, *Ujamaa: The Hidden History of Tanzania's Socialist Villages* (London: Crossroads Books, 2014).

105 David Scott, 'The Archaeology of Black Memory: An Interview with Robert A. Hill', *Small Axe*, 5 (March 1999), 97–99 [80–150]. For more on George Myers (who used the pseudonym Joseph Edwards), see Matthew Quest (ed.), *Workers' Self-Management in the Caribbean: The Writings of Joseph Edwards* (Atlanta, GA: On Our Own Authority!, 2014). 'Black Stalin', the name adopted by the legendary political Trinidadian calypsonian Leroy Calliste, might also speak to this grassroots popular anti-capitalist philosophy. See Louis Regis, *Black Stalin: Kaisonian* (Kingston: Arawak, 2007) and the documentary film *Come With It, Black Man: A Biography of Black Stalin's Consciousness* (2012).

106 The tensions between Marxism and Rastafarianism continued to be a theme in the Black Power movement in Jamaica as it developed into the 1960s, as can be seen by the chapters by Rupert Lewis and Anthony Bogues in Kate Quinn (ed.), *Black Power in the Caribbean* (Gainesville, FL: University of Florida, 2014).

107 David Scott, 'On the Very Idea of the Making of Modern Jamaica', *Small Axe*, 54 (2017), 43–47.

108 David Austin, 'Introduction: The Dialect of Liberation' in David Austin (ed.), *Moving Against the System: The 1968 Congress of Black Writers and the Making of Global Consciousness* (London: Pluto Press, 2018), 73.

109 Ruth Wilson Gilmore, 'Abolition Geography and the Problem of Innocence' in Gaye Theresa Johnson and Alex Lubin (eds), *Futures of Black Radicalism* (London: Verso, 2017), 225–240, quote on 228.

110 Austin, 'Introduction: The Dialect of Liberation', 73.

111 David Roediger, *Class, Race, and Marxism* (London: Verso, 2017), 19.

112 Roediger, *Class, Race, and Marxism*, 1.

113 Sivamohan Valluvan, *The Clamour of Nationalism: Race and Nation in Twenty-First Century Britain* (Manchester: Manchester University Press, 2019).

114 Kirill Medvedev, 'Europeans and Russia Should Remember what Bound them Together: Anti-Fascism', *Guardian*, 8 May 2020: www.theguardian.com/world/commentisfree/2020/may/08/europeans-russians-together-anti-facism [accessed 10 May 2020].

115 Cathy Bergin and Anita Rupprecht, 'History, Agency and the Representation of "Race": An Introduction', *Race & Class* 57:3 (2016), 3–17, quote on 12.

I

Racism, resistance and revolution

1

Claude McKay's Bolshevisation in London

Winston James

If there was no romance for me in London, there was plenty of radical knowledge.

Claude McKay, 1937

Claude McKay's sojourn in London marks one of the pivotal moments in his political and intellectual evolution. Yet it remains one of the most obscure, underexplored and poorly understood. This, no doubt, is partly due to McKay's own misleading statements and silences about his time in Britain. But the ignoring and ignorance of valuable archival resources by ostensible McKay scholars, and until recently the unavailability of other relevant sources of information have certainly also played their part. My intention here is, therefore, to apprehend more fully the dimensions of McKay's London moment by drawing on these overlooked and new archival resources. In particular, I hope to illuminate the radical milieus in which McKay lived and operated, the social and political circles in which he moved, the friendships, networks and contacts he established, and to document and analyse the manner in which his 'English innings', as he called it, proved crucial in deepening his radicalisation, to the extent that he became a fully and publicly committed Bolshevik – a relatively rare phenomenon among black intellectuals at the time.[1]

The road to London

McKay arrived in London in early December 1919 and returned to New York over a year later in January 1921. But his journey to Britain had certain distinct and important characteristics. First, unlike virtually all the other Caribbean intellectuals who made their way to Britain, McKay's journey to London was indirect: he travelled not from Kingston, Jamaica, but from New York City and after an absence of more than seven years from his native Jamaica.[2] Second, he was not simply an intellectual migrating to

Britain. He had in fact been a member of America's black proletariat ever since he dropped out of college after just two years in 1914, earning his living in the US, as his close friend Max Eastman put it, 'in every one of the ways that northern Negroes do, from "pot-wrestling" in a boarding-house kitchen to dining-car service on the New York and Philadelphia Express'.[3] Moreover, McKay regarded and explicitly identified himself as 'not only a Negro but also a worker',[4] and his American poetry reflected that world, as would his novels. Prior to going to Britain, then, McKay had experienced a double exposure setting him further apart from the other Caribbean intellectuals who went to England in the nineteenth and twentieth centuries: he had travelled indirectly after having lived not only as a black person in a virulently racist America, but also as a member of its black working class, one of its millions of 'Negro' menials.

Partly because of this prior American life, by the time he arrived in London, McKay was no 'black Briton' except in the most nominal sense of that term. And even that, he would later disavow: 'I've never *felt* I was legitimately British, which I'm not after all.'[5] He was from the British Caribbean but his self-identification had expanded well beyond such tight confines through experience, travel and conscious decision. He identified himself as a Pan-Africanist (one who recognised the common experience, condition and struggles of black people the world over) *and* a revolutionary socialist – a race man and a class man, not merely a West Indian.[6] He had entered the US as a Fabian socialist and freethinker. But during the next seven years he had been further radicalised by the shocking brutality of racism in the US; the catastrophe of the First World War; and the hope engendered by the outbreak of revolution in Russia, revolutionary upheavals elsewhere in Europe and especially the Irish and Indian anti-colonial struggles. His British sojourn would significantly deepen and consolidate these allegiances.

McKay's reflections on Britain and the British (especially the English) were overdetermined by his experience of racism, and they mark a historic departure. They break with the adulatory and often cloying celebration of Britain, characteristic of previous black writings – including William Wells Brown, Frederick Douglass and Ida B. Wells-Barnett – anticipating a sensibility that was to become more pronounced in black British writing and political practices half a century later. McKay's distinguished Caribbean predecessors, such as Henry Sylvester Williams and Theophilus Scholes, were critical of Britain, but focused on imperial matters unfolding outside Britain itself. McKay was arguably the first Caribbean intellectual to provide a detailed description and analysis of what it meant to be black in Britain.[7] He wrote with anger and bitterness, pre-empting sentiments expressed half a century later by writers such as George Lamming, reaching a crescendo in the work of Linton Kwesi Johnson and a later generation.[8] McKay's anti-British feelings remained with him and intensified the older he got.

The man who went to London

Best known for his pioneering role in the so-called 'Harlem Renaissance' of the 1920s, Claude McKay was born in Jamaica into an uncommonly prosperous peasant family in 1889. He was educated by his eldest brother, Uriah Theodore, who had been a prize student at Mico College (the Caribbean's leading teacher training college). Seventeen years Claude's senior, U. Theo (as he was known to all) became one of the island's outstanding schoolmasters. Exceptionally widely read, worldly and cosmopolitan, and progressive in outlook, U. Theo trained Claude in the virtues of socialism, feminism and militant rationalism. After a brief stint in the constabulary, which radicalised him further, McKay immigrated to the United States in 1912 to study scientific agriculture at Tuskegee Institute.[9] Hating the 'semi-military, machinelike existence' of Booker T. Washington's school, he transferred to Kansas State College.[10] But in 1914 he gave that up too, for New York. Before leaving Jamaica, he had earned a reputation as a poet and published two volumes of verse to critical acclaim at home and abroad. To make a living in New York, he laboured at the tasks described by Eastman, stealing time on the job to work at the craft of poetry. His first American poems appeared in 1917; by 1919 he had become famous (and notorious) throughout the US, mainly because of his militant sonnet, 'If We Must Die'.[11]

American racism shocked and appalled him. 'I had heard of prejudice in America but never dreamed of it being so intensely bitter', he wrote.[12] He was attracted by Garvey's Universal Negro Improvement Association (UNIA), and wrote for its newspaper, *Negro World*, but never joined the organisation. However, while working in a Manhattan factory, McKay did join the Industrial Workers of the World (IWW), the most radical, internationalist and inclusive working-class organisation in the US. The IWW welcomed and embraced skilled and unskilled workers, men and women, and – going against the American grain – white, black, Asian and all others who wished to join, regardless of race and ethnicity.[13]

Before he left the US, two events had crucially affected McKay and contributed to his deepening radicalisation. The first was the mass carnage wrought by the First World War. This 'great catastrophe', as he called it, had proven the 'real hollowness of nationhood, patriotism, racial pride and most of the things which one was taught to respect and reverence'. The war, he averred, epitomised the 'blind brute forces of tigerish tribalism which remain at the core of civilized society'.[14]

But out of that catastrophe came the second event that inspired McKay. This was the Russian Revolution. 'Holy' Russia, as he dubbed Soviet Russia, had given McKay back his 'golden hope'.[15] Before the second anniversary of the revolution he was debating the subject with the black nationalist Garveyites. He vigorously promoted the relevance of Bolshevism to the struggles of black people the world over. 'Every Negro', he wrote in a letter to the *Negro World*,

> who lays claim to leadership should make a study of Bolshevism and explain its meaning to the colored masses. It is the greatest and most scientific idea afloat in the world today that can be easily put into practice by the proletariat to better its material and spiritual life. Bolshevism ... has made Russia safe for the Jew ... It might make these United States safe for the Negro.[16]

McKay was not alone in advocating black liberation through Bolshevism. But he was one of the first black people to do so in the US, and he did so vigorously and openly, which drew the attention of the authorities.[17]

The pogroms and attempted pogroms against black people in the United States, the so-called 'race riots' of 1919, also had a profound impact on McKay. White mobs, led mainly by ex-servicemen, went on a rampage of unparalleled breadth and savagery. Almost thirty outbreaks with their blood and fire, death and destruction, convulsed urban America. These events of 1919 were dubbed the 'Red Summer' by James Weldon Johnson, black poet and executive secretary of the National Association for the Advancement of Colored People (NAACP).[18] The Red Summer had a catalytic effect on McKay, helping to transform him into a revolutionary. It was his open, militant and courageous response to it that first brought McKay into the limelight. 'If we must die', he implored a besieged Afro-America,

> – oh, let us nobly die,
> So that our precious blood may not be shed
> In vain; then even the monsters we defy
> Shall be constrained to honor us though dead!
>
> Oh, kinsmen! We must meet the common foe;
> Though far outnumbered, let us still be brave,
> And for their thousand blows deal one death-blow! ...
> Like men we'll face the murderous, cowardly pack,
> Pressed to the wall, dying, but – fighting back![19]

And it was for this reaction to 1919 that he is most widely remembered. Important though these experiences were, the key to the distinctiveness of McKay as a black intellectual in Britain is not only his political formation and trajectory prior to his arrival in London, but also the milieu in which he lived, chose to live and operate, and the friendships he established while in London.

As in the US, McKay was shocked at the racism he encountered in London. He was denied long-term lodgings – and during his time in England he rented from foreign landladies, who, in at least one instance, were taunted by their English neighbours for doing so. He was refused service in pubs. He was insulted while accompanying white female comrades in the streets, physically attacked on more than one occasion and 'nearly mauled in Limehouse'. McKay was forced to conclude of England: 'One must always be on one's guard.'[20] At the time he had lodgings with a German family at Provence Street in Islington, but a few months later decided to move to West London, where it was 'a little safer' and '[t]he grown-ups are more sensible & the children are not so disgustingly provocative & bad-mannered'.[21] In London McKay often felt like a man under siege. And he was disgusted by the smug racism of the British intelligentsia as revealed in the tone and language of the reviews of his *Spring in New Hampshire and Other Poems*, published in London in 1920.[22]

Little wonder then that McKay described his time in London as an 'ordeal', 'that most miserable of years'.[23] Even the 'suffocating' fog of London – which 'not only wrapped you around but entered your throat like a strangling nightmare' – seemed to McKay more welcoming than the Londoners themselves: 'The feeling of London was so harshly unfriendly to me that sometimes I was happy in the embrace of the unfolding fog.' 'Oh blessed was the fog that veiled me blind!' he rejoiced in a poem on the city. To him, the English as a whole were 'a strangely unsympathetic people, as coldly chilling as their English fog'.[24]

Despite the misery, McKay acknowledged that he got something of value from his time in London, for which he was eternally grateful: 'plenty of radical knowledge'.[25] This was not an abstract knowledge, but as we shall see, it was one that he gained through *praxis* – the linking of theory to practice. For McKay became politically engaged in the most practical sense of the term for the first time in his life. He was an active member of the Central Branch of the Workers' Socialist Federation (WSF), the very first time that he became a disciplined party activist.

Three groups and institutions were crucial in the process of his accumulating this 'radical knowledge'. The first was the group around Sylvia Pankhurst, the WSF, which she founded and led, and its organ, the *Workers' Dreadnought*; the second was the Hoxton-based International Socialist Club (ISC), in London's East End; and the third was a club based in central London's Drury Lane, catering to black, non-white and colonial veterans of the First World War. His experience in these three (sometimes overlapping) milieus played a crucial role in McKay's political development and radicalisation.[26]

McKay's British milieus

Sylvia Pankhurst, the Workers' Socialist Federation and the Workers' Dreadnought

American friends provided him with contacts in London and letters of introduction to Charles Ogden, editor of the *Cambridge Magazine*, Grant Richards, the publisher, and George Bernard Shaw, among others.[27] But the first person that McKay contacted in London was not one of these eminent men of Britain's literary and publishing world. It was Sylvia Pankhurst. McKay was not a complete stranger to Pankhurst. In September 1919, a few months before they met face to face, Pankhurst's newspaper, the *Workers' Dreadnought*, had carried a prominent spread of five poems written by McKay (including 'If We Must Die'), under the caption, 'A Negro Poet', describing him as 'a negro of Jamaica, who when he wrote them, was a waiter in an American dining car'.[28] McKay's connection to Max and Crystal Eastman, American friends of Pankhurst and editors of the *Liberator* magazine, from which the poems were republished, no doubt also helped.[29] McKay began work on the *Workers' Dreadnought* within weeks of his arrival, thus becoming, so claimed Peter Fryer, 'Britain's first black reporter'.[30]

McKay's published recollection of his first meeting with Pankhurst is unreliable, however. Writing almost twenty years after the event, he reported that he met her after a letter he had written to the *Daily Herald* in April 1920 had been rejected. But, in fact, Pankhurst had employed him before she left for a tour of Italy and Germany in the autumn of 1919, as he confided to Ogden. He had published his revolutionary poem 'Samson' as early as the 10 January 1920 issue of the *Dreadnought*, over four months before the date he claimed to have become associated with Pankhurst and her paper. Furthermore, his article 'Socialism and the Negro' adorned the front page of the *Dreadnought* the same month.[31] Thus when he wrote of his job on the *Dreadnought* as an 'opportunity to practice a little practical journalism [which] was not to be missed', McKay failed to disclose his membership in the Central Branch of Pankhurst's WSF and also that he had quickly become one of the organisation's leading comrades.[32] In the summer of 1920 he more than likely attended (though the evidence is not definitive) the historic Communist Unity Convention in London, which laid the foundations for the formation of the Communist Party of Great Britain.

McKay's job at the *Dreadnought* formally entailed covering the volatile labour situation at the London docks, which had been the scene of racist riots in the summer of 1919, getting news from the non-European as well as white seafarers and writing from a point of view which would be fresh and different. He was also assigned the task of reading the foreign newspapers from the US, India, Australia, Africa and other parts of the British Empire, with an eye to items that might interest *Dreadnought* readers. In this latter task he worked closely with a 'Comrade Vie', who read the foreign-language newspapers, mainly French and German. Comrade Vie, who events later proved to have been a young Comintern agent, would compare his articles with McKay's, criticising the latter's point of view and McKay Vie's English.[33] But in reality, McKay did much more than that at the *Dreadnought* office. He effectively became the paper's labour relations correspondent, covering events from the annual conference of the Trades Union Congress to a strike at an East End sawmill. He wrote on the plight and struggles of the unemployed, racism among the British working class, the colour bar in South Africa, socialism and black liberation, the Irish struggle and the international money crisis. He wrote book reviews on topics from the shop stewards movement to Gorki on Tolstoy; and he published a large number of poems, including some of his most revolutionary. He used his own name as well as a large number of pen names; many of his articles, especially the ones on international affairs, though attributable, went unsigned.[34] All told, McKay published at least nine articles and nineteen poems (including the five published before he arrived in London), some of them among his most militant, in the *Dreadnought*.

Pankhurst entrusted him with great responsibility. As he later noted, apart from reporting, he corrected proofs, wrote and rewrote articles and sold papers.[35] He privately complained in October 1920 of being overworked at the *Dreadnought* office. 'I should have written before', he told Ogden,

> but I have been kept so frightfully busy by Sylvia Pankhurst since she came back [from Russia]. She has been experiencing all sorts of domestic and business difficulties, due to her own erratic nature, & all the routine work of getting out the paper falls upon me in consequence.[36]

As a good revolutionary, McKay also attended WSF meetings and other party functions. As he told Max Eastman, he did 'propaganda work among the colored soldiers'.[37] As early as February 1920, he was telling a London friend: 'Although weak, I must also do my part to keep my poor people awake and discontented.'[38] McKay's political agitation was wide-ranging. He was, for example, responsible for selling his quota of *Dreadnoughts* and other 'red literature' on the streets of London. He vividly recalled selling the paper along with Pankhurst's pamphlet, *Rebel Ireland*, and Herman Gorter's *Ireland: The Achilles Heel of England* at a big Sinn Fein rally in Trafalgar Square in the summer of 1920. He fondly recounted donning a green tie and being amused when he was welcomed light-heartedly as 'Black Murphy' or 'Black Irish' by the Sinn Feiners. He could hardly keep up with the 'hearty handshakes and brief chats with Sinn Fein Communists and regular Sinn Feiners'.[39] As we will see, he even recruited and cultivated disaffected members of the British armed forces to the revolutionary cause, to the great alarm of the authorities, military and civilian, whose intelligence branches kept him under close surveillance. Indeed, McKay's activities with radical sailors led directly to police raids on the *Dreadnought* office in the autumn of 1920, ending with Pankhurst's arrest and subsequent imprisonment for sedition.

McKay's involvement with the *Dreadnought* group was neither trivial nor innocuous. British intelligence exaggerated when they later alleged that McKay had entertained ambitions of taking over the leadership of the WSF from Pankhurst, for there is no evidence to support this.[40] But the accusation itself is an index of McKay's deep involvement with the British far left. Indeed, McKay was the author of one and had a big hand in another of the three articles that brought down the wrath of Scotland Yard on Pankhurst and the *Dreadnought* in October 1920. The motives behind the understatement of his revolutionary activities in Britain is open to speculation, and need not detain us here; amnesia, however, is implausible.

The WSF had emerged organically out of Pankhurst's efforts among working-class women in London. The organisation had developed out of a split within the mainstream suffragette movement. Pankhurst, McKay noted, had left the 'suffragette legion' for the working-class movement, 'when she discovered that the leading ladies of the legion were not interested in the condition of working women'.[41] It is therefore not surprising that the WSF was a predominantly women's organisation based on working-class support, primarily in the East End of London.[42] Recognising that working-class women were not only oppressed as women but also exploited as workers, Pankhurst 'came to see that women's liberation required more than the vote; it needed the overthrow of capitalist society'. And they fought an 'unrelenting struggle, often coming into conflict with the forces of law and order'.[43] Harry Pollitt described the members of the WSF as 'the most self-sacrificing and hard-working comrades it has been my fortune to come in contact with'.[44] And this he wrote while general secretary of the Communist Party of Great Britain (CPGB), which had long denounced Pankhurst.

The Bolshevik revolution had its most enthusiastic British supporters in Sylvia Pankhurst and the WSF.[45] Indeed, the WSF was one of only two

British left-wing organisations to wholeheartedly welcome the outbreak of revolution in Russia. And it was the first British organisation to affiliate to the Communist International (Comintern) or Third International, founded in Moscow in March 1919.[46] The WSF renamed itself the 'Communist Party (British Section of the Third International)' within less than three months after the founding of the Comintern, a decision that was too fast even for Lenin, who would have preferred the amalgamation of all the British far-left forces into one party before affiliation.

Thus, in the WSF, Britain had the most radical of its left-wing formations. 'Left-wing communists', Lenin called them, as he chided Pankhurst and her followers for boycotting parliamentary elections and rejecting affiliation to the Labour Party. Such behaviour was the symptom of an 'infantile disorder' declared Lenin.[47] But it is perhaps for that very reason – its uncompromising political stance, its contempt for the dirty business of *Realpolitik* – that many respected, if not followed, Pankhurst and her group. As Raymond Challinor noted: 'In the supreme test – that of its attitude to revolution – the Workers' Socialist Federation acquitted itself well.' Resolutely anti-imperialist, of all the British groups on the left, the WSF came out by far the most strongly in support of the Irish Easter Uprisings.[48] And when the group changed its name in 1918 from the Workers' Suffrage Federation to the Workers' Socialist Federation it explicitly called for self-determination not only for Ireland, but India too.[49]

Under Pankhurst's moral leadership, the *Dreadnought* was far and away the most principled and explicitly anti-racist organ on the left. From reading Guy Aldred's anarchist organ, *The Spur*, one would never know that the blood of black men flowed in the streets of Liverpool, London, Cardiff, Glasgow and elsewhere in 1919; that black men were stabbed to death and many more badly beaten, burnt out of their homes, chased on the streets by mobs. In 1920 another full-scale riot occurred in Hull and a smaller one in Limehouse, a part of the East End that McKay frequented.[50] *The Spur*, which was radical on everything, did not report let alone condemn the racist rampage on the part of white workers. In marked contrast, at the height of the madness in June 1919, Pankhurst did so in a bold and clear editorial in her paper. 'I was returning home one evening down the East India Dock Road, and I found the place thronged', she recalled. 'I asked, "What is the matter?" and I was told, "They are stabbing coloured men." Some were killed that night, and for three nights the thing went on in Poplar. Out of work soldiers and other unemployed were stabbing coloured men.'[51]

In 'Stabbing Negroes in the London Dock Area', Pankhurst 'submitted', as she put it, 'a few questions for the consideration of those who have been negro hunting':

Do you think that the British should rule the world or do you want to live on peaceable terms with all peoples?

Do you wish to exclude all blacks from England?

If so, do you not think that blacks might justly ask that the British should at the same time keep out of the black peoples' countries?

Do you not know that capitalists, and especially British capitalists, have seized, by force of arms, the countries inhabited by black people and are ruling those countries and the black inhabitants for their own profit? ...

Are you afraid that a white woman would prefer a blackman to you if you met her on equal terms with him?

Do you not think you would be better employed in getting conditions made right for yourself and your fellow workers than in stabbing a blackman ... ?[52]

Uncommonly decent and courageous, Pankhurst sought to challenge and to lead – not follow; to break the prejudice among some of her own constituents in the East End, rather than pander to it or remain silent, as so many others did. Small wonder, then, that in hers, McKay found the most congenial political home in London.

Although he bluntly registered a notable political climbdown on her part,[53] McKay liked, respected and admired Pankhurst. Like many others, he did not get on with her closest friend and ally, 'the upper-middle-class' Nora Smyth, with whom he worked at the *Dreadnought* offices in the Old Ford Road.[54] But he remembered Pankhurst with kindness and admiration. He recalled her as 'a plain little Queen-Victoria sized woman with plenty of long unruly bronze-like hair. There was no distinction about her clothes, and on the whole she was very undistinguished. But her eyes were fiery, even a little fanatic, with a glint of shrewdness.'[55]

He noted, as others had before and since, that Pankhurst was 'a good agitator and fighter, but she wasn't a leader. She had the magnetism to attract people to her organization, but she did not have the power to hold them ... It was a one-woman show.'[56] And this judgement did not only come in hindsight. As early as October 1920 he had privately disclosed to a comrade:

I am working quite close to Sylvia & the more I see of her & study her manner & gauge her intellect, the more I recognise how hopeless & what madness it is for her to aspire to be a leader. She is no doubt a sharp, clever woman, quick at grasping & sizing up current events ... Her work is to be an editor and agitator & no more.[57]

He accused Pankhurst and her group of 'rather hysterical militancy', and judged that the WSF was perhaps, in hindsight, 'more piquant than important'. But he conceded that Pankhurst had a personality 'as picturesque and passionate as any radical in London'. She had committed herself to working women, the poor and exploited women of the East End of London. And in the labour movement she was always 'jabbing her hat pin into the hides of the smug and slack labor leaders'. Her weekly, McKay thought, might have been called 'the Dread Wasp'. He observed that she had to deal with the 'male-controlled radical groups', which were 'quite hostile' to her and her group. But despite it all, to her eternal honour, wherever imperialism 'got drunk and went wild among native peoples, the Pankhurst paper would be on the job'.[58] McKay gave her credit for having been one of the first leaders in Britain to 'stand up for Soviet Russia'. He praised her for founding the People's Russian Information Bureau, begun as early as 1918, which, he said, 'remained for a long time the only source of authentic news from Russia'. He was very protective of Pankhurst and came to her defence when he met up again with her former-comrade-turned-nemesis, Arthur McManus, in Moscow in 1922. McManus, who knew and had worked with McKay in London, repeatedly described Pankhurst as 'intellectually dishonest' in one of his 'vodka-heated' rants, to which McKay took exception.[59]

McKay's work and membership of the Pankhurst group provided him with important insights into various dimensions of the British scene. First, his association with the *Dreadnought* group placed him, as he put it, in the 'nest of extreme radicalism in London'.[60] He got to know the politics and personalities of Britain's various far-left groups intimately, not just Pankhurst's. Second, he became acquainted with different sections of the trade union movement and especially the shop stewards movement, which appealed to his syndicalist predilections. He also met and got to know many of the key figures in the working-class movement. Third, McKay became deeply familiar with London proletarian life. Pankhurst and the WSF had their base in one of the most deprived areas of the East End. He worked for much of his time in London at the production office of the *Dreadnought* in the Old Ford Road in Bow. For a time he also lived in the neighbourhood. His reporter's brief included coverage of struggles in the area, especially the docklands. He had friends in the area and he was rather fond of visiting Chinatown in Limehouse, about which he wrote with characteristic insight and compassion.[61] The ISC, at 23 East Road in Hoxton, of which he became a member and habitué soon after arriving in London, was also an East End locale.

Finally, because of his remit on the *Dreadnought*, McKay accelerated and deepened his knowledge of international affairs, especially as they pertained to the British Empire. Over the years he augmented this storehouse of knowledge, which served him well in analysing the international system. During his time with Pankhurst, he also became highly informed about the anti-colonial struggle, especially in India and Ireland – a part of his duty on the paper. But McKay not only wrote for the *Dreadnought*; he also read the *Dreadnought*, and Pankhurst's paper provided schooling in revolutionary socialism. Apart from her own remarkable contributions, others from Lenin, Trotsky, Kamenev, Rosa Luxemburg, Clara Zetkin, Alexandra Kollantai and – especially during and after 1920 when Pankhurst started to explicitly express disquiet over Bolshevik domestic and foreign policy – from left Communists such as Anton Pannekoek and Herman Gorter, found a welcoming home in the *Dreadnought*.[62] Theoretical, strategic and tactical questions were all discussed to the highest level of sophistication and openness, not only among the comrades at the ISC, but also in the pages of the *Dreadnought*, and McKay was one of the beneficiaries of Pankhurst's Marxist cornucopia.

During his time with the *Dreadnought* McKay acquired a greater appreciation of the perils of revolutionary work, narrowly escaping arrest by the British Secret Service, MI-5. On 18 and 19 October 1920, the *Dreadnought* offices were raided by Scotland Yard.[63] McKay evaded arrest, but Pankhurst was arrested. She was charged and later convicted of sedition for four articles published in the issue of 16 October: 'Discontent on the Lower Deck', 'How to Get a Labour Government', 'The Datum Line' and 'The Yellow Peril and the Dockers'. In at least two of these, McKay had a direct hand.

'Discontent on the Lower Deck' emerged as an article from material furnished to McKay by Douglas Springhall, a 19-year-old sailor in the Royal Navy. Springhall, who met McKay in early September 1920, had entered the navy at 15, but developed both physically and intellectually. An avid reader of the *Dreadnought* and other revolutionary propaganda, Springhall informed McKay that other men on his ship were also 'eager for more stuff about the international workers' movement'. Disillusioned by the horrors of the war, disgruntled over wages and conditions in the navy and inspired by Bolshevik Russia, some sailors had leapt to the side of revolution. Impressed with his ardour, on Springhall's visit to the Bow offices of the *Dreadnought*, McKay provided him with many copies of the paper to share with his comrades. Before leaving, Springhall promised to send some navy news for the paper. He made good on his word and sent McKay various items for the paper and an article, 'a splendid piece of precious information', that was so incendiary that McKay waited for the material to be approved by Pankhurst on her return from her trip to Russia. She was 'enthusiastic' and personally edited what became 'Discontent on the Lower Deck'.[64]

Under the pseudonym 'S.000 (Gunner), H.M.S. Hunter', the article, covering the entire front page of the *Dreadnought* and adorned with a portrait of Marx (recently discovered in the Tsar's archives) in the middle, concluded:

To the rank and file of the Navy I say: You are the Sons of the Working Class, therefore it is your duty to stand by that class and not the class and Government which is responsible for the starving of your ex-service brothers. Therefore, hail the formation of the Red Navy, which protects the interests of the working class, and repudiate the dirty financial interests which you are protecting now.[65]

The second article, 'The Yellow Peril and the Dockers', was written by McKay himself under the pen name of 'Leon Lopez'. It addressed the racist objection of white seafarers and dockers to Chinese seafarers being employed on British ships and in British ports. The authorities took especial exception to the final paragraph:

The dockers, instead of being unduly concerned about the presence of their coloured fellow men, who like themselves, are victims of Capitalism and Civilisation, should turn their attention to the huge stores of wealth along the water front. The country's riches are not in the West End, in the palatial houses of the suburbs; they are stored in the East End, and the jobless should lead the attack on the bastilles, the bonded warehouses along the docks to solve the question of unemployment.[66]

McKay and Pankhurst were the only ones at the *Dreadnought* who knew the identity of the source for 'Discontent on the Lower Deck'. And Pankhurst refused to name McKay as the author of 'The Yellow Peril and the Dockers'. In her appeal hearing she vigorously defended the article and the right of this 'coloured man', the author, to speak out against racist propaganda and violence.[67] Her appeal rejected, she served five terrible months at Holloway until she was released a month early in May 1921 on grounds of ill health.

When the detectives raided the Fleet Street offices of the *Dreadnought*, Pankhurst's private secretary tipped McKay off as he was leaving the top floor of the building. He quickly returned upstairs to his office and gathered the material that Springhall had sent him, tucking the papers into his socks. Pankhurst's office on the ground floor had been turned 'upside down'. 'And what are you?' the detective asked McKay. 'Nothing, Sir', he replied with a 'big black grin'. The detective chuckled and let him pass. McKay left the building, entered another, went to the toilet, tore up the papers and flushed them away. Another detective was waiting for him at his lodgings in Bow Road when he got home: 'He was very polite and I was more so. With alacrity I showed him all my papers, but he found nothing but lyrics.'[68]

Thinking that he had outwitted the authorities, McKay was rather pleased with himself.[69] What he did not realise, was that the authorities knew far more about his activities than he could have imagined. They had intercepted his correspondence with Springhall and another radical sailor, George

Crook, and had even cracked the different pseudonyms used. McKay, to put it mildly, was not half as clever as he thought in such matters. The authorities must have had another chuckle when they observed that the 'letters of a suspicious nature' to Springhall 'were sent by a man from Bow, London, who signed himself U. B. WARE in one letter and "Claude McKay (my real name)" in another'. They had discovered this by 3 November 1920, if not earlier.[70] In short order, they had noted in Springhall's file that he had been 'receiving Communist literature and letters from Claude McKAY @ C.E. EDWARDS @ U.B. WARE ... a negro Communist from Jamaica'.[71]

It is a mystery as to why McKay was not arrested. But the authorities might have decided that they had already got Pankhurst, the big fish, and also knew that McKay was about to leave the country. In one of his last intercepted letters McKay told Springhall that 'he is going to the Continent as it is getting too hot for him in London'. In another he wrote that he would be leaving for America in the next few weeks.[72] Apparently, they were happy to simply be rid of the troublemaker, letting him leave the country under his own steam and at his own expense.

Stoker Douglas Springhall and able seaman George Crook were discharged from the navy by mid-November 1920. But that did not stop Springhall.[73] Comrade Vie was apprehended with incriminating documents a week after Pankhurst's arrest, sentenced to six months and then deported to Russia. He turned out to have been a Finnish-born agent (real name Erkki Veltheim) of the Comintern. On his release, Pankhurst's secretary followed him to Russia where they were married. McKay met them in Moscow during his 'magic pilgrimage' in 1922.[74]

The International Socialist Club

The ISC served as McKay's primary redoubt in London. Crystal Eastman almost certainly told him about the club before he left the United States. Eastman was in Britain in the summer of 1919, only months before McKay sailed, and she knew the radical scene there well.[75] McKay joined the club soon after arriving in London and quickly became a familiar presence. At one point he went there every day and even used it as an address for his mail. 'No', he told a friend, 'I am not living at the Club but I go by every day.' It was at the ISC that he established some of his most enduring friendships across the Atlantic, and it was there, he said, that he made his most interesting contacts in Britain.[76] He heard Britain's most distinguished left-wing orators of the day at the ISC, including J.T. Walton Newbold, the first person elected to parliament on the Communist Party ticket; Indian-born Shapurji Saklatvala, who in 1922 was first elected an MP for Battersea as an independent and then switched to the Communist Party; A.J. Cook of the

Miners' Federation, of which he later became leader; Jack Tanner, a leader of the shop stewards movement; Guy Aldred, the editor of the anarchist organ, *The Spur*; Arthur McManus and William Gallacher, labour agitators from the Clyde, Glasgow; George Lansbury, editor of the *Daily Herald*; and Sylvia Pankhurst herself. A strong supporter of women's liberation since childhood, McKay probably also attended the 1920 ISC conference on 'Birth Control for the Workers', featuring Rose Witkop and Margaret Sanger as the main speakers.[77]

McKay painted a vivid portrait of life at the ISC. It was, he said, 'full of excitement with its dogmatists and doctrinaires of radical left ideas: Socialists, Communists, anarchists, syndicalists, one-big-unionists and trade unionists, soap-boxers, poetasters, scribblers, editors of little radical sheets which flourish in London'.[78] There were 'lectures, concerts, dancing and always group discussions of social problems'. There were 'outstanding interesting personalities', and there were some 'suspicious persons [who] had nefarious schemes such as the promotion of a big robbery to help the proletarian cause'.[79] He noted that foreigners formed the majority of the membership, among which Jews predominated. 'The Polish Jews and the Russian Jews were always intellectually at odds', he observed, while the German Jews tended to be aloof.[80] Czechs, Italians, Irish nationalists, French, Serbs, wartime prisoners, deportees from America and British Wobblies (members of the Industrial Workers of the World) were among its members. The ISC, he noted, 'was like a piece of foreign territory on English soil'.[81] There were also, McKay recalled, 'rumors of spies' and agent-provocateurs – and British intelligence reports show that they were not mere rumours; they were very real and apparently plentiful.[82]

But cosmopolitan though it was, when McKay joined the ISC he was the only 'African', as he described himself, among its members.[83] McKay took it upon himself to introduce other black people to the club. Among them was a 'Reverend Negro' whose great hope was to establish a church for the black population of London. He liked the place and returned again and again, and was soon busy sending '*billets-doux*, old style' to the female comrades who welcomed him with a cordial smile. McKay also introduced a Trinidadian student from Oxford. He, too, enjoyed the place.[84] It was different with the young medical student from Dulwich. One visit and sitting through a lecture was enough for him: '[h]e disapproved of the club and the reckless and impertinent discussions of economic problems and established authority'. He lectured McKay about 'taking the wrong turn'. He invited McKay one Sunday to his home in Dulwich, only to take him to church, 'the first and only time I ever attended religious service during my stay in London. That pious long-faced congregation singing so solemnly those salvation hymns remains among my memories unforgettable.'[85]

McKay also introduced some of his black friends from the Drury Lane club to the ISC. He mentioned three soldiers and a couple of boxers. But undoubtedly the most important black figure McKay introduced to the club was a man whom he simply describes in his 1937 memoir as 'a mulatto sailor from Limehouse' – probably to protect his identity.[86] His name was Reuben Gilmore. He figured prominently in East End and North London radical politics in the aftermath of the First World War, but with the notable exception of Ken Weller, has been overlooked by historians.[87] A 21-year-old ship's steward, Gilmore was a member of the Pankhurst group and by 1920 was the secretary of the Poplar Unemployed Workers' Committee (PUWC).[88] He was the first of twenty taken into custody on 3 January 1921, for being among the assault party that tried to seize Islington Town Hall during a massive unemployed workers' demonstration, which attracted national attention. Gilmore was arrested with a rush basket containing three bottles of petrol and copies of the *Workers' Dreadnought* hidden under his coat. He was rescued by the crowd, but was recaptured by the police who charged with truncheons. Among the fourteen men who attempted to rescue Gilmore was his close friend and comrade, John O'Sullivan (also known as Jack Sullivan), chairman of the PUWC. For his effort, O'Sullivan was arrested and the police found five rounds of ammunition on his person. Gilmore and O'Sullivan were each bound over with two sureties of £10 with six weeks imprisonment in default. The attempted assault on the town hall occurred in the aftermath of the occupation of the Essex Road library in Islington by unemployed people demanding an increase in their allowance.[89]

Gilmore was a close associate of Lillian Thring, editor of *Out of Work*, newspaper of the unemployed movement. A militant suffragette and socialist, Thring worked closely with Pankhurst and was herself a leading member of the WSF.[90] She was a member of the ISC, and according to Scotland Yard she 'took an active part in the Islington riot in January, 1921, when she suggested burning down the Town Hall and claimed that the incendiary mixture, found on the half-caste Gilmour [sic], was made in her rooms'.[91] Gilmore attended the first national conference of the unemployed held at the ISC on 15 April 1921. As a merchant seaman, but with deep roots in the East End, Gilmore travelled widely and would have taught McKay much, including easing his way around some of the rougher parts of London, including Limehouse, his birthplace.

The men corresponded with each other up to at least the end of 1936, when their surviving correspondence breaks off. Decades had passed, but Gilmore remained as militant and indignant as ever. Unemployed in January 1934, he wrote to McKay from his home in Poplar, complaining during the Depression of having to 'sell' himself to 'Capitalist Shipowners whenever possible[,] that possibility only occurring at very long intermittent intervals and as I have not lived at home for a period upwards of thirteen years[,] life has shown me more uncongenial spots than otherwise'.[92] Almost three years later, he wrote from a ship off Bermuda, telling McKay that he was working in the 'menial capacity of "Second Cook & Baker," all work and very little play, but what can one do, one must live'.[93]

On a lighter note, Gilmore shared news of their mutual friends – Christmas with Frank and Francine Budgen and another friend, Nancy, in 1933 – 'the best I have spent for years'; he wrote to Springhall but without reply; Jack Sullivan, he of the PUWC, 'whom you knew as a somewhat callow boy is now a very much married man with two children'. And bringing out the audacious, proletarian, autodidactic strain that was on display at the ISC during McKay's time, Gilmore related that Sullivan had 'for some years been working on a scientific idea which is more or less a refutation of Einstein's theory of Relativity based on a newer kind of mathematics'. He had been to Russia twice in an effort to develop the idea in a 'practical manner'. But Gilmore confessed that although he had 'always held a great faith in his [Sullivan's] method I still cannot help thinking now at this stage that his time would have been better occupied had he concentrated on his undoubted literary ability'.[94] No one knew where Edgar Whitehead (a leading member of the WSF) had gone, but rumour had it that he had 'dropped out of the movement altogether'. And Francine and Frank Budgen had had a son. Gilmore tells McKay of his ship's visit to Jamaica and Haiti and other parts, including Vancouver, where he wandered around its streets and naturally checked out its 'Chinese quarter where I glean great interest'.[95] He had read McKay's 1933 novel, *Banana Bottom*, 'and to an extent, enjoyed your somewhat realistic style. When your new book is published I intend to give you my patronage, if I can find three dollars.' Because of his travels at sea in 1936, he thought that McKay's enquiries about the British political scene would be better answered by Sullivan, whose Poplar address Gilmore provided. 'In any case I think he would appreciate a letter. What kind of line are you hearing in New York just now and have you finished your book[?] I eagerly await your reply.'[96] The men almost certainly remained in touch beyond this, their last surviving letter dated 1 December 1936.

The ISC had a two-fold impact on McKay, one political, the other intellectual, but both interconnected. He recalled later that it was the 'first time' that he had found himself in an atmosphere in which people 'devoted themselves entirely to the discussion and analysis of social events from a radical and Marxian point of view'. And there were 'always group discussions of social problems'. At the ISC he noticed 'an uncompromising earnestness and seriousness about those radicals that reminded me of an orthodox group of persons engaged in the discussion of a theological creed'. His contact with the ISC, he wrote, 'stimulated and broadened my social outlook and plunged me into the reading of Karl Marx'. McKay sought his reading ticket from the British Museum primarily to keep up with the comrades at the club. 'I felt intellectually inadequate', he confessed, 'and decided to educate myself.' He put his reading ticket to good use, and earnestly ploughed through volumes one and two of Marx's *Capital* and much else. It 'wasn't entertaining reading' and he felt like one 'studying subjects you dislike, which are necessary to pass an examination'. He, however, felt pride in 'mouthing' that he was a 'Marxian student'. He certainly learned enough to appreciate the greatness of Marx: 'I marveled that any modern system of social education could ignore the man who stood like a great fixed monument in the way of the world.'[97]

It was during his stay in London that, for the first time since his student days in Kansas, McKay had the opportunity to engage in sustained intellectual activity. In the US he was obliged to work long shifts in physically demanding jobs, including as a Pullman waiter, with little time and energy to fully engage in a life of the mind. And in his poetry, he repeatedly returned to the toll on the body of the work he did, most notably in 'The Tired Worker' and 'On the Road'.[98] Now, thanks to a stipend from his Dutch friend and benefactor, Johannes Ezerman, and the income he earned at the *Dreadnought*, he had the time to read, attend exhibitions, museums, the theatre, concerts, and to engage in the political life and lively discussions at the ISC.[99]

But it was not all Marx and no play at the ISC. The comrades liked their concerts and dances and so did McKay. Many of the events were fund-raising ones, but no less fun. On 6 November 1920, for instance, the Pankhurst-led Communist Party (British Section of the Third International) held a 'Social and Dance' in aid of the *Workers' Dreadnought* at the ISC.[100] The manager of the ISC asked McKay's boxing friends from the Drury Lane club to put on a boxing exhibition. The men, one coffee brown, the other bronze, their bodies gleaming as if they were painted in oil, did not disappoint, 'showing marvelous foot and muscle work, dancing and feinting all over the stage'.[101] When Jack Tanner returned from his visit to Russia in 1920 he brought back with him a remarkable collection of posters and photographs of Bolshevik Russia. The ISC mounted an exhibition of this collection in the autumn of 1920.[102] McKay was especially impressed with the photographs and invited the art-loving C.K. Ogden to take a look.[103]

On a more practical level, the ISC provided a vital service for McKay. It was from the comrades there that he was able to secure lodgings in London, including one of the last places he stayed, which was the home of a French woman who used to serve at the ISC.[104] McKay established friendships at the ISC that endured well beyond his London days. As we have seen, he kept in touch with Reuben Gilmore. Henry Bernard, artist, writer and cartoonist for the anarchist publication *The Spur*, was a particularly close friend. It was Bernard's relatives who provided McKay with his first lodgings, the one in Islington. The painter Frank Budgen (friend and biographer of James Joyce) and his wife Francine, both of anarchist persuasion, were also very close to McKay and kept in touch with him for many years after he left Britain. They interceded on McKay's behalf when he was being harassed by French and British authorities in Morocco in the 1930s.

The ISC provided succour to many more than McKay and in very tangible ways. It provided loans to the unemployed and, according to McKay, almost went bankrupt on account of its inability to recoup the money due to the post-war recession. In November 1920 in an apparent cost-cutting measure, it drastically reduced its opening hours – by half, closing at 6 p.m. instead of midnight.[105]

But it was not all sweetness and light at the ISC. The Trinidadian student McKay introduced to the club had 'atrocious' manners and caused a spot of bother which required McKay's intercession to smooth things over. There was apparently at least one racist incident, of a 'horrid cockney type' trying 'to stir up race prejudice in the club', and McKay brought charges against him to the management committee of the ISC.[106] During the latter part of August 1920, he kept his distance from the club for a while: the CID had been 'haunting' the place because 'certain clever young criminals' had been using the ISC as a rendezvous to disguise their activities.[107] But on the whole, the experience of the ISC was a positive one for McKay. When, back in New York, he heard that his friend Joseph Freeman, the young poet, journalist and contributor to the *Liberator*, was going over from Paris to London, he recommended the ISC: 'If you ever want to meet some real proletarians in London who have no regular passport to intellectualism, I know of a club in City Road where you could drop in. It's a real den for revolutionary working folk, quite rough but once in a while one meets "artists" and "intellectuals" there.'[108]

Having witnessed the operation of and benefits provided by the ISC, not surprisingly McKay sought the creation of a similar club in New York. Thus, after he was appointed co-editor of the *Liberator* soon after his return in 1921, McKay made strenuous attempts to establish a 'Liberator Club' in Manhattan. He also attempted to organise social events along the lines of those he had observed and participated in at the ISC to raise funds for the financially strapped *Liberator* magazine.

Because of the prominence of the ISC in his London life, McKay operated within a largely foreign milieu. He had never secured lodgings in a British, let alone English, home. He spent time with black soldiers at and from the Drury Lane club. And most of his spare time was spent at the ISC. Because of his membership of these two clubs, which were 'overwhelmingly foreign', McKay felt most of the time that he was 'living on foreign instead of English soil'.[109] His friends were mainly foreigners or outsiders in one way or another. Among his 'little group that stuck together' at the ISC, Frank Budgen was the only white Englishman. Brought up in a strange and tiny religious sect called the Lampeter Brethren, which he renounced for socialism in his teens, Budgen had spent many years in France, Switzerland and Germany studying and practising painting.[110] Budgen's wife, Francine, was Jewish and Belgian; Henry Bernard was half-German and Jewish. In addition to these, McKay mentioned a seamstress and a fur dealer who were Jewish. Gilmore was black, as was the Trinidadian student. Jack Sullivan, close comrade of Gilmore's and arrested with him in Islington, was of Irish descent if not birth. Arthur McManus, who became even closer to McKay in Moscow, was a Belfast-born Glaswegian. Springhall was based in Plymouth until he was kicked out of the navy towards the end of McKay's stay. After he was told openly by prospective landlords and landladies that 'black guests were not accommodated', his comrades at the ISC came to the rescue, helping him secure lodgings from Italian, French and German families. The French woman from the ISC who provided lodging was the one taunted by her English neighbours for having a black person in her house.[111] '[A]lthough I could say I lived in London', McKay told Nancy Cunard, 'it was altogether in a foreign milieu – chiefly Russian-Jewish – except for the little time I worked with a Miss [Nora] Smythe [sic] on Sylvia Pankhurst's *Workers' Dreadnought*. But that was very uncongenial.'[112] This was the most cosmopolitan milieu in which he had ever operated, and as he acknowledged, it broadened his outlook.

McKay later reflected that he did not think he could have survived the 'ordeal' of his year-long London sojourn had it not been for his enjoying the freedom of two clubs, the ISC and the Drury Lane club.[113]

The Drury Lane club

The large amount of time McKay spent at the ISC was partly due to his being banned from another, the Drury Lane club. The club was founded by the YMCA during the troubles of 1919.[114] According to McKay it came into being because of 'the friction and mutual hatred' that existed between white American and coloured soldiers and, 'in a lesser, but nevertheless, ugly form, English and native colonials'. McKay detested the patronising and 'overwhelmingly churchy' ambience of the club. Mrs Newcombe, the woman who ran the place, insisted on referring to the men as her 'colored boys'.[115] She 'is one of those too-utterly-nice type of the English bourgeois',

McKay wrote in the *Negro World*. 'I didn't like her – the oleaginous way she talked about the Negro boys as if they were all a lot of silly children', McKay told Cunard.[116] 'She has traveled in the East and she knows a little of life and books. Apparently she takes some interest in dark people and is not averse to working among her swarthy brethren.' She has known 'great sorrow', McKay acknowledged: she lost her husband and two brothers in France during the war. But she is 'still narrow-minded enough to hate the German people and blame them for the terrible suffering that the imperial exploiters have brought upon a blindly submissive world'. The club consisted of 'three small and rather mean rooms', and McKay noticed among the many cards on the wall, one in particular. It read: 'Remember Booker T. Washington. Follow his leadership.' The little library had only a few books. He remembered seeing a copy of Huxley's *Man's Place in Nature*, a few back numbers of the *Crisis* and 'some old newspapers from America and the West Indies that had no guts'. He donated copies of both the American and English *Nation* magazines, *Workers' Dreadnought*, *One Big Union Monthly*, the *Negro World* itself and 'also some I.W.W. and other revolutionary literature'. He reported the unhappiness of some of the men with the place, and noted in particular the obsequious behaviour of one black churchman who conducted a Christmas service in 1919 ending with the presentation of a gift to Mrs. Newcombe wrapped in cloying words.[117]

In time, a copy of the *Negro World* containing McKay's article arrived at the club. Mrs Newcombe was not pleased, and declared McKay *persona non grata* at Drury Lane.[118] But before he was banished, McKay had an opportunity to listen to the soldiers' stories of the war. He learned, as he told Trotsky a couple of years later, that the men had all been 'disillusioned' by the war. They kept on having 'frightful clashes' with British and American soldiers. On top of this, the authorities treated them 'completely differently from the white soldiers'. Radicalised, they were 'deeply aroused' by the Garvey movement.[119] 'I am glad', he wrote in the *Negro World*, 'that in the hearts of black men the "grievance against things British" is rapidly growing greater instead of disappearing'. He went on:

> We should rejoice that Germany blundered, so that Negroes from all parts of the world were drawn to England to see the Lion, afraid and trembling, hiding in cellars, and the British ruling class revealed to them in all its rottenness and hypocrisy.[120]

McKay invited the most 'forward-thinking' Drury Lane men to the ISC.[121] He was thus able to maintain close contact with at least some members of the club, including the boxers, as we have seen. He became deeply attached to them. Even their Caribbean creole speech provoked a nostalgic and visceral response from McKay. He explained to Ogden, who asked for some creole-language poems for McKay's forthcoming anthology, that he had forgotten the 'melody of the dialect'. In the US he mainly associated with African Americans, so 'when I met some West Indian soldiers here speaking the dialect, it gave me a strange, pleasant sensation as of regaining some precious thing long lost'.[122] His contact with West African soldiers at the club apparently triggered a desire in him to go to Africa. 'I am thinking seriously of working my way to Africa before I return to America!' he wrote Ogden. It was in this context that he expressed his desire to do his part in keeping his 'poor people awake and discontented'.[123]

He recalled in his memoir the painful challenges these men faced in England and gave a telling example. One of the boxers, who came from the Caribbean, gave McKay a ticket to a boxing match that he had in Holborn. The fight was with a white Englishman and McKay's friend won. Some of the men from the club had gone to support their comrade. After the match McKay and the rest of the group gathered around their friend with congratulations. They proposed going to a black restaurant off Shaftesbury Avenue for a celebration. At that moment a white man pushed his way through the crowd to offer congratulations to the boxer: 'Shake, Darkey, you did a clean job; it was a fine fight.' The boxer shook hands and thanked his admirer. A 'modest type of fellow', the boxer

> then turned to a little woman almost hidden in the group – a shy, typically nondescript and dowdy Englishwoman, with her hat set inelegantly back on her head – and introduced her to his white admirer: 'That is my wife.' The woman held out her hand, but the white man, ignoring it, exclaimed: 'You damned nigger!' The boxer hauled back and hit him in the mouth and he dropped to the pavement.

They hurried off to the restaurant. 'We sat around, the poor woman among us, endeavoring to woo the spirit of celebration. But we were all wet. The boxer said: "I guess they don't want no colored in this damned white man's country."' He moaned: 'I hate dis damn country ... Yet I doan' want to go back to de damn West Indies. Ah doan' know wha' fe do.'[124] The boxer 'dropped his head down on the table and sobbed like a child. And I thought that that', McKay added, speaking of his friend, 'was *his* knockout'.[125]

Race, class, nation

The pervasiveness of such pernicious racism disgusted and pained McKay. He gave many examples of his personal encounters with it in London, but it hurt him even more to see it meted out to others – 'for misery / I have the strength to bear but not to see'.[126] And it was for that reason that he felt impelled to publicly respond to E.D. Morel's 'Black Horror on the Rhine' campaign, primarily disseminated by the *Daily Herald*, the newspaper of the British labour movement. Morel, and to a lesser extent George Lansbury, the *Herald*'s editor, used the most inflammatorily racist and sexualised language against black French troops on the Rhine: sexually unrestrained and unrestrainable black, barbaric savages, thrusting into Europe and defiling white womanhood.[127] Worse still, from the very start it was clear that Morel had little regard for evidence and proof when it came to his incendiary charges. It was apparent then, and more so subsequently, that lies and misinformation formed the basis of Morel's campaign aimed at the withdrawal of French troops from the Ruhr, placed there under terms established by the Versailles Treaty. Still, the damage was done and what concerned McKay most was the impact it would have on a London and Britain that had seen widespread racist mob violence the previous summer.[128] McKay wrote to the *Herald* but Lansbury refused to publish his letter. 'Like a little cat up against a big dog, the *Workers' Dreadnought* was always spitting at the *Daily Herald*', McKay observed.[129] Pankhurst was glad to have it, however, and printed the letter. 'Why all this obscene, maniacal outburst about the sex vitality of black men in a proletarian paper?' McKay asked.

> I do not protest because I happen to be a negro (I am disgusted when I read in your columns that white dockers would prohibit their employers using Chinese and Indian labour), I write because I feel that the ultimate result of your propaganda will be further strife and blood-spilling between the whites and the many members of my race, boycotted economically and socially, who have been dumped down on the English docks since the ending of the European War.

As McKay told Trotsky two years later, the propaganda was still under way and he pointed to the fact that even the British Communist Party had become one of its purveyors, carrying Morel's propaganda in its daily, *The Communist*, in 1922.[130]

On top of the hurt of the racist propaganda in the press, the disillusionment of the black men of the Drury Lane club – their sense of isolation, their anguish, their painful experience of racism in the theatre of war and on the streets of London – moved McKay deeply. Their hurt and anger became his own. And he transmuted them into verse as well as prose. 'Enslaved', one of his most powerful sonnets, was written at that time, probably soon after the Holborn incident:

> Oh when I think of my long-suffering race
> For weary centuries despised, oppressed,
> Enslaved and lynched, denied a human place

In the great life line of the Christian West;
And in the Black Land disinherited,
Robbed in the ancient country of its birth, –
My heart grows sick with hate, becomes as lead,
For my race, my race, outcast upon the earth.
Then from the dark depths of my soul I cry
To the avenging angel to consume
The white man's world of wonders utterly:
Let it be swallowed up in earth's vast womb,
Or upward roll as sacrificial smoke
To liberate my people from its yoke![131]

McKay wanted the anger and energy of such men to be joined with the world revolutionary movement. As he explained to Garvey soon after his arrival in London,

> radical Negroes should be more interested in the white radical move-
> ments. They are supporting our cause, at least in principle … [T]hey are the
> great destructive forces *within*, while the subject races are fighting without …
> [T]hey are fighting their own battle & so are we; but at present we meet on
> common ground against the common enemy. We have a great wall to batter
> down and while we are working on one side we should hail those who are
> working on the other.[132]

Tellingly, contemporaneously with his letter to Garvey, McKay sought to enlighten his English comrades on the black nationalist and anti-colonial movements. In 'Socialism and the Negro', he explained that although he is an 'international Socialist' he is supporting the Garvey movement. He chided the English comrades who disparaged the Irish and Indian movements because they are nationalistic. The British Empire, he argued, was the greatest obstacle to international socialism, and any of its subjugated parts succeeding in breaking away from it would be helping the socialist cause. The breaking up of the empire 'must either begin at home or abroad; the sooner the strong blow is struck the better it will be for all Communists'. McKay argued that the nationalist anti-colonial struggles would not stop at the bourgeois phase; would not 'tamely submit' to a new capitalist order for the old one. Therefore, unless one believes in the absurd monstrosity of a 'Socialist British Empire', the Irish, Indian and Garvey movements and other nationalist currents ought to be supported by English socialists.[133]

Thus in these two texts – in effect, a diptych – McKay tried to bring together black nationalist and anti-colonial militants, on the one hand, and English socialists, on the other, to a common understanding and solidarity, if not deliberate collaboration. McKay's revolutionary socialism was organically tied to the black liberation struggle, and vice versa. And that was why he invested such great hopes in the Bolshevik revolution and bringing others to its cause. He sought to tap the race's 'undeveloped energy' and transmute it into a revolutionary force.[134] Accordingly, in one of his London poems he cried, 'Ethiopia! Awake! / In the East the clouds glow crimson with the new dawn that is breaking ... / O my brothers and my sisters, Wake! Arise! / ... Wake from sleeping; to the East turn, turn / your eyes!'[135] He was working on his side of the 'wall'.

It is important to note that, during McKay's time in New York and also London, his black friends and associates were overwhelmingly working class, not members of the black middle class, not even the black intelligentsia. When he arrived in London in 1919, McKay stayed at a hotel located at 39 Woburn Place, a stone's throw away from Student Movement House, the newly established meeting place for 'coloured' students at 32 Russell Square. Yet nowhere does he mention ever going there. He probably knew students who frequented the place but apparently kept away from it. This is not entirely surprising given McKay's utter contempt for Christianity. The centre in Russell Square was run by the Student Christian Movement, a white, philanthropic organisation that had seen the isolation of non-white students in London and sought a place for them to meet with dignity, among themselves as well as members of the enlightened British public.[136]

He certainly would have heard of the Coterie of Friends, a London-based, black-supported organisation begun in the spring of 1919 by Edmund Jenkins, a brilliant African-American student-teacher at the Royal Academy of Music, and several other students from the Caribbean and West Africa. Jenkins's achievements were often featured in the press and McKay probably even heard him perform at one of Jenkins's many outings on the London concert scene.[137] For McKay, as his rich correspondence with Ogden shows, frequently went to the theatre and music halls. He certainly went to see the Southern Syncopated Orchestra, which toured Britain and 'took London by storm' during 1919 and 1920.[138] Ogden even reviewed one of their concerts in the *Cambridge Magazine* and would later draw a parallel between the orchestra's achievements in music and McKay's in poetry.[139] Given his wide reading and contacts, he would also have known of the African Progress Union and the Society of Peoples of African Origin and the journal they produced, the *African Telegraph*, yet there is no mention of them either. Similarly, there is no mention of Dusé Mohamed Ali, who lived in London up to 1921, or his journal, the *African Times and Orient Review*, which McKay almost certainly would have read. He certainly would have heard of the distinguished black London resident and fellow Jamaican, Dr Harold Moody, and perhaps even met him in the city; virtually every black person in London at the time knew Moody. And as we have seen, McKay visited Dulwich, where Moody lived, and even dropped in at a church there.[140] Why then this lack of meaningful contact with black organisations and the individuals who ran them?

The likelihood is that McKay regarded them as too conservative. And as far as he was concerned they were all too involved in the 'amusing, but very pathetic' business of petitioning the British government, which he thought was utterly futile.[141] He was at the time also in his most enthusiastically Bolshevik phase. Even the man with whom he shared most in common, Felix Hercules of the Society of Peoples of African Origin, would have been too conservative for him. For the platform enunciated by the *African Telegraph*, edited by Hercules, was not one that McKay could have endorsed:

> We stand, first and foremost, for the maintenance of our connection with Great Britain, and, for this reason, we shall resist any and every effort that may be made from whatever quarter to imperil this connection, because we regard Great Britain as the best and truest friend of the native races within the Empire.

It went on: 'We are not going to be led astray by vague notions of self-determination ... Self-determination for us means the *ultimate* goal of political autonomy within the British Empire, which we hope to attain under the tutelage of Great Britain.' The document concluded by distancing the journal from those whom it describes as 'irresponsible agitators' whose one object is to 'embarrass and to retard our development'.[142]

McKay was way to the left of such people. He probably would have tolerated them during his Fabian days, before he 'became Bolshevik'.[143] But McKay now wanted the destruction of the British Empire – not 'autonomy' under its tutelage. He yearned for its 'disintegration and the birth of a proletarian order'.[144] Hercules would have counted McKay among the 'irresponsible agitators'. In any case, by the time McKay arrived in London, Hercules was in the Caribbean, estranged from his London colleagues who regarded him as too radical, and never returned to Britain. By 1920 the *African Telegraph* was dead.[145]

Conclusion

Despite the doubtless pain and bitterness coming out of his English experience, his sojourn in London generally helped to develop McKay in various ways.

First, his time in London destroyed any residual notion he may have had about his Britishness: to white Britons he was at best a 'darkey' – not British at all. This realisation contributed mightily to McKay's Pan-Africanist and anti-imperialist outlook on life, including the newly expressed desire to go to Africa and do revolutionary work there. For it was in London, not Marseilles, as is commonly believed, that McKay first developed a power-ful identification with Africa. It was there that he first described himself as 'African'; there that he expressed a desire to visit his ancestral homeland. His befriending of West African soldiers at the Drury Lane club, combined with British racism, contributed to that yearning. Almost a decade before the publication of *Banjo*, McKay confided to Ogden his intention to go to Africa before returning to the US, and his wanting to 'keep my poor people awake and discontented'.[146] His more profound identification with Africa in London stimulated even further his interest in African history and culture, particularly African art, about which he systematically edu-cated himself, especially among the rich collection he found at the British Museum's ethnological division.[147]

Second, it also contributed to McKay's revolutionary socialist politics and world view. To him, imperialism, colonialism and racism required the strong medicine of revolutionary socialism of the Bolshevik variety to be thoroughly expunged. And he was not at all sentimental about the process. He did not mind working with the 'poor white devils', even when they called him 'darkey', as long as they got on with the demolition of their side of the capitalist and imperialist wall.

McKay brings this hard absence of sentimentality to the fore in fic-tional form in a striking, but overlooked, passage in *Banjo*. Ray, McKay's alter ego, berates a French waiter for calling him 'Joseph' (equivalent to American white racists calling every black man 'George'). The waiter later compounds the discourtesy by addressing him with the French familiar *tu*. Crosby, Ray's white British friend, is shocked at the ferocity of Ray's rebuke of the waiter. In the course of their discussion, Crosby says to Ray: 'I thought *you* were a proletarian', to which Ray replies: 'Sure. That's my politics. But you never asked me why I prefer Proletarian to Liberal, Democrat or Conservative.' Crosby wants to know, so Ray tells him in a rather Socratic exchange:

'Because I hate the proletarian spawn of civilization. They are ugly, stupid, unthinking, degraded, full of vicious prejudices, which any demagogue can play upon to turn them into a hell-raising mob at any time. As a black man I have always been up against them, and I became a revolutionist because I have not only suffered with them, but have been victimized by them – just like my race.'

'But you have no real faith in the proletariat,' said Crosby. 'Then what can you expect from proletarian politics?'

'I have never confused faith with politics. I should like to see the indecent horde get its chance at the privileged things of life, so that decency might find some place among them. I am not fond of any kind of hogs, but I prefer to see the well-fed ones feeding out of a well-filled trough than the razor-backs rooting all over the place. That's why I am against all those who are fighting to keep the razor-backs from getting fat and are no better doing it than fat swine themselves.'

Crosby is taken aback by Ray's response. 'Your being politically proletarian from hatred's got me stumped', he says. 'I thought you loved the proletariat.' Ray replies: 'I love life – when it shows lovable aspects.'[148]

Though he found the Irish proletariat more lovable than Ray makes out,[149] McKay followed the same ruthless but compelling political logic when it came to the Indian and Irish nationalist struggles. At the Sinn Fein rally in Trafalgar Square, McKay heard the bourgeois Irish nationalist refrain – a racist one – that Ireland is the only 'white' nation left under the yoke of foreign imperialism. 'There are other nations in bondage, but they are not of the breed; they are colored, some are even Negro.' McKay not only let it pass, but even expressed a little sympathy for their position.[150] What was significant about the Irish nationalists, even the bourgeois ones, was that they were contributing to the break-up of the British Empire. They were working on the wall, and that was all that mattered. His British experience – including being chased by a working-class mob down Old Street subway station, his boxer friend being called a 'damned nigger' for having a white wife, and his observation of Irish nationalism at close quarters – pushed him to such an unsentimental view of the socialist and anti-imperialist struggle. And it strengthened his commitment to the socialist cause.

Third, it was in London that McKay became properly acquainted with the socialist classics, including reading and studying the first two volumes of *Das Kapital* at the British Museum. In addition, both the *Workers' Dreadnought* and the ISC expanded his knowledge of revolutionary currents and anti-imperialist struggles around the world.

Fourth, McKay submitted himself to the membership and discipline of a revolutionary party (Pankhurst's WSF) for the first time. On his return to the US, he would soon join the Workers' Party of America (the US affiliate to the Communist International, later becoming the Communist Party) and its de facto black section, the African Blood Brotherhood (ABB), headquartered in Harlem. He would serve on the executive committee of the ABB.

Fifth, McKay was so well equipped by his journalistic work on Pankhurst's *Workers' Dreadnought* that, on his return to New York in January 1921, Max Eastman, the co-editor of the *Liberator*, America's leading socialist magazine, not only appointed McKay associate editor, but made him de facto managing editor.

Sixth, McKay was so enamoured of his experience at the ISC that soon after returning to New York he exerted himself in an attempt to establish an American equivalent, which he called the Liberator Club, affiliated to the *Liberator* magazine. (It never really took off, but that was not due to any lack of effort on McKay's part.)

Finally, London was the place where McKay wrote not only his most nostalgic, but also his most revolutionary poems, especially in the pages of the *Cambridge Magazine* and *Workers' Dreadnought*. 'The Spanish Needle' and 'Samson' are merely a couple from either category.[151]

In short, though it only lasted just over a year, the impact of McKay's sojourn in Britain on his political and artistic development can hardly be overstated. The experience was in many ways searing, but it accelerated McKay's maturation as a revolutionary and as an engaged artist, and overdetermined his political trajectory in the subsequent decades. London, in short, played a critical role in the Bolshevisation of Claude McKay, thanks in large measure to the rich and varied connections and networks he established there.

Notes

1 W.A. Domingo, and the editors of *The Messenger* magazine, A. Philip Randolph and Chandler Owen, were early and vocal supporters of the Bolshevik revolution, but none of them joined the American affiliate of the Communist International (Comintern), the Workers' Party or the later Communist Party. They chose to remain members of the Socialist Party. Cyril Briggs and much of the leadership of the African Blood Brotherhood (including Grace Campbell, Harry Haywood, Richard B. Moore and Lovett Fort-Whiteman) also became forthright supporters of the Bolshevik revolution and later joined the Workers' Party, which later became the Communist Party. In France, the young Martinican lawyer, Joseph Gothon-Lunion, was one of the first black adherents of Bolshevism, attending the Fifth Congress of the Communist International (Comintern) as a delegate in 1924. The early black responses to the Bolshevik revolution are analysed in Winston James, 'To the East Turn: The Russian Revolution and the Black Radical Imagination in the United States, 1917–1924,' *American Historical Review* 126: 3 (2021). That article originated as the keynote address to 'The Red and the Black' conference organised by the Institute for Black Atlantic Research (IBAR), University of Central Lancashire, Preston in October 2017.

2 The few notable exceptions are: Trinidadian radical George Padmore, who left the US in the late 1920s for Moscow, moved to Berlin and Paris before settling in London in the 1930s; Guyanese Ras Makonnen migrated from the US to Britain in the 1930s, as did Eric Walrond (via Paris); and before them, Henry Sylvester Williams moved from Canada to London in the 1890s.

3 Max Eastman, 'Introduction' to Claude McKay, *Harlem Shadows: The Poems of Claude McKay* (New York: Harcourt, Brace, 1922), xvi–xvii.
4 McKay to Eastman, 23 March 1939, McKay Manuscripts, Manuscripts Department, Lilly Library University, Bloomington, Indiana. The McKay/ Eastman correspondence cited in this chapter is from this collection.
5 McKay to Eastman, 18 June 1932.
6 These facts escape Wayne Cooper and Robert Reinders, who, in their pioneering article on McKay's visit to England, frame their argument around the notion of a black Briton coming home only to be disillusioned. It is as if McKay remained unchanged between 1911, when he wrote the poem 'Old England', and December 1919, when he arrived in London. Wayne Cooper and Robert Reinders, 'A Black Briton Comes "Home": Claude McKay in England, 1920', *Race*, 9 (1967), 67–83.
7 In 1909 a Sierra Leonean, A.B.C. Merriman-Labor, published *Britons Through Negro Spectacles or A Negro on Britons* (London: Imperial and Foreign Company, n.d. [1909]). Though it carries interesting anecdotes, it lacks analysis.
8 George Lamming, *The Pleasures of Exile* (London: Michael Joseph, 1960); Linton Kwesi Johnson, *Dread Beat and Blood* (London: Bogle-L'Ouverture Press, 1975). 'Inglan is a bitch / dere's no escapin it / Inglan is a bitch / a noh lie mi a tell, a true', Johnson shouted in his notorious poem, 'Inglan is a Bitch'.
9 Winston James, *A Fierce Hatred of Injustice: Claude McKay's Jamaica and His Poetry of Rebellion* (London: Verso, 2000).
10 Claude McKay, 'Claude MacKay [sic] Describes His Own Life: A Negro Poet', *Pearson's Magazine*, 39:5 (1918), 275–276, quotation on 276.
11 Claude McKay, 'Sonnets and Songs', *Liberator*, 2:7 (1919), 20–21, poem quoted on 21.
12 McKay, 'Claude MacKay [sic] Describes His Own Life', 275.
13 Melvyn Dubofsky's *We Shall Be All: A History of the Industrial Workers of the World* (Chicago: Quadrangle Books, 1969) remains the best general history of the union. But also see the wonderful collection: Peter Cole, David Struthers and Kenyon Zimmer (eds), *Wobblies of the World: A Global History of the IWW* (London: Pluto Press, 2017).
14 McKay, 'Claude MacKay [sic] Describes His Own Life', 275; Claude McKay, *A Long Way from Home* (New York: Lee Furman, 1937), 55.
15 Claude McKay, 'To "Holy" Russia', *Workers' Dreadnought* (hereafter abbreviated as *WD*), 28 February 1920.
16 *Negro World*, 20 September 1919, quoted in A. Mitchell Palmer, *Letter from the Attorney General Transmitting in Response to a Senate Resolution of October 17, 1919, a Report on the Activities of the Bureau of Investigation of the Department of Justice Against Persons Advising Anarchy, Sedition, and the Forcible Overthrow of the Government* (Washington, DC: US Government Printing Office, 1919), 163–164. The original of this issue of the *Negro World* has not been located and likely has not survived.

17 Theodore Kornweibel, *No Crystal Stair: Black Life and The Messenger, 1917–1928* (Westport, CT: Greenwood Press, 1975), and *'Seeing Red': Federal Campaigns Against Black Militancy, 1919–1925* (Bloomington, IN: Indiana University Press, 1998), and Winston James, *Holding Aloft the Banner of Ethiopia: Caribbean Radicalism in Early Twentieth-Century America* (London: Verso, 1998), and 'Being Red and Black in Jim Crow America: On the Ideology and Travails of Afro-America's Socialist Pioneers, 1877–1930', in Charles Payne and Adam Green (eds), *Time Longer than Rope: A Century of African American Activism* (New York: New York University Press, 2003), 336–399.

18 James Weldon Johnson, *Black Manhattan* (New York: Knopf, 1930), 246, and *Along This Way: The Autobiography of James Weldon Johnson* (New York: Viking Press, 1933), 341.

19 Claude McKay, 'If We Must Die', *Liberator*, July 1919, 21.

20 McKay to Ogden, 2 April 1920; Claude McKay 'Up to Date' (1934, 2). [Fragment of an unpublished sketch of his time in Britain], Nancy Cunard Collection, Harry Ransom Humanities Research Center, University of Texas at Austin.

21 McKay to Ogden, 2 April 1920.

22 McKay, *A Long Way From Home*, 86–91.

23 *Ibid.*, 303.

24 McKay, 'London', in his manuscript, 'Cities', Claude McKay Papers, James Weldon Johnson Collection, Beinecke Rare Books and Manuscript Library, Yale University (hereafter, McKay Papers, Yale University); McKay, *A Long Way From Home*, 66–67.

25 McKay, *A Long Way From Home*, 69.

26 McKay also visited the '1917 Club', a redoubt of the 'Bloomsbury Set' in Soho, but primarily as a rendezvous spot for meeting with C.K. Ogden (about whom more below). He never liked it and felt uncomfortable there. In any case, the 1917 Club was artistic and Fabian, not radical, in politics. See Winston James, 'A Race Outcast from an Outcast Class: Claude McKay's Experience and Analysis of Britain', in Bill Schwarz (ed.), *West Indian Intellectuals in Britain* (Manchester: Manchester University Press, 2003), 77–79.

27 Frank Harris to Grant Richards, 8 November 1919, Frank Harris Papers, Albert H. Small Collections Library, University of Virginia. Fuller to Ogden, 11 November 1919; McKay to Ogden, 17 August 1920; both in C.K. Ogden Fonds, William Ready Divisions of Archives and Research Collections, Mills Memorial Library, McMaster University. All other cited correspondence between McKay and Ogden is from this collection. McKay and Ogden (1889–1957) became close friends. Ogden effectively acted as McKay's literary agent, promoter and editor of *Spring in New Hampshire and Other Poems* (1920), McKay's first anthology since leaving Jamaica. For more on the relationship see James, 'A Race Outcast from an Outcast Class', 77–79.

28 *WD*, 6 September 1919.

29 Pankhurst had known both Crystal Eastman, a socialist and ardent feminist, and her younger brother Max who at the time of Pankhurst's 1911 US tour

was secretary and treasurer of New York State's Men's League for Woman Suffrage. Sylvia Pankhurst, *The Suffragette Movement* (London: Virago, 1977), 349; Max Eastman to Sylvia Pankhurst, 11 May [1911?], Estelle Sylvia Pankhurst Papers, International Institute of Social History, Amsterdam.

30 Peter Fryer, *Staying Power: The History of Black People in Britain* (London: Pluto Press, 1984), 318.

31 McKay to Ogden, 25 February 1920; 'Samson', *WD*, 10 January 1920; 'Socialism and the Negro', *WD*, 31 January 1920; McKay, *A Long Way From Home*, 76.

32 McKay, *A Long Way From Home*, 76. On 23 October 1920, for instance, the *Dreadnought* reported on a 'very lively meeting' which finished at 11 p.m. at the WSF's Soho branch, and explicitly mentioned 'Comrades McKay, Bishop, and others from the Central branch' as visitors.

33 McKay, *A Long Way From Home*, 76–77.

34 E. Edwards, Hugh Hope, C.E.E., C.E., C.E. Edwards, C.M. and Leon Lopez were among the pseudonyms used. Wayne Cooper was mistaken about 'Ness Edwards' being one of McKay's pen names. Ness Edwards (born Onesimus Edwards [1897–1968]) was at the time a Welsh revolutionary miner, a leading member of both the South Wales Miners' Federation and the South Wales Socialist Society, and close associate of Pankhurst and the *Dreadnought* group. (He later became a Labour MP.) See Wayne Cooper, *Claude McKay: Rebel Sojourner in the Harlem Renaissance* (Baton Rouge, LA: Louisiana State University Press, 1987), 117, 394–395n; and *The Labour Who's Who, 1927* (London: Labour Publishing Co. Ltd., 1927), 62.

35 McKay, 'Up to Date', 1.

36 McKay to Ogden, 9 October 1920.

37 McKay to Eastman, 18 May 1923, McKay MSS.

38 McKay to Ogden, 25 February 1920.

39 Claude McKay, 'How Black Sees Green and Red', *Liberator*, June 1921, 17, 20–21.

40 McKay, however, did believe that Pankhurst ought to have been removed from her position as head of the revolutionary left, but not by himself. He saw William Gallacher as the person equipped to do so, since Pankhurst lacked the qualities of a 'great leader'. In a letter to Gallacher marked 'Private', he sought to enlist Gallacher for the role. McKay told him that he, Gallacher, 'ought to be the man to weld the little warring forces together who are now wasting their energy fighting among themselves'. McKay to Gallacher, 10 October 1920, Papers of William Gallacher, CP/IND/GALL/02/04, Labour History Archive and Study Centre, People's History Museum, Manchester.

41 McKay, *A Long Way From Home*, 77. Pankhurst herself tells of the break in *The Suffragette Movement*, esp. book ix, chap. iv.

42 Raymond Challinor, *The Origins of British Bolshevism* (London: Croom Helm, 1977); Mary Davis, *Sylvia Pankhurst: A Life in Radical Politics* (London: Pluto Press, 1999); Katherine Connelly, *Sylvia Pankhurst: Suffragette, Socialist and Scourge of Empire* (London: Pluto Press, 2013).

43 Challinor, *The Origins of British Bolshevism*, 129, 168.

44 Harry Pollitt, *Serving My Time: An Apprenticeship to Politics* (London: Lawrence & Wishart, [1940] 1950), 110.

45 Walter Kendall, *The Revolutionary Movement in Britain, 1900–1920: The Origins of British Communism* (London: Weidenfeld and Nicolson, 1969), 198; Ian Bullock, *Romancing the Revolution: The Myth of Soviet Democracy and the British Left* (Edmonton: AU Press, 2011), 24–27.

46 Kendall, *The Revolutionary Movement in Britain*, 196–197; Challinor, *The Origins of British Bolshevism*, 176.

47 Vladimir Ilyich Lenin, *'Left-Wing' Communism, An Infantile Disorder* (Moscow: Progress Publishers, 1970), 60–73. Lenin's pamphlet was first published in June 1920 in time for the Second Congress of the Comintern. For the most detailed discussion of Pankhurst's and other anti-parliamentary Communists' disagreement with Lenin, see Mark Shipway, *Anti-Parliamentary Communism: The Movement for Workers' Councils in Britain, 1917–45* (Basingstoke: Macmillan Press, 1988), chaps 1–4; also see Ian Bullock, 'Sylvia Pankhurst and the Russian Revolution: The Making of a "Left-Wing" Communist', in Ian Bullock and Richard Pankhurst (eds), *Sylvia Pankhurst: From Artist to Anti-Fascist* (Basingstoke: Macmillan, 1992), 121–148.

48 Challinor, *The Origins of British Bolshevism*, 168; Geoffrey Bell, *Hesitant Comrades: The Irish Revolution and the British Labour Movement* (London: Pluto Press, 2016), 12–13.

49 *WD*, 1 June 1918. Significantly, her position on the struggle in Ireland was one of the issues that contributed to Pankhurst's split with her mother Emmeline and sister Christabel, leaders of the Women's Social and Political Union, in 1913. Pankhurst had earned the opprobrium of her mother and sister for appearing on a platform supporting Irish workers fighting for unionisation during the Dublin Lockout that year. See Bell, *Hesitant Comrades*, 6.

50 Robin Cohen and Roy May, 'The Interaction between Race and Colonialism: A Case Study of the Liverpool Riots of 1919', *Race & Class*, 16:2 (1974), 111–126; Neil Evans, 'The South Wales Race Riots of 1919', *Llafur: Journal of Welsh Labour History*, 3:1 (1980), 5–29; Neil Evans, 'Across the Universe: Racial Violence and the Post-War Crisis in Imperial Britain, 1919–25', *Immigrants and Minorities*, 13:2–3 (1994), 59–88; Jacqueline Jenkinson, 'The 1919 Race Riots in Britain: A Survey' in Rainer Lotz and Ian Pegg (eds), *Under the Imperial Carpet: Essays in Black History* (Crawley: Rabbit Press, 1986), 182–207; Jacqueline Jenkinson, 'Black Sailors on Red Clydeside: Rioting, Reactionary Trade Unionism and Conflicting Notions of "Britishness" Following the First World War', *Twentieth Century British History*, 19:1 (2007), 29–60; Jacqueline Jenkinson, *Black 1919: Riots, Racism and Resistance in Imperial Britain* (Liverpool: Liverpool University Press, 2009). For a rare and perhaps unique account of the riots from a black eye-witness and victim, see Ernest Marke, *Old Man Trouble: The Memoirs of a Stowaway, Mutineer, Bootlegger, Crocuser and Soho Club Owner* (London: Weidenfeld and Nicolson, 1975), 25–32.

51 'The Appeal of Miss Sylvia Pankhurst Against the Sentence of Six Months Imprisonment', Guildhall, City of London, 5 January 1921, 16–17, folder 254, Estelle Sylvia Pankhurst Papers, International Institute of Social History, Amsterdam.

52 *WD*, 7 June 1919.

53 McKay, *A Long Way From Home*, 77–79. In *A Long Way From Home*, McKay reported that during a strike at a sawmill owned by George Lansbury 'scabs' (strike-breakers) were used. He wrote an article for the *Dreadnought* exposing the situation and Lansbury's hypocrisy. But Pankhurst, he claimed, objected to its publication and killed the article because, she said, the *Dreadnought* owed Lansbury £20. In a letter to Lee Furman, McKay's publishers, Pankhurst said that she took 'strong exception' to many statements in the book and in particular the sawmill story, which she claimed was 'absolutely untrue' and that McKay had libelled her. She requested that Furman 'immediately withdraw the book from circulation and delete those passages'. She concluded: 'It is a pity that Claude McKay should have chosen to libel one who has treated him with consideration and kindness.' E. Sylvia Pankhurst to Lee Furman, 22 May 1937, in Box 6, Folder 177, Claude McKay Collection, James Weldon Johnson Manuscripts, Yale Collection of American Literature, Beinecke Rare Book and Manuscript Library.

54 McKay, *A Long Way From Home*, 78. Speaking of Smyth, Pankhurst's former secretary testified that 'people didn't care for her'. She was arrogant, and the fact that her family had an estate in Ireland with '30 servants' did not endear her to many East Enders. Lucia Jones, 'Interview with Nellie Rathbone', 27 June 1972, appended to Lucia Jones, 'Sylvia Pankhurst and the Workers' Socialist Federation: The Red Twilight, 1918–1924', MA thesis, Warwick University, 1972.

55 McKay, *A Long Way from Home*, 76.

56 *Ibid.*, 87. British intelligence were fully aware of Pankhurst's strengths as well as her weaknesses. One of their agents, reporting on the secret Communist conference in Manchester in September 1920 aimed at unifying the far-left forces, wrote confidently: 'This need not disturb us over much for no one has yet succeeded in working amicably with Sylvia Pankhurst.' CAB 24/112, National Archives, Kew, UK (hereafter TNA).

57 McKay to Gallacher, 10 October 1920.

58 McKay, *A Long Way from Home*, 76–77.

59 *Ibid.*, 198.

60 *Ibid.*, 76.

61 Leon Lopez [Claude McKay], 'The Yellow Peril and the Dockers', *WD*, 16 October 1920. There is also an article on Limehouse published in *The Spur*, that was almost certainly written by McKay, though the author's name is given as 'W. Winter': 'More Limehouse', *The Spur*, October 1920, 105.

62 Bullock, 'Sylvia Pankhurst and the Russian Revolution'; Shipway, *Anti-Parliamentary Communism*; Herman Gorter, Anton Pannekoek, Sylvia Pankhurst and Otto Ruhl, *Non-Leninist Marxism: Writings on the Worker's*

Council (St Petersburg, FL: Red and Black Publishers, 2007); Philippe Bourrinet and International Communist Current, *The Dutch and German Communist Left: A Contribution to the History of the Revolutionary Movement, 1900–1950* (London: Porcupine Press, 2001).

63 'Sylvia Pankhurst Arrested', *WD*, 23 October 1920.

64 McKay, *A Long Way from Home*, 81–82. See item, 'D. F. Springhull [sic] @ Silverhill' in Douglas Springhall file, TNA: KV 2/1594.

65 'Discontent on the Lower Deck', *WD*, 16 October 1920.

66 'The Yellow Peril and the Dockers', *WD*, 16 October 1920.

67 'The Appeal of Miss Sylvia Pankhurst', esp. 16–17.

68 McKay, *A Long Way from Home*, 81–83.

69 *Ibid.*, 82–83.

70 L.C. Lampen, Commander-in-Chief's Office, Devonport, to 'My dear Peel', 3 November 1920, TNA: KV 2/1594.

71 'D. F. Springhull [sic] @ Silverhill'.

72 Unsigned intelligence report, 25 November 1920; intercepted and transcribed letter from McKay to Springhall, [no date, but envelope stamped in Bow, '4-pm 25 Nov. 20'], TNA: KV 2/1594.

73 Springhall rose up the ranks to become the national organiser of the CPGB by 1940; he was sentenced to seven years in prison for spying for the Russians in 1943. He died in Moscow in 1953 and was buried in China. (See the Douglas Springhall files, TNA: KV 2/1594.)

74 McKay, *A Long Way from Home*, 85–86; Kendall, *The Revolutionary Movement in Britain*, 246–248.

75 See Blanche Wiesen Cook (ed.), *Crystal Eastman on Women and Revolution* (New York: Oxford University Press, 1978) for a good sample of Eastman's writings, including some excellent analyses of the British political scene.

76 McKay to Ogden, 25 November [1920]; McKay, 'Up to Date', 4.

77 McKay, *A Long Way from Home*, 69–70; Ken Weller, *'Don't be a Soldier!': The Radical Anti-War Movement in North London, 1914–1918* (London: Journeyman Press and the London History Workshop Centre, 1985), 79–80; William J. Fishman, *East End Jewish Radicals, 1875–1914* (London: Duckworth, 1975), 269.

78 McKay, *A Long Way from Home*, 68.

79 McKay, 'Up to Date', 4.

80 McKay, *A Long Way from Home*, 68.

81 McKay, 'Up to Date', 4.

82 McKay, *A Long Way from Home*, 68; McKay, 'Up to Date', 4. During McKay's time in London the British cabinet received, via the Directorate of Intelligence at the Home Office, a detailed document at least once a month, entitled 'Report on Revolutionary Organisations in the United Kingdom'. Hundreds pertaining to the revolutionary ferment during and after the First World War have been preserved. See TNA series CAB 24. Many of these relate to the goings on at the ISC, which was regarded by the government as the headquarters of the Communist Party in the early 1920s. One report in September 1921 claimed

that the ISC was 'entirely controlled by the Communist Party, which has paid 1,000 [pounds] towards its up-keep'. TNA: CAB 24/128, Report No. 123.

83 McKay, *A Long Way from Home*, 70; McKay, 'Up to Date', 4.

84 McKay, *A Long Way from Home*, 70; McKay, 'Up to Date', 4. McKay to Ogden, 30 April 1920.

85 McKay, *A Long Way from Home*, 70; McKay, 'Up to Date', 4. McKay to Ogden, 30 April, 1920. Professor David Killingray, who is writing a biography of Dr Harold Moody, informs me that the medical student in question was probably a Jamaican named I.O.B. Shirley. As Dr Shirley he entered into partnership with Moody in 1929 but it was dissolved in 1933. (Killingray to James, 1 June and 17 July 2002.)

86 McKay, *A Long Way from Home*, 70; The man referred to was still active at the time McKay wrote his memoir, *A Long Way from Home*. See below.

87 Barbara Winslow mistakenly called him Reuben Samuels and incorrectly stated that he was a correspondent for the *Dreadnought*. Barbara Winslow, *Sylvia Pankhurst: Sexual Politics and Political Activism* (London: UCL Press, 1996), 128, 211n. Others – notably Patricia Romero, *E. Sylvia Pankhurst: Portrait of a Radical* (New Haven, CT: Yale University Press, 1990), Davis, *Sylvia Pankhurst* and Connelly, *Sylvia Pankhurst* – do not even mention him.

88 'Islington Riots: More Stories', *Globe*, 5 January 1921; *Daily Gazette* (Islington), 5 and 6 January 1921; Ken Weller, 'Direct Action and the Unemployed, 1920–21', *Solidarity* (July 1964), 24–30. McKay's biographical profile of a 'Comrade Gilmore', 'The Leader of the Bristol Revolutionaries', *WD*, 7 August 1920, is of a different man. (See also *WD*, 31 July 1920 for a report on the march from Bristol and rally in Trafalgar Square.) The Gilmore who led a tramcar strike and the ex-servicemen's march to London is cited variously in the *Bristol Observer* and *Bristol Evening Post* as 'G. Gilmore' or 'J. Gilmore' and is never referred to as 'coloured' or 'a man of colour' indicating he was black, as was the media custom at the time when referring to non-white people. The McKay profile made no reference to this 'Comrade' Gilmore's colour.

89 *Holloway & Hornsey & Harringay & Muswell Hill Press*, 8 January 1921; *Daily Gazette* (Islington), 5 and 6 January 1921. Gilmore's defence claimed that the petrol was for the purpose of 'making tea' when the Essex Road library, occupied previously by the unemployed (from which the authorities forcibly expelled them), was 'recovered'. *Daily Gazette* (Islington), 6 January 1921.

90 'Islington Riot: Startling Document', *Globe*, 4 January 1921; Weller, 'Direct Action and the Unemployed, 1920–21'; Weller, *'Don't Be a Soldier!'*, 43–44, 76–80.

91 Directorate of Intelligence, 'Report on Revolutionary Organisations in the United Kingdom', 15 September 1921, 5; TNA: CAB 24/128.

92 Three letters from Gilmore to McKay have survived but none from McKay to Gilmore. See Reuben Gilmore to McKay, 5 January 1934 (quoted); 1 November 1936; 1 December 1936; McKay Papers, Yale University.

93 Gilmore to McKay, 1 November 1936.

94 Gilmore to McKay, 5 January 1934.

95 Gilmore to McKay, 5 January 1934; 1 November 1936.

96 Gilmore to McKay, 1 November 1936; 12 December 1936.

97 McKay, 'Up to Date', 1, 4; McKay, *A Long Way from Home*, 68–69; McKay to Eastman, 16 September 1946, McKay MSS.

98 *Liberator*, August 1919, 46; March 1922, 22.

99 McKay, 'Up to Date', 3–4. McKay met J.L.J.F. Ezerman (1869–1949), a radical and maverick Orientalist (he worked on Indonesia), in New York in August 1919. He employed McKay to do research for him at the New York Public Library. Ezerman was called to Holland on family business and invited McKay to accompany him, paying his passage. From Holland they went to London in December 1919, where the relationship broke down. Ezerman, however, gave McKay his return passage and £50 towards the publication of his book of poems. The wages from the *Dreadnought* only covered McKay's board in London. McKay to Ogden, 25 February, 23 June, 4 August 1920; J.L.J.F. Ezerman to McKay, 18 June 1920, Ogden Fonds; McKay, *A Long Way from Home*, 87. McKay's recounting of a mysterious couple, 'the Grays', providing him with the passage to Europe (*A Long Way from Home*, 38–44) should not be taken literally. He probably used the device to conceal Ezerman's involvement.

100 Advert in *WD*, 23 October 1920.

101 McKay, *A Long Way from Home*, 70. Over the years, the *Dreadnought* carried many adverts for social events at the ISC.

102 Opened on 21 October, the exhibition was advertised in the *Dreadnought*, 23 October 1920.

103 McKay to Ogden, 30 October 1920.

104 McKay to Cunard, 30 April 1932.

105 McKay to Ogden, 25 November 1920.

106 McKay to Ogden, 30 April 1920; McKay to Francine Budgen [August? 1920], quoted in Cooper, *Claude McKay*, 130–131.

107 McKay to Ogden, [mid-August] 1920.

108 McKay to Joseph Freeman, 19 March 1921, Joseph Freeman Papers, box 29, file 35, Hoover Institution Archives, Stanford University.

109 McKay, *A Long Way from Home*, 67.

110 Budgen tells his own remarkable story in an engaging autobiography: Frank Budgen, *Myselves When Young* (London: Oxford University Press, 1970).

111 McKay, 'Up to Date', 2.

112 McKay to Cunard, 30 April 1932.

113 McKay, *A Long Way from Home*, 67.

114 Writing in January 1920, McKay claimed the club was 'about three months old', but the 14 June 1919 issue of the magazine *West Africa* carried a report on the operations of the club (444). See McKay, 'Our London Letter'. Although McKay's 'letter' – in fact a long article on the club – was published in the *Negro World* of 13 March 1920, it is datelined 'London, Jan. 14, 1920'. For an analysis of the context and the reprinted document itself, see Winston James, 'Letters

from London in Black and Red: Claude McKay, Marcus Garvey and the *Negro World*', *History Workshop Journal*, 85 (2018), 281–293.

115 McKay, *A Long Way from Home*, 67; McKay, 'Our London Letter'.

116 McKay to Cunard, 30 April 1932.

117 McKay, 'Our London Letter'. He appended the Rev Matthias's words to his article sent to the freethinking Hubert Harrison who was then an editor on the *Negro World*. The report in *West Africa* (14 June 1919) corroborated McKay's description of the place as 'overwhelmingly churchy'. The magazine reported that the club had a reputation as a 'no drinking club'. And one of its officials advised the men to 'keep smiling', telling them: 'The average Englishman does not understand coloured men, never having seen crowds of them, so is apt to stare and perhaps pass remarks. Don't let it get your goat' (444).

118 McKay, *A Long Way from Home*, 67–68.

119 'Pismo Mek-Kaia Tovarishu Trotskomu' ['Letter from McKay to Comrade Trotsky'], *Pravda*, 1 April 1923. Though *Pravda* carried it in April, McKay's letter was dated 20 February 1923.

120 McKay, 'Our London Letter'.

121 Letter to Trotsky.

122 McKay to Ogden, 12 March 1920.

123 McKay to Ogden, 25 February 1920.

124 McKay, *A Long Way from Home*, 70–71; McKay, 'Up to Date', 3.

125 McKay, *A Long Way from Home*, 71.

126 Claude McKay, 'The Castaways', *Cambridge Magazine*, Summer 1920, 58.

127 *Daily Herald*, especially 9 and 10 April 1920; and E.D. Morel, *The Horror on the Rhine* (London: Union of Democratic Control, 1920).

128 Sally Marks, 'Black Watch on the Rhine: A Study in Propaganda, Prejudice and Prurience', *European Studies Review*, 13:3 (1983), 297–334; Keith L. Nelson, 'The "Black Horror on the Rhine": Race as a Factor in Post-World War I Diplomacy', *Journal of Modern History*, 42:4 (1970), 606–627; James, 'A Race Outcast from an Outcast Class', 82–83; Peter Collar, *The Propaganda War in the Rhineland: Weimar Germany, Race and Occupation after World War I* (London: I.B. Taurus, 2013).

129 McKay, *A Long Way from Home*, 78.

130 Claude McKay, 'A Black Man Replies', *WD*, 24 April 1920; Claude McKay, 'Letter to Comrade Trotsky', *Communist*, 8 April 1922.

131 Claude McKay, 'Enslaved', *Liberator*, July 1921, 6; 'Africa Enslaved' is the title of one of the poems McKay sent to Ogden in a letter dated 17 August 1920. (The enclosure was not retained.) It is almost certainly the one later published as 'Enslaved'.

132 McKay to Marcus Garvey, 17 December 1919, Hubert H. Harrison Papers, Box 2, Folder 66, Rare Book and Manuscript Library, Columbia University Library. Reprinted in James, 'Letters from London in Black and Red'.

133 Claude McKay, 'Socialism and the Negro', *WD*, 31 January 1920.

134 McKay to Ogden, 25 February 1920.

135 Claude McKay, 'To Ethiopia', *Liberator*, February 1920, 7.

136 Jeffrey Green with Randall Lockhart, '"A Brown Alien in a White City": Black Students in London, 1917–1920' in Rainer Lotz and Ian Pegg (eds), *Under the Imperial Carpet: Essays in Black History* (Crawley: Rabbit Press, 1986), 208–216; Paul Rich, 'The Black Diaspora in Britain: Afro-Caribbean Students and the Struggle for a Political Identity, 1900–1950', *Immigrants and Minorities*, 6:2 (1987), 151–172.

137 Jeffrey Green, *Edmund Thornton Jenkins: The Life and Times of an American Black Composer, 1894–1926* (Westport, CT: Greenwood Press, 1982), 64–70.

138 McKay saw the Southern Syncopated Orchestra in December 1919 at the Coliseum. He was not as taken with Buddy Gilmore as most of the critics were. '[H]is drum was more than noisy & practically drowned the whole band. There was no balance.' McKay to Ogden, n.d. but marked 'Saturday' [June/July 1920 (between 23 June and 7 July 1920)]; Green, *Edmund Thornton Jenkins*; Howard Rye, 'The Southern Syncopated Orchestra' in Rainer Lotz and Ian Pegg (eds), *Under the Imperial Carpet: Essays in Black History* (Crawley: Rabbit Press, 1986), 217–232.

139 *Cambridge Magazine*, 16 August 1919, 913, and Summer 1920, 55.

140 W.F. Elkins, 'Hercules and the Society of Peoples of African Origin', *Caribbean Studies*, 11:4 (1972), 47–59; Ian Duffield, 'Duse Mohamed Ali and the Development of Pan-Africanism, 1866–1945', PhD dissertation, Edinburgh University, 1971; Fryer, *Staying Power*; David A. Vaughan, *Negro Victory: The Life Story of Dr Harold Moody* (London: Independent Press, 1950); Winston James, 'The Black Experience in Twentieth-Century Britain' in Philip D. Morgan and Sean Hawkins (eds), *Black Experience and the Empire* (Oxford: Oxford University Press, 2004), 347–386; David Killingray, '"To Do Something for the Race": Harold Moody and the League of Coloured Peoples' in Bill Schwarz (ed.), *West Indian Intellectuals in Britain* (Manchester: Manchester University Press, 2003), 51–70.

141 McKay to Garvey, 17 December 1919.

142 'What We Stand For', *African Telegraph*, July–August 1919, 271; emphasis added.

143 McKay to Ogden, 26 March 1920.

144 Claude McKay, 'English Journalists Investigate Bolshevism', *Crusader*, 4:4 (1921), 18–19.

145 Elkins, 'Hercules and the Society of Peoples of African Origin'; James, 'The Black Experience in Twentieth-Century Britain', 58–60.

146 McKay to Ogden, 25 February 1920.

147 See McKay's insightful and moving discussion of African art in his correspondence with Ogden, and in Claude McKay, *The Negroes in America* (Port Washington: Kennikat Press, [1923] 1979), 56–59.

148 Claude McKay, *Banjo: A Story Without a Plot* (New York: Harper and Brothers, 1929), 269–271.

149 'I react more to the emotions of the Irish people than to those of any other whites', he wrote soon after his London sojourn. '[T]hey are so passionately primitive in their loves and hates. They are quite free of the disease which is

known in bourgeois phraseology as Anglo-Saxon hypocrisy. I suffer with the Irish. I think I understand the Irish. My belonging to a subject race entitles me to some understanding of them. And then I was born and reared a peasant; the peasant's passion for the soil possesses me, and it is one of the strongest passions in the Irish revolution.' McKay, 'How Black Sees Green and Red', 20.

150 McKay, 'How Black Sees Green and Red', 17. McKay's profound sympathy with the Irish comes through powerfully in the article; see also Hugh Hope [McKay], 'A Hero of the Wars', *WD*, 17 April 1920, and C.E.E. [McKay], 'Under the Iron Heel', *WD*, 14 August 1920 and C.E.E. [McKay], 'The Martyrdom of Ireland', *WD*, 9 October 1920. Bell (*Hesitant Comrades*, 125–126) noted how exceptionally radical the *Workers' Dreadnought* was on the Irish question, and applauded and quoted at length the latter article without knowing and therefore acknowledging that it was by McKay.

151 'The Spanish Needle', *Cambridge Magazine*, Summer 1920, 55; 'Samson', *WD*, 10 January 1920.

2

From Russian colonies to black America … and back: Lenin and Langston Hughes

Matthieu Renault

In the summer of 1920, the highlight of the Second World Congress of the Comintern, held in Moscow, was a debate organised by Lenin on 'national and colonial questions'. Lenin laid down the terms of the debate in a series of theses, asking his 'comrades' to communicate their remarks on a list of issues: Ireland, national minorities from Central Europe and the Balkans, Russian Turkestan (Central Asia), the 'peoples of the Orient' and 'Negroes in America'. For him, these were all 'nations […] without equal rights'.[1] On 28 July, during the fifth session of the Congress, John Reed, the American journalist, spoke on the situation of black people in the United States, the practice of lynching, and the Jim Crow laws. He highlighted the simultaneous emergence of race *and* class consciousness in black American populations since the Mexican–American War (1898) and through their migration north. This new consciousness, he explained, was motivating blacks to take action for black social and political rights *as Americans*. This suggested that attempts to encourage national independence would be futile – a notion put forth a decade later by the Comintern and promoted by the Communist Party of the United States (CPUSA). Instead, blacks would have to be convinced to ally with the white proletariat.[2]

As the capitalistic hegemony of the United States grew, the global anti-imperialist struggle became increasingly urgent. In response, the Second Congress conceived a strategy in which black liberation played a central role. The strategy encouraged former slaves from the 'New World' to identify with the colonised masses of Asia and, to an even greater degree, of Africa, who toiled under the yoke of European imperialism. Indeed, black Americans would soon be defined as a *colonised people from within*. This history is well documented. What is less well known is that connections between the 'colonial question' and the 'Black question' had already been established, in a different way and with different implications, in Lenin's little-known pre-1917 writings on the internal colonisation of the Russian Empire's borderlands.

On internal colonisation or in praise of capitalist expansion

In 1907, Lenin confided to a friend that 'I know so little of Russia: Simbirsk, Kazan, Saint Petersburg, and that's all'.[3] Simbirsk (today's Ulyanovsk): a southern city in 'Europe's Russia', bathed by the Volga, where Lenin was born and spent his childhood; Kazan: a bit further north along the Volga, the historic Muslim centre and capital of what would become the Republic of Tatarstan, where he studied law at the Imperial University before being expelled for participating in demonstrations against the Tsarist bureaucracy; and Saint Petersburg, where he strengthened his Marxist training and engaged in revolutionary activism before being arrested, detained and then sentenced to exile in Siberia in 1897. Lenin's silence on his experience in Siberia, where he spent three years (in exile), will, as we will see, prove symptomatic of his view of the Russian Empire's borders.

An illustration of this view can be found in Lenin's first major work, *The Development of Capitalism in Russia* (1899), which he in fact completed while in exile. In the preface, Lenin explains that his book will be limited to 'the standpoint of the home market, leaving aside the problem of the foreign market', and 'interior, purely Russian gubernias [provinces]', bracketing peripheral spaces and their varying degrees of national minorities (non-Russians).[4] As the following remarks in the final chapter make clear, these two restrictions are tightly bound:

> [W]here is the border line between the home and the foreign market? To take the political boundaries of the state would be too mechanical a solution – and would it be a solution? If Central Asia is the home market and Persia the foreign market, to which category do Khiva and Bokhara belong? If Siberia is the home market and China the foreign market, to which category does Manchuria belong? [...] What is important is that capitalism cannot exist and develop without constantly expanding the sphere of its domination, without colonising new countries and drawing old non-capitalist countries into the whirlpool of world economy. And this feature of capitalism has been and continues to be manifested with tremendous force in post-Reform Russia.[5]

Lenin was well aware that the (economic) trend towards expansion and *colonisation* at work within capitalism and its (political) expressions around the imperial world made the borders between home and foreign markets extremely porous and shifting. That is why the borderlands excluded at the outset of his analysis inevitably make a return, for instance when he focuses on the commercial cultivation of grain – the heart of whose production had moved from the 'central zone of Black Earth' to the 'Lower Volga steppe provinces'. The shift was the result of vast migrations towards southern Russia: 'in the post-Reform period the outer steppe regions have been *colonies* of the central, long-settled part of European Russia. The abundance of free land has attracted an enormous stream of settlers, who have quickly increased the area under crops.' These new 'colonies' provided 'central Russia' with wheat, receiving in exchange manufactured goods and labour: 'The extensive development of commercial crops was possible only because of the close economic ties of these colonies with central Russia, on the one hand, and the European grain importing countries, on the other.' Further on, as he refers to a work by Nikolaï Remezov on Bashkortostan, a predominantly Muslim area, Lenin enthusiastically describes 'coloniser[s] fell[ing] timber for shipbuilding and transform[ing] the fields "cleared" of "wild" Bashkirs into "wheat factories"'. For Lenin, this process, based on a structural division of production into centres and borderlands, is a reflection of Marx's theses on the 'capitalist colony' in the third volume of *Capital*: 'This is a sample of colonial policy that bears comparison with any of the Germans' exploits in a place like Africa.'[6]

For Lenin, any differences stem from a *delay* in capitalist colonisation in the realm of politics due to the recent arrival of Russia into the league of capitalist nations, as well its persistent feudalism and 'the domination of the Asian way of life'. In his view, the political conquest still to be achieved was one of internal colonisation, a notion he probably borrowed not only from Prussian bureaucratic language, but also from Russian historiography, notably from a historian he refers to elsewhere: Vasily Klyuchevsky. This latter, in an extension of the work of his own predecessor – the chair of the University of Moscow, Sergey Solovyov – posited that '[the] history of Russia is the history of a country that colonizes itself'.[7] For Klyuchevsky, the history of *all* of Russia – including its centre – should be viewed as a form of *self-colonisation*, with migrations towards Siberia, Central Asia and the Pacific Coast embodying the latest episode of the saga.[8] For Lenin, domestic colonisation is relevant in any place with 'unoccupied, free lands, easily accessible to settlers'. In such a context, peasants driven out of agricultural lands and into populated areas are not forced to join the ranks of the industrial army or go abroad. They can also emigrate to 'new lands' *within* the country. That explains why capitalism takes on two forms of development: a development of 'depth' that advances capitalist relations (industrialisation) where they already exist (in the centre), and a development of 'breadth' through *geographic expansion* (towards the borderlands): 'Post-Reform Russia affords us an example of the two processes going on simultaneously.'[9]

This 'term colony', Lenin goes on, 'is still more applicable to the other outer regions, for example, the Caucasus', where population growth had expanded massively and the land area used for agriculture increased considerably. This change went hand in hand with the devastation of local craftsmanship due to competition with goods imported from central Russia and abroad. That in turn led to the 'decline in the making of drinking-horns because of the decay of the feudal system in Georgia and of the steady disappearance of her memorable feasts', as well as to a *Europeanisation* of mentalities and practices. As a synonym of 'civilisation', Europeanisation was embodied by changes in fashion: 'Russian capitalism has thus been drawing the Caucasus into the sphere of world commodity circulation, obliterating its local peculiarities – the remnants of ancient patriarchal isolation – and providing itself with a market for its factories [...] Mr Coupon [the capitalists] has been ruthlessly divesting the proud mountaineer of his picturesque national costume and dressing him in the livery of a European flunkey.' And Lenin adds that 'similar phenomena' can be found at work in the further flung regions of Central Asia and Siberia. In that respect, Russian capitalism's capacity for expansion exceeded that of Western European countries: 'Russia is in a particularly favoured position as compared with other capitalist countries, due to the abundance of free land accessible for colonisation in her border regions.'[10]

Lenin's laudatory view of colonisation is simply an expression, in *Marxist geography* terms, of a deep conviction inherited from Kautsky and Plekhanov of the fundamentally progressive character of capitalism, despite its devastating effects. It also reflects what was for him a 'historic mission' to generate and nourish forces capable of toppling it. This enthusiasm can also be seen in another essay, 'Once More on the Theory of Realisation', published in March 1899, where he highlights, in addition to the historic evolution that led to the emergence of 'great mechanical industry' in the 'old countries' of Western Europe, the 'mighty drive of developed capitalism to expand to other territories, to populate and plough up new parts of the world, to set up colonies and to drive savage tribes into the whirlpool of world capitalism'. Russia, whose 'capitalist period' (a period inextricably linked to internal colonisation) had begun with the end of serfdom (1861), had no reason to be any different: 'The south and south-east of European Russia, the Caucasus, Central Asia, and Siberia serve as something like colonies for Russian capitalism and ensure its tremendous development, not only in depth but also in breadth.'[11]

In Russia, as in Western European colonial possessions, a key factor and indicator of colonial expansion and its spatial sprawl was the *development of railways*. Just like Western capitalists, who 'stretched out their paws towards [...] Asia, of which only until recently only India and a small section of the coastal regions had been closely connected with the world market', and began a mad race to 'build massive railroads', Russian capitalists began to establish solid connections with the country's furthest flung provinces: 'The Transcaspian Railway began to "open up" Central Asia for the capitalists. The "Great Siberian Railway" [...] opened up Siberia.'[12] Lenin was well aware of the rail industry's particularly oppressive conditions and of the fact that the 'furious global race toward new and unknown markets', as spearheaded by railways, was already on its way to creating a crisis that could only worsen. But this was the iron law of capitalism and a gruelling stage that could not be avoided, unless one deluded oneself with populist illusions or other fantasies.

Lenin ignores the fact that, prior to capitalist expansion, the initial aim behind the construction of the Transcaspian (which crosses Russian Turkestan and was finished in 1906 with the line linking Moscow to Tashkent) was to facilitate the Russian imperial army's missions against local Muslim populations and Great Britain's imperialist interests – which was not lost on Lord Curzon, a British Conservative statesman, in his book, *Russia in Central Asia* (1889).[13] This is still a long way from Lenin's later thinking, which would lead him to posit a *consubstantiality between capital and war* ('conquest, pillage, and banditry') in the era of imperialism, to view 'access to *railroads*' and the 'inequality of [their] development' as the fundamental material and geographical infrastructure of financial and monopolistic capitalism, and to declare that the 'division of the world' was now complete.[14] In this sense, the need for 'free' internal or external land was no longer an issue: 'the colonial policy of the capitalist countries has *completed* the seizure of the unoccupied territories on our planet. For the first time the world is completely divided up, so that in the future *only* redivision is possible, i.e., territories can only pass from one "owner" to another, instead of passing as ownerless territory to an "owner".'[15] At the turn of the twentieth century, however, Lenin was still convinced that nothing could stop the inevitable march of capitalist colonisation to the far reaches of the Russian empire.

Serfs and slaves: Russia mirrored in the United States

During debates on the 'agrarian question' gripping Marxists in Russia following the revolution in 1905, Lenin returned to the theme of internal colonisation with the aim of broadening the fomenting *bourgeois* revolution. A section of 'The Agrarian Programme of Social Democracy in the Russian Revolution' focuses on the problem of colonisation, shifting the reader's attention from European Russia to 'the entire Russian Empire'. But here Lenin is no longer concerned with telling the story of capitalism as a colonial force. Instead, he focuses on showing the barriers slowing down capitalist expansion. He posits that, although 'these figures plainly show how vast is the land area of Russia', many areas are unproductive due to a lack of irrigation. But that is a lesser obstacle. The main obstacle to a 'rational economic use of the bulk of [Russia's] borderlands' is the persistence, *in the centre of the country*, of feudal latifundia (remnants of serf society), which '[keep] the Russian peasantry in a downtrodden state', preventing both 'technical progress' and 'the mental development of the mass of the peasants [...], as also their activity, initiative, and education', and the enterprising spirit necessary for the colonisation of far-flung free lands. The true problem was therefore rooted in '*social* conditions of agriculture in Russia', rather than in '*natural* properties of this or that borderland':

> All these millions of dessiatins [a land measurement unit] in Turkestan, as well as in many other parts of Russia are 'awaiting' not only irrigation and reclamation of every kind. They are also 'awaiting' the emancipation of the Russian agricultural population from the survivals of serfdom, from the yoke of the nobility's latifundia, and from the Black-Hundred dictatorship in the state [...] Russia possesses a gigantic amount of land available for colonization, which will be rendered accessible to the population and accessible to culture, not only by every technological advance of agriculture, but also by every advance in the emancipation of the Russian peasantry from the yoke of serfdom.[16]

For Lenin, the growth of capitalism in Russia was reliant on *Europeanisation*, which needed to further expand, including in Russia's 'semi-Asian' centre. However, he now turned to the United States, not Europe, to understand the most advanced model of agricultural practice. Lenin's interest in agrarian capitalism probably began with his reading of Kautsky's *Agrarfrage* [*The Agrarian Question*] (1899),[17] but it did not begin appearing regularly in his work until after 1905. For him, the bourgeois development of the agrarian economy in Russia would most likely take one of two paths: either the 'reorganization of landlord farms' – the way of 'reform' – or 'the elimination of feudal latifundia' – the way of 'revolution': 'Those two paths of objectively possible bourgeois development we would call the Prussian path and the American path.' Although these two 'paths' overlapped in central Russia, 'where landlord and peasant farming exist side by side', the division between the centre and borderlands provided 'the spatial or geographical distribution of the localities in which one or the other type of agrarian evolution prevails'. 'American'-style expansion to the far reaches of Russia, through internal colonisation, was different and faster than in 'the central provinces [...] burdened by the survivals of serfdom'. For Lenin, Russia's bourgeois revolution should follow the 'American style' rather than modelling itself on the 'countries of Western Europe, which our Marxists so often draw upon for thoughtless and stereotyped comparisons', even though in European countries 'all the land was already occupied in the epoch of the bourgeois-democratic revolution'.[18]

Lenin promoted these ideas until at least 1915, when he wrote a long essay on American capitalism in which he refers to the 'remarkably detailed' census data compiled by the American government, and particularly to a report on Southern agriculture drafted by the unknown-to-him African-American intellectual and activist W.E.B. Du Bois.[19] The United States, he writes, is a 'leading country of modern capitalism' and should serve as 'the model for our bourgeois civilization and its ideal'. For him, it was also a country where one could simultaneously observe all '*forms* of capitalist penetration into agriculture', within the borders of a single territory, with a 'vast area [...] only slightly smaller than the whole of Europe'. For Lenin, the United States is a space where differences between European states, with all their historic density, can be projected and re-examined in an *external* setting. The 'industrial North' represents Western Europe in America: 'We find here areas which have long been settled, highly industrialised, highly intensive, and similar to most of the areas of civilised, old-capitalist Western Europe'; the former slave region of the South is strikingly similar to central Russia and its legacy of serfdom; the West represents an opportunity for large-scale colonization – the settlement and exploitation of that land in many respects provides a road map for colonising Russian borderlands, particularly on its eastern margins. The thick limits of Russian geography are more similar to the American *frontier* than to the thin border lines of Western European countries. In an even greater evolutionist compari-son, Lenin suggests that the economic *geography* of the United States is a modern spatial repetition of the *history* of capitalism in Europe: 'This is a remarkable diversity of relationships, embracing both past and future, Europe and Russia.'[20]

In a remark that would later have been unthinkable, Stalin rightly wrote in 1924, in his *Foundations of Leninism*, that the 'style of Leninism' is the combination of two features: 'Russian revolutionary fervor' and 'American practical sense'.[21] In 1915, Lenin, who was an admirer of the American revolutionary tradition (from the War for Independence to the Civil War[22]), declared the following in a critique of the notion of a United States of Europe, his thinking steeped in the 'evolution [...] of America': 'The times when the cause of democracy and socialism was associated only with Europe alone have gone forever.'[23] It may seem surprising today, but in the early twentieth century, this way of looking towards the United States, which very few European Marxists were prepared to do, was in essence a way of *provincialising* (Western) *Europe*.

This does not suggest, however, that Lenin was an enthusiastic supporter of American capitalism. It is true that 'the Civil War of 1861–65 and the abolition of slavery' dealt 'a decisive blow [...] at the latifundia of the slave-owners' and encouraged the development of 'small farms', notably owned by former slaves. The rapid proliferation of such farms reveals 'the particu-lar energy' with which the 'Negro urge to emancipation from the "planta-tion owners" half a century after the "victory" over slave-owners is still marked by an exceptional intensity'; a nearly simultaneous end to serfdom in Russia did not result in the same revolution. Yet it is important to note the equally generalised growth of the sharecropping system, which com-bined the legacy of slavery with the most advanced methods of capitalist oppression. According to Lenin, American sharecroppers, the vast majority of whom were black, were 'semi-slaves', exploited in a 'typically Russian, "purely Russian"' fashion. Former Russian serfs, who were chained to the 'labour-service system' and rotting away in latifundia, and former slaves, who were still attached to the former plantations, shared a common fate.[24]

Lenin learned of racial oppression in the United States at a young age. His favorite childhood book was none other than Harriet Beecher Stowe's *Uncle Tom's Cabin*.[25] In 1913, he wrote an article titled 'Russians and Negroes' in which he emphasised that 'the emancipation of the American slaves took place in a less "reformative" manner than that of the Russian slaves' and that 'the Russians still show *many more* traces of slavery than the Negroes'. However, the illiteracy rate was significantly higher in the South (in 'American "Russia"') than in the North ('American non-Russia'), and more generally the 'position of the Negroes in America', 'unworthy of a civilized country', were proofs that 'capitalism *cannot* give either *complete* emancipation or even complete equality'. And in conclusion, he writes: 'Shame on America for the plight of the Negroes!'[26] In the same year, during another episode in his long fight against supporters of cultural national autonomy (the Bundists – a general union of Jewish workers – being his primary target), he stated that the condition of blacks in the United States, in the 'Southern, former slave states of America', where schools were segre-gated, provided sufficient evidence that the plan for the 'nationalization of Jewish schools' in Russia would only further reinforce inequalities.[27]

Three decades later, the Caribbean Marxist historian C.L.R. James would praise Lenin's ideas on 'agriculture and the Negro question', applauding him for comparing the economic evolutions of two starkly contrasting societies, 'Tsarist Russia and the United States'.[28] Nevertheless, Lenin's quasi-identification of former Russian serfs (more marginally, Jews from Russia) and black former slaves in the United States makes his neglect of other groups more glaring: natives (non-settlers) of the Russian border-lands, particularly national (non-Russian) minorities; or 'nationals', whom he mentions occasionally in his notes on the debates in the Duma on the agrarian question,[29] but which never appear as true protagonists.

Lenin's arguments on the colonisation of the Russian Empire's margins echo, more than Marx's work, John Locke's legitimation of colonial expansion in America two centuries earlier. Locke's argument is based on the notion of virgin lands – uninhabited, or at least unexploited spaces – or *terrae nullius* which beckon entrepreneurial individuals capable of making them profitable and extracting the greatest value/capital. The colonial logic behind Lenin's call to populate a massive swathe of free land is based, perhaps, not on a virgin land free of civilisation, but on a world in which there are only 'Indians' scattered here and there. These 'Indians' (as in the case of the 'savage' Bashkirs) are invited either to clear the land for settlers or are destined (like the Georgian peasants), perhaps not for elimination, but for assimilation and *denationalisation* by external capitalist relations. Lenin not only demonstrates an American style of 'practical sense', but also the American *colonial imagination*. As such, he is simply walking in the footsteps of the 'father of Russian socialism' (an influence he himself makes explicit), Alexander Herzen, who wrote in 1835: '[W]hat is Siberia? – here is a land you do not know at all [...] Do you realize that Siberia is an entirely new country, an America *sui generis* [...]? Here all are exiles and all are equal. [...] Back there [in European Russia] life is more enjoyable, and there is enlightenment, but the more important points are: freshness and newness.'[30]

Beginning in 1914, Lenin's writings on national self-determination (as a *political* right of separation) introduce an important distinction between 'oppressive nations' and 'oppressed nations'. Here, he depicts Russia as a vast 'prison of peoples' and defends the revolutionary trend towards 'national wars' against imperialism. After 1916, all references to internal colonisation would completely disappear from his discourse. However, traces can still be found, and the fact that these two discursive strains could exist simultaneously in his work presages the contradictions the Bolsheviks would face in the borderlands when performing the dual task of promoting the socialist revolution and decolonising the Russian Empire.

From one cotton field to another: Langston Hughes in Central Asia

In June 1932, the African-American poet Langston Hughes, then aged 30, boarded the *Europa* liner in New York for Moscow. He was walking in the footsteps of Claude McKay, a seminal figure in the Harlem Renaissance, who had gone to Russia ten years earlier to participate in the Fourth World Congress of the Communist International.[31] Two years after Hughes, it was the actor and singer Paul Robeson's turn to tread over Soviet soil, on the invitation of Sergei Eisenstein, as part of a quickly abandoned idea for a movie on the Haitian revolution. Hughes's visit was also linked to a movie, *Black and White*, to be produced by the German–Russian production company Mezhrabpom. The aim of this never-made film was to expose racial oppression in the United States. Hughes was to be the scriptwriter, and he was joined on his trip to Moscow by twenty-one other 'Black artists'.[32]

After the project was abandoned, half of the group, including Hughes, who had been invited to visit a Soviet region of their choice, opted to see 'where the majority of the colored citizens lived, namely Turkmenistan in Soviet Central Asia'.[33] Unsatisfied by this brief and tedious official visit, Hughes left his travel companions in Ashgabat, where he happened to meet the Hungarian journalist Arthur Koestler (who would later become known for his critique of Stalinism, but who was then a member of the Communist Party of Germany). The two men travelled for a time together, but Hughes is clear about their differing *views* of the Soviet Orient in his autobiography, *I Wonder as I Wander* (1956): 'I was trying to make him understand why I observed the changes in Soviet Asia with *Negro* eyes. To Koestler, Turkmenistan was simply a *primitive* land moving into twentieth-century civilization. To me it was a colored land moving into orbits hitherto reserved for whites.'[34]

This comparison between black America and the Muslim Soviet East, which radically displaces the parallel Lenin draws between (former) serfs from central Russia and (former) American slaves, dominates the articles published by Hughes in *Izvestia* during his several-month trip to Central Asia. These writings were collectively published on his return in a small volume titled *A Negro Looks at Soviet Central Asia*. In the book, he recounts his journey by train between Moscow and Tashkent, which he views more as a journey south than east: 'For an American Negro living in the northern part of the United States the word *South* has an unpleasant sound, an overtone of horror and of fear [...] I wanted to study the life of these people [from Central Asia] in the Soviet Union, and write a book about them for the dark races of the capitalist world.' And he contrasts the segregated trains in the United States, where 'if you are yellow, brown, or black, you can never travel anywhere without being reminded of your color', with Soviet trains, where 'Jim Crow laws' or their equivalent under the Tsarist empire had been abolished. Skin colour acts as a vehicle of identification throughout Hughes's narrative, in which he provides hopeful glimpses of emancipation: 'there [are] many cities in Central Asia where dark men and women are in control of the government'; and while illiteracy rates in 'colonies of tsarist Russia [...] were higher than in "today's Alabama" before the Revolution', schools now flourished there.[35]

There is one striking similarity between Central Asia and the American South: the ubiquity of *cotton growing*. In the former, cotton was a pillar of the imperial economy; the extension of this monoculture was necessarily strongly linked to the kind of internal colonisation that interested Lenin. In the latter, 'in Georgia, Mississippi, and Alabama', cotton was the cornerstone of the slave system. But while in the American South, slavery continued with the practice of sharecropping – with all its methods of terror, particularly lynching – Soviet cotton production, organised into kolkhozes, was, according to Hughes (who claims to have filled notebooks with figures and data), freed from oppression and oppressors: 'How different are the cotton lands of Soviet Central Asia! The beys are gone – the landlords done with forever. I have spoken to the peasants and I know. They are not afraid to speak like the black farm-hands of the South.'[36]

Even twenty years later, Hughes would continue to assert that 'the disappearance of the color line in Soviet Asia' was one of the greatest accomplishments of the Russian Revolution. Another great accomplishment for him was 'the unveiling of the harem women in Turkestan',[37] which he equated with an emancipation of religious subjugation and participation in public life. This theme can already be found in *A Negro Looks at Soviet Central Asia*, particularly in the chapter on the former emirate of Bukhara (attached to the Republic of Uzbekistan when it was founded in 1924), in which he writes of the terrible fate of women under the cruel tyrant. For him, women freed of their headscarves was the symbol of an emerging 'new people': 'New times demand new people, and [...] new [women] are coming into being.'[38] Hughes is even clearer on the matter in 'In an Emir's Harem', an article published in *Woman's Home Companion*:

> That strange Bolshevik revolution commenced at once smashing the customs of hundreds and hundreds of years, shattering the oldest traditions of the Orient, deposing beys and emirs, unfrocking mullahs, educating children and freeing women. Everywhere – in Bukhara, in Samarkand, in Ferghana, in Osh – women were leaving the harems, casting off their veils, walking alone in the streets, working in factories and going to school.[39]

However, for Hughes, this change of garment also *revealed* the limits of the ongoing revolution. Although he was initially silent on his reservations, he would later write in his autobiography that 'the native officials everywhere tried too hard to convince us of the progress made under the new regime [...] [T]housands of women were still in harems in spite of the new decrees, and veiled from head to foot in public. Muezzins still called to prayer from tall towers. Bazaars were still filthy.' While mocking Koestler who repeatedly argued, tongue in cheek, that 'if the Revolution had only occurred in Germany, at least it would have been a clean one', Hughes also noted the extreme poverty that continued to grip large swathes of Central Asia and the palpable 'dark frontiers of progress'. The 'frontiers of revolution'[40] were first and foremost visible in the margins of the (former) empire.

Although the parallels drawn by Hughes between the condition of black Americans and that of (formerly) colonised 'coloreds' in the Russian Empire[41] provide interesting insights, his vision of emancipation in the Soviet East is troubling – not because of his praise of Stalinist collectivisation (which was common at the time and would not appear in his work after the early 1930s), but because of the *orientalism* that dominates his image of Central Asia as a massive harem. In particular, he seems to ignore or have nothing to say on the fact that the massive unveiling of Muslim women was far from a sign of a burgeoning revolutionary consciousness, but instead part of a targeted offensive begun in 1927 with Stalin's so-called Hujum campaign (literally, 'the attack' in Turkic languages), which only resulted in generating resistance to the Soviet order.[42] As early as the beginning of the 1920s, Alexandra Kollontaï, the feminist intellectual then at the head of the Russian Department of Women (*zhenotdel*), stated: 'I have been laughed at because so far I have brought here only a few women from the harems of Turkestan. These women have thrown aside their veils [...] How else would we get in touch with Mohammedan women except through women?'[43] In 1924, during the third anniversary of the opening of the Communist University of the Toilers of the East (KUTV), Trotsky underlined the emancipation of Muslim women as a vital part of the process of *translating* the revolution eastwards:

> [T]he Eastern woman who is the most paralyzed in life, in her habits and in creativity, the slave of slaves, that she, having at the demand of the new economic relations taken off her cloak will at once feel herself lacking any sort of religious buttress; she will have a passionate thirst to gain new ideas, a new consciousness which will permit her to appreciate her new position in society.[44]

If there was one thing even the most stubborn enemies in the Bolshevik Party could agree on, it was the need to free the 'Eastern woman' from male and religious subjugation. It is doubtful that Lenin would have supported such policies. In his fight against the persistent great-power chauvinism among Russian Communists, and as an advocate for a *policy of prudence*, he called for 'a wise and circumspect line' that could serve as an example for the whole Muslim East, even beyond the borders of the (former) Russian Empire.[45] In a letter to Georgy Chicherin dated March 1921, he says he 'completely agrees' with Chicherin on the topic of sending a message to encourage the party's local chapters to be tactful and avoid offending Muslims.[46] In addition, during this period, Lenin supported Georgy Safarov, an adviser on the 'Eastern issue' at the Comintern, who, in direct conflict with the Soviet powers in Turkestan, was uncompromising in his task of restoring land to local populations that had previously been expropriated by settlers. Safarov, in reference to Klyuchevsky, believed that liquidating the legacy of domestic colonisation in the case of the Russian 'Orient' was vital.[47]

But could Lenin, who had long promoted the internal colonisation of the empire's borderlands, make a clean break with this legacy? Following the Civil War, the primary concern for the Soviet power was to repair damaged railways and restart industrial production. In this context, 'Turkestan' became synonymous with cotton: 'Everybody knows that the textile industry is at a complete standstill because today we have no cotton – it has to be imported – owing to the fact that Western Europe, too, is suffering from an acute shortage of raw materials. Our one source of supply is Turkestan.'[48] In 1918, Lenin began taking part in discussions on an irrigation programme in Central Asia, and in 1922 he inquired as to the progress of the work and experiments performed as part of that programme. The expansion, or simple survival, of the Soviet regime then seemed inconceivable without a reinvestment in the economic and material infrastructure built by Russian imperialism; in other words, without extracting natural resources from the colony. This necessarily contradicted a no less vital political need for national self-determination, which, from Lenin's mouth, was never an empty promise.

Stalin's solution to this contradiction would not be to reduce the sphere of colonisation, but instead to extend it to the *entire* Soviet territory, reproducing, in the opposite direction, the movement laid out in Klyuchevsky's *History of Russia*, and providing the conditions for the possibility of what Foucault would call 'state racism'.[49] From this perspective, the question was no longer who were Russia's 'Blacks' – the peasants living in the centre under the remnants of serfdom (Lenin) or the 'colored' Muslims of Central Asia (Hughes). They both were, as were many other groups. African Americans, as mentioned in the introduction to the chapter, have often imagined their situation as an internal colonisation. To conclude, I would like to hypothesise, conversely, that re-examining Soviet internal (re)colonisation in the light of the African American experience could provide unexpected insights into the history of the demise of the October revolution.

Notes

1 V.I. Lenin, 'Preliminary Draft Theses on the National and the Colonial Questions (For the Second Congress of the Communist International)' [1920], *Collected Works*, Vol. 31 (Moscow: Progress Publishers, 1966), 145, 149.

2 John Reed, *Second Congress of the Communist International: Minutes of the Proceedings*, Vol. 1 (London: New Park Publications, 1977), 121–124.

3 Lenin, cited in Robert Service, *Lénine* (Paris: Perrin, [2000] 2016), 294.

4 V.I. Lenin, *The Development of Capitalism in Russia* [1899], *Collected Works*, Vol. 3 (Moscow: Progress Publishers, 1960), preface to the first edition, 25.

5 *Ibid.*, 593–594. Khiva and Bukhara (today in Uzbekistan), a khanate and emirate respectively, were annexed in 1873 and 1868 by the Tsarist armies and then had the status of protectorates of Imperial Russia.

6 *Ibid.*, 257–258.

7 Vasily Klyuchevsky, cited in Jean-Louis Buer, *La Russie* (Paris: Le Cavalier bleu, 2009), 29.

8 See Alexander Etkind, *Internal Colonization: Russia's Imperial Experience* (Cambridge and Malden: Polity Press, 2011), 67.

9 Lenin, *The Development of Capitalism in Russia*, 680, 647–648.

10 Lenin, *The Development of Capitalism in Russia*, 680–682.

11 V.I. Lenin, 'Once More on the Theory of Realisation', *Collected Works*, Vol. 4 (Moscow: Progress Publishers, 2008), 92.

12 V.I. Lenin, 'The Lessons of the Crisis', *Collected Works*, Vol. 5 (Moscow: Progress Publishers, 2009), 90.

13 George N. Curzon, *Russia in Central Asia in 1889 and the Anglo-Russian Question* (London: Longmans, Green and Co., 1889).

14 V.I. Lenin, *Imperialism, the Highest Stage of Capitalism* [1916], 'Preface to the French and German Editions' [1920], *Collected Works*, Vol. 22 (Moscow: Progress Publishers, 1964), 190.

15 *Ibid.*, 254.

16 V.I. Lenin, 'The Agrarian Programme of Social Democracy in the First Russian Revolution, 1905–1907' [1908], *Collected Works*, Vol. 13 (Moscow: Progress Publishers, 1962), 248–254.

17 See V.I. Lenin, 'Capitalism in Agriculture (Kautsky's Book and Mr Bulgakov's Article)' [1899], *Collected Works*, Vol. 4, Digital Reprints, 2008 (Moscow: Progress Publishers, 1977).

18 Lenin, 'The Agrarian Programme of Social Democracy', 239–241, 254.

19 See 'Lenin, V.I. (1870–1924)', in Gerald Horne and Mary Young (eds), *W.E.B. Du Bois: An Encyclopedia* (Westport, CT: Greenwood Publishing, 2001), 122.

20 V.I. Lenin, *New Data on the Laws Governing the Development of Capitalism in Agriculture, Part One: Capitalism and Agriculture in the United States of America* [1915], *Collected Works*, Vol. 22 (Moscow: Progress Publishers, 1964), 19, 22, 100–101.

21 Stalin, cited in Jean-Jacques Lentz, *De l'Amérique et de la Russie* (Paris: Le Seuil, 1972), 91.

22 See especially V.I. Lenin, 'Letter to American Workers' [1918], *Collected Works*, Vol. 28 (Moscow: Progress Publishers, 1965), 62–76.

23 V.I. Lenin, 'On the Slogan for the United States of Europe' [1915], *Collected Works*, Vol. 21 (Moscow: Progress Publishers, 1964), 342.

24 Lenin, *New Data on the Laws Governing the Development of Capitalism in Agriculture*, 25, 28, 29, 92.

25 Service, *Lénine*, 79.

26 V.I. Lenin, 'Russians and Negroes' [1913], *Collected Works*, Vol. 18 (Moscow: Progress Publishers, 1963), 543–544.

27 V.I. Lenin, '"Cultural-National" Autonomy' [1913], *Collected Works*, Vol. 19 (Moscow: Progress Publishers, 1963), 504.

28 C.L.R. James, 'Lenin on Agriculture and the Negro question' [1947], in Scott McLemee (ed.), *C.L.R. James on the 'Negro Question'* (Jackson, MS: University Press of Mississippi, 1996), 130–132.

29 Lenin, 'The Agrarian Programme of Social Democracy'.

30 Alexander Herzen, letter to N.I. Sazonov (18 July 1835), cited in Mark Bassin, *Imperial Visions: Nationalist Imagination and Geographical Expansion in the Russian Far East, 1840–1865* (Cambridge, New York and Melbourne: Cambridge University Press, 1999), 65. Original version: http://gertsen.lit-info.ru/gertsen/letters/1832–1846/letter-41.htm [accessed 5 February 2021].

31 Claude McKay, 'Soviet Russia and the Negro' [1923–24], *Crisis*, 27:2 (December 1923), 61–74, 27:3 (January 1924), 117.

32 Langston Hughes, *Autobiography: I Wonder as I Wander* [1956] in Joseph McLaren (ed.), *The Collected Works of Langston Hughes*, Vol. 14 (Columbia and London: University of Missouri Press, 2003), 95–121.

33 *Ibid.*, 123.

34 *Ibid.*, 135.

35 Langston Hughes, *A Negro Looks at Soviet Central Asia* (Moscow and Leningrad: Co-operative Publishing Society of Foreign Workers in the USSR, 1934), 5–6, 8, 33. My reference here is a copy in Yale University Library's Hughes archives (http://brbl-dl.library.yale.edu/vufind/Record/3581372 [accessed 5 February 2021]). I have included the author's handwritten corrections.

36 Hughes, *A Negro Looks at Soviet Central Asia*, 12–15.

37 Hughes, *Autobiography*, 233.

38 Hughes, *A Negro Looks at Soviet Central Asia*, 20–28, 49.

39 Langston Hughes, 'In an Emir's Harem', *Woman's Home Companion*, September 1934, 92, http://brbl-dl.library.yale.edu/vufind/Record/3528048 [accessed 5 February 2021].

40 Hughes, *Autobiography*, 126, 134, 147–148.

41 Also see David C. Moore, 'Local Color, Global "Color". Langston Hughes, the Black Atlantic and Soviet Central Asia, 1932', *Research in African Literatures*, 27:4 (1996), 49–70.

42 Douglas T. Northrop, *Veiled Empire: Gender & Power in Stalinist Central Asia* (Ithaca and London: Cornell University Press, 2004).

43 See Louise Bryant, *Mirrors of Moscow* (New York: Thomas Seltzer, 1923); 'Madame Alexandra Kollontaï and the Woman's Movement': www.marxists.org/archive/bryant/works/1923-mom/kollontai.htm [accessed 18 February 2021].

44 Leon Trotsky, 'Perspectives and Tasks in the East', speech on the third anniversary of the Communist University for Toilers of the East, 21 April 1924: www.marxists.org/archive/trotsky/1924/04/perspectives.htm [accessed 5 February 2021].

45 V.I. Lenin, 'To: M.P. Tomsky' [1921], *Collected Works*, Vol. 45 (Moscow: Progress Publishers, 1976), 246–247.

46 V.I. Lenin, 'To: G.V. Chicherin' [1921], *Collected Works*, Vol. 45 (Moscow: Progress Publishers, 1976), 68.

47 Georgy Safarov, 'The East and the Revolution': https://cosmonaut.blog/ 2019/08/11/evolution-of-the-national-question-and-the-east-and-revolution-by- safarov/ [accessed 5 February 2021].

48 V.I. Lenin, 'Speech Delivered at the Third All-Russian Congress of Textile' [1920], *Collected Works*, Vol. 30 (Moscow: Progress Publishers, 1965), 519–525.

49 Michel Foucault, 'Society Must Be Defended', *Society Must Be Defended: Lectures at the Collège de France, 1975–1976* (New York: Picador, 1997).

3

African-American literature in the Soviet Union, 1917–1930s: contacts, translations, criticism and editorial policy

Olga Panova

Mutual attraction between the Soviet Union and Afro-America became apparent soon after the 1917 October revolution. For the African-American left, Soviet Russia seemed to be a 'promised land' for national and ethnic minorities and a complete contrast to the United States with its system of segregation and discrimination.[1] As Claude McKay put it, 'the Russian workers, who have won through the ordeal of persecution and revolution, extend the hand of international brotherhood to all the suppressed Negro millions of America'.[2]

On the other hand, travel books written by Soviet writers who went to the United States – Vladimir Maiakovsky's *My Discovery of America* (1926), Boris Pilnyak's *OK: An American Novel* (1931), Ilf and Petrov's *American Road Trip* (1937) – always included chapters (or at least fragments) specially devoted to the 'Negro problem', black literature, folklore, music and art. Thus Maiakovsky writes about Harlem, jazz, and dwells at some length on the Pushkin literary award announced by the *Opportunity*, discussing its foundation and its winners.

The architects of the Russian Revolution kept an eye on the 'Negro problem' in the USA. An idea of a worldwide congress of black people (as opposed to the Pan-African movement and its congresses) emerged in the Comintern as early as 1919.[3] In December 1919, John Reed made a detailed report on the situation of African Americans and the current tasks of the world Communist movement.[4] Lenin, in his 'Draft Thesis on the National and Colonial Question', prepared for the Second Congress of the Comintern (1920), included the item 'Negroes in America' in the list of acute problems and stressed that all Communist parties must directly support the revolutionary upheaval of oppressed nations and national minorities (the Irish in Great Britain and African Americans).[5] The Negro Bureau of the Eastern Secretariat of the Comintern Executive Committee, created at the turn of 1922–23,[6] dealt with matters relating to Africa and the countries with African diaspora, including the USA. There are 102 files on the Negro Bureau in the Russian State Archive of Social and Political History (RGASPI),[7] which give a good idea of early Comintern activity in this field: lots of protocols, reports, instructions, decisions, reviews, research articles, newspaper and journal clippings; files devoted to the black press (the *Negro Voice*, the *Negro Worker*, etc.); documents on the American Negro Labor Congress (1925); voluminous correspondence between Comintern officials and black leftist leaders, members of socialist and Communist parties, radical political figures like David Ivon Jones, Lovett Fort-Whiteman (James Jackson), and many others. Almost every Comintern congress adopted a resolution on the situation of black people in the USA.

The 'Negro problem' was a key focus of attention in the USSR; lamentations against racial oppression in the USA flooded the Soviet press of the 1920s and 1930s. Political strivings, propaganda and ideological guidelines had a direct influence over Soviet cultural policy and cultural diplomacy, including Soviet–black American literary contacts, translations and publishing of African-American writers.

The situation of black people in America had long been a subject of concern for educated Russians. *Uncle Tom's Cabin* by Harriet Beecher Stowe and Joel Chandler Harris's *Tales of Uncle Remus* had been favourite books in Russia since the nineteenth century; in the Soviet Union, however, they were regarded as children's books and appeared in so-called 'juvenile editions'. African-American literature used to be *terra incognita* for Russian readers before the revolution, so first of all it had to be introduced, and then duly interpreted – meaning that making an ideologically bound image of 'American Negro literature' was on the agenda.

In the 1920s, Soviet officials working for the literary institutions, as well as Soviet publishers, literary critics and readers, began to get acquainted with African-American literature. In the chaotic years that followed the revolution, publishing in general was in decline because of the Civil War, intervention, shortages of paper and equipment. But the New Economic Policy (NEP, 1922–28) brought forth a flood of books, both native and translated. Deming B. Brown gives the following data: at least 900 printings of translated American books during the NEP period as compared to a total of 38 American books under War Communism (1918–21).[8] In the period of commercial book publishing, the selection of American books for translation was more eclectic than it had ever been before in Russia (or would ever be again in the USSR), thanks to the private enterprise enjoying relative freedom of choice, and an amnesty for non-proletarian literature between 1924 and 1929.

Lots of private publishing houses were competing for the literary market,[9] trying to keep their fingers on the pulse and to quickly publish the most interesting, outstanding and/or commercially successful books. For the private publishers the key figure was the translator, who usually chose and recommended books (usually he or she managed to get the books from abroad with the help of friends or acquaintances there). The Soviet Union didn't join the Copyright Convention, so foreign books were frequently shortened and abridged in order to simplify imported works or edit them in accordance with ideological guidelines.[10]

In the 1920s black American authors were being published by the private as well as state publishers. The key figures of the decade were W.E.B. Du Bois, Walter White, Jessie R. Fauset and Claude McKay. Before the 1930s there appeared Russian editions of six African-American novels – W.E.B. Du Bois's *Quest of the Silver Fleece*,[11] Walter White's *Fire in the Flint*[12] and *Flight*,[13] Jessie R. Fauset's *There is Confusion*[14] and two novels by Claude McKay – *Home to Harlem*[15] and *Banjo*.[16] Collections of African-American poetry (that comprised poetic works by Countee Cullen, Claude McKay and Langston Hughes) appeared in various newspapers, journals and magazines.

The best translators of the decade facilitated public access to the black literary heritage. Among them were people with remarkable biographies, such as Piotr Okhrimenko, who translated Claude McKay's poetry, short stories and *Negroes in America* (1923). Okhrimenko was born into a family of peasants, attended a parochial school and worked in a factory; Leo Tolstoy helped him to start his literary career. Another 'star' of that generation, Mark Volosov, translator of Jessie Fauset's novel and McKay's *Home to Harlem*, was a sailor, who spent a decade working in the USA, taught himself English and became a successful translator after returning to Russia.

In the 1920s black American literature began to attract the attention of Soviet critics (among them such reputed experts as Ivan Kashkin, Sergei Dinamov and Nikolay Efros), with book reviews and short essays on particular authors and books being published over this decade. Paradoxically, *The Quest of the Silver Fleece* passed almost unnoticed – with no reviews at all, just occasional references to it in the press – although Du Bois was well known in the USSR both as a writer and an outstanding scholar and activist, co-founder of the National Association for the Advancement of Colored People (NAACP) and the *Crisis* magazine. His name appeared in various draft lists of invitees to the Congress of Friends of the Soviet Union that took place in Moscow (10–12 November 1927) during the celebration of the anniversary of the October revolution. The lists of invitees – delegates to the congress – compiled by the Comintern Executive Committee and VOKS (All-Union Society for Cultural Relations with Foreign Countries) included several outstanding black leaders: James Weldon Johnson, A. Philip Randolph, a leader of the labour movement, Robert S. Abbot, the founder of *Chicago Defender*, John Max Barber, the president of John Brown Memorial Association, William Pickens from the NAACP and Eugene Kinkle Jones, an active member of the National Urban League and the founder of *Opportunity* magazine.[17] None of these figures came to Moscow. W.E.B. Du Bois's 1926 visit to the Soviet Union left no traces inside the Soviet Union (or at least any traces remain unknown so far) – in contrast with his post-war visits, which received considerable press coverage. His earlier visit was most probably not considered a remarkable event by the Soviet officials.

As for the two writers that were close to Du Bois – Jessie Fauset and Walter White – the former remained in the shadows of the latter, obviously due to his activism in NAACP where he directed a broad programme against segregation and investigated lynchings in the South (sometimes passing for white). Both White's novels were reviewed in the Soviet press. A short review of *Fire in the Flint* by literary critic, editor and Communist functionary Sergei Dinamov appeared in the bibliographic journal *Knigonosha* (*Book Fetcher*). The review characterised White as a leading black writer, whose works (together with Du Bois's and McKay's) mark the beginning of the 'Negro American literature' that had at last replaced folklore – 'anonymous plaintive songs' – due to the 'decreasing of rural Black population, growth of Black proletariat and rise of class consciousness'.[18] Dinamov believed that *Fire in the Flint* was an excellent protest novel, but argued that the writer treats the 'Negro problem' as simply racial, neglecting its class basis – which he declared to be obviously his weak point.

K. Loks, in his review of White's work in the bibliographical journal *Pechat' i revoliutsia* (*The Press and the Revolution*), comes to the conclusion that the author sticks to real facts and tries to be honest, but unfortunately lacks taste and talent:

> The author defends the Negro, and his book could have been marvelous, if the writer had been talented enough to tell such a story. Seems like real facts make the basis of the novel, but they are daubed in such a coarse manner, that the whole thing makes you think of a cheap popular print. Its style is that of a dime novel stuffed with awful accidents, rapes and murders. Despite all this however, *Fire in the Flint* seems to be sincere and truthful, and inspires confidence.[19]

A brief note in another bibliographic journal, *Kniga i profsyuzy* (*The Book and the Trade Unions*), describes Walter White's *Flight* as a novel 'that contains vivid and impressive scenes of disenfranchisement and humiliations the Negroes are subject to in the so-called free country'. The critic stressed that the writer understands the race problem 'as a representative of the Negro bourgeoisie and intelligentsia', and therefore 'idealizes the Negro' and 'urges Blacks to break with the white culture – a position that doesn't make any sense'.[20]

W.E.B. Du Bois and his circle were assessed by Soviet critics as 'inconsistent' in their attitudes: they were spokesmen for the oppressed Negro people and at the same time liberal petty bourgeois intellectuals. As for the schism among the Harlem Renaissance literati (Du Bois's followers against the Van Vechtenites, named after Carl Van Vechten, author of *Nigger Heaven*), Soviet critics reacted to it in a very particular manner.

Van Vechten's *Nigger Heaven* was published in Russian immediately after its American edition: the first translation appeared in 1927,[21] the second in 1928,[22] and soon after the reputed critic and translator Evgeny Lann responded through a review published in *Pechat'i revolutsia* (*The Press and the Revolution*). Lann described Van Vechten as an apprentice to the 'four godfathers of aesthetism' (Theophile Gautier, Jules Barbey d'Aurevilly, Joris-Karl Huysmans and Oscar Wilde), a refined stylist and a 'European aesthete'. Lann argued that Van Vechten made a great mistake when he decided to write about the race problem – such a book was doomed to be a complete failure despite its 'excellent composition and superb legerity of narration':

> Carl Van Vechten is totally unable to solve problems. He always tended to ignore problems – and it used to be his forte ... Van Vechten spoiled his book because he decided to treat the Negro problem ... He wished to raise it and solve it showing Negro intellectuals and bourgeoisie in Harlem cabarets and dance halls. No doubt he has the right to it, and we are not going to reproach him that he hasn't shown proletarians of the 'nigger heaven' he was writing about ... Van Vechten is an aesthete, who would have failed to show proletarians, so these self-imposed restrictions are definitely to his advantage ... we are not going either to demand of him any socio-political judgements ...[23]

Despite adopting a quite tolerant tone (which was very unusual for Soviet critics, who in their reviews tended to instruct and teach authors how to write), Lann nevertheless pointed to the 'greatest mistake' made by Van Vechten: 'all the characters are torn between two ways – that of Booker T. Washington and that of William Du Bois'. They cannot overcome the deadlock and break through to the third way, because Van Vechten fails to see 'the intellectuals that hack the Negro problem cutting the Gordian knot with the help of class – not color – consciousness'.[24]

Thus both Booker T. Washington and W.E.B. Du Bois are criticised by Lann (and some other Soviet critics) as spokesmen for the black bourgeoisie and black petty-bourgeois intellectuals. As for the mantra to 'solve the race problem according to the class approach', this became a cornerstone in Soviet critical assessments of African-American writers and their texts. In the 1920s Claude McKay won recognition as the writer pioneering both in relation to proletarian themes in black literature (having depicted a black proletarian in *Home to Harlem* and *Banjo*) and in Soviet–African American literary contacts.

McKay's visit to the USSR has been studied in so much detail[25] that only a few additional remarks would be appropriate in this case. It is well known that on his arrival at Petrograd McKay had to fight for his right to be a delegate to the Comintern Congress; John Carr (pseudonym of Ludwig E.A. Katterfeld, the head of the American delegation to the Fourth Congress and the representative of the CPUSA in the Comintern) objected to it. McKay was successful thanks to Sen Katayama, the leading Japanese Communist, who had close links with the American left and John Reed's circle. McKay's links with the African Blood Brotherhood (ABB) were another reason that probably helped McKay to get the mandate of Comintern delegate. On the eve of the Fourth Congress, one founder of the South African Communist Party, David Ivon Jones,[26] whose authority on the 'Negro question' was beyond doubt, characterised the ABB as an ally to Soviet Russia, capable of being an alternative pole of attraction to Garvey's Universal Negro Improvement Association:

> Garvey and his UNIA show [the] immaturity of the Negro people that are now at the very first stage of their awakening. One cannot, however, trick [the] steadily growing group of progressively thinking Negroes, who in their struggle direct their eyes at Soviet Russia. They go under the banner of the African Blood Brotherhood [and are] in close contact with the white workers in America, imbued with class feeling, they show the way to proletarian freedom – the only way for their oppressed Black brothers in Africa and America.[27]

Claude McKay himself in his letter to the Secretariat of the Comintern Executive Committee (spring 1923),[28] which was written at the request of Comintern in order to clarify his relations with the Third International and the details of his trip to the Congress, does not mention Sen Katayama. In the letter McKay observes that he was sent to Moscow by his comrades from the African Blood Brotherhood, and they tried to raise funds for his trip by 'selling my recent collection of poetry [*Harlem Shadows*]', but failed to get enough money; on arrival to Russia he produced his mandate as a member of the ABB and the Workers' Party of America, but John Carr 'claimed he had never ever heard of the ABB, although 8 of its members were at the same time members of both legal and the illegal party organizations of the CP USA'. McKay states that he 'was included in the list of delegates 10 days later when another Negro delegate [Otto Huiswoud], a member of ABB and illegal part of the Communist Party arrived and verified that my documents were authentic'. McKay explains that he was supposed to go back to the USA with the American delegation: he mentions Huiswoud and Alexander

Figure 3.1 Claude McKay and Sen Katayama at the Fourth Congress
of the Communist International

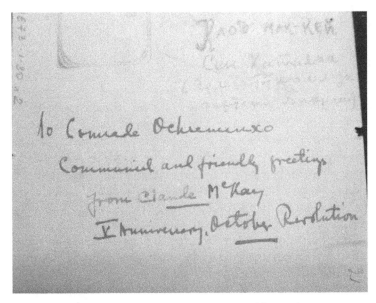

Figure 3.2 Claude McKay's inscription to Piotr Okhrimenko on reverse
of Figure 3.1

Trachtenberg who were responsible for the departure; McKay planned to leave Russia with them, but 'had to stay to collect materials for the book'.

Claude McKay spent almost seven months in the Soviet Union – he came to Petrograd on the eve of the Fourth Congress that began on 5 November 1922; he then went to Moscow where the Congress continued until 5 December. Staying mainly in Petrograd, McKay was busy writing his book *Negroes in America*, attending meetings, visiting museums and bohemian cafes.[29] Because of bureaucracy he had to wait for a long time to leave the USSR (which he finally did at the end of May 1923).[30] Two letters mailed to Piotr Okhrimenko, McKay's translator, one from Petrograd and the other on McKay's arrival in Berlin, give some additional information about McKay's last weeks in Russia.[31]

McKay's visit stirred interest in his poetry.[32] Russian translations appeared in several magazines.[33] Three poems (among them the famous 'If We Must Die') translated by T. Levit entered the anthology *Revolutionary Poetry of the Contemporary West* (Moscow: Moskovsky rabochiy publ., 1927).

Claude McKay's literary reputation in the Soviet Union underwent a considerable change during the 1920s. Initially Soviet literary critics attempted to depict McKay as a leader of black American literature, a writer who treated the 'Negro problem' from the point of view of Marxism and class struggle. In the early 1920s he was introduced to the Soviet public as a revolutionary black American author writing about the black proletariat, and a friend of the Soviet Union.[34] The situation changed drastically in the late 1920s when *Home to Harlem* and *Banjo* were published in Russia.

The first novel got an ambivalent response. Ivan Kashkin, influential literary critic and translator,[35] drew parallels between Van Vechten and McKay, but insisted that the former was a stranger, an observer, while the latter wrote his novel on the basis of his personal experience. Kashkin emphasised that McKay's novel 'contains many scenes depicting physical labor'; he characterised Jake as a 'Negro dandy, a straightforward, primitive, healthy, honest, and innocent guy', while Ray is positioned as McKay's alter ego, a type of proletarian intellectual, and especially stresses his love of Russian classical literature. The critic also praised McKay's 'charming simplicity, musicality and plasticity of artistic expression'.[36]

Other critics were less indulgent, describing Jake as 'a proletarian who lacks class consciousness', who was 'indifferent to racial and social problems',[37] and Ray was depicted as 'an intelligent neurotic Negro ... with shattered nerves, useless for social struggle'.[38]

McKay is also severely criticised as a Van Vechtenite who created a picturesque but distorted image of Harlem, full of 'primitive, naïve realism', poor and biased in comparison with Walter White's social prose or Theodore Dreiser's *Nigger Jeff*.[39] *Home to Harlem*, the novel written by the Comintern delegate, is also compared to the works of 'bourgeois syco-phants' and 'decadents' like Paul Morand, a French belletrist, whom Soviet critics used to denounce as a racist, and fascist reactionary scribbler. McKay was criticised for his depictions of 'animalistic Negro temper, African atavistic features thus extending his hand to Paul Morand, hyper-elegant Negrophobe, author of *Magie noire*'.[40]

McKay's second novel was unanimously regarded as ideologically harmful and a complete failure artistically. Critics stigmatised McKay, once a fellow traveller, as a 'Bohemian lumpen-intellectual' and a 'petty bourgeois Black nationalist'. Both reviews – by Boris Pesis[41] and Abel Startsev[42] – are uncompromisingly hostile. Critics were unhappy about the characters in the novel – 'Negro sailor-vagabonds', 'social drop-outs' with their 'good-for-nothing freedom of outlaws', unable to understand that 'white exploiters can oppress them as much as they like'. Jake and Banjo are 'primitive animalistic samples of the Negro race that are so much praised in bourgeois belles-lettres', 'social misfits, helpless victims of bourgeois civi-lization'.[43] But the main preoccupation of the critics is Ray's 'cloudy and ambiguous racial and political philosophy'[44] – a mixture of Leo Tolstoy's 'Confucius' and Gandhi's ideas without any reference to Marxism and the Russian Revolution. Boris Pesis's text is a chain of derogatory epithets: 'unsteady libertine Ray' with his 'snobbery and hedonism of a music-hall frequenter' and 'philistine piggishness'.[45] Ray's individualism, his distrust in the white world and his contempt for the proletariat is interpreted as bourgeois black nationalism and, therefore, a dead-end way:

> Ray speaks directly about the ineradicable basis of racial differences ... Race chauvinism extends its hand to imperialism ... McKay unmasks his attitude making Ray believe that the whites are doomed because of their class society and idealise the primitive life of the Blacks ... Home to Harlem therefore? Or, maybe, back to Africa? Back to nature, to the wild Negro tribes? Harmful, reactionary point of view![46]

Statsev stresses that McKay, who 'fell into a trap prepared by the right-ist reactionary forces', does not belong to the working class but to leftist lumpen-intellectuals, and that is why he tends towards exotics and 'racial chauvinism'.[47] Pesis is convinced that McKay is a renegade who 'will stray away from the wide stream of revolutionary literature and will soon mingle in American and European bourgeois literature'.[48]

Class instinct did not betray the Soviet critics and enabled them to foresee McKay's dangerous drifting away from the only 'omnipotent and true doc-trine': instead of becoming a fiercely loyal Stalinist, the poet finally arrived at Catholicism.

There is another piece of evidence which sheds light on Claude McKay's evolution. Nikolay Chukovsky, who worked as a guide and interpreter for McKay in Petrograd, in his enthralling memory essay 'A Poet from the Island of Jamaica' brings out several significant details. First, he stresses that Claude McKay was extremely sensitive and vulnerable as far as racial oppression and racial prejudices were concerned.

> As every Russian I have read a lot about the discrimination of Negroes in America and was aware of it … Nevertheless when McKay started to talk about it I was shocked with his outbreak of hatred and pain.[49]

Chukovsky reports that one day McKay, having noticed white American tourists in the Hermitage, went away from the paintings, sat on a bench in a corner of the museum room and remained there until the tourists left the place:

> White Americans! McKay stared at them, silent, frozen to the spot, pressing my hand harder every minute. He seemed paralyzed with hatred. He didn't stir nor move a muscle while they were viewing paintings – until they finally left the room.

This burning hatred discouraged Chukovsky, who tried to persuade McKay with the help of Marxist arguments – but all in vain:

> He hated whites and I failed to convince him that Blacks hating whites is as absurd as whites hating Blacks … I tried again and again, I kept explaining that one must hate capitalism, not whites. Actually not me, but he as a delegate to the Congress of Comintern, was supposed to tell me that. But he was absolutely deaf to my preaching, he didn't even object, he just ignored it.

Chukovsky quickly realised that Communism, Comintern and the Soviet Union were of importance for McKay primarily because they contributed to the struggle against racial oppression. He even started to suspect that it was 'someone's mistake' to send McKay to the Congress of Comintern:

> I don't think American communists did the right thing when they chose him as a delegate to the Congress of Comintern. He was unable to tell me about the Congress and in general paid very little attention to it.

Chukovsky was struck by McKay's absolute ignorance of Marxist theory:

> He didn't have a slightest idea of what Marxism is. Shocked, I started to tell him about class society, workers' solidarity, internationalism … He listened inattentively and obviously lacked interest. He seemed absolutely impenetrable to Marxism. He liked our country for two reasons: first, people here treated Negroes well and, second, our national poet Pushkin had Negro blood in his veins.[50]

Although Chukovsky's evidence cannot be regarded as absolutely true and objective, it is clear, nevertheless, that McKay concentrated on racial issues, not Communism/Marxism – the former being a vital problem for him, and the latter primarily a means that might help to solve this problem.

After 1931 no reviews or essays on McKay appeared in the Soviet press and none of his new works were published either (besides several poems in the anthologies of black poetry that appeared in the 1930s). By that time Langston Hughes had won the title of the Best Black Friend of the USSR.

African-American literature attracted much more attention in the USSR by the end of the 1920s than in the early 1920s – obviously due to the impact of the Harlem Renaissance. Growing interest is clear from the increase in the number of essays that offer 'panoramic views' of black American letters. Soviet literary critics analysed the phenomenon of the 'Harlem school' (*Garlemskaia shkola*), and 'the whites writing up the black' – Carl Van Vechten, Howard W. Odum, Michael Gold, Albert Halper, etc.

Nikolay E. Efros's survey, 'Negro Theater', appeared as early as 1923 in the magazine *Sovremenny zapad* (*Contemporary West*).[51] After a brief introduction devoted to the 'Negro topic' in eighteenth- and nineteenth-century Anglo-American theatre, Efros writes about 'recent novelties' – among them, so-called 'Negro plays' by white playwrights of the 1910s, such as Frederic Ridgely Torrence's *Plays for a Negro Theater* (*Granny Maumee, The Rider of Dreams, Simon the Cyrenian*), published by Macmillan in 1917 and produced by the Negro Players; *Children* by Guy Bolton and Tom Carlton (produced by the Washington Square Players, 1916). Eugene O'Neill's *Emperor Jones* is briefly mentioned, as well as two plays by African-American authors – W.E.B. Du Bois's *The Star of Ethiopia* (1911) and Angelina Grimke's *Rachel* (1915). Efros's review is descriptive and devoid of ideological bias, and follows pre-revolutionary traditions – most probably because Efros used a set of materials from *Choses de thèâtre*, the Paris theatre monthly periodical, as a basis for the piece.

In 1928 there appeared several surveys of African-American literature, some written by Soviet critics, others translated from English. One of them was published in *Na literaturom postu* (*On Literary Guard*), the organ of RAPP – the Russian Association of Proletarian Writers – which was seizing literary hegemony for itself and followed the principle 'to scourge and chastise', i.e. censor literature on ideological grounds.[52] In full accordance with the canonical rules, the survey started with a sociopolitical preamble devoted to the 'situation of Negroes in the United States' – racial discrimination, segregation, lynching, Jim Crowism. The critic gives a misleading explanation of the latter term: 'The system of racial discrimination is called "Jim Crowism" because someone called Jim Crow invented these anti-Negro practices in the past century.'[53] After the introductory passage (quite long and commonplace), the critic starts with Doctor W.E.B. Du Bois (who is described as a 'founding father of Negro American literature') and the writers 'belonging to Du Bois' circle' – Walter White and Jessie R. Fauset. Next comes Claude McKay – a 'former communist', and 'one of the best Black poets'. *Home to Harlem* is praised as the first novel that has 'a Negro worker' as a protagonist. The critic is happy with the 'social character of the contemporary Negro American literature', although there are some 'followers of mysticism and individualism' like Jean Toomer and Eric Walrond. James Weldon Johnson is also severely criticised as 'religiously minded' – probably because of his recently published *God's Trombones* (1927).

The concluding part of the essay offers a classification of whites writing about blacks: 'racists', like Thomas F. Dixon Jr (his surname is misspelled in the article); 'writers mocking the Negro' who employ clichéd images of 'happy darkies' taken from blackface minstrel shows and plantation novels, like Octavus Roy Cohen, author of stories, plays and scripts, some of which concerned themselves with African Americans; finally there are those who depict black people as exotic primitives. Among them the critic names Van Vechten and, strangely enough, Thomas Sigismund Stribling: his 'exotic' novels (*Fombombo*, 1922; *Red Sand*, 1923) are about Venezuela, while his novel *Birthright* (1921–22), the story of a young educated African American trying to effect some change in a small Southern town, is a serious social novel, highly praised by both white and black critics, and has nothing to do with exoticism.

Despite some mistakes which are the result of the critic's superficial knowledge of the subject, the conclusion of the survey epigrammatically sums up a thorny problem of the Harlem Renaissance: 'Only Negro clowns and cabaret entertainers can win recognition from the American bourgeois public'.[54] It is well known that this leitmotif is omnipresent in African-American prose and poetry of the 1920s.

In 1928 *Vestnik inostrannoi literatury* (*Herald of Foreign Literature*, founded in January 1928), the organ of the IURW (International Union of Revolutionary Writers), published three long surveys of African-American literature in its first few issues. One of them was written by Ivan Kashkin, while others were translations from English – William Wilson's essay on contemporary African-American poets,[55] and a survey of contemporary black literature, theatre and arts by Williana 'Liana' Burroughs (known also under her pen name 'Mary Adams'), a Communist organiser, radical political activist and journalist who often visited the Soviet Union. Both Kashkin's and Burroughs's essays are crammed with information and lots of names that were new or almost unknown to the Soviet reader – Countee Cullen,

Angelina Grimke, Arna Bontemps, Sterling Brown, Ann Spencer, Walter Everett Hawkins, Lewis Alexander, George Schuyler, Helen Johnson. This gave an idea of black American literature as a vast, rich and diverse phenomenon. Williana Burroughs's survey[56] is devoted to the funds and collections of Harlem Public Library, Schomburg Center, and black periodicals – *Crisis, Opportunity, Chicago Defender, The Messenger, Negro World.* She also gives a brief survey of black arts (mentioning Aaron Douglas and Augusta Savage) and black theatre: the National Ethiopian Art Theater (NEAT), the Krigwa Players Little Theatre Group and African-American playwrights such as Willis Richardson, Mary P. Burrill and Eulalie Spence. Williana Burroughs avoids straightforward assertions and propagandistic clichés; it is obvious, however, that she doesn't approve of the assimilationist attitudes of some Harlem Renaissance authors like Countee Cullen, and praises a quest for identity based on 'the beauty, force, and hard pulse of the life of the Negro masses'.[57]

Ivan Kashkin in his survey[58] concentrates on four novels, two of them by black writers – McKay's *Home to Harlem* and *Quicksand* by Nella Larsen. The third part of Kashkin's article is devoted to McKay's novel,[59] but only one paragraph to Nella Larsen – a writer at that moment absolutely unknown to Russian readers; however, that one paragraph was enough to condemn the book as both 'bad' and 'useless'. For no obvious reason Kashkin calls Nella Larsen 'a white bourgeois Scandinavian writer' and claims that the novel is devoted to the 'universal problems' instead of the race problem, that it doesn't show racial oppression and discrimination and therefore that 'it cannot be viewed as a novel of Negro life'.

Kashkin also writes about two other works written by white authors. Both of them are based on African-American folklore with black vagabonds as protagonists, and trace their origin to the minstrel show type. Howard Washington Odum's *Rainbow Round my Shoulder: The Blue Trail of Black Ulysses* (1928) is the first part of his Black Ulysses trilogy. Kashkin calls the book by this famous sociologist and folklorist 'a picaresque novel' that is made up of huge blocks of folk material connected with 'binders' – fragments written by the author; grammatically correct, literary language in these parts contrasts with the black dialect used by the character – 'Ulysses' very particular, lively pidgin talk'.[60] Kashkin thinks that the best thing in the novel is that it abounds with folk songs and humour: 'The book sparkles with laughter, jokes and genuine folk musicality.'[61]

Michael Gold's play *Hoboken Blues: or The Black Rip Van Vinkle: A Modern Negro Fantasia on an Old American Theme* produced by the New Playwrights Theater (founded by Michael Gold, John Dos Passos and Howard Lawson) in 1928 is also highly praised by Kashkin: 'it is really a musical fantasia – great material for an artful stage director. Its energetic bright and dynamic action unites its episodes into a whole, and its leitmotif is music, of course.'[62] Kashkin's review is accompanied by an editor's note that is intended to rectify the reviewer's benign attitude:

> In his play Michael Gold sticks to the traditional 'white' idea of the Negro as a lazy idle dreamer, etc. It is remarkable that Michael Gold has decided to choose such an out-of-date theme. Michael Gold and the New Playwrights Theatre shouldn't pay so much attention to purely formal things.[63]

This rebuke can be easily explained: the editorial board knew very well about the negative reaction in the American leftist press to Michael Gold's play; among its critics were John Dos Passos (who visited the USSR a year before, in 1927)[64] and Paul Robeson. Having been invited to act the titular part, the famous actor and singer refused to play a good-for-nothing loafer, a Harlemite who instead of working keeps dancing and strumming the banjo.[65] In the end the roles were played by a team of blackface white actors and the staging was *a la* minstrel show.[66]

Towards the end of the 1920s the tone of criticism started to shift, and some new demands were put forward following the changing ideological doctrine. In 1930 *Vestnik inostrannoi literatury* published Albert Halper's essay 'Whites Writing Up the Black'.[67] Albert Halper criticised 'the Negro vogue' of the 1920s, the fact that black culture had become a mainstream interest – and mainly a commercial one – for white people. Halper ridiculed banalities and clichés (Vodou, black mystic, 'black fingers strumming the banjo, dark-skinned girls in flame-colored dresses',[68] etc.), that contrast with the serious realistic writing that helps to comprehend and solve the 'Negro problem'. The editor's foreword 'On the Negroes only?' criticised *Dial* magazine which printed Halper's essay – 'a magazine of a leftist group of intellectuals with its *sotto voce* protest'; 'a breeding ground for individualism and discontent', where Waldo Frank, Sherwood Anderson and other bohemian rebels made a name for themselves and later switched their attitudes to more conservative and reactionary ones after having overcome their adolescent crises.[69] Halper's essay, however, was interpreted as a forerunner of the coming changes that were inevitable because of the end of the period of economic prosperity:

> the torrent of standard sentimental (*a la* Dickens) Negro literature and white literature about the Negro that has flooded the American literary market won't be in demand any more, and soon will be replaced with social critical realistic analysis of the Negro problem in American literature.[70]

In the USA the end of the 1920s became a borderline between the Age of Prosperity and the Great Depression, and after 1929 the Harlem Renaissance made way for the protest novels of the Red Thirties. The Soviet

Union at the turn of the 1920s and 1930s was between two Ages too – autonomy was gradually giving place to heteronomy. The New Economic Policy, with private enterprise and relative freedom of expression in political, social and literary spheres, was approaching its end, to be replaced with strict centralisation, statism and dictatorship. In this context writers and literature became, step by step, totally subdued to the ideological dogmas, and the Soviet image of African-American literature started to change as well.

Even in the 1920s, despite the elements of the commercial 'capitalist free market' introduced in the NEP period, ultimate responsibility for the choice of books and their publishing by state and private enterprises belonged to the Soviet government, which through the Commissariat of Education, and its censorship organ *Glavlit*, examined, sanctioned and controlled publishing activity. Since 1929 the Great Turn ended the NEP and led to the totalitarian Stalinist regime, meaning the liquidation of private ventures, total state control of publishing, censorship and centralised management in the sphere of literature and art.

With the first Five-Year Plan the circulation of American books began to drop. According to Deming Brown's data, a steady decrease started in 1928 and continued until the mid-1930s.[71] Alongside this, while Soviet literary doctrine was sharpening, the character of American literature published in the USSR was changing. The choice of American literature reflected the writing on political and social discontent that was typical in the 1930s, which was influenced by a strong Marxist orientation and protest literature (Grace Lumpkin, Albert Maltz, Pearl S. Buck, Jack Conroy, Josephine Herbst, Erskine Caldwell, Clifford Odets, etc.). The stream of black American literature, by contrast, swelled in the 1930s. New names and works of both black writers and white authors writing about black people were being translated and published during the decade, among them John L. Spivak,[72] Edwin DuBose Heyward,[73] Roark Bradford,[74] Langston Hughes, Angelo Herndon[75] and Richard Wright. Soviet publishers in the 1930s were alert for the appearance of new books by or about African Americans, particularly those with a strong ingredient of social protest.

If Claude McKay was the most popular black American writer in the 1920s, the key figure of the 1930s was Langston Hughes, and, at the turn of the 1930s to the 1940s, Richard Wright. Langston Hughes was the most extensively translated and published black American author in the 1930s thanks to his significant conformity to Soviet ideological demands. There were numerous publications of his poetry and short prose in the periodicals,[76] but his editions in book form appeared only in the post-war period. The translator who specialised in Hughes's poetry was Yulian Anisimov: an *homme de lettre* of the Russian Silver Age (1890–1917), he published several books of poetry; after the revolution he became a very successful translator and *Kulturträger* of American, and, more precisely, black American poetry. Anisimov and Hughes exchanged letters, and Hughes several times mentioned the Soviet translator in his essays. Hughes's poems were printed at least twenty-two times between 1932 and 1940 in various Soviet periodicals, such as *30 dnei (30 days)*, *Krasnaia nov'(Red New Soil)* – the first Soviet thick literary magazine founded after the revolution (1921) – and of course in the *International Literature* magazine, organ of the IURW.[77]

Langston Hughes's 1932 trip to Soviet Central Asia and his stay in Moscow have been the topic of many studies.[78] Much less is known about the important role he played in Stalin's ambitious project for the worldwide overinflated celebration of the Pushkin centenary in 1937. Hughes became a member of the American Pushkin Committee (its activity was directed by the Soviet literary and political institutions) and was a founder of the Negro American Pushkin Committee created in 1936. He invited many outstanding figures to be part of the centenary, including William Stanley Braithwaite, Alain Locke, Zora Neal Hurston, Arthur Schomburg, Ethel Waters, Gilpin Players actors and Williana 'Liana' Jones Burroughs (who by this time was a programme editor at Radio Moscow). The Negro American Pushkin Committee Exhibitions organised performances, publications in press, concerts and many other activities in the New York Public Library and Schomburg Center, Howard and Tuskegee universities, which made the Pushkin centenary a remarkable event in African-American cultural life of the late 1930s. Leading black American newspapers and journals contributed to the celebration, for example the *Crisis*, the *Opportunity* and the *Negro Worker*, where William L. Patterson published the essay 'The Negro People and the Centenary of Pushkin',[79] and the *Chicago Defender* which printed Chatwood Hall's[80] interview with Pushkin's great-granddaughter Ekaterina Pushkina.[81] Hughes himself published reports of the Pushkin celebrations in the *International Literature* magazine and helped the black repertory theatre Gilpin Players to stage a play devoted to Pushkin.[82]

The last impressive project connected with black American literature that was carried out by the Soviet literary institutions before the Second World War was the 'discovery' of Richard Wright in 1938, and an extensive promo-campaign of the black Communist writer was launched in 1940–41 – just on the verge of the German invasion.

The correspondence between Richard Wright and *International Literature (Interlit)* started in 1935: Wright sent his poems to the magazine, and the editor-in-chief Sergei Dinamov wrote back to the young writer with thanks. In 1936 Wright sent a letter telling the *Interlit* about himself and asking about the possibility of publishing his works in the magazine. Wright had an ideal autobiography for a revolutionary black American writer – a childhood in the racist American rural South, a poor family, early experiences of class and racial oppression, an interest in Marxism and membership of Chicago's John Reed Club. In 1938 Wright's *Uncle Tom's Children* was translated by a group of excellent professionals (Ivan Kashkin's disciples) and published in the *Interlit*.[83] In November 1938 the new editor-in-chief of the *Interlit*, Timofey Rokotov, wrote to Richard Wright:

> I am happy to inform you that your *Uncle Tom's Children* is enjoying remarkable success in the USSR. *Pravda*, the central organ of our Party, published an extremely favorable review of the stories ... The book has been accepted by the State Literary Publishing House (Goslitizdat) for publication in full. We will be glad to hear from you soon and still gladder to receive your new literary work.[84]

The Soviet translators and publishers started their work on the Russian edition of *Native Son* in 1939, and the novel was printed in the *Interlit* (1941, nos 1–2). The foreword was written by the American Communist poet, literary critic and translator Isidor Schneider, who in 1937–38 worked for the *Interlit* during his stay in the USSR; the novel was followed by Wright's essay 'How Bigger was Born'. Wright's fame in the USSR had reached its peak.

The correspondence between Richard Wright, the *Interlit* and the Foreign Commission of the Union of Soviet Writers became regular and very active. Wright was thinking of travelling to the Soviet Union; he planned to take his wife Dimah with him and spend a year in Crimea working on his new novel – 'the book dealing with the question and plight of Negro women' in the US.[85] He asked whether it would be possible to earn money with literary work, and Rokotov offered him a positon on the staff of the *Interlit*. Soviet officials forwarded all the documents necessary for the Soviet visa to the Soviet Consulate in New York, Wright applied for his passport and was already packing things – but the war changed his plans. Three years later, in 1944, Wright published 'I Tried to Be a Communist' in the *Atlantic Monthly*, broke with the Communist Party, emigrated to France and disappeared from the horizon of Soviet readers and literary officials. His next publication in the Soviet Union appeared forty years later. It was a 1981 collection of prose that comprised, among other things, his novel *Native Son* and his tale *The Man who Lived Underground*.[86]

Soviet editors, publishers, translators and readers have been accustomed to think of black American literature as a literature of protest, militant revolutionary activism, anti-imperialist solidarity. 'The Negro writers' were considered the best friends of the Soviet Union, fighting against racial oppression and social inequality, and struggling for internationalism, socialism and Communism. That stereotype formed in the 1920s–1930s was true to a certain extent – but it was not the whole truth about African-American literature. For decades Soviet literary institutions ignored various names, currents, forms and phenomena of African-American literature that failed to fit into the paradigm of protest literature. Ralph Ellison's *Invisible Man*, Chester Himes's *The Primitive*, Richard Wright's post-war novels, James Baldwin's *Giovanni's Room, Another Country* and *Tell Me How Long the Train's Been Gone* were silenced and passed unnoticed. Some of them came to the Russian reader in Brezhnev's era (late 1970s to early 1980s), during Perestroika and in the post-Soviet period together with the new generation of African-American writers such as Toni Morrison, Alice Walker and Gloria Nailor – and helped to restore the landscape of black American prose as much more versatile, rich and multifaceted than early depictions of black literature.

Notes

1 See Astrid Haas, '"To Russia and Myself": Claude McKay, Langston Hughes and the Soviet Union' in Christa Buschendorf and Astrid Franke (eds), *Transatlantic Negotiations* (Heidelberg: Winter Verlag, 2007), 111–113; Kate A. Baldwin, *Beyond the Color Line and the Iron Curtain: Reading Encounters between Black and Red, 1922–1963* (Durham, NC: Duke University Press, 2002), 1, 14, 21.

2 Claude McKay, 'Soviet Russia and the Negro', *Crisis*, 27:2 (1923), 64.

3 Rossiiskii Gosudarstvenyi Arkhiv Sotsial'no-Politicheskoi Istorii (RGASPI), *fond* (*f.*) 495, *opis* (*o.*) 155, *delo* (*d.*) 1, *list* (*l.*) 56. The Small Bureau of the Executive Committee of the Communist International to Reed, Janson, Scott and others, 25 February 1919 (in Russian).

4 RGASPI, *f.* 495, *o.* 155, *d.* 1, *fol.* 3–11. John Reed's report on the Negro Question in the USA, attn. Grigory Zinoviev, 12 December 1919 (in Russian).

5 V.I. Lenin, 'Draft of the Theses on the National and Colonial Question (for the II Congress of the Communist International', *Collected Works*, Vol. 41 (Moscow: Izdatel'stvo politicheskoi literatury, 1981), 161–168 (in Russian).

6 RGASPI, *f.* 495, *o.* 155, *d.* 2. Statement of the Comintern Executive Committee on the Negro Question, 18 December 1922 (in Russian).

7 RGASPI, *f.* 495, *o.* 155.

8 Deming Brown and Glenora W. Brown, *A Guide to Soviet Russian Translations of American Literature* (New York: Columbia University King's Crown Press, 1954), 8.

9 Among them *Mysl'* (*Thought*), *Vremya* (*Time*), *Seyatel'* (*Seeder*) in Leningrad (Petrograd), and *Zemlya i Fabrika* (*Land and Factory*) in Moscow, which published mainly foreign books.

10 See, for example, the excellent research reconstructing the history of the Vremya publishing house in Leningrad: Maria E. Malikova, '"Vremya": History of the

Leningrad Corporate Publishing House' in Maria E. Malikova (ed.), *The End of the 1920s Cultural Institutions in Leningrad* (Moscow: Novoe Literaturnoe Obozrenie publ., 2014), 129–331 (in Russian).

11 W.E.B. Du Bois, *Quest of the Silver Fleece*, trans. A.S. Polotska (Leningrad: Seyatel' publ., 1925).

12 There were two Russian editions of the novel: Walter White, *Fire in the Flint*, trans. D. Zaslavsky (Leningrad: Priboi Publ., 1925; abridged version) and Walter White, *Fire in the Flint*, trans. A. Sviazheninov (Moscow: Nedra publ., 1926; full version).

13 Walter White, *Flight*, trans. L. Vsevolodskaia (Leningrad: Mysl' publ., 1927).

14 The novel appeared under the title *Black Skin* (trans. M. Volosov, Moscow: Gosizdatp, 1927).

15 First published in *Vestnik inostrannoi literatury*, 10 (1928), trans. Z. Vershinina; then as a book edition: Claude McKay, *Home to Harlem*, trans. M. Volosov (Moscow, Leningrad: Zemlia & Fabrika publ., 1929).

16 Claude McKay, *Banjo*, trans. Z. Vershinina (Moscow: Gosizdat publ., 1930).

17 RGASPI, *f.* 495, *o.* 99, *d.* 19, *fol.* 6, 78 (in Russian).

18 Sergei Dinamov, review of Walter White, *Fire in the Flint* (Leningrad, 1925), *Knigonosha*, 5 (1926), 34 (in Russian).

19 K. Loks, review of Walter White, *Fire in the Flint* (Moscow, 1926), *Pechat' i revoliutsiia*, 8 (1926), 214 (in Russian).

20 S., review of W. White, *Flight* (Leningrad, 1927), *Kniga i profsoiuzy*, 1 (1928), 27 (in Russian).

21 Carl Van Vechten, *Nigger Heaven*, trans. V.O. Tsederbaum (Khar'kov: Proletarii publ., 1927) (in Russian).

22 Carl Van Vechten, *Nigger Heaven*, trans. A.V. Shvyrov and A.N. Gorlin (Leningrad: Gosizdat publ., 1928) (in Russian).

23 Evgeny Lann, review of Carl Van Vechten, *Nigger Heaven* (Leningrad, 1928), *Pechat' i revoliutsiia*, 6 (1928), 218 (in Russian).

24 *Ibid.*, 219.

25 See, for example, Baldwin, *Beyond the Color Line and the Iron Curtain*; John L. Garder, 'African Americans in the Soviet Union in the 1920s and 1930s: The Development of Transcontinental Protest', *Western Journal of Black Studies*, 23:3 (1999), 190–200; Haas, '"To Russia and Myself"'; Fiorenzo Iuliano, 'Claude McKay tra Stati Uniti e Unione Sovietica: identità afroamericana e utopia socialista', *Between*, 5:10 (2015): http://ojs.unica.it/index.php/between/article/view/1507/1885 [accessed 5 February 2021]; Marian B. McLeod, 'Claude McKay's Russian Interpretation: *The Negroes in America*', *CLA Journal*, 23:3 (1980), 336–351; William J. Maxwell, *New Negro, Old Left: African-American Writing and Communism Between the Wars* (New York: Columbia University Press, 1999); Tatiana A. Tagirova-Daley, *Claude McKay's Liberating Narrative: Russian and Anglophone Caribbean Literary Connections* (New York: Peter Lang, 2012); Tatiana A. Tagirova-Daley, '"A Vagabond with a Purpose": Claude McKay and his International Aspirations', *FIAR. The Journal of the International Association of Inter-American Studies*, 7:2 (2014), 55–71; Tyrone

Tillery, *Claude McKay: A Black Poet's Struggle for Identity* (Amherst, MA: University of Massachusetts Press, 1992); Jacob A. Zumoff, 'Mulattoes, Reds, and the Fight for Black Liberation in Claude McKay's *Trial by Lynching* and *Negroes in America*', *Journal of West Indian Literature*, 19:1 (2010), 22–53.

26 David Ivon Jones (1883, Aberystwyth, Wales – 1924, Yalta, USSR) left Wales in 1909 and went to New Zealand and then South Africa, joining the local workers' movement; he was a delegate to the Second and Third Comintern Congresses, and helped to create the Negro Bureau; he translated Lenin's works into English. Buried in Moscow, Novodevichy cemetery.

27 RGASPI, *f.* 495, *o.* 155, *d.* 3, *fol.* 16–17. David Ivon Jones's remarks on the worldwide congress of black people to be convened in Moscow, 18 June 1922 (in Russian).

28 RGASPI, *f.* 495, *o.* 261, *d.* 3993. Claude McKay's dossier (in German).

29 McKay describes his stay in Russia and his contacts with Soviet writers and artistic intelligentsia in his memoir *A Long Way from Home* (1937) and his Russian travelogue 'Soviet Russia and the Negro', 61–65; *Crisis*, 27:3 (1924), 114–118.

30 In the above cited letter to the Secretariat of the Comintern Executive Committee, McKay says that when he felt it was time to leave Russia it was found that his name was not in the list of Comintern delegates, which caused legal problems.

31 Claude McKay's letters to Piotr F. Okhrimenko, 18 May and 30 June, 1923. Published in Olga Panova, 'Exotic Visitor: Claude McKay in the Soviet Union', *Literature of the Americas*, 6 (2019), 243–248 (in English and in Russian): http://litda.ru/images/2019-6/LDA-2019-6_220-256_Panova.pdf [accessed 12 June 2019].

32 The division of manuscripts of the A.M. Gorky Institute of World Literature of the Russian Academy of Sciences keeps Claude McKay's autograph – his poem *In Bondage* handwritten on a sheet of paper with a drawing McKay made for his Russian friends.

33 Several Russian translations of his poetry appeared in various periodicals: Claude McKay, 'America. In Bondage. Enslaved. Tired Worker', trans. V. Vasilenko and P. Okrimenko, *Krasnaia niva*, 2 (1923), 22; Claude McKay, 'North and South. Poems', trans. M. Zenkevich, *Vestnik inostrannoi literatury*, 2 (1929), 186; Claude McKay, 'Enslaved', trans. V. Bryusov, *Sovremenny zapad*, 2 (1923), 112; Claude McKay, 'Poems', trans. Yulian Anisimov, *Literaturnaia gazeta*, 19 February 1931.

34 V. V[asilenko], 'Claude McKay', *Krasnaia niva*, 1 (1923), 15; M. Kozytsyn, 'Claude McKay', *Literaturny ezhenedel'nik*, 8 (1923), 16 (in Russian).

35 Later in the 1930s he became famous for his correspondence with Hemingway, who gave Kashkin's name to a character in the novel *For Whom the Bell Tolls*.

36 K–n [Ivan A. Kashkin], 'Novelties of the Negro Literature', *Vestnik inostrannoi literatury*, 10 (1928), 143–149 (in Russian).

37 S. Vinogradskaia, review of Claude McKay, *Home to Harlem* (Moscow, Leningrad, 1929), *Kniga i revolutsia*, 8 (1929), 59 (in Russian).

38 Ia. Frid, review of Claude McKay, *Home to Harlem* (Moscow, Leningrad, 1929), *Novy mir*, 6 (1929), 238 (in Russian).

39 *Ibid.*

40 *Ibid.*

41 Boris Pesis, 'Rearward', *Kniga i revolutsia*, 29–30 (1930), 16–18 (in Russian).

42 Abel Startsev, 'To Harlem! To Harlem!', *Oktyabr'*, 4–5 (1931), 236 (in Russian).

43 Pesis, 'Rearward', 16, 17.

44 Startsev, 'To Harlem! To Harlem!'.

45 Pesis, 'Rearward', 16.

46 Startsev, 'To Harlem! To Harlem!'.

47 *Ibid.*

48 Pesis, 'Rearward', 18.

49 Nikolay Chukovsky, 'A Poet from the Island of Jamaica', in Nikolay Chukovsky, *Literary Memoirs* (Moscow: Sovetskyi pisatel' publ., 1989), 204 (in Russian).

50 *Ibid.*, 205, 207, 205–206.

51 N.E. [Nikolay Efros], 'Negro Theater', *Sovremennyi zapad*, 3 (1923), 223–224 (in Russian).

52 N., 'Negro Literature in America', *Na literaturnom postu*, 13–14 (1928), 79–80 (in Russian).

53 *Ibid.*, 79.

54 *Ibid.*

55 William Wilson, 'Contemporary Negro Poets', *Vestnik inostrannoi literatury*, 6 (1928), 146–148 (in Russian).

56 Liana Burroughs, 'Negro Culture in America', *Vestnik inostrannoi literatury*, 10 (1928), 146–149 (in Russian).

57 *Ibid.*, 146.

58 [Kashkin], 'Novelties of the Negro Literature', 143–146.

59 See above Kashkin's criticism of McKay's *Home to Harlem*.

60 [Kashkin], 'Novelties of the Negro Literature', 145.

61 *Ibid.*

62 *Ibid.*, 146.

63 *Ibid.*

64 John Dos Passos, 'Did the New Playwright's Theatre Fail?', *New Masses*, 5:3 (1929), 13.

65 Richard Tuerk, 'Michael Gold's *Hoboken Blues*: An Experiment that Failed', *MELUS*, 20:4 (1995), 3.

66 Tuerk, 'Michael Gold's *Hoboken Blues*'; Brooks E. Hefner, *The World on the Streets: The American Language of Vernacular Modernism* (Charlottesville, VA: University of Virginia Press, 2017), chapter 3.

67 'On the Negroes Only? Albert Halper, "Whites Writing Up the Black"', *Vestnik inostrannoi literatury*, 1 (1930), 172–173 (in Russian). Halper's essay was originally published as: Albert Halper, 'Whites Writing Up the Black', *Dial*, 86:1 (1929), 29–30.

68 'On the Negroes Only?', 173.

69 *Ibid.*, 172.

70 *Ibid.*
71 'In 1929 the number of American authors in new Russian printings was only half of that of 1928. The number continued to dwindle steadily, until in 1932 the works of only 9 Americans were published in book form as compared to 52 in 1927. Even more striking is the contrast in printings: in 1927 there were 177; in 1932 there were 14' (Brown and Brown, *A Guide to Soviet Russian Translations*, 18).
72 John L. Spivak, *Georgia Nigger*, trans. A. Gavrilov, foreword by W. Carmon (Moscow: Khudozhestvennaia luiteratura publ., 1933) (in Russian).
73 E. DuBose Heyward, *Porgy*, trans. V.A. Dilevskaia, ed. A. Smirnov (Leningrad: Vremia publ., 1930) (in Russian).
74 Roark Bradford, *Ol' Man Adam an' His Chillun'*, trans. D.L. Maizels and I.I. Solovieva (Moscow, Leningrad: Goslitizdat publ., 1931) (in Russian).
75 There appeared three Soviet editions of Angelo Herndon's *Let me Live* in 1938 (all in Russian): trans. M. Astrakhan and E. Romanova, foreword by I. Schneider (Moscow: Goslitizdat publ., 10,000 copies). Next followed Zhurgas publ. (Moscow, 25,000 copies), and Molodaia Gvardia publ. (Moscow, 25,000 copies). Fragments of the book were published in several journals and magazines; many reviews were devoted to the 'remarkable story, told by the victim of bourgeois justice'. See, for example, 'Victims of bourgeois justice', *Sputnik agitatora*, 17 (1938), 41–43 (in Russian).
76 See Valentina A. Libman, *Russian Translations and Criticism of American Literature: Bibiliography 1776–1975* (Moscow: Nauka publ., 1976), 310–318 (in Russian); Brown and Brown, *A Guide to Soviet Russian Translations*, 98–101.
77 After the dissolution of the IURW in 1935 it became the organ of the Foreign Commission of the Union of Soviet Writers. The *International Literature* fund in RGALI (Russian State Archive of Art and Literature) contains interesting correspondence with the key figures of African-American literature of the 1930s – Langston Hughes and Richard Wright – as well as with many journalists, artists, scholars, political activists etc. such as Eugene Gordon, William L. Patterson, Professor of Howard University Eugene Clay Holmes and Paul Robeson. The magazine published several collections of 'Negro poetry' rendered into Russian by famous translators – Mikhail Zenkevitch and Ivan Kashkin. Vera Toper, Nina Daruzes and Evgenia Kalashikova, who belong to the so-called 'Kashkin's school', worked on the translations of Hughes's and Wright's prose.
78 See, among the recent ones, a chapter on Hughes and the USSR in Steven S. Lee, *The Ethnic Avant-Garde: Minority Cultures and World Revolution* (New York: Columbia University Press, 2015); Kate A. Baldwin, 'Revolution and Langston Hughes' Central Asian Writings', *Literature of the Americas*, 3 (2017), 90–105: http://litda.ru/images/2017-3/LDA-2017-3_90-105_Baldwin.pdf (in English) [accessed 10 June 2019], and Elena Ostrovskaya, 'Langston Hughes in Correspondence with *International Literature* Magazine', *Literature of the Americas*, 3 (2017), 106–126: http://litda.ru/images/2017-3/LDA-2017-3_106-126_Ostrovskaya.pdf (in Russian) [accessed 10 June 2019].

79 William L. Patterson, 'The Negro People and the Centenary of Pushkin', *Negro Worker*, 7:4 (1937), 7, 14–15.

80 Pen name of Homer Smith, who in 1932 came to the USSR with Langston Hughes and a group of African Americans to make a film, *Black and White*, and stayed in the Soviet Union until 1946. See more on him in: Jan G. Carew, *Blacks, Reds and Russians: Sojourners in Search of the Soviet Promise* (New Brunswick, NJ: Rutgers University Press, 2008), 79–85.

81 Chatwood Hall, '*Defender*'s Moscow Correspondent Great Interview with Pushkin's Descendant', *Chicago Defender*, 22:1 (1936), 24. Later Homer Smith described his acquaintance Ekaterina Pushkina in his memoir: Homer Smith, *A Black Man in Red Russia* (Chicago, IL: Johnson Publishing, 1964). For more on Homer Smith and Pushkin's descendant see Alexander Adamov, 'Branch', *Slovo* [*Word*], 78 (2013): http://magazines.russ.ru/slovo/2013/78/a1.html (in Russian) [accessed 5 February 2021].

82 Langston Hughes, 'Here in Cleveland', *International Literature*, 4 (1937), 239 (in Russian). On African-American celebrations of the 1937 Pushkin anniversary see Olga Panova, '"Pushkin has Become the Hottest Topic of the Day": Stalinist Celebrations of Pushkin Death Centenary in the USA, 1937' in *Russian Literature in the Mirror of World Culture: Reception, Translations, Interpretations* (Moscow: IMLI RAN publ., 2015), 705–779 (in Russian).

83 Richard Wright, 'Uncle Tom's Children', trans. V. Toper, N. Daruzes, T. Ozerskaia and E. Kalashnikova, foreword by I. Schneider, *Internatsionalnaia literatura*, 7 (1938), 3–85, 175–177 (in Russian). In book form *Uncle Tom's Children* was published in 1939 (Moscow: Goslitizdat publ.) with Isidore Schneider's foreword (in Russian).

84 Timofey Rokotov's letter to Richard Wright, 5 November 1938, cited in Olga Panova, 'Richard Wright's Might-Have-Been Travel to the USSR', *Literature of the Americas*, 3 (2017), 199–200 (in Russian): http://litda.ru/images/2017-3/LDA-2017-3_176-228_Panova.pdf [accessed 12 June 2019].

85 Richard Wright's letter to Timofey Rokotov, 24 August 1939, cited in Panova, 'Richard Wright's Might-Have-Been Travel to the USSR', 207–209 (in English).

86 See more about Richard Wright's Soviet contacts in Panova, 'Richard Wright's Might-Have-Been Travel to the USSR' (in Russian). Richard Wright's correspondence with the Soviet officials (in English and in Russian) is published in the Addendum.

II

Spreading the revolution across the Black Atlantic

4

Bolshevism and African-American agency in the African-American radical press, 1917–24

Cathy Bergin

In this chapter I focus very specifically on the way in which the black radical press mobilised the concept of Bolshevism to speak to the paramountcy of black agency; how the Russian Revolution was represented as an event which proffered a model for transnational black liberation. In engaging with radical black history we are not only addressing the damaging legacies of white supremacy which are inherited and inhabited by the descendants of the enslaved and colonially oppressed, but also how those subjects have inaugurated forms of resistance and liberatory politics. The relationship of black radicals to the Russian Revolution illuminates a very particular moment in the interconnectedness of the ideas and struggles that have informed anti-racist and anti-colonial histories. In addition to uncompromising anti-racism, these writers and activists eschewed and ridiculed liberal paradigms which could not account for either the sheer violence of white supremacism or the importance of black agency and resistance.

The radical black press of the post-First World War period precisely exemplifies a black claim on particular visions of what socialism might mean. This is not just about freedom from racist oppression or class exploitation, or indeed both. It is about a vision of liberation which draws on and extends the rich traditions of black radicalism and the anti-colonial and anti-capitalist politics of the present; a politics which is attuned to both race and class and brings them into a relationship which stretched the common understandings of both terms. The Bolshevik revolution is thus understood within a very particular and illuminating concept of agency in relation to both class and race. The prolific Jamaican emigrant activist and writer W.A. Domingo asked and answered the question of Bolshevism's relevance to black liberation in the black socialist newspaper *The Messenger* in September 1919. Domingo speaks of internationalism in local idioms, which we see again and again in the pages of the black press, not least in the constant references to lynching which are ubiquitous in the writings of black activists in the post-war US.

Will Bolshevism accomplish the full freedom of Africa, colonies in which
Negroes are in the majority, and promote human tolerance and happiness
in the United States by the eradication of the causes of such disgraceful
occurrences as the Washington and Chicago race riots? The answer is deduc-
ible from the analogy of Soviet Russia, a country in which dozens of racial
and lingual types have settled their many differences and found a common
meeting ground, a country, which no longer oppresses colonies, a country
from which the lynch rope is banished and in which racial tolerance and
peace now exist.[1]

The writings that are the focus of this chapter come from black authored
newspapers, the *Emancipator*, the *Messenger*, the *Crusader*, *Negro World*
and the *Crisis*.[2] Writing for these papers were some of the most notable
black writers and activists of the early twentieth century. They articulated
a rich and ambitious race-centred class politics and a class-centred race
politics. Even in early editions of the Garveyite *Negro World* the Russian
Revolution is celebrated, and not just by socialist writers like Hubert
Harrison and W.A. Domingo who wrote for it. Marcus Garvey himself
wrote in March 1919 that 'The Russian people have issued a proclamation
of sympathy towards the labouring people of the world.' While stressing
that black people were not 'concerned as partakers' in the revolution, he
saw in it 'a breathing space to declare our freedoms from the tyrannical rule
of oppressed overlords'.[3] Similarly, the supposedly 'moderate' the *Crisis*,
in addition to publishing seminal articles about the revolution by Claude
McKay, could claim in 1921 that 'everywhere in the world Socialism ... is
dominating', and furthermore that 'this is the future which the world faces
and its success is the success of civilisation'.[4]

For the more avowedly socialist press the revolution was the occasion for
untrammelled anti-colonial, anti-capitalist fervour, with a particular role
for a black vanguard in international revolution. The black working class
were envisioned as central to the maintenance of world capitalism, both
in terms of the historic role of black labour and as potential revolutionary
agents of transnational liberation. The writings of these radicals were not
just cognisant of the centrality of race to class politics; they fought to insist
on it against a plethora of obstacles which would deny this reality.[5]

There are many problems with the Cold War truisms about the relationship between the left and black radicals in the US between the wars, but
crucially the mischaracterisation of that relationship must ignore the sheer
impact of black radical thought on the left and on anti-colonial politics for
over two decades at the very least.[6] As many contemporary historians have
meticulously demonstrated, these black radicals *shaped* the anti-racist, anti-
colonial politics of the period; they did not parrot them in the idioms of
Communism.[7] They forced a sometimes hostile left to recognise the black

claim on class politics and *enabled* rather than were duped by the race/class politics which emerged from this period.

The most glaring absence in the press is a gendered one. The voices of important black women activists like Grace Campbell, Maude White, Williana Burroughs and Louise Thompson Patterson are wholly under-represented in the black radical press. One of the limitations of focusing on the black radical press is that this vital counter public sphere does not reflect the work of black women activists whose contribution to these politics remains oblique in terms of public representation. To note this absence is not simply a gestural nod to the aporia of women's voices in the black radical press (and indeed the radical press of the time more widely). The form of address in these newspapers is a carefully cultivated one which speaks on registers of class and race where both concepts are gendered. This gendering is less the invisibilising mobilisation of 'man' to mean humankind which is ubiquitous in this period and beyond, and more of an active assertion of the raced classed subject as a black man.[8] Although the case for women's suffrage is covered widely in the papers (especially *The Messenger*), in general the concept of liberation is usually imagined in relation to black men reclaiming traditional masculinity denied them by the pathologically fixated gendered racism of white supremacism.[9]

In this discourse of liberation the symbolism of the Bolshevik revolution was central in the mobilisation of a delineating politics of race. It was a politics of race in the US that was presented as intimately connected to the politics of empire and a broader anti-colonial struggle. Here the status of many of these writers as Caribbean migrants to the US who grew up under European colonial rule cannot be overstated. Winston James's pioneering work on these radicals has transformed our understanding of race politics in the African diaspora in the first decades of the twentieth century.[10] The frameworks offered to imagine black liberation at home were intimately bound up with the struggles in the diaspora, and in certain cases (Ireland, Russia and India) anti-colonial struggles outside of ones which directly affected those of African descent. Claude McKay, Cyril Briggs, Wilfred Domingo, Hubert Harrison, who dominate the pages of these newspapers, are all Caribbean migrants to the US, and their particular brand of anti-colonialism imbues their race writings with a multilayered transnational politics of liberation.

The reason this chapter talks about these politics in terms of an *African-American* context is not to deny the wide-ranging and diasporic origin of their *inauguration* but to concentrate on the terms of their mode of address in the black press. The transnational structure of these writings is clear but their enunciation is generally audience-specific in relation to address-ing the contemporary experiences of black life in the US – even amongst

Caribbean-born activists.[11] While the commitment to internationalism in these writings is palpable, they are also pointedly local in terms of the urgency of resisting white supremacy in the US on a day-to-day level and their seriousness in nuancing their discursive appeal.

Yet despite, or because of, the ever present danger in the US to daily black life, politics and history, the writers and activists who wrote for the radical press fought to give specific voice to a politics that was adequate to the ambition of mobilising an interracial, international class politics which forefronted the racialised nature of capitalism itself. The point here is not about their *immediate* success in such an endeavour – that is both a shorter and a longer story. It is about how we might understand this moment in relation to lived black experience in the US, for both US-born and Caribbean migrants, and in relation to the visions of international solidarity instituted by the Bolshevik revolution.

These radicals were fighting against a concept of race in which black labour exploitation was marginalised and against a concept of class which was limited to the industrial labour organisations from which the majority of African Americans were excluded. They were attempting to give voice to a utopian, or at least untested, vision of a politics which was based on imaginative solidarity rather than an articulated historical experience of such solidarity. There is nothing spontaneous about class solidarity for even the most romantic anti-capitalist, and this is even more pronounced in the context of US racial history. For the black radicals of the period their vision of solidarity was premised on a commitment to internationalism both abstract and concrete (in relation to the Comintern). This concept of internationalism was indeed a radical one for black communities in the US between the wars, when it often meant making connections with a variety of struggles whose relationship to race was, on the face of it, quite oblique. Significantly, internationalism was not just imagined in terms of extending solidarity outwards to those suffering oppression in the colonial world or those potential global class allies, but it was to structure the understanding of racism in the United States itself. An article in *The Messenger* in July 1919 clearly expressed this:

> That the above title is not our opinion hardly needs to be stated by men who are internationalists ... No, lynching is not a domestic question, except in the rather domestic minds of Negro leaders, whose information is highly localized and highly domestic. The problems of the Negroes should be presented to every nation in the world, and this sham democracy, about which Americans prate, should be exposed for what it is – a sham, a mockery, a rape on decency and a travesty of common sense. When lynching gets to be an international question, it will be the beginning of the end. The sooner the better. On with the dance![12]

Despite the diversity of black voices in the press, there is a consistency in the determination to address *both* the racist discrimination of the everyday in US life *and* the racist history of wealth distribution which ensures black poverty and dispossession. This is thus an *anti-capitalist* politics – one in which questions of black agency are inextricably tied to confronting the social and material structures of racism. Yet in the context of African-American experience of US racism this necessitated some complex rhetorical negotiation and a deeply nuanced articulation of interracial class solidarity.

The question which haunts these writings is what to do with the white American worker (as opposed to the Russian worker or the white American socialist)? Unlike the black Communist press in the 1930s, we do not have extensive articles about historic examples of black and white class solidarity or a plethora of articles on John Brown.[13] Throughout the pages of the black radical press of this period there is an insistence on the objective position of the white worker as a *potential* ally, with a stark acknowledgement of the racism which pervades the labour movement in the US. As Domingo notes, 'for many years a majority of Negroes have looked askance at labor Unions. They have avoided and opposed them. This attitude is in many cases a natural reaction to the prejudiced conduct of the unions themselves.'[14] It is worth noting that in comparison to current racist mobilisations of the concept of '*the white working class*' the black radical press talked about 'white workers' or 'white labor' – the distinction is extremely important. In *The Messenger* and the *Crusader*, the working class itself was always imagined in multicultural if not exclusively black terms. The migration of over three-quarters of a million African Americans from the South to the North between 1915 and 1920 saw an enormous swelling of the ranks of the urban black working class, and the concept of the African American *as a worker* is one which dominates the radical black press of the period. Socialist and trade union organiser Frank R. Croswaith insists that 'race prejudice' is the 'child of capitalism' and thus in

> whatever land under whatever flag found, the Negro unquestionably occupies the lowest rung in the social, political, educational and economic ladder; placed there consciously by those whose aim it was and is to keep the iron battalions of labor from realizing their identity of interest. Yes, placed there consciously so they can better play their game of dividing and robbing, dividing and ruling … No, the Negro does not own for a living, all that he has owned so far is the position of 'doormat' of the other races and his labor power.[15]

For the *Crusader*, the historic role of black labour has placed the black worker as the ideal revolutionary subject to wage battle against both capitalism and a vampiric imperialism which imperils black labour and black life:

No race has less of the idle non-producing rich than the Negro race. No race would be more greatly benefited proletariat than the Negro race, which is essentially a race of workers and producers. With no race are the interests of Labor so clearly identified with racial interests as in the case of the Negro race.

No race would be more greatly benefited by the triumph of Labor and the destruction of parasitic Capital Civilization with its Imperialism incubus that is squeezing the life-blood out of millions of our race in Africa and the islands of the sea, than the Negro race.[16]

This insistence here on the black worker as the vanguard of class politics is a foregrounding of both the importance of black labour and the implied limitations of competing models of liberation – either black reformist or colour-blind socialist. As Du Bois famously expressed it in *Black Reconstruction*, 'The emancipation of man is the emancipation of labor and the emancipation of labor is the freeing of that basic majority of workers who are yellow, brown and black.'[17]

Concurrently the category of whiteness itself was somewhat fluid. In the press of the period, Russians, the Irish and Jews are often represented outside of the categories of 'white'. The Russians are characterised as the liberators of the Jews and colonial subjects, the Irish are imagined as brothers in arms against 'Anglo-Saxonism' and Jews as both victims of racialisation and exemplars of self-organisation. Writing in *The Messenger*, J.A. Rogers insisted that in relation to oppression 'what has been said of the Jews also applies to the Irish ... as long as there is any oppression around no minority group can call itself safe. The dragon having eaten the weakest victim reaches out for the next.'[18] In the context of the onslaught of racism in the US, 'the American psychology of discriminating against black toilers', the black radical's sometimes stated commitment to working-class unity did not and indeed could not find expression in any ideal form, but in the politics of pragmatism.[19] Interracial class unity is imagined first and foremost as a *tactic* to break the monolith of whiteness. Moreover it provides a powerful role for black activists in wrenching apart the bonds of white fraternity. As *The Crusader* states it in November 1921,

WE MUST AIM to encourage existent divisions and even to foster new divisions in the ranks of the white race ... We must aim to keep White Labor and Capital apart by showing White Labor that its interests are identical with our own, inasmuch as we are both seeking freedom from Capitalist oppression and exploitation and neither the Negro nor White Labor can achieve that freedom without the aid of the other.[20]

The lived experience of 'race' in the US complicated any ideal discursive formation of white workers as *natural* allies. Briggs insists 'Not love or hatred, but identity of interest at the moment dictates the tactics of practical people.'[21] It is not accurate to say that the entire left, or indeed all white workers in the US, were racists in this period. Indeed organisations such as the Wobblies (the Industrial Workers of the World) were avowedly anti-racist, as were many individuals in the Socialist and nascent Communist Parties.[22] But the question of race was one that was often imagined, with a few exceptions, even by the most committed anti-racists as mostly a class question where economic struggles against capital would vanquish racism, and thus *specific* mobilisations around race were not necessary.[23] What we find in the black radical press is an attempt to *make* race a class question, not by disregarding the structural function of race in American life by the deferral of race to some limit time after the revolution, but by insisting on the necessity of racism for international class rule to operate. We also see that there are very particular conditions set out in relation to interracial class solidarity. According to the *Crusader*

> It is always possible to apply the acid test of friendship, and that test in the case of the white person professing friendship for the Negro is simply whether that person is willing to see the Negro defend himself with arms against aggression, and willing even to see Negroes killing his own (white) people in defence of Negro rights.[24]

So, this is not a triumphant story of uncomplicated interracial solidarity. Rather it is recognition of the limitations of the left in the US and the black radical insistence on resistance to racist violence being the starting point for any interracial class alliance.

What is significant here, however, as many commentators on this period have emphasised, is that it was the Comintern rather than the local left which seemed to hold out an internationalist model for black liberation.[25] According to the editor of the *Crusader*, Cyril Briggs, reflecting on his early activism, his Communism was 'inspired by the national policy of the Russian Bolsheviks and the anti-imperialist orientation of the Soviet State birthed by the October revolution'.[26] The relationship between black activists and the Comintern is not uniform, nor does it need re-rehearsing here, but the early Comintern's explicit demand that anti-colonialism was a precondition to anti-capitalism was crucial to the coverage of the Bolshevik revolution in the radical press. Moreover, as Minkah Makalani has argued, the Comintern's race politics were themselves influenced by Asian radicals which 'informed how the Comintern approached anticolonial struggles', and further that 'the ABB and Asian radicals thus introduced race and nation into international communism at its inception'.[27]

Bolshevism dominates the black radical press. In particular this comes in the form of reports from Russia about Bolshevik anti anti-semitism as well as responses to the onslaught of anti-Bolshevism in the dominant culture, which the black press consistently lampooned in relation to questions of race at home and colonialism abroad. Bolshevism seemed to offer a vision of liberation in which questions of national and racial oppression would be central. As McKay stated it in Garvey's *Negro World*

> Every Negro who lays claim to leadership should make a study of Bolshevism and explain its meaning to the colored masses. It is the greatest and most scientific idea afloat in the world today that can be easily put into practice by the proletariat to better its material and spiritual life. Bolshevism ... has made Russia safe for the Jew. It has liberated the Slav peasant from priest and bureaucrat who can no longer egg him on to murder Jews to bolster up their rotten institutions. It might make these United States safe for the Negro.[28]

McKay's vision of Bolshevism here is not merely that it has the capacity to vanquish racism, but also that it has a role in breaking the monolith of race through its *class* politics. It is hardly a stretch here, to read the 'Slav peasant' in terms of the 'poor white'. These early articulations of the connections between class and 'race' in the service of a politics which refused to collapse 'race' into class reductionism are extremely significant in terms of the very particular purchase that black radicals placed on the dynamics of 'race' and class. As I have mentioned, articulations of interracial class solidarity were sometimes complex in terms of the concrete conditions of American racism. But in Bolshevism these radicals identified a model of politics that presented an active role for the black working class in liberating both themselves and *potentially* their deluded racist white counterparts. Bolshevism, according to Domingo in *The Messenger*, 'succeeded in making Soviet Russia unsafe for the mobocrats, but safe for Jews and other oppressed racial minorities' but, crucially, only 'after a few executions of lynchers and race-rioters'.[29]

Thus the engagement with the Bolshevik revolution was a way to delineate a new form of assertive and effective race/class politics which spoke in the idioms of resistance to localised racist terror and yet was part of a transnational project of what Hubert Harrison calls 'we Africans of the dispersion'. In his piece on Bolshevism in Barbados, Harrison warns:

> Let the white Englishman learn that justice exists not only for white Englishmen, but for all men. Let him get off the black man's back, stand out of the black man's light, play the game as it should be played, and he will find very little need for wasting tons of print paper and thousands of pounds in a crusade against the spectre of Bolshevism.[30]

In addition to an insistence that the spectre of Bolshevism speaks to black life and black history in very specific ways, Harrison expresses himself here through the tropes of English 'fair play' which are particularly resonant for subjects of British colonialism. British colonialism is also omnipresent in W.A. Domingo's short-lived newspaper *The Emancipator*, where the anti-colonial possibilities inaugurated by the Russian Revolution are forefronted:

> England, with the blood of numberless Indians, Negroes, Egyptians and Irishmen upon her grasping, greedy hands, looks with nervous apprehension at the approach of Bolshevism to her Eastern Colonies. Everywhere Bolshevism brings terror to the heart of imperialism ...[31]

The *Crusader* loudly proclaimed its Bolshevik sympathies in its signature declamatory style which speaks in a register that disdains understatement:

> Bolshevist is the epithet that present-day reactionaries delight to fling around loosely against those who insist on thinking for themselves and on agitation for their rights. We do not know exactly what the reactionaries desire to convey by the term – we do not think they know themselves. However, if, as appears by its frequent use against those who are agitating in the people's interests and for justice for the oppressed, the term is *intended* to cover those 'bad agitators' who are not content that the people shall forever be enslaved in the clutches of the cut-throat, child-exploiting, capitalist-imperialist crew, then assuredly we are Bolsheviks. This epithet nor any other holds any terrors for us. If to fight for one's rights is to be Bolshevists, then we are Bolshevists and let them make the most of it.[32]

Here, as elsewhere in the *Crusader*, Bolshevism is carefully mobilised in the service of black political agency and resistance. To 'fight for one's rights' to be a 'bad agitator' in the service of anti-capitalism *and* anti-imperialism is what is key.

In this chapter I am concerned not with *actual* Bolsheviks or indeed specific events in Russia in the aftermath of the revolution. *The Messenger* in particular does detail reports from Russia in the context of global geopolitics of the period, but Bolshevism is more often spoken of as a model of political identity which can speak to issues of race and anti-colonialism as well as questions of class. As Domingo insists in his defence of Bolshevism in *The Messenger*: 'there is a great connection between the future of the Negro race the world over and the success of the theories – now under trial in Russia – which are collectively known as Bolshevism'.[33]

Significantly, these words are not formed in the context of revolutionary upsurges informed by the October revolution that we see in Germany for example. Indeed these are years of vicious reaction for African Americans in relation to the 'Red Summer' of 1919 and its aftermath. Bolshevism is a rallying call for racialised subjects in an environment where worker's revolution seems tangential indeed to the daily humiliations of life in the US. Yet the Bolshevik revolution is reported as a world-changing event in the black radical press precisely because it is represented as an event which has a particular vanguard role for black workers in the lexicon of class politics. Throughout the coverage of the October revolution is the insistence on black agency – defined both in terms of the particular role of black labour and the importance of black self-defence. Moreover this agency is often starkly enunciated in opposition to liberal politics of 'inclusion' or 'tolerance'.

As Harrison argued in *Negro World*, in a scathing address to white liberals penned in a newspaper defined by its black readership:

> one way for Negroes to put down lawless violence is by resisting it to the full with the lawful violence of self-defense. If you and other so-called white friends of the Negro are opposed to this, then you simply stand in the position of one who would look on and see a friend get his throat cut without offering him a gun or a knife to prevent that throat cutting; but as soon as he grabs a gun or takes a knife to save his throat, you will always be found ready and willing to run up and offer against his self-defense the protest which you never offered against the original aggression. And for such frightful friendship the good white people of this country might just as well understand that the Negro of America today does not care two pins.[34]

Harrison has the full measure of righteous whiteness. The rejection here of liberal paternalism and the insistence on an assertive politics of black self-defence in the face of white supremacy was pervasive in the radical press and prefigures the Black Power discourses of the late 1960s and elements of the contemporary Black Lives Matter movement. It also demands the right to name the terms of any potential solidarity from white Americans. The myriad of articles which speak of white supremacist violence hold American racism to account while also insisting on the centrality of black labour. Here is Harrison again:

> Here in America, we who are of African ancestry and Negro blood have drunk this cup of gall and wormwood to the bitter dregs. Our labor built the greatness of this land in which we are shut out from places of public accommodation: from the church, the ballot and the laws' protection. We are Jim-Crowed, disfranchised and lynched without redress from law or public sentiment, which vigorously exercises its humanity on behalf of the Irish, Armenians and Germans thousands of miles away, but can find no time to concern itself with the barbarism and savagery perpetrated on black fellow citizens in its very midst.[35]

The 'savagery' of white supremacy is such that it must be resisted by any means necessary, or as Briggs puts it 'organized force is the only language intelligible to all the world (the only language that Europeans understand in dealing with Colored races) and the foundation upon which all white civilisation is in reality based'.[36]

In this context Russian workers are placed outside of the taxonomy of the 'European' to serve as exemplars of active agents of a diverse society of variously oppressed peoples who are forging alternatives to racialised capitalism *and* colonialism. As Domingo argued in *The Messenger*:

> Bolshevism – Socialism – is the only weapon that can be used by Negroes effectively to clip the claws of the British lion and the talons of the American eagle in Africa, the British West Indies, Haiti, the Southern states and at the same time reach the monsters' heart (they have a common one) in London, Paris, New York, Tokyo and Warsaw.[37]

Far from being a foreign import, Bolshevism is a weapon to be wielded in black hands for liberation of the entire black world.

It has not been my intention to suggest that this was a breezy and easy formulation, despite the compulsive expressiveness of these writers. As the other chapters in this book suggest, there were all sorts of complex and tortuous routes through which the Bolshevik revolution was brought into dialogue with anti-racist and anti-colonial struggles. The black radical press is *one* very particular articulation of the relationship between left-wing politics and race politics and it is generally celebratory – these are proclamative writings, a call to arms. In the FBI files, internal Communist Party bulletins, speeches, letters, Comintern documents and memoirs, alternative annunciations of this relationship emerge, and they too are part of this story. However, the black radical press is so interesting precisely *because* of its mode of address – its attempt not to 'report' the times but to shape them, to speak to an imagined readership in a manner which would strike a chord with the lived experience of race in the US. This was a configuration of race which sought to encompass the possibility that that experience was not *just* one of wretchedness, although the wretchedness was not minimalised. Being the object of racialisation also enabled one to be a subject of revolution; not just any subject of revolution but a privileged subject of revolution. The black worker was the exemplar of 'a race of toilers', an agent of anti-colonial, anti-racist and anti-capitalist rebellion in a unique way.[38]

In the Christmas issue of *The Messenger* published in January 1918 the editorial had a distinctly un-festive message. 'We expect neither your Xmas to be merry or your New Year Happy. We expect this to be the saddest and most miserable Xmas and new year which you will have ever experienced.' Speaking about black poverty, empty chairs of those who have died on the Western front, poor-quality clothing and shoes and Christmas cake lacking sugar, this editorial implores its readers, 'don't think we are pessimists. Not at all.' In its concrete exposition of the miseries of black poverty and its wilful anti-consumerist tone it continues in this vein to proclaim: 'We see no Utopia. We have no dream. We are not obsessed with any fancy.' Yet, the editorial insists, the spatial and temporal coordinates of black life and black history are connected to the present fight of Russian workers:

> But the trend of the times is so sure and definite that the worst reactionaries are warning of the next change in human and in property rights. Down the dark future we see vistas rise. We see the Russian peasants raise up a government destined to achieve the [sic] social welfare. We see them beset on all sides by the agents of the passing system of rottenness, corruption and greed ... The World's discontent grows. Brave men and brave women point the way. They are lynched, murdered, horsewhipped ... We close our eyes. We listen. What do we hear but the martial tread of millions, marching not in the armies of destruction, but in the armies of progress.[39]

The readers are then assured that because of the Russian Revolution Merry Xmas and a Happy New Year is being shouted by the proletariat all year round and they need to 'join the great radical army'.[40] *The Messenger*'s seemingly dour exaltation of the hope that inheres in the Russian Revolution, framed within the grimly acknowledged miseries of the lived experience of working-class African Americans, beautifully captures the very specific registers of these writings. While Briggs and Harrison address a readership where the explicit racialised violence of the state does not need theorising, here the violence of racialised poverty is also presupposed and it places the black worker as a part of a collective army of global resistance.

To argue that these writings have much to tell us about contemporary politics of race and class is not to make a set of trite connections about the 'then' and the 'now'. It is to note that contemporary forms of racialisation are increasingly premised on rending apart those 'intertwined histories' and 'overlapping territories' which these activists insisted on as necessary for liberation.[41] In the extraordinarily chilling moment in which we find ourselves today, with the global normalisation of an emboldened racist far right, and their deployment of the concept of a specifically disenfranchised *white working class*, the black radical press' rigorous insistence on the paramountcy of black labour in the making of the modern world is imperative.

The whitening of the working class is *not* new, even if its current mobilisations are a frightening development. Indeed the racialised discourses of liberal history have not only marginalised black and brown labour and black and brown resistance – but the liberal narrative is dependent on such erasures, where enslavement and colonialism are presented as aberrations of liberal democracy as opposed to constitutive of it.[42]

Afro-Caribbean and African-American writers and activists represented the Bolshevik revolution as a prototype with which to smash *racial* capitalism and to mount a challenge to traditional politics of race reform. These writings are integral to subsequent socialist and black radical traditions. Interviewed in the late 1960s, the co-editor of *The Messenger*, A. Phillip Randolph, argued in relation to Black Power that:

> The black militants of today are standing upon the shoulders of the '[N]ew Negro radicals' of my day – the '20s, '30s and '40s. We stood upon the shoulders of the civil rights fighters of the Reconstruction era and they stood upon the shoulders of the black abolitionists. These are the interconnections of history and they play their role in the course of development.[43]

For all of his complicated relationship to black radicalism by this time, Randolph delineates a black radical history of resistance while also inserting into that history the often occluded black radicals of the left in the early to mid-twentieth century. The pioneers of these esoteric and ambitious liberation politics were determined to pursue the interconnectedness of a global system of oppression which necessitates making links to other groups who are exploited and oppressed. This is why the Bolshevik revolution, as both internationalist and anti-colonialist, is so very important. It is why the perceived anti-racism of the Bolsheviks in relation to Jews and the former subjects of the Tsarist empire speaks so redolently to the resistances against white supremacism in the US. In the black radical press we can see the attempt to forge those links and the opening up of a space in which the specific nature of racialised capitalism is attested in all its complexity.

Notes

1 W.A. Domingo, 'Did Bolshevism Stop Race Riots in Russia', *The Messenger*, September 1919, 26–74.

2 With the exception of the *Emancipator*, these papers were explicitly attached to political organisations: the *Messenger* (Socialist Party), the *Crusader* (African Blood Brotherhood), *Negro World* (Universal Negro Improvement Association), and the *Crisis* (National Association for the Advancement of Colored People). *The Emancipator* was edited by W.A. Domingo, who also wrote for *The Messenger* and *Negro World*. I am grateful to Peter Hulme who located and generously shared *The Emancipator*.

3 Marcus Garvey, cited in Colin Grant, *The Negro with the Hat: The Rise and Fall of Marcus Garvey* (Oxford: Oxford University Press, 2008), 135.

4 W.E.B. Du Bois, 'The Spread of Socialism', *Crisis*, 22:5 (1921), 200.

5 Joyce Moore Turner, *Caribbean Crusaders and the Harlem Renaissance* (Urbana and Chicago: University of Illinois Press, 2005), 71–78.

6 Cathy Bergin, *African American Anti-Colonial Thought, 1917–1937* (Edinburgh: Edinburgh University Press, 2016), 2–3.

7 Robin D.G. Kelley, *Race Rebels: Culture, Politics, and the Black Working Class* (New York: Free Press, 1996), 7–13.

8 Erik S. McDuffie, *Sojourning for Freedom: Black Women, American Communism and the Making of Black Left Feminism* (Durham, NC: Duke University Press, 2011); Michelle Stephens, *The Black Empire: The Masculine Global Imaginary of Caribbean Intellectuals in the United States 1914–1962* (Durham, NC: Duke University Press, 2005); Kate Weigand, *Red Feminism: American Communism and the Making of Women's Liberation* (Baltimore and London: Johns Hopkins University Press, 2001).

9 See Lydia Lindsey, 'Gendering the Black Radical Tradition: Grace P. Campbell's Role in the Formation of a Radical Feminist Tradition in African American Intellectual Culture' in David Featherstone, Christian Høgsbjerg and Alan Rice (eds), *Revolutionary lives of the Red and Black Atlantic since 1917* (Manchester: Manchester University Press, 2022).

10 Winston James, *Holding Aloft the Banner of Ethiopia: Caribbean Radicalism in Early Twentieth-Century America* (London: Verso, 1998).

11 This is an interesting tension and it emerges in a nasty attack on Domingo as a 'West Indian' in the pages of *The Messenger* during the Garvey wars of 1922–23. See *The Messenger* (March 1923).

12 'Lynching, a Domestic Question', *The Messenger*, July 1919, 7.

13 Cathy Bergin, *'Bitter with the Past but Sweet with the Dream': Communism in the African American Imaginary* (Leiden: Brill, 2015), 65–68.

14 'Labor Unions and the Negro', *The Emancipator,* 20 March 1920, 4.

15 Frank R. Crosswaith, 'Declare Yourselves', *The Emancipator*, 20 March 1920, 4.

16 Cyril Briggs, 'Make their Cause Your Own', *Crusader*, July 1919, 6.

17 W.E.B. Du Bois, *Black Reconstruction in America 1860–1880* (New York: Free Press, 1999), 16.

18 J.A. Rogers, 'The Irish and the Negro', *The Messenger*, November 1924, 350.

19 W.A. Domingo, 'The I.W.W.', *The Emancipator*, 27 March 1920, 4.

20 Cyril Briggs, 'Lessons in Tactics for the Liberation Movement', *Crusader*, November 1921, 15.

21 Cyril Briggs cited in Robert A. Hill, 'Racial and Radical: Cyril V. Briggs, *The Crusader* Magazine and the African Blood Brotherhood 1918–1922' in *The Crusader* (New York: Garland, 1987), lxviii.

22 Paul Heideman (ed.), *Class Struggle and the Color Line: American Socialism and the Race Question 1900–1930* (Chicago, IL: Haymarket, 2018), 1–39.

23 Bergin, *'Bitter with the Past but Sweet with the Dream'*, 58.

24 Cyril Briggs, 'The Acid Test of White Friendship', *Crusader*, July 1921, 9.

25 Mark Solomon, *The Cry was Unity: Communists and African Americans, 1917–1936* (Jackson, MS: University of Mississippi Press, 1998), 38–52.

26 Briggs cited in Hill, 'Racial and Radical', xxv.

27 Minkah Makalani, *In the Cause of Freedom: Radical Black Internationalism from Harlem to London, 1917–1939* (Chapel Hill, NC: University of North Carolina Press, 2011), 73–74.

28 Claude McKay, *Negro World*, 20 September 1919, quoted in Bill Schwarz (ed.), *West Indian Intellectuals in Britain* (Manchester: Manchester University Press, 2003), 73.

29 Domingo, 'Did Bolshevism Stop Race Riots in Russia', 26–27.

30 Hubert Harrison, 'Bolshevism in Barbados' in Hubert H. Harrison, *When Africa Awakes* (Baltimore, MD: Black Classic Press, [1920] 1997), 111.

31 W.A. Domingo, 'Bolshevism and the Darker Races', *The Emancipator*, 13 March 1920, 4.

32 'Bolshevist!!!' editorial, *Crusader*, October 1919, 9.

33 Domingo, 'Did Bolshevism Stop Race Riots in Russia', 26.

34 Hubert Harrison, 'Frightful Friendship vs Self-Defence', *Negro World*, 18 July 1921, 6.

35 Hubert Harrison, 'Wanted – A Colored International', *Negro World*, 28 May 1921, reprinted in Jeffrey B. Perry, *A Hubert Harrison Reader* (Middletown, CT: Wesleyan University Press, 2006), 223–228.

36 Cyril Briggs, 'Aims of The Crusader', *Crusader*, November 1918, 1.

37 W.A. Domingo, 'Will Bolshevism Free America?', *The Messenger*, September 1920, 86.

38 Frank R. Crosswaith, 'Building a Negro Empire', *The Emancipator*, 10 April 1920, 4.

39 Philip Randolph and Chandler Owen, 'Xmas and the New Year', *The Messenger*, January 1918, 16–17.

40 *Ibid.*, 17.

41 Michelle Stephens, 'Re-Imagining the Shape and Borders of Black Political Space', *Radical History Review*, 87 (2003), 178.

42 Cathy Bergin and Anita Rupprecht, 'History, Agency and the Representation of "Race"', *Race & Class*, 57:3 (2016), 7.

43 'A. Philip Randolph: Labor's Grand Old Man', *Ebony*, May 1969, 31.

5

International Communist trade union organisations and the call to black toilers in the interwar Atlantic world

Holger Weiss

Early in 1931, The *International Negro Workers' Review* informed its readers about the struggles of the German harbour workers in Hamburg against intended wage cuts. In Britain and Japan, shipowners were planning an attack against seamen and harbour workers. The leaders and bureaucrats of the national unions of maritime transport workers, branded as 'social fascist', were accused of betraying the workers by siding with the capitalist owners in backing the reduction of wages and splitting the maritime working class. This was no surprise, the journal reminded its readers: the reformist and 'social fascist' trade union bosses had 'always betrayed the Negro and coloured seamen'. However, a new era of radical international solidarity among the maritime workers, the journal assured readers, had started with the establishment of the International of Seamen and Harbour Workers. This organisation, the journal declared, was the only one that was prepared to fight back against wage cuts and the reduction of living conditions on board – regardless of race, creed or colour. The announcement ended by calling on black seamen and harbour workers throughout the world to join in the united front with the Hamburg harbour workers and, even more importantly, to enlist in the militant sections of the International of Seamen and Harbour Workers: 'UNITE IN INTERNATIONAL SOLIDARITY! STRUGGLE AGAINST IMPERIALIST WAR!'[1]

A similar but much longer call for radical international solidarity among maritime workers was published half a year later in the *Negro Worker*. Two main points were raised in the article. First, the struggle against the 'imperialist war' (i.e. the campaign against the (presumed) 'imperialist' plan to attack the Soviet Union) was part of the daily struggle of the maritime transport workers for bettering their conditions on ships, in ports and in the transport industry. Second, the most exploited ones on board as well as ashore were the colonial seamen: 'they are nothing but slaves to the ship-owners'. The trade unions affiliated to the Amsterdam International – the International Federation of Trade Unions with its headquarters in Amsterdam, and the International Transport Workers' Federation – were branded as lackeys of the capitalist owners and 'storm brigades and war inciters against the Soviet Union', as well as backing the exploitation of colonial workers and propagating race hatred between black and white maritime workers. The only organisation which championed proletarian international solidarity among black and white maritime workers, the journal stressed, was the International of Seamen and Harbour Workers.[2]

The International Negro Workers' Review and the *Negro Worker* were the mouthpieces of the International Trade Union Committee of Negro Workers (ITUCNW). This organisation had been formed in July 1930. Its main task was to establish and maintain contact with trade union organisations in the Black Atlantic. The ITUCNW was the brain child of the combined efforts of the Communist International (Comintern), the Red International of Labour Unions (RILU) and a handful of African-Caribbean/American activists. The headquarters of the ITUCNW were located at 8 Rothesoodstrasse in Hamburg. This was also the address of the International Seamen's Club and Hamburg Port Bureau – and the International of Seamen and Harbour Workers (ISH). The latter organisation was also part of the RILU and had been established in October 1930.[3]

Although the author of the calls to the 'Negro' seamen is not known, it is evident that they had been drafted by someone at the ISH headquarters, as the ISH used the journal of the ITUCNW as a propaganda vehicle. A textual analysis of the articles and notes published in the journal clearly indicates that the two calls differed in style and language, using the specific Communist language during the 'class-against-class' period, including phrases such as 'social fascist' and calling for the unity of black and white workers. This comes as no surprise as the ITUCNW and the ISH had received strict orders from Moscow to cooperate; in fact, one of the tasks of the ITUCNW was to assist the ISH in its agitation and propaganda work among black seamen.[4]

The Comintern and its trade union wing, the RILU, were slow in adopting a resolute position towards the Black Atlantic. Although the Communists had recognised the importance of 'Negro work', addressing the exploitation of black workers and calling them to join the Communist sections in the trade unions as well as to enlist in the Communist Party in the USA and in South Africa during the 1920s, other parts of the Black Atlantic, such as sub-Saharan Africa, Latin America, the Caribbean or Europe, remained blank spots on the mental map of the Comintern and RILU leadership. In addition, the activities of the Communist Parties in the USA, Brazil and South Africa left large parts of the black population untouched.[5] Not least because sub-Saharan Africa was a blind spot in Moscow and vice versa: only a few Africans lived in Moscow during the 1920s.[6]

However, a remarkable change occurred in Moscow in 1928 with the establishment of a specific body focusing on work in the Black Atlantic. This was the International Trade Union Committee of Negro Workers of the RILU, or ITUCNW. In contrast to existing Pan-Africanist organisations such as the Universal Negro Improvement Association or the National Association for the Advancement of Colored People, or anti-colonial African ones such as the Ligue de Défense de la Race Nègre, the ITUCNW presented itself as a class organisation for black workers only.[7] The ITUCNW belonged to a group of new committees and organisations of the RILU that came into existence during the so-called Third Period when the Comintern inaugurated its 'class-against-class' doctrine. Among others, the new policy was a broadside attack against reformist and social democratic trade unions and parties, targeting them as 'social fascist'. In comparison with the previous 'United front from below' tactics that had given a limited space for cooperation between Communist and reformist labour organisations, the new tactic turned the RILU and its organisations to call for a vigorous 'revolutionary' opposition politics within the labour unions.[8] The 'class-against-class' tactics were to be fully applied in those countries where Communist parties existed and/or where Communists were members of trade unions. While this was the case throughout Europe as well as in the Americas and Asia, a different situation prevailed in sub-Saharan Africa.[9]

The ITUCNW was an attempt by the RILU and its leading propagandists to sensitise and radicalise black workers in sub-Saharan Africa and the Caribbean and, ultimately, to promote a class-conscious proletarian solidarity and support the anti-colonial aspirations of black urban and rural workers. In contrast, the Comintern and especially its main body which dealt with the so-called 'Negro Question', the Negro Bureau/Secretariat of the Eastern Secretariat, focused on matters concerning the radicalisation and organisation of black workers in the USA and South Africa as well as on the anti-colonial agenda and outreach of the Belgian, British and French Communist parties. As a consequence, Communist activities in the Atlantic world took a dual direction during the interwar period. While the Negro Bureau and its main propagandist, the African-American Communist Harry Haywood, focused on the 'American Atlantic' by promoting the so-called Black Belt thesis, the ITUCNW attempted to encompass a larger radical 'African Atlantic'. Together with various other political and intellectual networks of Pan-African activists and movements, they formed the Black Atlantic of the interwar period.[10]

The relationship between Moscow and the Black Atlantic reflected uneven power relations and geographies during the interwar period.[11] Radical black workers and intellectuals in the Atlantic world were disappointed by the unfulfilled promises of Wilsonian internationalism and the prospects for the self-determination of colonial people in 1919.[12] Inspired by the Bolshevik revolution, black intellectuals and workers turned to the Communist alternative, the radical agenda of racial justice and equality and national independence.[13] However, the 'race-first' perspective of black internationalism and radical political Pan-Africanism was at odds with the 'class-first' interpretations of revolutionary socialism, class struggle and class-against-class of the Comintern and the Communists.[14] Although the Communists in American, British and French labour unions tried to fuse red and black radical agendas, most of the black workers remained lukewarm to the Communist call and most black 'fellow travellers' turned their backs on the Communists during the latter half of the 1930s.[15] The turning point for the Communist thrust into the Black Atlantic was the Italo-Ethiopian crisis in 1935 when the Comintern remained inactive and paved the way for black internationalism and political Pan-Africanism.[16]

The Comintern and the Black Atlantic

The Pan-Africanists' focus on race and colour was a challenge for the Communists. At the Fourth World Congress of the Comintern in 1922, a specific resolution, the *Theses on the Negro Question*, was adopted that dedicated the international Communist movement to the task of promoting revolution among the world's black population. Although the plight of the Africans in the colonies was acknowledged, their political readiness for revolution was unclear, especially as, seen from the perspective of Moscow, there was not much of an African working class – apart from South Africa, where a Communist Party had been established as early as 1921. Nevertheless, the *Theses* called for the formation of an international black movement to be organised in order to join the three corners of the Black Atlantic world: in the United States, in sub-Saharan Africa as well as in Central America and the Caribbean.[17] Ultimately, the 1922 *Theses* highlighted the leading role of African Americans in the global struggle against colonialism.[18]

The position of the Comintern with regard to the Black Atlantic was further elaborated at its Fifth World Congress in 1924. The Congress adopted two resolutions that were directed towards the special challenges in the African Atlantic. Whereas the first document dealt with the 'Negro Question' in the USA,[19] the second focused on Africa. The main emphasis of the second document, *Resolution Concerning the Negro Question in the Colonies*, was on the deployment of African troops against European workers, especially during the French occupation of the Ruhr in 1923. Also, the resolution repeated the call for the emancipation and political self-determination of the

African colonies and the establishment of independent African governments under the leadership of workers and peasants.[20]

The establishment of an international organ in Moscow to direct agitation and propaganda work in the Black Atlantic had to wait until the aftermath of the Sixth World Congress of the Comintern which convened in Moscow from 17 July to 1 September 1928. The Congress officially inaugurated the new class-against-class strategy which had a direct consequence for work in the 'semi-colonies' and colonies. A new strategy was outlined in the *Theses on the Revolutionary Movement in the Colonial and Semi-Colonial Countries*, better known as the *Colonial Theses*. The *Colonial Theses* proclaimed a closer unity between revolutionary movements in the colonies and the Soviet Union, and underlined the need for an alliance between the Soviet Union, the Western industrial proletariat and the oppressed masses in the colonial and semi-colonial countries. Consequently, the *Colonial Theses* called for the creation and development of Communist parties as well as workers' and peasants' unions in the colonial areas and rejected all collaboration with nationalist movements.[21]

The Sixth World Congress was a turning point in the Comintern's relationship with the Black Atlantic. During the Congress, the African-American trade union activist James W. Ford had strongly criticised the lack of focus, if not neglect, by the Comintern and the metropolitan Communist parties on the plight of the oppressed masses in the Black Atlantic. Even worse, Ford claimed that neither the Comintern leadership nor the metropolitan parties had fully understood the global importance of activating the oppressed masses throughout the African world.[22] One consequence of Ford's criticism was the establishment of a special 'Negro Commission' at the Congress. However, the Commission mainly discussed the 'Negro Question' in the USA and eventually drafted a resolution on the issue. The most disputed part of this resolution was the call for national liberation of the African-American population in the US South (the famous Black Belt thesis). Only one paragraph clearly stressed the link between the conditions in the USA and the oppression of the black race in the Atlantic world.[23]

The question in Moscow was how to organise work in the Atlantic world as the Negro Commission had been dissolved after the Congress. A first solution was the establishment of two special 'Negro Bureaus' at the Comintern headquarters in December 1928. The Negro Commission of the Anglo-American Secretariat was mainly to focus on the 'Negro Question' in the USA and South Africa. The Negro Bureau of the Eastern Secretariat, on the other hand, was to focus on the Colonial Question – i.e. the African and Caribbean colonies.[24] In principle, the activities of the two bureaus were supposed to be integrated. However, it was soon realised that neither of the two were working very effectively, which resulted in several changes during 1929. Finally, the two bureaus were merged in November 1929 and continued thereafter as the Negro Section of the Eastern Secretariat.[25] The crux of the matter was that the Negro Section of the Eastern Secretariat had few, if any links and contacts to radical activists and potential agitators in the Atlantic world. The radicalisation and mobilisation of the black working class in the Atlantic world was to be the task of another organisation, the International Trade Union Committee of Negro Workers of the RILU.

Calling the toilers in the Black Atlantic

The RILU's engagement with the Black Atlantic had oscillated between non-existence (sub-Saharan Africa and the Caribbean) and, at most, a lukewarm attitude (USA and South Africa) during larger parts of the 1920s. For the RILU, too, 1928 marked the beginning of a new era in the approach towards the Black Atlantic. In March 1928, Ford attended the Fourth Congress of the RILU in Moscow where he highlighted the need for revolutionary work in Africa and criticised the RILU and its sections for underestimating, if not totally neglecting, work among the black workers.[26]

Ford's criticism started a process which culminated a few months later. Concurrent with the Sixth World Congress of the Comintern, the RILU's Executive Committee held a separate meeting in July 1928, resulting in the organisation of the 'International Trade Union Committee of Negro Workers of the RILU' or the ITUCNW. Its objective was to engage black workers throughout the African Atlantic in the labour and trade unions. New joint unions of white and black workers were to be created, or, if this was not possible due to racial discrimination in the unions, independent black ('Negro') unions were to be established. Much emphasis was laid on the establishment of a global network – 'the work of setting up connections with the Negro workers of the whole world and the unification of the wide masses of Negro workers on the basis of class struggle'.[27]

The ITUCNW was the 'Negro Bureau' of the RILU and vehemently articulated a class-against-class rhetoric in its mouthpiece, the *Negro Worker*.[28] Its first issue publicised the RILU resolution on the establishment of the ITUCNW, including the aims and tasks of the organisation. Black workers were warned about the International Federation of Trade Unions, also known as the Amsterdam International. Little help was to be received from reformist unions, where black members either had to face white chauvinism and open racism or were forbidden to join at all. The RILU and its sections, in contrast, were presented as colour-blind: 'The RILU includes in its ranks workers of all races. It takes steps to combat all forms of reformism and all white chauvinism.'[29] In the same issue, the Trinidad-born and CPUSA member George Padmore highlighted the 'class-before-race' perspective of this international proletarian solidarity: 'Negro workers of the world! Organize your labour power and join hands with the class-conscious white workers of the world and oppressed colonial peoples, Chinese, Indians, Indonesians, etc. for the overthrow of capitalism, imperialism, and the liberation of the working class.'[30] The main enemy of the black working class were the 'Negro bourgeois leaders' who were branded as traitors of black workers. Accused of serving as the 'tools of the bourgeois imperialists',[31] Padmore was very frank when he declared that 'Negro reformism', most notably 'Garveyism', was the biggest obstacle for sensitising the class struggle among the black working class in the Atlantic world: 'In the struggle between the imperialist ruling classes, and the oppressed Negro workers and peasants there can be no middle road, but only the road of class struggle.'[32]

The political language used in the *Negro Worker* was that of the Third Period. Almost monthly, the journal published attacks against 'reformism' and Pan-Africanist activists as well as calls for a global united front of workers irrespective of their colour. In April 1930, Harry Haywood urged readers to combat all forms of 'national reformism among Negro toilers'.[33] One month later, RILU Secretary General Alexandre Lozovsky declared that 'the Negro workers are part and parcel of the whole international proletariat', and underlined that 'without the class struggle it is impossible, nor can it be possible, to abolish race oppression'.[34] In October 1930, George Padmore bashed: 'The social-fascist parties and trade union organizations whether affiliated with the Amsterdam and II International or the American Federation of Labour in the United States, have not defended the interests of the black and white workers.'[35]

Ford's political vision was 'Pan-African' in the sense that it embraced the total Atlantic world. The tasks to be achieved in the struggle against imperialism were independence and self-rule in all countries with a black population, including West, Central and East Africa as well as the Caribbean. In line with official Comintern doctrine, he propagated the idea of establishing an independent 'Native South African Republic' based on workers' and peasants' organisations, with full safeguards and equal rights for all nationals, including white and minorities, and for self-determination of the black population in the 'Black Belt' of the US South. Last, but not least, he called for full and complete political, economic and social rights of 'Negro subjects' in 'Central American' countries. Whether these countries in his mental map also included Brazil and other Latin American countries remains unclear.[36]

Apart from launching an agitation and propaganda campaign for the radicalisation of the working class in the Black Atlantic through the *Negro*

Worker, Ford's second task was to organise a world congress of black workers. Initially planned for 1929, the congress convened in Hamburg in early July 1930. The congress resulted in the establishment of a new 'independent' organisation – or rather re-establishment of an already existing one: The International Trade Union Committee of Negro Workers.[37] Its headquarters was placed in Hamburg, with Ford as the person in charge of its Secretariat.[38] After the congress, most of the African, Caribbean and African-American participants travelled to Moscow where they attended the Fifth World Congress of the RILU. This congress, too, highlighted the mobilisation of the black working class in the Atlantic world and issued two resolutions on the 'Negro Question', with a special focus on sub-Saharan Africa.[39]

The most notable outcome of the 1930 congresses in Hamburg and Moscow was the reorganisation of work at the RILU headquarters. As the ITUCNW was to be presented as a 'new' organisation, the unit in Moscow was renamed the Negro Bureau of the RILU (and claimed to have existed since 1928); the person in charge of the unit in Moscow was George Padmore.[40] The ITUCNW was to publish its own journal whereas the *Negro Worker* remained the official organ of the Negro Bureau of the RILU. The task of the RILU Negro Bureau was, first, to stimulate the revolutionary opposition groups within the existing – mainly reformist-dominated – trade unions in Europe, America and South Africa to reach out to and organise black workers throughout the Atlantic world. Second, it was to promote the revolutionary trade union movement in sub-Saharan Africa and the Caribbean as well as to combat white chauvinism and race prejudice in the trade unions. Third, its task was to combat 'Negro bourgeois nationalism'.[41]

The outcome of the reorganisation was a hierarchical relationship between the two organisations, with the ITUCNW being subordinate to the RILU Negro Bureau. The main task of the ITUCNW was to establish and maintain contact with trade union organisations in sub-Saharan Africa and the Caribbean and to coordinate their activities. Of equal importance was the objective to stimulate the organisation of trade unions in the African Atlantic in countries where none existed. Its official organ was *The International Negro Workers' Review*. Echoing the RILU Negro Bureau's mouthpiece, the ITUCNW journal was to denounce the 'reactionary principles of Negro bourgeois nationalism' and black trade union reformism in the USA and South Africa as well as that of the Amsterdam International and the International Labour Office.[42] The specified guidelines in January 1931 dictated further that the new organisation was to comply with the 'class-before-race' approach of the Comintern and RILU: 'No initiation or affiliation fees shall be collected by the Committee from the different organisations that will come into relations with it as this might create the impression that the ITUC of NW is a Black International conducted on racial lines and not based on the class struggle.'[43] In spring 1931, however, the RILU Negro Bureau decided to stop the publication of its journal and thus to camouflage its links to the Black Atlantic. Instead, the ITUCNW journal was renamed the *Negro Worker* and became the sole vehicle for Communist agitation and propaganda. The ITUCNW, Padmore stressed, was to promote the programme of 'militant class struggle'.[44]

However, the RILU never envisioned the ITUCNW establishing itself as an independent actor in the Black Atlantic. Instead, the organisation was to be supervised by the European Secretariat of the RILU and adhere to instructions which were prepared in Moscow by the RILU Secretariat, the RILU Negro Bureau or the Executive Committee of the Communist International (ECCI). In addition, the ITUCNW was to cooperate closely with the Secretariat of the International of Seamen and Harbour Workers and the International Secretariat of the League Against Imperialism.[45] Initially, and in contrast to the guidelines of January 1931, Ford's ambition seems to have been to engage the ITUCNW in the agitation and propaganda work among black workers in the USA and Latin America.[46] However, these ideas were heavily criticised in Moscow, not least by Padmore, who reminded him that the ITUCNW was not allowed to engage or interfere in US American labour union affairs as this was the duty of the Trade Union Unity League, while the Confederación Sindical Latino-Americana was directing activities on Cuba and Haiti.[47]

What followed was a lengthy debate in Moscow at the RILU headquarters about the geographical outreach of the ITUCNW. In October 1931, the ECCI finally intervened and decided that the activities of the ITUCNW were limited to the British, French, Belgian, Dutch and Portuguese colonies in Africa and the Caribbean.[48] When Padmore replaced Ford as secretary for the Hamburg Committee in November 1931, the objectives of the ITUCNW remained unchanged – being a class not a race organisation, 'organizing and leading the fight in the interests of Negro workers in Africa, the West Indies and other colonies', as well as fighting against 'white chauvinism, social-reformism and the reformist programmes of Negro capitalist misleaders' in the USA, South Africa and the Caribbean.[49] The challenge of the ITUCNW was to expose and denounce the 'Negro reformists', underlined the Surinamese Communist Otto Huiswoud who had replaced Padmore as head of the RILU Negro Bureau.[50]

Kopie aus dem Bundesarchiv

Figure 5.1 The 'Negro toiler breaking his chains' and ITUCNW call
'Free the colonies'

Postscript: Communism or Pan-Africanism?

It took the political theorists in Moscow ten years to formulate an agenda
to address the black workers in the Atlantic world but only one year to
narrow the focus of the ITUCNW from a 'maximal' to a 'limited' vision
of activity. Two perspectives were to clash. The first one was articulated in
Moscow and by the (white) functionaries at the RILU units in Berlin and
Hamburg who monitored and supported the activities of the ITUCNW –
the European Secretariat of the RILU and the International Secretariat of
the ISH. Here, the official Comintern and RILU dogma dictated theoretical considerations and political actions, marked by the combination of an
uncompromising attitude against political and trade union reformism on

the one hand and on the other, anti-colonial and anti-imperial agitation and support for the fight for national self-determination and independence of 'semi-colonial' and colonial subjects.[51]

The second position was that of Padmore at the ITUCNW headquarters in Hamburg. Initially, he backed cooperation with the ISH and published an appeal to African and Caribbean seamen and harbour workers in the *Negro Worker* in April 1932. In line with the official RILU position, the appeal started by underlining the unity of 'White, Black and Yellow water transport workers' and invited them all to participate at the forthcoming world congress of the ISH. Noting that the 'Negro workers in Africa, England, France, America, and the West Indies are among the worst paid and treated slaves of the ship-owners and other capitalists', the invitation to participate was especially directed to them. The appeal reminded readers that the reformist national unions in the United Kingdom and France had turned their backs on the black workers. Instead, the black maritime workers were reminded that the only organisation that defended their rights and called them to join its ranks was the ISH and its affiliated national sections in the USA, United Kingdom, France and South Africa.[52] Soon, however, Padmore declared that the ITUCNW and its journal were not the propaganda vehicles of the ISH. At the ISH World Congress in Altona in May 1932, the rift became an open one when he and like-minded black Communist and radical agitators vehemently criticised the chauvinist and racial attitudes of British party and union activists.[53] Instead, the ITUCNW during Padmore's term as secretary increasingly turned to address issues of a racial rather than class character throughout the Black Atlantic, such as the international Scottsboro campaign.[54]

The two positions on the objectives of Communist agitation and propaganda in the Black Atlantic clashed in 1933. Starting with the Nazi takeover and the crushing of Communist organisations and structures in Germany in that year, the political changes in Europe prompted a re-evaluation of the uncompromising stands of the Communists towards the Social Democrats and paved the way for experimenting with the Popular Front between left-wing and liberal bourgeois parties in France and Spain in 1934. Officially, however, Comintern policy had not changed. Finally, at the Seventh World Congress of the Comintern in August to September 1935, the class-against-class policy was scrapped and replaced by the Popular Front tactics.

The ITUCNW was directly affected by the changes in tactics in Moscow. Padmore, who had moved the ITUCNW headquarters from Hamburg to Paris in March 1933, wanted to scrap the class-against-class approach and apply his version of a 'united front' approach. He started to cooperate with black activists, and together with Garan Kouyaté planned to call for a 'Negro World Unity Congress' and the formation of a universal organisation 'destined to direct the future of the Negro movement in all countries' – i.e. a Black International.[55] However, the plan did not receive any backing in Moscow. Instead, Padmore was accused of sidestepping official policies and was replaced by Otto Huiswoud as secretary of the ITUCNW in spring 1934. Padmore was finally expelled from the CPUSA and the Comintern in March 1934, accused by the International Control Commission of having declined Moscow's order as well as undermining the 'class unity of Negro toilers'.[56]

In the United States, the old policy was to stay with the official guidelines throughout 1934. Harry Haywood, the head of the CPUSA Negro Department, declared the struggle against black nationalism as a major priority and condemned any rapprochement with 'Negro reformists'.[57] Padmore was publicly discredited by black Communists in the USA for being a renegade and having sided with the enemies of the black working class.[58] Ford was amongst them and authored a pamphlet in which he denounced him.[59] Huiswoud, too, attacked Padmore for having betrayed the black working class.[60] Padmore, in turn, accused his former comrades for being 'Little Red Uncle Toms' and condemned the Comintern and the Soviet Union for having sold out the workers in the Black Atlantic.[61]

The cause of the ITUCNW and Communist engagement in the Black Atlantic received a decisive blow in 1935. Padmore's radical political Pan-Africanist approach was to triumph over the inability of Huiswoud, the ITUCNW and the Comintern to launch a global campaign against Italian imperialism in Ethiopia.[62] Ford, who participated at the Seventh World Congress of the Comintern, had together with other black delegates called for the establishment of a new platform, termed the International Negro Liberation Committee. In accordance with the new Popular Front policies of the Comintern, the black delegates envisioned a kind of 'broad united people's front among the Negro people'.[63] In their mind, the ITUCNW had lost its role in the Black Atlantic. Nevertheless, the plan was rejected by the Comintern. Huiswoud now wanted to transform the ITUCNW into a Black International but this plan, too, was scrapped.[64] By 1936, the ITUCNW was barely still in existence and was quietly dissolved by the ECCI in 1937.

An assessment of ITUCNW as a vehicle for the radicalisation of the black working class in the Atlantic world gives conflicting conclusions. Moscow's aim clearly ended in a cul-de-sac, if not outright collapse. This was the standpoint of, among others, George Padmore and C.L.R. James, who claimed that the ITUCNW-initiated struggle against colonial exploitation and racism, and for self-determination and political freedom in the Black Atlantic had been sacrificed by Stalin and Soviet Realpolitik after 1933.[65] A similar critical assessment was presented by William L. Patterson in 1936: after the debacle in 1935, the ITUCNW had few, if any, connections to activists and organisations in the Black Atlantic.[66] The indirect impact of the ITUCNW, and especially its mouthpiece the *Negro Worker*, in the radicalisation and ideological mobilisation of black activists is much more difficult to assess.[67] By the end of 1932, the journal had reached 5,000 copies per issue and was spread – and read – throughout the Black Atlantic. However, by March 1934, the journal's print run had to be reduced to 2,000 copies.[68] The reactions of its readers are difficult to trace. A few of them sent letters to the editors (who sometimes published them), but most of the correspondence is lost (only part of Padmore's is kept in the Comintern archives in Moscow). A critical assessment of the impact and legacy of the *Negro Worker* is yet to be made.

Notes

1 NN, 'Negro Seamen and the German Harbour Workers', *The International Negro Workers' Review*, 1:1 (1931), 5.

2 NN, 'August First and the Negro Toilers', *Negro Worker*, 1:7 (1931), 4–6 (quotation from page 6).

3 On the ISH, see further Holger Weiss, 'The International of Seamen and Harbour Workers – A Radical Global Labour Union of the Waterfront or a Subversive World-Wide Web?' in Holger Weiss (ed.), *International Communism and Transnational Solidarity: Radical Networks, Mass Movements and Global Politics, 1919–1939* (Leiden and Boston: Brill, 2017), 256–317; Holger Weiss, *För kampen internationellt! Transportarbetarnas globala kampinternational och dess verksamhet i Nordeuropa under 1930-talet* (Helsinki: Työväen perinteen ja historian tutkimuksen seura, 2019); Holger Weiss, *A Global Waterfront: The International Propaganda Committee of Transport Workers and the International of Seamen and Harbour Workers, 1921–1937* (Leiden and Boston: Brill, 2021).

4 Resolution on the Work of the Hamburg Committee, draft, 18.10.1931, *fond* (*f.*) 534, *opis* (*o.*) 3, *delo* (*d.*) 668, 44–46, Russian State Archive of Social and Political History (hereafter: RGASPI), Moscow, and Resolution on the Work of the Hamburg TU Committee, draft, 13.12.1931, *f.* 495, *d.* 155, *o.* 100, 29–31, RGASPI. On the (complex) cooperation between the ITUCNW and ISH, see further David Featherstone, 'Maritime Labour and Subaltern Geographies of Internationalism: Black Internationalist Seafarers' Organising in the Interwar Period', *Political Geography*, 49 (2015), 7–16; Holger Weiss, 'Against Japanese and Italian Imperialism: The Anti-War Campaigns of Communist International Trade Union Organizations, 1931–1936', *Moving the Social: Journal of Social History and the History of Social Movements*, 60 (2018), 121–146; Holger Weiss, '"Unite in International Solidarity!" The Call of the International of Seamen and Harbour Workers to "Colonial" and "Negro" Seamen in the early 1930s' in Stefano Bellucci and Holger Weiss (eds), *The Internationalisation of*

the Labour Question: Ideological Antagonism, Workers' Movements and the ILO since 1919 (Basingstoke: Palgrave Macmillan, 2019), 145–162.

5 See further Edward T. Wilson, *Russia and Black Africa Before World War II* (New York: Holmes & Meier, 1974); Mark Solomon, *The Cry was Unity: Communists and African Americans, 1917–1936* (Jackson, MS: University Press of Mississippi, 1998); Marika Sherwood, 'The Comintern, the CPGB, Colonies and Black Britons, 1920–1938', *Science and Society*, 60:2 (1996), 137–163; Hakim Adi, 'The Comintern and Black Workers in Britain and France 1919–37', *Immigrants and Minorities*, 28:2–3 (2010), 224–245; Irina Filatova and Apollon Davidson, *The Hidden Thread: Russia and South Africa in the Soviet Era* (Johannesburg and Cape Town: Jonathan Ball Publishers, 2013); Jacob A. Zumoff, *The Communist International and US Communism, 1919–1929* (Leiden, Boston: Brill, 2014); Aruã Silva de Lima, 'Comunismo contra o racismo: autodeterminação e vieses de integração de classe no Brasil e nos Estados Unidos (1919–1939)', PhD thesis, Universidade de São Paolo, 2015; Margaret Stevens, *Red International and Black Caribbean Communists in New York City, Mexico and the West Indies, 1919–1939* (London: Pluto Press, 2017).

6 Woodford McClellan, 'Africans and Black Americans in the Comintern Schools, 1925–1934', *International Journal of African Historical Studies*, 26:2 (1993), 371–390; John L. Gardner, 'African Americans in the Soviet Union in the 1920s and 1930s: The Development of Transcontinental Protest', *Western Journal of Black Studies*, 23:3 (1999), 190–201; Holger Weiss, 'The Making of an African Bolshevik: Bankole Awoonor Renner in Moscow, 1925–1928', *Ghana Studies*, 9 (2006), 177–220; Woodford McClellan, 'Black Hajj to Red Mecca: Africans and Afro-Americans at KUTV, 1925–1938' in Maxim Matusevich (ed.), *Africa in Russia, Russia in Africa: Three Centuries of Encounter* (Trenton, NJ: Africa World Press, 2007), 61–83; Maxim Matusevich, 'Black in the USSR: Africans, African-Americans, and the Soviet Society', *Transitions*, 100:1 (2009), 56–75; Maxim Matusevich, '"Harlem Globe-Trotters": Black Sojourners in Stalin's Soviet Union' in Jeffrey O.G. Ogbar (ed.), *The Harlem Renaissance Revisited: Politics, Arts, and Letters* (Baltimore, MD: Johns Hopkins University Press, 2010), 211–244.

7 Jonathan Derrick, *Africa's 'Agitators': Militant Anti-Colonialism in Africa and the West, 1918–1939* (London: Hurst, 2008); Minkah Makalani, *In the Cause of Freedom: Radical Black Internationalism from Harlem to London, 1917–1939* (Chapel Hill, NC: University of North Carolina Press, 2011); Hakim Adi, *Pan-Africanism and Communism: The Communist International, Africa and the Diaspora, 1919–1939* (Trenton, NJ: Africa World Press, 2013); Holger Weiss, *Framing a Radical African Atlantic: African American Agency, West African Intellectuals and the International Trade Union Committee of Negro Workers* (Leiden, Boston: Brill, 2014). See also the roundtable discussion on Pan-Africanism and Communism in *Black Perspectives*, www.aaihs.org/introduction-roundtable-on-pan-africanism-and-communism-by-hakim-adi/ [accessed 30 March 2017].

8 On the Third Period, see Matthew Worley (ed.), *In Search of Revolution: International Communist Parties in the Third Period* (London, New York: I.B. Tauris, 2004). On the RILU, see Reiner Tosstorff, *The Red International of Labour Unions (RILU) 1920–1937* (Leiden, Boston: Brill, 2016).

9 John Callaghan, 'The Communists and the Colonies: Anti-Imperialism Between the Wars' in Geoff Andrews, Nina Fishman and Kevin Morgan (eds), *Opening the Books: Essays on the Social and Cultural History of the British Communist Party* (London: Pluto Press, 1995), 3–22; John Callaghan, 'Storm over Asia: Comintern Colonial Policy in the Third Period' in Matthew Worley (ed.), *In Search of Revolution* (London, New York: I.B. Tauris, 2004), 18–37; Josephine Fowler, 'From East to West and West to East: Ties of Solidarity in the Pan-Pacific Revolutionary Trade Union Movement, 1923–1934', *International Labor and Working-Class History*, 66 (2004), 99–117; Carolien Stolte, 'Bringing Asia to the World: Indian Trade Unionism and the Long Road Towards the Asiatic Labour Congress, 1919–37', *Journal of Global History*, 7:2 (2012), 257–278; Klaas Stutje, 'To Maintain an Independent Course: Interwar Indonesian Nationalism and International Communism on a Dutch-European Stage', *Dutch Crossing: Journal of Low Countries Studies*, 39:3 (2015), 204–220.

10 Weiss, *Framing a Radical African Atlantic*, 144–145; Hakim Adi, *Pan-Africanism: A History* (London: Bloomsbury, 2018), 61–88; Holger Weiss, 'Framing Black Communist Labour Union Activism in the Atlantic World: James W. Ford and the Establishment of the International Trade Union Committee of Negro Workers, 1928–1931', *International Review of Social History*, 62:2 (2019), 1–30.

11 David Featherstone, *Solidarity: Hidden Histories and Geographies of Internationalism* (London: Zed Books, 2012).

12 Erez Manela, *The Wilsonian Moment: Self-Determination and the International Origins of Anticolonial Nationalism* (Oxford: Oxford University Press, 2007).

13 Barbara Keys, 'An African-American Worker in Stalin's Soviet Union: Race and the Soviet Experiment in International Perspective', *The Historian*, 71:1 (2009), 31–54; Makalani, *In the Cause of Freedom*, 5; Joy Gleason Carew, 'Translating Whose Vision? Claude McKay, Langston Hughes, Paul Robeson and the Soviet Experiment', *Intercultural Communication*, 23:2 (2014), 1–16.

14 Roderick Bush, *The End of White World Supremacy: Black Internationalism and the Problem of the Color Line* (Philadelphia, PA: Temple University Press, 2009), 88–131; Makalani, *In the Cause of Freedom*, 135–136.

15 Adi, 'The Comintern and Black Workers'; Brent Hayes Edwards, *The Practice of Diaspora: Literature, Translation, and the Rise of Black Internationalism* (Cambridge, MA: Harvard University Press, 2003); Susan D. Pennybacker, *From Scottsboro to Munich: Race and Political Culture in 1930s Britain* (Princeton, NJ: Princeton University Press, 2009); Leslie James, *George Padmore and Decolonization from Below: Pan-Africanism, the Cold War, and the End of Empire* (Basingstoke: Palgrave Macmillan, 2015).

16 Barbara Bush, *Imperialism, Race and Resistance: Africa and Britain, 1919–1945* (London, New York: Routledge, 1999); Joseph Fronczak, 'Local People's Global

Politics: A Transnational History of the Hands Off Ethiopia Movement of 1935', *Diplomatic History*, 39:2 (2015), 245–274; Tom Buchanan, '"The Dark Millions in the Colonies are Unavenged": Anti-Fascism and Anti-Imperialism in the 1930s', *Contemporary European History*, 25:4 (2016), 645–665; Neelam Srivastava, *Italian Colonialism and Resistances to Empire, 1930–1970* (London: Palgrave Macmillan, 2018); Weiss, 'Against Japanese and Italian Imperialism'.

17 *Theses on the Black Question*: www.marxists.org/history/international/comintern/4th-congress/black-question.htm [accessed 20 February 2021].

18 Roger E. Kanet, 'The Comintern and the "Negro Question": Communist Policy in the United States and Africa, 1921–1941', *Survey: A Journal of East & West Studies*, 19:4 (1973), 86–122, esp. 104–107; Wilson, *Russia and Black Africa*, 127–136; Solomon, *The Cry Was Unity*, 42–43.

19 Report on the American Negro Question (V. Congress; typewritten document, no date, no author), *f. 495, o. 155, d. 20*, 3–4, RGASPI.

20 Resolution zur Negerfrage in den Kolonien (V. Congress: typewritten document, no date, no author), *f. 495, o. 155, d. 20*, 1–2, RGASPI.

21 Roger Edward Kanet, 'The Soviet Union and Sub-Saharan Africa: Communist Policy Toward Africa, 1917–1965', PhD thesis, Princeton University, 1966, 85–88; Wilson, *Russia and Black Africa*, 166–167, 171–172.

22 Extract from Ford's speech at the Sixth Congress, published in *International Press Correspondence*, 3 August 1928, reproduced in James S. Allen and Philip S. Foner (eds), *American Communism and Black Americans: A Documentary History, 1919–1929* (Philadelphia, PA: Temple University Press, 1987), 182.

23 On the Black Belt thesis, see further Cedric J. Robinson, *Black Marxism: The Making of the Black Radical Tradition*, foreword by Robin D.G. Kelley (Chapel Hill, NC: University of North Carolina Press, [1984] 2000); Susan Campbell, '"Black Bolsheviks" and the Recognition of African-America's Right to Self-Determination by the Communist Party', *Science and Society*, 58:4 (1994/1995), 440–470; Oscar Berland, 'The Emergence of the Communist Perspective on the "Negro Question" in America: 1919–1931. Part One', *Science and Society*, 63:4 (1999–2000), 411–432; Oscar Berland, 'The Emergence of the Communist Perspective on the "Negro Question" in America: 1919–1931. Part Two', *Science and Society*, 64:2 (2000), 194–217; Beverly Tomek, 'The Communist International and the Dilemma of the American "Negro Problem": Limitations of the Black Belt Self-Determination Thesis', *WorkingUSA: The Journal of Labor and Society*, 15:4 (2012), 549–576.

24 Protokoll Nr. 14 der Sitzung des Politsekretariats des EKKI, 10.12.1928, *f. 495, d. 3, o. 70*, 2, RGASPI.

25 Williams, Memorandum, dated 5.11.2929, *f. 495, d. 155, o. 80*, 107, RGASPI. See further Weiss, *Framing a Radical African Atlantic*, chapter 3.1.

26 Ford, Life and activities (1932), page 6, *f. 495, d. 261, o. 6747*, 67, RGASPI. See further Weiss, *Framing a Radical African Atlantic*, chapter 3.2.

27 Resolution of the Executive Bureau of the RILU on the Organisation of the International Trade Union Committee of Negro Workers, *f. 534, d. 3, o. 359*, 1–6, RGASPI.

28 See, further, Susan Campbell, 'The *Negro Worker*. A Comintern Publication 1928–37. An Introduction': www.marxists.org/history/international/comintern/negro-worker/index.htm [accessed 10 February 2021].

29 'Organisation of an International Negro Trade Union Committee by the RILU', *The Negro Worker: Bulletin of the International Trade Union Committee of Negro Workers of the RILU*, 1:2 (August–September 1929), 1.

30 [George] Padmore, 'Problems of Negro Workers in the Colonies – USA', *The Negro Worker: Bulletin of the International Trade Union Committee of Negro Workers of the RILU*, 1:2 (August–September 1929), 15.

31 J. Reed, 'Anti-Imperialist Struggle of the Negro Workers', *The Negro Worker: Bulletin of the International Trade Union Committee of Negro Workers of the RILU*, 2:5 (December 1929), 1–2.

32 George Padmore, 'Report & Resolution on the Economic Struggles and Task of Negro Workers', *Negro Worker, Vol 3 – Special Number: The Hamburg Conference* (15 October 1930), 7.

33 Harry Haywood, 'Forward to the London Conference of Negro Toilers', *The Negro Worker: Bulletin of the International Trade Union Committee of Negro Workers of the RILU*, 3:6 (April 1930), 1–3.

34 A. Lozovsky, 'Negro Workers Awakening', *The Negro Worker: Bulletin of the International Trade Union Committee of Negro Workers of the RILU*, 3:7 (May 1930), 1.

35 Padmore, 'Report & Resolution', 7.

36 [James W.] Ford, 'The Negro Question. Report to the IInd World Congress of the League Against Imperialism', *The Negro Worker: Bulletin of the International Trade Union Committee of Negro Workers of the RILU*, 2:4 (August 1929), 8–9.

37 See, further, Hakim Adi, 'Pan-Africanism and Communism: the Comintern, the "Negro Question" and the First International Conference of Negro Workers', *African and Black Diaspora: An International Journal*, 1:2 (2008), 237–254; Adi, *Pan-Africanism and Communism*; Weiss, *Framing a Radical African Atlantic*.

38 'Aims of the ITUCNW', *Negro Worker, Vol. 3 – Special Number: The Hamburg Conference* (15 October 1930), 16.

39 'Tasks of the Revolutionary Movement in Africa' and 'Resolution on Work among Negroes in the US and the Colonies', both published in *Negro Worker: Special Number on the Fifth Congress of the RILU* (1 November 1930).

40 Weiss, *Framing a Radical African Atlantic*, 286–288.

41 'Statement to our readers', *Negro Worker: Special Number on the Fifth Congress of the RILU* (1 November 1930), 1.

42 'Tasks of the ITUCNW', *Negro Worker, Vol. 3 – Special Number: The Hamburg Conference* (15 October 1930), 17; ECCI, The organisation and functions of the International Trade Union Committee of Negroes in Hamburg, 16.11.1930, *f*. 495, *d*. 155, *o*. 87, 432–433, RGASPI.

43 Resolution of the Organisation and Functions of the International Trade Union Committee of Negro Workers, 24.1.1931, *f*. 495, *o*. 155, *d*. 96, 10–13, RGASPI.

44 G[eorge] P[admore], 'Editor's Note', *Negro Worker*, 1:8 (August 1931).

45 Plan of Work and Immediate Tasks of the International Trade Union Committee of Negro Workers at Hamburg, undated and no author, *f.* 534, *o.* 3, *d.* 668, 6–7, RGASPI.

46 'Our Aims', *The International Negro Workers' Review*, 1:1 (1931), 1.

47 Padmore to Ford, 13.2.1931 and 17.3.1931, *f.* 534, *o.* 3, *d.* 668, 57 and 60, RGASPI.

48 Protokoll Nr. 187 der Sitzung der Politischen Kommission des Pol.Sekr am 13.10.1931, *f.* 495, *d.* 4, *o.* 145, 1–2, RGASPI. See further Weiss, *Framing a Radical African Atlantic*, 292–298. The debates in Moscow concerning the outreach of the ITUCNW are not discussed by Adi. Makalani, *In the Cause of Freedom*, 163 and 173, claims that the ITUCNW had been a product of '(t)he black radical vision of a diasporic international' and that black Communists, including Ford and Padmore, prospected the ITUCNW to develop into a black international.

49 'What is the International Trade Union Committee of Negro Workers?', *Negro Worker*, 1:10–11 (1931), 45.

50 O.E. Huiswoud, 'The Economic Crisis and the Negro Workers', *Negro Worker*, 2:4 (1932), 25–27; Weiss, *Framing a Radical African Atlantic*, 298–299.

51 See, further, Weiss, *Framing a Radical African Atlantic*.

52 NN, 'Appeal to Negro Seamen and Dockers', *Negro Worker*, 2:4 (1932), 20–24.

53 For more on this, see Sherwood, 'The Comintern, the CPGB, Colonies and Black Britons' and Featherstone, 'Maritime Labour and Subaltern Geographies' as well Christian Høgsbjerg, 'Mariner, Renegade and Castaway: Chris Braithwaite, Seamen's Organiser, Socialist and Militant Pan-Africanist', *Race & Class*, 53:2 (2011), 36–57; David Featherstone, 'Harry O'Connell, Maritime Labour and the Racialised Politics of Place', *Race & Class*, 57:3 (2016), 71–87.

54 On the international campaign to free the nine 'Scottsboro Boys' who had been sentenced to death by a local court in Alabama, USA, see further James A. Miller, Susan D. Pennybacker and Eve Rosenhaft, 'Mother Ada Wright and the International Campaign to Free the Scottsboro Boys, 1931–1934', *The American Historical Review*, 106:2 (2001), 387–430; Pennybacker, *From Scottsboro to Munich*; James A. Miller, *Remembering Scottsboro: The Legacy of an Infamous Trial* (Princeton, NJ: Princeton University Press, 2009); and Weiss, *Framing a Radical African Atlantic*, 392–397.

55 See further Edwards, *The Practice of Diaspora*, 269, 275–282.

56 Statement of the International Control Commission, 20.3.1934, *f.* 495, *d.* 261, *o.* 4718, 3, RGASPI.

57 Mark Naison, *Communists in Harlem During the Depression* (Chicago, IL: University of Illinois Press, 2005), 108–109.

58 See further Naison, *Communists in Harlem*, 131–132.

59 James W. Ford, *World Problems of the Negro People: (A Refutation of George Padmore)* (New York: Harlem Section of the Communist Party, [1934?]).

60 [Otto Huiswoud,] 'A Betrayer of the Negro Liberation Struggle', *Negro Worker*, 4:3 (1934), 6–10.

61 George Padmore, Open letter to Earl Browder, no date [*c*.1934], *f*. 495, *o*. 155, *d*. 102, 123–125, RGASPI.

62 See further Weiss, 'Against Japanese and Italian Imperialism'.

63 (Declaration,) The International Negro Liberation Committee, no author, no date [*c*.1935], *f*. 495, *d*. 155, *o*. 102, 25–26, RGASPI.

64 See further Weiss, *Framing a Radical African Atlantic*, 698–699.

65 C.L.R. James, *World Revolution, 1917–1936: The Rise and Fall of the Communist International* (Durham, NC: Duke University Press, [1937] 2017); George Padmore, *Pan-Africanism or Communism?: The Coming Struggle for Africa* (London: Dennis Dobson, 1956).

66 See Weiss, *Framing a Radical African Atlantic*, 709–711.

67 Brent Hayes Edward's claim that the *Negro Worker* emerged as the key channel for Padmore's radical Pan-African vision rather than a vehicle for orthodox rhetoric is a valid one, but the 'class-before-race' perspective should not be lost in articles authored by Padmore and other black/non-black Communists. See Edwards, *The Practice of Diaspora*, 257.

68 Weiss, *Framing a Radical African Atlantic*, 533–566, 633.

6

Firebrands, trade unionists and Marxists: the shadow of the Russian Revolution, the colonial state and radicalism in Guyana, 1917–57

Nigel Westmaas

In a letter sent to the Comintern publication *Negro Worker* in 1933, the pioneer Guyanese labour leader Hubert Critchlow wrote a letter to the 'Secretariat International Red Aid' in Moscow, USSR. Signing his name 'comrade', he outlined his actions following his return from a visit to the USSR. Referring to a public meeting he held in Georgetown, Guyana after his return he noted that the 'hall was taxed to the utmost capacity, many persons standing'. Critchlow said 'I have forwarded you copies of newspapers with report of meeting and criticisms. I will like you to read carefully the criticisms written about the USSR.'[1]

This letter is an especially relevant trope for the fairly slender shadow of the Russian Revolution on the Guyana process throughout the period under enquiry, from 1917 to 1957. And the operative term in Critchlow's correspondence, 'criticisms written about the USSR', is a fair template from which to interrogate the impact (or lack thereof) of the Russian Revolution on Guyana over time.

The contribution of the early (or colonial) radical movements and individuals in British Guiana (now Guyana) to the anti-colonial, labour movement and nationalist movement, is largely unrecorded. Early radicalism in Guyana was varied in organisation, scope, duration and cause. I contend that in this general assessment of anti-systemic movements and individuals, the broad descriptive 'radical' was ideologically diffuse and fundamentally pliable given the powerful hegemonic forces at work in the colony and the region. This chapter explores the contribution of some of the early radical movements, and goes on to provide a summary of their activity and ideological outlooks, and potential collective influence on the development, by the 1950s, of a popular national party, the People's Progressive Party (PPP) with its Marxist and anti-colonial orientation.

The story of these radical movements' (and individuals') role in influencing change in the colony is conveniently identified for the scope of this chapter in three phases: before the First World War (and the 1917 Russian Revolution); between 1917 and the Second World War; and from 1945 to 1957. The year 1957 provides a convenient symbolism as the year of a formal split in the national movement after the anti-colonial shock election of 1953 which witnessed perhaps the only left-wing political party come to power in the British Empire.

David Scott's revisionist take[2] on the 'conventional narrative' of colonial historiography in the Caribbean, or Jamaica to be more precise, is a relevant and valuable examination of the hazards of the 'familiar chronology' of anti-colonial and nationalist teleology and 'moments', and the itemisation and repetition of important events in the life of nations. In his critical musing, Scott laments 'the exhausted nation-state' periodisation, giving examples such as the 1938 labour rebellions and the 1944 adult suffrage struggles in modern Jamaican history as recurring episodes in the Jamaican historical narrative.

As for Jamaica, the focus of Scott, the danger of this lazy narrative also exists for Guyana. In Guyana's case, historians and public commentators have been partial to the traditional narratives in respect of the 1953 suspension of the constitution (as a result of the anti-colonial struggle and success of what was called the left-wing PPP) and the '1950s'. This period is considered the alpha and omega of the country's 'main event' history from which all the anti-colonial nationalism gloss, repression and deep racial problems sprang. In repeating this teleology a researcher is in danger of falling into the same conventional narrative of which Scott warns. I try to avoid this by extending the range with other national organisations, individuals and their respective activities in defining the role and activity in Guyana's radical past. Nonetheless, reality indicates that this chapter can only partially avoid the drawbacks of the kind of historiography that Scott warns against. In sum, it is undeniably next to impossible to circumvent the embracing empirical and metaphoric '1953' and its hallowed position in the collective memory and impact on modern Guyanese history.

Prelude

Before 1900, British Guiana was defined by the effects of the termination of slavery in 1838 and the post-emancipation hiatus. The many socio-historical disturbances in this interregnum, including the struggles of the underprivileged and labour's response, together with the onset of the village movement, made the early post-slavery phase a fertile ground for radical instincts. Indubitably, the first known public comment on 'socialism' in Guyana is credited to an article in the London *Times* newspaper that derisively described the incipient post-slavery village movement of 1839 as 'little bands of socialists'.[3] Advanced as criticism, the reference amounted, for the tenor of the time, to high praise for the impulse and creativity of the early villagers and labourers in Guyana. In the nineteenth century other individuals, both black and white, Guyanese and Europeans, were designated 'socialists' or radicals by the spokespersons of the colonial state and the press on account of the radicalism of their views for the time. Two other significant social disturbances occurred in the interregnum. These revolts, interchangeably baptised as 'riots' and 'disturbances', stood out: the 1856 Angel Gabriel riot, and the 1889 Cent Bread riot.[4]

The Indian immigrant, Bechu, was another firebrand who caught the attention of the colonial authorities by the end of the nineteenth century. In his regular letter writing – his forte – Bechu consistently exposed the horrors and limitations of the indentureship system and its effect on the people.[5] Walter Rodney has registered the activities of the Rev. Henry John Shirley,[6] who had arrived from England in 1900 to serve in the New Amsterdam mission church, for the response he evoked from the colonial press. For stating, among other things, that it was the intention of the British colonial authorities to keep 'the black and coolie people in ignorance' and calling for trade union organisation, the Rev. Shirley was dubbed a 'socialist demagogue', and was placed under Special Branch surveillance after the speech in which he made that call.[7]

Bechu and the Rev. Shirley were by no means alone. The rebellious Guyanese population would speckle the colonial landscape with strikes and riots from the end of the nineteenth to the early twentieth century. Later, two militant Indian newspapers, *Ghadar* and *Bande Mataram*,[8] were intercepted and banned from the colony in 1908 on account of their contentious reporting on local issues.

Of the major revolts, the 1905 riot[9] was in many ways a powerful signpost for the future radical movement in Guyana. In 1905 Guyana was still a valued British colony. It was one of the largest sugar producers in the world, and one that Victorian novelist Anthony Trollope famously characterised as a 'mild despotism tempered by sugar'.[10] By the time the 'streets exploded' in 1905, the background to the rebellion had been well and truly established. The mishmash of the history of sugar, slavery, rice, indentureship, gold and sweat all commingled on the streets of the capital city Georgetown. Kimani Nehusi, in assessing the origins of the 1905 rebellion (or riot), identifies four main causes: 'high taxation, low wages, lack of political participation and adequate representation; and the intransigence of the plantocracy in the face of change'.[11] All of these factors were in one way or another testimony to the dominance of sugar production in the lives of the people. By the time of the 1905 rebellion there was large-scale diversification in Guyana's economy. Wages were down and there was no formal trade union or political representation. Workers thus took their own independent strike action in 1905. The first two days of the strike witnessed its slow spread across sectors as street activity in support picked up. By the third day, labour historian Ashton Chase reports that 'hoodlums and gangs of work shirkers took matters ... out of the hands of strikers, and by their frequent acts of violence at various wharves. It was plain that the strike had turned into a riot.'[12] Rodney's account of the riot is more passionate, lively and less critical of the 'hooliganism'. He focused instead on the causes and the justifications of the actions of an oppressed and suppressed working population.[13] The rebellion was eventually crushed and the police 'mopping up' operations were described as 'swift and brutal', involving 'hundreds of arrests'.[14] The arrival of two British warships and the placement of street power back into the hands of the authorities, restored 'order'. Patrick Dargan, a radical politician for his time, called for the two senior police officers in command of the repression to be 'indicted for manslaughter'.[15]

Another chapter of ferment in British Guiana, still in 'unorganized' form, could be said to have commenced with the onset of the Russian Revolution of 1917. Taking one of their cues from the memory of the 1905 rebellion, Guyanese newspapers from the moment of the Russian Revolution were peppered with reports of the 'Dangers of Bolshevism'. Several *Daily Argosy* editorials were devoted to the dangers of 'Bolshevism' and the impact of the Russian Revolution – not only in Europe but also the effects in the colonies. These fears were grossly overstated and merged with other perceived threats such as Garveyism and general 'agitators' in the colony.

While the reaction to the Russian Revolution in a colony like Guyana is not easily quantified, the event impacted Hubert Critchlow, who saw the revolt as a victory for the working class. In 1919, not long after the Bolshevik revolution, Critchlow, in consort with others, had founded the British Guiana Labour Union (BGLU). The BGLU, locally derived and inspired, created quite a stir in the colony and in the anglophone Caribbean. The external influence was also tangible. The British Labour Party was a formidable force by 1919 and the works of the Fabian socialists, Sidney and Beatrice Webb, were identified as a threat by the local British Guiana authorities. Other non-socialist groupings assisted in providing for the atmosphere of challenge to things colonial.

Others gave movements like Garveyism its due: 'Garveyism left a lasting mark on Guyana', one researcher declared.[16] Perhaps the high mark of the Garvey organisation's strength on the ground in British Guiana was the visit of Marcus Garvey himself to the colony in 1937. In any event, Hubbard noted that 'when Garveyism was at its zenith, the British administration took such alarm at the strength of its impact in Georgetown, and the possibility of its growth and extension to the rural areas, that a Bill was introduced into the Legislature to ban the importation and distribution of the Garvey publications'.[17]

This Seditious Publications Ordinance (Prohibition Order) of 1919, a very repressive piece of legislation, was directly introduced, by all accounts, to prevent Garvey's *Negro World* from circulating in the colony.[18] The Seditious Bill was met with fierce resistance from many quarters. The vigorous debate and opposition it stimulated coincided with the rise to public office of non-white middle-class politicians and legislators who were slowly overcoming the structural, political and social hindrances and seeking political representation in the highest organs of the colony. A letter from lawyer John Johnson lamented the Bill's purported goal to target 'American coloured newspapers' circulating in the colony.[19] Even the usually conservative *Daily Argosy* condemned the Sedition Bill, deeming it in an editorial headline a 'Menace to Honest Criticism'.[20] Alfred Athiel Thorne, Barbados-born Guyanese politician, journalist and labour leader, in response to the Bill affirmed his support for the circulation of the African-American *Crisis* and Garvey's *Negro World*.

The 1920s

By the 1920s local political activism was actively shaped by the likes of several political militants. Among them was A.A. Thorne, an omnipresent figure in early twentieth-century Guyana and a passionate advocate for many issues including education, and the economic and social progress of working people. Consequently, at one time or another, he was given the designation 'socialist' by colonial officials and the conservative press. Thorne was active in the post-war period in the international campaign for black dignity.

> In a racy speech ... Mr Thorne showed that [sic] the Labour Party had done for the working people of this Colony in 1919, and the interest they had been taking in them continuously since. He impressed on them the great advantage of forming a proper organisation to be affiliated to the Labour party which is now the Government of Great Britain. He emphasized the fact that for the first time in the history of Great Britain there was government by the people, and he gave them information from correspondence to satisfy them that the present Government in Great Britain was keenly interested in the condition of the masses in this colony, and was desirous of improving their condition.[21]

Other political figures, Nelson Cannon (a white politician of local birth), A.R.F. Webber, R.E. Brassington and J.P. Santos, were active in the Popular

Party – an organisation considered quite radical for its time. But even prior to the activity of organisations like the Popular Party there were other organisations and characters who fought for social progress in the colony. Their social and political space was limited, however, not only by the franchise, but also by the ethos of the time which as individuals they found difficult to transcend. As Nehusi explains:

> The political organisations which emerged in Guiana between 1887 and 1928 have been characterized as short-term affairs which fought for limited gains and disappeared immediately after their electoral purposes were fulfilled …[22]

Individual prestige has been discussed as one of the motivating factors impelling these men to seek public office. In the 'requisitioning of candidates' system, a candidate was formally invited by prominent citizens to consent to nomination to a particular constituency.[23] The constitutional framework in which they operated shaped the activity of these middle-class politicians. In order to enter the orbits of power, they were forced to genuflect at times to colonial authority. At other times, mass pressure and their own prestige forced them to confront the government.

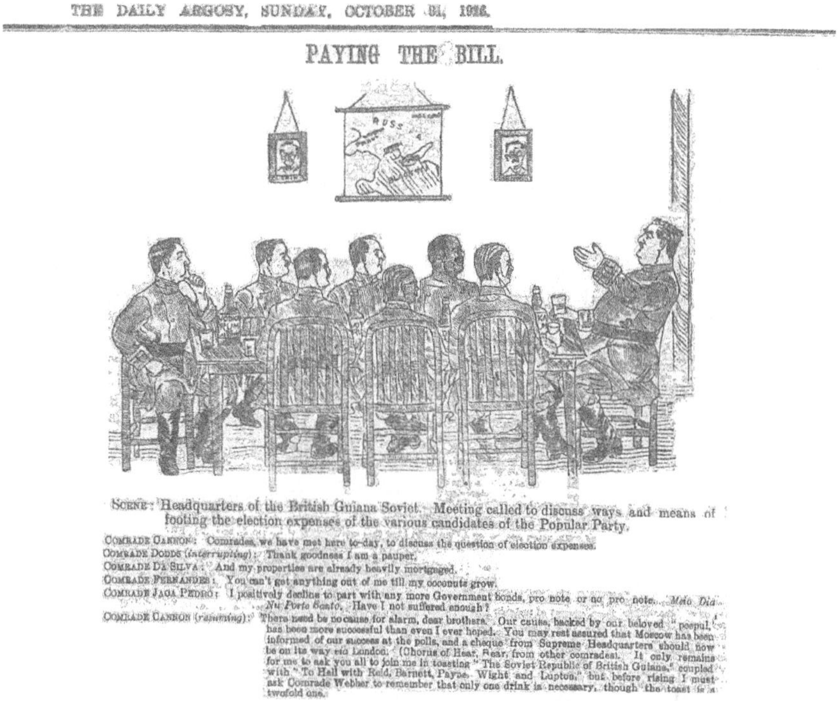

Figure 6.1 'Paying the bill', cartoon in the *Daily Argosy* (31 October 1926)

After a victory of the Popular Party in the 1926 elections, even moderate attempts at reform led to hostility from conservative newspapers and the colonial hierarchy, and rivalry among the men and women who ran the Popular Party. In 1928 a setback occurred with the introduction of modifications in the colony's constitution and the advent of 'Crown Colony rule' that was 'singularly hostile to the formation of even reformist political organisations'.[24]

Several ethnic populist groupings were similarly active in the 1920s including Marcus Garvey's Universal Negro Improvement Association (UNIA), the Negro Progress Convention (NPC) and the British Guiana East Indian Association (BGEIA). All of these organisations played their role in the early nationalist and labour movement. Nonetheless, while these individuals and groups contributed to the anti-colonial sparks, at least one scholar conceded, 'they failed to comprehend the fundamental conflict between labour and capital in the society'.[25]

Women were by no means excluded from among these early firebrands and radicals. From their visible and leading presence in the 1889 and 1905 riots, all manner of names were placed on them by the colonial press. The many unemployed women who participated in these and other demonstrations were deemed 'amazons', 'idle ruffians' and 'women of the street'. In some cases, they were more feared and loathed than the 'socialists' in the colony. In 1931, the Guyanese woman activist Gertie Wood was prolific in her calls for women to 'throw off the shackles of slavery, prepare yourselves to fight your own battles and read every book and paper you can get hold of, ask questions about all sorts of things ...'[26] It was not difficult to establish why Wood was seeing British Guianese society from two angles, as charitable worker and as an activist against subservience to the male order. Her coherent and far-seeing social and political contributions were even more stellar in her language and expressions. On the conditions of women workers in the shops Wood had this to say:

> now we come to the question of 'sweated labour', I want to say that in Georgetown, woman and woman only bears the lash of this damnable scourge ... in homes and in the shirt factories, by women and girls who are bravely trying to help out the situation, by doing their bit, but who are being crushed, sent down to perdition, ruined physically and morally, by having to submit to work under conditions known as 'sweated labour'. Oh woman of Guiana, throw off the shackles that bind you, there must be something you want to say for yourselves ... It is high time for British Guiana women to stop following men and taking whatever they say for granted – step out from behind and lead out somewhere, somehow, over rough and thorny places perhaps, it matters not so long as the goal is reached.[27]

Wood was also head of the local committee that hosted the second Inter-Colonial Conference of Women Social Workers (founded in 1936) in Georgetown in 1938. She complained during the proceedings that 'one section of the press appeared not in favour of the conference'.[28]

Another firebrand whose brief career in resistance has been lost to formal history is the self-styled Rev. Claude Smith of the 'Church Army of America'. While the local newspapers at the time were sceptical and critical of Smith and deemed him 'a demagogue', he appeared more attuned to assisting the poor and led an 'army of the unemployed' against colonial conditions while making representations on behalf of the people – mainly of Georgetown. While Smith's aberrant local actions and troubles with the law were sensationalised, this hid his underlying social activism. A reading through the press suggests that Claude Smith and his followers made an impact on the body politic between 1929 and 1933. The *Daily Argosy* with grudging backhand respect, deemed him the 'avowed champion of the oppressed'.[29]

Hubert Critchlow's activism

While not all labour unions were accorded the 'radical' brush, it was the BGLU, and especially its general secretary Hubert Critchlow, who was certainly ahead of his time. He became the target of a hostile press which drew associations of his activism with the pursuit of socialism and Communism. And Critchlow did not dispel these associations with his travel activity and approximate statements. After calling for 'universal manhood suffrage', he proceeded on a trip to London in 1931. After London, he visited Germany and Soviet Russia. On his return to Guyana, Critchlow is reported to be the first individual to introduce the term 'comrade' to the colony, and began to uphold the Red symbols in May Day marches. An editorial in the *Daily Chronicle* in early 1932 was critical of his connections with the moderate international trade union organisation, the International Confederation of Free Trade Unions, and his alleged familiarity with socialism. The editorial wryly suggested that 'Critchlow was one of the few persons in the colony that understands socialism, but his knowledge is so profound that much of what he says passes over our heads.'[30] It was certainly Critchlow's intent to aim for those heads when, in one of his speeches in the 1930s, he called for the organisation for workers to 'demonstrate against the system of the economic exploitation of the masses'.[31] Critchlow later gave a stirring speech titled 'Jesus and Labour' in a Guyana church. In this speech, mindful of local political conditions, and an audience distant from Soviet Russia, he connected his belief in class struggle to the teachings of Jesus:

In our trade unions, friendly Societies, and cooperative societies to get on, the ambition to climb, makes cowards of us all, and impels us often to forget the teachings of Christ or of the founders of our movement. Yes, let who will declare the contrary, the class war is here in our midst. Those of us who declare this fact, or, as it said, preach it, are not the inventors of the hideous system. It has come down to us from the past. We neither minimize its existence not obscure its evils by declaring its nonexistence.[32]

Statements like these emphasise the myriad ways in which radical ideas were pursued in Guyana in the 1930s. And the colonial authorities were alarmed. One of the newspapers angrily editorialised about Critchlow's activity, stating:

We do not know to what exploiters he is referring; we do not know that there is as yet in British Guiana any organised 'power' or 'might' of the workers – a fact which we sincerely regret; we do not know – since we have often heard it said that British Guiana needs them – who are the capitalists against whom Mr Critchlow complains. We admit our inability to apply to British Guiana with the deftness of other folk the broad principles of socialism as laid down by the Karl Marxes, the Lenins and the Bernard Shaws. Very probably the Marxians and the Soviets and the Shavians are more ignorant of economic conditions in undeveloped British Guiana than people like Mr Critchlow and ourselves are of economic conditions in industrialised Europe.[33]

The Second World War and Guyana – the shadow of Soviet Russia

A further phase in the development of the radical movement emerged with the Second World War and its aftermath. This was also the era in which the major colonial powers and the USA became deeply enmeshed in the fortunes of Guyana. In the 1940s a trade unionist in the colony, Jocelyn Hubbard, and a few of his friends, presumably the first group of self-conscious Marxists in the colony, formed what has traditionally been called the Marxist circle. The victories of the Red Army in Europe over Hitler appeared to have stimulated (essentially middle-class) individuals like Hubbard to bring into question the 'pre-war propaganda of an inefficient and hungry Russian nation'.[34] In his work, *Race and Guyana*, Hubbard also referenced the birth of the Victor Gollancz Left Book Club, named after a prominent British socialist (see Cardoso-da-Silva's chapter in this volume). This group held regular classes and studied the works of Karl Marx, Lenin and other Communists and socialists. It is noteworthy that there were already Marxist circles operating in Jamaica and Trinidad around the same period. Left publications had begun to penetrate the colony by this time. Some of these works included Edgar Snow's *Red Star Over China*, Hewlett Johnson's *The Soviet Power* and John Reed's *Ten Days that Shook the World*. Ashton Chase credits Hubbard with becoming a Marxist when it was unfashionable and also dangerous: 'he had a background of studying Marxism on his own'.[35] Hubbard, for his part, explained that the 'sickening realities of life in the colony' had led him first to 'a critical examination of the great religions, and eventually, by way of sociology to Marxism.'[36] Hubbard was also one of the earliest to identify the radical currents in British Guiana at the time, namely Garveyism, trade unionism and Marxism.

The formation of the Political Affairs Committee (PAC) in 1946 was another significant milestone for the radical movement. It is a now well-established narrative that with the coalition of Cheddi Jagan, Jocelyn Hubbard, Ashton Chase and Janet Jagan, the PAC was born – the first explicitly Marxist political group ever to be established in the colony. Among the goals of the original PAC was the need to:

> assist in the growth and development of labour and progressive movements of British Guiana to the end of establishing a strong, disciplined and enlightened party, equipped with the theory of scientific socialism; to provide information, and to present scientific political analysis on current affairs, both local and international, and to foster and assist discussion groups, through the circulation of bulletins, booklets and other printed matter.[37]

The PAC developed rapidly after this, significantly assisted by Cheddi Jagan's militant advocacy inside and outside the halls of power from 1947. It attracted other individuals, including a young lawyer, Forbes Burnham, who would later become one of the leaders of the People's Progressive Party and a major figure in the political life of independent Guyana. After spending time in England, he had returned in 1949 and was reputed to have maintained some political contact with the British Communist Party.

The rise of the PPP

A further point was scaled with the formation of the People's Progressive Party in 1950. One of the noticeable features of the nascent PPP was its heterogeneous make-up. The party's multiracial support base included members and supporters that included small shopkeepers, government workers, middle-class professionals, small farmers, sugar workers and the unemployed. Within this coalition of interests, a Marxist core that allegedly identified with the principles of Marxism–Leninism was unmistakable. The core personnel that sprang from the early PAC were essentially responsible for the theoretical preparation of the PPP leadership. The rhetoric emerging from the PPP leaders and the proliferation of references to left-wing causes and to the theory of Marxism have led many to wrongly conclude that the early PPP was 'Marxist–Leninist' along the lines of the Communist organisations in Europe and Latin America. The PPP's outlook in the early 1950s was in fact more modest. As Eusi Kwayana (formerly Sydney King), one of the leaders of the PPP, observed of the period:

> There was not a shred of evidence that the elected ministers sought orders from the Soviet Union, tried to link the currency to the rouble, a matter which was not under the control of an elected minister at any rate, sought to obtain military experts from that country, or any such thing, and this applied to all ideological tendencies among the elected ministers. I do not use the word cabinet, because there was no cabinet. It was a power-sharing cabinet between the old colonial officials led by the governor and elected ministers led by Cheddi Jagan and L.F.S. Burnham.[38]

Another account proposes that the ideology of the early PPP, while Marxist, was restricted to a few of the senior leaders and expressed itself in the desire for political independence and other social goals, in 'everyday language'.[39] This, he suggests, accounts for the popularity of the organisation. This pragmatism, however, did not mean that the PPP relied solely on the receptiveness of the masses to their message. Kwayana identified another source of influence from the Communist world. Apart from the number of left-wing pamphlets circulated in the colony, he advised that party activists should listen to Radio Moscow on the 'Berec' radio in the early 1950s.[40]

There was evidence of material and financial support from the Soviet Union and the British Communist Party. But even here the evidence suggests mild side play with 'Communism'. Even the British Security Service reported in 1951 that there was 'no evidence that the PPP is controlled or directed by any communist organisation outside the colony'.[41]

The Marxists – some say the true Marxists – were active and concentrated within a small group of individuals in the colony who would become known as the 'Anira group'.[42] Martin Carter, popular poet and scribe, was an early member of the PPP and belonged to the Anira group. His activity would lead him to prison, along with others. Carter was one of the shrewdest readers of people and events around him – and his poetry reflected this astuteness. Ben Carter describes their older brother Keith (Carter) as the person who 'converted Martin into socialism and Communism'.[43] Keith Carter left Guyana to read law at Oxford University in the late 1940s, and he would send home the latest Communist publications from the UK. His passion and the constant flow of material, including the *Communist Manifesto* and issues of the *Daily Worker*, the UK Communist publication, persuaded Martin Carter 'that politics was as important as the literature that had already captured his attention'.[44] E.R. Burrowes, artist and teacher, was influenced by and in turn influenced the burgeoning labour and working-class orientation and the conditions of the people. While his organisation was titled 'Working People's Art Class', Burrowes himself was not directly part of the political movement or any political party. Nevertheless, in the tenor of the time, a simple subscription to the *Daily Worker* caught the attention of the colonial authorities.[45]

In the general elections of 1953, the PPP won eighteen out of twenty-four seats and formed the government.[46] As a left-wing organisation working in a hostile colonial administration and in a hemispheric climate characterised by anti-Communism, its impact and success at the polls were remarkable. That very 'success' highlighted latent weaknesses in the movement. At both the level of experience and organisation the PPP had little time to gel before it thrust itself on the political scene. As it introduced 'radical' measures, there were still considerable limitations and restrictions on the PPP's room for manoeuvre and 'independence' in the colonial polity. Yet in giving history a 'shove' in 1953 the PPP appeared to harness multiple processes: the popularity of some of its individual leaders; anti-colonial sentiments; and strong labour roots. But when it began to implement reforms aimed at benefiting the working people, the British government, with hyperbolic fervour, suspended the constitution and removed a government that had occupied office for a mere 133 days.

While one of the reforms undertaken by the PPP revoked anti-Communist legislation, this regulation was more comparable with global anti-colonialism than with a reach for Communism. In short, the PPP was operating under a system of limited self-government where any idea of socialist transformation would have been impossible. Yet, to establish a Communist conspiracy the British, in making public their accusations against the short-lived PPP government, listed eleven major charges in a White Paper after the removal of elected ministers and detention of leading PPP members.[47] One of the charges was 'the removal of the ban on the entry of West Indian communists' by the 1953 government.[48] When the PPP government was suspended, it received little regional solidarity from other governments in the anglophone Caribbean. In fact, regional leaders like Alexander Bustamante, Grantley Adams, and Norman Manley were generally supportive of the British action to suspend the constitution.

One of the consequences of the PPP's removal from office became apparent later. After a period of 'marking time', solidarity within the party – always tenuous – collapsed, and in 1955 the organisation split into two wings, each claiming hegemony over the original PPP amid racial competition. It is from this formative period in British Guiana that we glimpse some of the perturbations that engulfed the Marxist movement and, by extension, the country over time. The overall pressure of the British move against the

PPP, which included the dispatch of troops to Georgetown, together with the weaknesses in the social and programmatic composition of the PPP and personal ambitions in the leadership, resulted in the rupture in the organisation into two factions, PPP (B) and PPP (J) – PPP (Burnhamite) and PPP (Jaganite), reflecting the initials of the two rival leaders, Burnham and Jagan. Some commentators have represented the split between Burnham and Jagan as an ideological fissure. However, while it is clear that ideology played some part in the conflict, the issue of race casts a long shadow over the process. One key figure at the time agreed in general with this proposition. Eusi Kwayana suggested that the division in the PPP was 'brought about by competition for leadership with undertones of racial choice, ideology, tactics, and such considerations'.[49] The New World Group, an intellectual formation established in the early 1960s, zeroed in on another key weakness when it noted that: 'unable creatively to apply theoretically acquired terminology to local reality they hovered between revolutionary Marxist utterances and unimaginative action'.[50] The two factions, while both formally professing to be socialist, eventually formalised the division after the 1957 general elections when the PPP (B) changed its name to the People's National Congress (PNC). With the PPP (J) winning the elections of 1957, a rise in racial insecurity was detected as a split along racial lines in the political movement became more conspicuous. The PPP and the PNC were now more or less focused on winning elections in a bid to see who would first lead the country to independence.

Now that the main political parties were separate, the racial composition of the country was, for the most part, represented in the support base of the two organisations. But where did they stand now in relation to the left? For the American and British policymakers, the matter of ideology was of the utmost importance. In some measure, the British authorities, in their efforts to separate fish from fowl, made the distinction for the parties in question by identifying with the lesser of two 'evils'. In the event, the PNC, the more identifiably moderate of the two, was deemed 'socialist' and the PPP held onto its image as a 'Communist' organisation for decades afterwards. Consequently narratives were established, especially by political office holders, of the expected roles of education, ideology and public policy in the independence struggle as custodians of competing narratives of political and social history.

In summary, over the forty-year period from 1917 to 1957 radicalism in Guyana was characterised by an array of individuals and organisations who assisted, over time, in framing the modern Guyanese political consciousness. The most far-reaching of these gains were made by the band of socialists who gave history a shove in Guyana in 1953. It is, however, unlikely that this grouping would have been possible without the multidimensional

legacy of radical struggle inspired by the collective accretion of contributions of early firebrands, trade unionists and movements. Yet, the narrative
of this period should be subjected to even further reanalysis and revision.
What the Scott argument clamours for in Jamaica can be transferred
seamlessly to Guyana: namely the call for the 'de-normalization' of the
'distinctive organization of chronologies and personalities and events'.[51]
For at least a generation now 'the 1950s' has continued to be the centre
of narrative historiography of Guyana's subsequent political and social
development.

What in the preceding period, from 1917 as this chapter has attempted
to unravel, set the foundation for the expansive memorialisation of the
successes and failures of the left in the 1950s in Guyana's lore? And if the
earlier period was of such formative import why is its significant impact on
the 1950s so absent from the narrative? It is evident, for a clearer understanding of the present, that the events and process condensed between
1917 and 1957 require an even more detailed visitation than this chapter
allows.

Notes

1 'Negro Toilers Speak at the World Congress of ILD', *Negro Worker*, February–
   March 1933.
2 David Scott, 'On the Very Idea of the Making of Modern Jamaica', *Small Axe*,
   54 (2017).
3 Cited in Allan Young, *The Approaches to Local Self-Government in British
   Guiana* (Bristol: Longmans, Green and Co., 1958), 37. Young was citing the
   editorial in *The Times* (London) of 19 August 1845, which described the nascent
   village movement in British Guiana as the product of 'little bands of socialists'.
4 These two riots, while different in origins and outcome, were characterised in
   both cases by the destruction of mainly Portuguese property by angry African-
   Guyanese, preceded by economic and tension between the two ethnic groups.
5 Clem Seecharan, *Bechu: 'Bound Coolie' Radical in British Guiana 1894–1901*
   (Kingston: University of the West Indies Press, 1999).
6 The Rev. Shirley arrived in British Guiana in 1901 and was involved with at
   least three Guyana newspapers in the colony – one of his forms of agitation.
   Shirley died in 1933.
7 Walter Rodney, *A History of the Guyanese Working People, 1881–1905*
   (Baltimore, MD: Johns Hopkins University Press, 1981), 171.
8 A nationalist, English-language Indian newspaper founded in 1905 by Aurobindo
   Ghosh. It was first published on 6 August 1906.
9 At a wider level – and attempting to get into the debate in Walter Rodney's
   head – the question arises: what are the main differences between 'riot' and

'rebellion'? Does the former suggest disorganisation and an inchoate, perhaps pejoratively assumed response? And if so are we semantically privileging the interpretation of the 'powers that be' to wit, that a riot is a bad thing? And if 'rebellion' is the sought mantra – what qualifies it over 'riot'? Organisation? 'Clear' purpose? Leadership? 'Regulation' as against the pejorative 'riot'?

10 Quoted by Edwin Slosson, 'Why not Swap the Philippines for Something Near Home', *The Independent*, 28 February 1916.

11 Kimani Nehusi, 'The Causes of the Protest of 1905' in Winston McGowan, James G. Rose and David A. Granger (eds), *Themes in African Guyanese History* (Georgetown: Free Press, 1998).

12 Ashton Chase, *A History of Trade Unionism in Guyana 1900–1961* (Georgetown: New Guyana Company, 1966), 21.

13 See Rodney, *A History of the Guyanese Working People*.

14 Chase, *A History of Trade Unionism in Guyana*, 22.

15 A.R.F. Webber, *A Centenary History and Handbook of British Guiana 1831–1931* (Georgetown: The Argosy Co. Ltd., 1931), 330.

16 See Jocelyn Hubbard, *Race and Guyana: The Anatomy of a Colonial Enterprise* (Georgetown: New Guyana Company, 1969). Hubbard, with the image of 'communist sympathizer', sought a seat in the legislature but was defeated by J. Nicolson of the LCP (League of Coloured Peoples), who beat him in the North Georgetown constituency.

17 *Ibid.*, 48.

18 The Bill's penalty was draconian. One of the provisions allowed for life imprisonment: 'any person who is guilty of an offence against the Ordinance shall be liable to penal servitude for life, or to imprisonment with or without hard labour for a period not exceeding seven years'. 'Seditious Publications – Importation and Distribution a Criminal Offence', *Daily Argosy*, 6 September 1919.

19 Letter from John Johnson, *Daily Argosy*, 24 September 1919.

20 'Editorial: A Menace to Honest Criticism', *Daily Argosy*, 7 September 1919.

21 'The British Guiana Workers' League', *Daily Chronicle*, 25 May 1930.

22 Francis Drakes [Kimani Nehusi], 'The Middle Class in the Political Economy of British Guiana 1870–1928', *History Gazette*, 11 (August 1989), 7–8.

23 Harold Lutchman, *From Colonialism to Cooperative Republic* (Rio Piedras: Institute of Caribbean Studies, 1974), 74.

24 James Rose, 'The New Arrivant: Cheddi Jagan and the Politics of the 1940s', *Stabroek News*, 20 March 1997.

25 Francis Drakes [Kimani Nehusi], 'The Development of Guyanese Political Organisations up to 1953', *History Gazette*, 27 (December 1990), 2.

26 Gertie Wood, 'To Guianese Women', *Daily Chronicle*, 1 March 1931.

27 Gertie Wood, 'To Guianese Women', *Daily Chronicle*, 1 March 1931.

28 'Inter-Colonial Women Social Worker's Conference', *The Guiana Review*, 14 August 1938.

29 'Wild Words – Rev CN Smith's Unemployment Demonstration', *Daily Argosy*, 6 February 1930.

30 'Editorial: Dangerous Statements', *Daily Chronicle*, 11 February 1932.

31 'Relief for the Unemployed: Mr Critchlow to Stage Demonstration', *Daily Argosy*, 9 September 1930.

32 'Jesus and Labour: Interesting Address by Mr H. Critchlow', *Daily Chronicle*, 3 April 1932.

33 'Editorial', *Daily Chronicle*, 11 February 1932.

34 Hubbard, *Race and Guyana*, 50.

35 At a function to celebrate the 50th anniversary of the PAC, Freedom House, Georgetown, 12 February 1996.

36 Reminiscences in the Hubbard Files, Caribbean Research Library, University of Guyana.

37 People's Progressive Party, *21 Years, 1950–1971* [Anniversary Publication] (Georgetown: New Guyana Company, 1971), 1.

38 Eusi Kwayana, 'There was No Communist Plot in 1953', *Stabroek News*, 30 October 2005.

39 Maurice St Pierre, *Anatomy of Resistance: Anti-Colonialism in Guyana 1823–1966* (London: Macmillan, 1999), 88.

40 Phone conversation with Eusi Kwayana, 29 March 2019.

41 Christopher Andrew, *Defend the Realm: The Authorized History of MI5* (New York: Alfred Knopf, 2009), 460.

42 Kimani Nehusi and others place this small urban grouping's birth as 1950. This group, Nehusi indicates, began to 'disintegrate by 1956'. Kimani Nehusi, *A People's Political History of Guyana, 1838–1964* (Hertford: Hansib, 2018), 520.

43 Martin Carter, *University of Hunger: Collected Poems and Selected Prose*, ed. Gemma Robinson (Tarset: Bloodaxe Books, 2006), 20.

44 *Ibid.*

45 Nehusi, *A People's Political History of Guyana*, 342, cites Stanley Greaves as the source of this information.

46 The government in 1953 was a limited ministerial government. There was an Executive Council made up of six elected ministers from the PPP, one nominated member from the Upper House, the Attorney-General, the Chief Secretary and the Financial Secretary, with the Governor of the colony in the chair. The Governor was head of government and held veto power. The Executive Council could advise the Governor but he was not bound to accept the advice. The six PPP ministers were Dr J.P. Lachmansingh, Sydney King (Eusi Kwayana), L.F.S. Burnham, Dr Cheddi Jagan, Jainarine Singh and Ashton Chase.

47 The eleven charges in the White Paper included the following examples of this 'conduct': '(i) Fomenting of strikes for political ends; (ii) Attempting to oust established trade unions by legislative action; (iii) Removal of the ban on the entry of West Indian Communists; (iv) Introduction of a bill to repeal the Undesirable Publications Ordinance and the flooding of the territory with Communist Literature; (v) Misuse of rights of appointment to boards and committees; (vi) Spreading of racial hatred; (vii) Plan to secularize church schools and to rewrite textbooks to give them a political bias; (viii) Neglect of their administrative duties; (ix) Undermining of the loyalty of the Police;

(x) Attempts to gain control of the public service; (xi) Threats of violence.'
See British Government White Paper on the Suspension of the Constitution of
British Guiana (20 October 1953).

48 British Government White Paper on the Suspension of the Constitution of British
Guiana (20 October 1953).

49 Eusi Kwayana, 'Guyana's Race Problems and My Part in Them', *The Rodneyite*,
2 (1992).

50 David DeCaires and Miles Fitzpatrick, 'Twenty Years of Politics in Our Land',
New World Journal, Independence Issue (1966), 42.

51 Scott, 'On the Very Idea of the Making of Modern Jamaica', 46.

7

Racialising the Caribbean Basin: the Communist racial agenda for the American hemisphere, 1931–35

Sandra Pujals

Up until 1931, the race issue had not been a significant element in the Communist agenda for the Spanish-speaking territories of the Caribbean Basin. For the most part, the region's radical intellectual community was predominantly white, and non-black, indigenous populations were the most preponderant racial minority in the territory. The establishment of the Caribbean Bureau of the Comintern in New York in 1931, however, forced a reassessment of the subject, as the Communist Party of the United States' (CPUSA's) Colonial Department undertakings in the West Indies merged with the Caribbean Bureau's anti-imperialist blueprint. The result was an amalgamated anti-racism initiative, American as much as Caribbean, in which slavery served as a common denominator, while imperialism and capitalism provided the vehicle for the perpetuation of exploitation.

The new geographical latitude for the race issue was meant to extend the reach of the directives established for the CPUSA on the matter following the Sixth Congress of the Comintern in 1928. In practical terms, however, the inclusion of race in the Communist agenda caused a new round of clashes between Comintern agencies and radical networks in the Spanish-speaking Caribbean Basin, since the instructions attempted to enforce distinctly black elements such as a shared experience of slavery as a common denominator for the region, artificially designed and imposed from New York. Although the Comintern set aside its race agenda as the fascist threat became a primary focus by 1935, its early foundations for an anti-racism platform added colour to the post-Second World War era's decolonisation debates, particularly in the British Caribbean, while providing the new 'democratic' era with a cultural and political pantheon of leaders previously tied to its agencies and front organisations. In the Spanish-speaking Caribbean, however, the racial issue not only added to the already mounting friction between local and international Communism, but also accelerated the severing of the two spheres' traditional ties and maintained a racially segregated radical agenda for most of the region.

This chapter examines the role of the Caribbean Bureau of the Comintern in creating a Communist race agenda for the Caribbean Basin during the first half of the 1930s.[1] Its main objective is to add dimension and texture to the sort of simplistic, racially focused optic that sometimes distracts from more intricate, underlying circumstances far beyond the mere colour-schemed, i.e. Red/Black, encounter. The study discusses the development of a project that brought together elements of anti-imperialist campaigns in the Spanish Caribbean, anti-lynching struggles managed from CPUSA headquarters in New York, and anti-Garveyist Communist initiatives in the British West Indies. The analysis also provides glimpses into the political and social environment within which the region's Communist internationalist activity related to race evolved at a crucial stage of development. The discussion relies on the documentation of the Caribbean Bureau, the Comintern intermediary office in charge of organising the regional initiative for the Caribbean Basin in coordination with the CPUSA and black radical enclaves in New York. Complementary information from other trustworthy sources attest to the complexity of the Comintern's equivocal race agenda.[2]

Although the interaction between Communists of African descent and the Comintern has been studied extensively, inquiries concerning the repercussions of the 'Red and Black' Communist phenomenon in the Caribbean are still scarce in comparison.[3] Barry Carr, for example, has examined the role of West Indian immigrant workers in Cuba during the 1920s and 1930s, particularly in the sugar industry. His work on black migrant participation in radical activity and strikes on the island underscores a generally ignored legacy of these groups outside their own places of origin.[4] Historians have also documented the participation of British West Indian immigrants, particularly from Jamaica, in iconic black cultural phenomena like the 'New Negro' and the Harlem Renaissance, and their contributions to Communist radicalism in the US.[5] In general, the transnational aspect of the encounter seems to be a common denominator for most of these historical narratives related to race. Other works explore the ways in which the Caribbean sensibility as a personal experience merged with the ideological as two sides of a coin, or as forms of expression beyond limited political lines, as in the case of revered West Indians Claude McKay and Leonard 'Tim' Hector.[6] The interaction between the European and American radical communities, another transnational angle, has also contributed to an ever-expanding scope of action and activity for this particular sort of transversal exchange.[7] A recent work also poses a triangular interaction between New York, Mexico and the 'Black Caribbean', which is, for the most, not authenticated by solid documentation other than Communist periodicals and manicured official reports.[8] But despite numerous studies, the Caribbean experience with international Communism in relation to race is still represented by a scarce volume of geographically limited sources.

In addition to a restricted topography, an effective assessment of this particular episode of Caribbean history has also been hindered by limited methodological approaches, since many scholars dealing with the 'Black and Red' metaphor focus on the race issue theoretically. But how far can literary analysis and critical race theory take us in a historical vacuum, without a solid context of the contemporary Soviet political moment with regards to Communist internationalism? For example, in her interesting 'how to' reading guide on several black figures' experiences in the Soviet Union, Kate A. Baldwin points out the construction of imaginaries related to race and ideology as a crosspollination process. She fails to take into account, however, underlying realities that could lead to distorted conclusions when reading between the lines and 'beyond the colour line'.[9] In 1931, Stalin's letter to *Proletarskaia revoliutsiia* led to the establishment of a particular sort of censorship of historical texts based on ideological loyalty, according to central party *kult-prop* directives.[10] In 1934, the First Writers Congress made ideological loyalty mandatory for written texts in general. Works written by foreigners in the Soviet Union were also subjected to this regulation. Not keeping these political nuances in mind can result in misleading assessments of writings that might have been altered, since levels of censorship could fluctuate from elimination of words, sentences or paragraphs to rewriting, or even completely ghost-writing, texts.[11]

Except for studies that examine different aspects of the evolution of radical activity in black communities, surveys that focus on race in relation to ideology rarely incorporate the Communist ecosystem.[12] The dynamics of life within the Comintern network of front organisations and allied radical fiefdoms is either selectively set aside or not understood. Many authors have very little knowledge of significant catalysts such as behind-the-scene negotiations and bureaucratic manoeuvres, networks, hidden agendas or rivalries, particularly in the case of the Comintern or the Soviet *nomeklatura*'s back alleys of power. As a result, conclusions are sometimes tainted by a racially biased panorama of a white Communist power structure overcoming black ideals of equality and justice, which allows very little room for questions. The objectivity of a black Communist's views, for example, is not contested even when a financial link existed between an author and the Soviet regime, as in the case of Langston Hughes, whose exorbitant 2,000 rouble salary for a series of articles for *Izvestiia* coincide with the year of the First Writers Congress' resolutions.[13] The Comintern's possible agency in relation to travel expenses to and from New York to the Caribbean, Europe, and Moscow for many of the black activists during the Great Depression, or the possibility that some of them may have actually been agents in the Comintern's payroll, are other considerations rarely scrutinised when analysing their relationship to the ideology.

For the most part, racism and discrimination is still the common denominator when explaining the lack of success of the Black and Red juncture in the Americas. However, the documentation of the Comintern's Caribbean Bureau during its short period of operations between 1931 and 1935 affords a very different panorama in relation to international Communism's racial agenda and activity. The Caribbean Bureau's organisational structure, for example, suggests a complex, multilevelled dynamic in which race was perhaps one of the less commanding factors. However, while segregation may have been a common denominator as an inevitable by-product of traditional race perspectives and relations worldwide, distance and separation within the Communist network went beyond usual divisions based on colour.

Aside from contributing details concerning the development of a coordinated Communist project related to race beyond the usual colour binary, this chapter poses several significant points to consider from the start. First, Communists involved in making the Comintern racial agenda operative, both black and white, did not necessarily relinquish their distinct optic regarding race, or their own racial misapprehensions for that matter. As a result, the project willy-nilly recreated and perpetuated segregation, in view of the traditional stereotypes and hesitancy on both sides of the racial divide. After all, even a sensible observer as Claude McKay had not been able to look beyond his experience with racial discrimination as he explained that the (only?) reason for Otto Huiswoud's selection as CPUSA black delegate for the Fourth Comintern Congress was because of the latter's lighter skin.[14] Agents' different understanding of race in the Spanish-speaking Caribbean Basin as opposed to the British and French West Indies added another degree of separation, since the racial demarcations between blacks and whites were not as rigid in the Spanish Caribbean. In addition, Caribbean immigrants' experience in New York may have been different as well, since migrants from the Spanish Caribbean had access to a much more solid support system of social networks operating between the region and New York since the late nineteenth century.

The Caribbean region itself was characterised by innumerable differences which promoted and exacerbated fragmentation among the former colonies of three main European powers: Spain, France and Great Britain. The first layer of inevitable separation consisted of common elements related to conditions within the Caribbean Basin itself, such as geographical demarcations, and language and cultural differences long-since established by the imperial masters' particular nationalities. There was no common language or cultural bond connecting the three main Caribbean regions. The disparity of experiences was even more significant between the islands and the other regions of the Spanish Caribbean Basin, such as Central America, Mexico, Colombia and Venezuela. Another discrepancy involved the Spanish Caribbean's intricate, racial colour palette which, unlike in the other imperial domains, included a wide variety of skin tonalities and nuances in facial qualities still understood as 'white' features. British West Indies Communists' attempt to fuse the Spanish racial rainbow into the unified, distinctly 'black' identity they envisioned probably added another dimension of tension and possible conflict. In addition, within the area sometimes identified as the 'Black Caribbean', differences in conditions in view of economic and social development of the larger territories like Jamaica, perhaps created another level of segregation and distancing even among racially similar workers. Finally, the Bureau's agenda also contemplated the black experience in the United States, particularly in the Southern region, adding yet another layer of complexity and diversity to its race project.

Along with the particularities of racial sensibilities, Communist internationalism's intricate organisational machinery added another stratum of segregation. The tiered, decentralised administrative structure dictating directives and supervising operations, and a multicultural, multilingual staff scattered around the world became destabilising factors. Despite an apparent cohesive dynamic within the Comintern's organisational structure, the system and internal operations were highly fragmented and decentralised. Activity, for example, was divided into two basic functions, one connected with the establishment of Communist political organisations, such as parties and groups, and another to trade union activity. Management of these two main, mostly separate, enclaves was also divided between two principal agencies: the Comintern's umbrella edifice of front organisations such as International Red Aid in the political domain, and the Red International of Labour Unions, or Profintern, for trade union matters. Each agency had its own leadership, headquarters, agendas and committees, along with numerous departments in charge of specific tasks. In addition, throughout most of the 1920s, both conglomerates followed an 'offshoring' strategy, using already established local and regional organisations and leaders as allies or intermediaries for activities that responded to a rather generic radical agenda.

In the Spanish-speaking Caribbean Basin, which included the islands, Central America and Mexico, and the coastal countries in South America, Colombia and Venezuela, the Comintern's organisational infrastructure followed a similar 'offshoring' pattern. Throughout the second half of the 1920s, the Anti-Imperialist League of the Americas (LADLA) served as liaison for Communist internationalism as part of its 'offshoring' system. Until the structural reorganisation of the Comintern's regional operations in late 1930, and the establishment of the new centralised office in New York, the Caribbean Bureau of the Comintern, the LADLA covertly organised Communist groups and parties in the region, such as the Communist Parties of Colombia and El Salvador, and managed the iconic initiative *Manos Fuera de Nicaragua* (MAFUENIC) in support of Augusto César Sandino's struggle against US intervention in that Central American country. Communication and interaction between the LADLA and groups in the other Caribbean regions was rare, since radical activity in the British, Dutch and French West Indies was handled by Communist enclaves in their respective colonial metropolises.

The establishment of the Caribbean Bureau of the Comintern in New York brought an additional layer of divisions and organisational segregation. Local leaders, for example, had to acquiesce to instructions formulated by CPUSA agents in New York according to directives in Russian from the Latin American Secretariat, a *troika* that included a seasoned Soviet bureaucrat with extensive knowledge on China and Central Asia, Georgi Skalov (Sinani), and an Italian-Argentinian Communist, Vittorio Codovilla.[15] Needless to say, most members of this new consolidated leadership had very little knowledge of the Caribbean reality, let alone its intricate racial dimensions. They relied on the reports of a 'flying brigade' of selected, loyal agents, although not necessarily nationals of the region, sent on missions as *instruktors* and observers.[16] Finally, the Soviets' own grassroots agenda added another complexity: the government's policy towards their own ethnic, 'black' minorities in Central Asia, since it could prove beneficial as yet another clearly delineated 'у нас/у вас' demarcation of good and evil to identify the United States and the Soviet Union.[17] This compilation of numerous geographical, cultural and organisational factors, both local and international, was bound to create a perfect storm that inevitably would lead to the failure of the Comintern's consolidated race agenda in the Americas.

The race issue in the Comintern's American domain: the first decade

Ironically, race had itself been a very segregated issue within the US radical domain throughout the 1920s, mostly because black factory workers were still a minority, especially in industries which required particular skilled labour.[18] By the middle of the decade, a radical organisation with close allegiance to the Communist Party, the American Negro Labour Congress, began to represent the struggle for African-American workers' rights in several industrial hubs of the East Coast, while also identifying up-and-coming leaders that could be co-opted to party work. But in general,

African Americans' plight as part of the US proletarian population was still, for the most, invisible within the Communist establishment, as was the concept of 'racism' which was then defined as 'white chauvinism'.[19] Despite complaints from black delegates in several Comintern congresses during the early 1920s, the Soviets paid little more than lip service to the group's critical assessment of the party's own 'white chauvinist' deficiencies, or to their requests for more attention to the issue.

During the Sixth Comintern Congress in 1928, however, a group of Communist delegates of African descent began a lobbying campaign for the inclusion of race as an important item in the internationalist agenda. In particular, James W. Ford, an outstanding Communist organiser and party member then residing in New York, complained before the Congress about the lack of attention the party had given to black workers' deplorable living conditions and the abuse they experienced in the workplace. A Congress resolution several months later, 'On the Negro Question in the United States', granting high priority to the 'Negro question', was the starting point for a reorganisation campaign within the CPUSA in New York and the establishment of a Negro Department under the direction of a Dutch Guinean and Buffalo District organiser, Otto Huiswoud, who happened to also be the 'highest ranking person of African descent in the party'.[20]

The new line, although promising and spirited, generated more internal conflicts in the Communists' camp. Before the resolution had been adopted, the issue had already given way to polemics even among the black delegates, since not all of them favoured the supposedly Leninist theoretical formula of African Americans' right to national self-determination as an option. Once the new directives were put to the test in New York, the factionalist crisis inside the CPUSA came into play, as the resolution called for the eradication of 'white chauvinism' inside the party, which could be used as a weapon against political rivals such as the Lovestonite group. Communists' zeal in making the race issue a priority also resulted in confrontations between the local union chiefs and the CPUSA's central leadership. The party's 'inept and sloppy work' exacerbated tensions.[21] In 1929, for example, the CPUSA leadership insisted on a strong racial component in a textile strike in Gastonia, North Carolina, that was purely a 'white-on-white' conflict, causing a serious rift between the strike bosses and the New York leaders. As the local Communists resisted the imposition of a line that was far from the demographic reality they faced, several were charged with white chauvinism and even expelled from the party. In New York, the needle trade, composed of mostly Jewish and Italian immigrants, was also assaulted by white Communist champions of black workers' rights, which led to a series of noisy show trials against 'white chauvinism', like the one against August Yokinen, a Finnish worker at the Finnish Workers Club of Harlem.[22]

Despite the enthusiasm of the sporadic campaigns, the CPUSA's fight against 'white chauvinism' gave way to very few long-term results during its first decade of activity. In 1932, Earl Browder, the CPUSA general secretary, still complained that the party would not be successful in this struggle 'unless it begins by burying out of its own ranks every manifestation and trace of the influence of white chauvinism ... [and the belief of] Negro inferiority'.[23] Within the black camp itself, however, the work of the CPUSA Negro Department's feisty leadership led to slight but fundamental organisational victories. One of the most significant, perhaps, was the consolidation of a radical opposition faction within Marcus Garvey's Universal Negro Improvement Association (UNIA) as a first step to an alternative movement centred in Jamaica, allied to the Communists and the American Negro Labor Congress (ANLC). According to Otto Huiswoud's report on the 1929 UNIA convention, Garvey's mismanagement and corrupt financial dealings prepared the way for a heated standoff between him and Garvey himself on the subject of black labour and capitalism.[24] 'As a result of the debate', Huiswoud asserted, 'I managed to get a few statements in the press, but what is more important, some of the workers (Garveyites) came around asking me to help them form trade unions. I immediately seized the opportunity, organized a committee and scheduled a number of meetings.'[25]

The organisational strategy behind Huiswoud's new trade union formation followed the usual model of Communists' Trojan Horse tactics of infiltration and fragmentation from within an organisation. As the Communist rep himself admitted, 'I've had to work almost solely through members of the U.N.I.A.'[26] 'We appointed', he added, 'committees of all the trades represented, assigning them the task of carrying on the propaganda work in their respective trades, with the purpose of forming local trade unions. A larger committee ... is to aid and supervise the work of these local bodies and also to work out plans for the formation of a federation of the local unions to be formed.' Huiswoud also suggested a name for the new organisation: 'The Jamaica Trades and Labour Union', composed of an eclectic array of trades such as carpenters, masons, painters, tailors, domestic labourers, mechanics, dressmakers, sugar boiler workers, bakers, clerks and railroad workers. By the time the round of meetings was done, the group had a membership of 200 local workers.[27]

Meanwhile in Central America, the Venezuelan neophyte Communist Ricardo Martínez embarked in a pilgrimage throughout several territories in an attempt to consolidate another zone of trade union activity in the Americas for the Comintern front organisation, the Red International of Labour Unions or Profintern. In 1927, Martínez, who was founder of an organisation of Venezuelan exiles in New York, had won notoriety for his outstanding speech against US intervention in Nicaragua during the fifth

Congress of the American Federation of Labour's sister conglomerate, the Pan-American Labour Federation (PALF).[28] As a result, he was invited to participate in the Profintern's Fourth Congress in Moscow, and elected member of its Executive Committee. As new organiser for the Profintern, Martínez's mission in Central America focused on establishing unions affiliated to the Communists and recruiting delegates for the 1929 founding congress of the *Confederación Sindical Latino Americana* (CSLA) which was meant to compete with the PALF for trade union hegemony in the region.

By December 1930, a Caribbean Subcommittee began working in New York as organisational overseer for radical trade-union activity in the region, promoting a 'systematic relationship' with the CSLA, affiliated to the Profintern. One year later, an expanded version of the group was already operating as an official Comintern intermediary agency, the Caribbean Bureau of the Comintern, a subregional appendage linked to the Latin American Secretariat in Moscow, with Ricardo Martínez as one of its leading figures.[29] The new agency was meant to consolidate activity and finances by attaching itself to the CPUSA's Colonial Department, which, in turn, expanded the geographical scope of activity to the British and French Caribbean territories. As the new decade began, Comintern-affiliated radical ventures in the Spanish-speaking Caribbean Basin, such as the Anti-Imperialist League of the Americas, as well as their management and network, had either disappeared or been restructured as part of the newly established regional office operating in New York.

First things first: assessing race in the Caribbean Bureau's domain

The point of departure for the development of a unified race agenda for the Caribbean Basin coincides with the establishment of the Caribbean Bureau of the Comintern in 1931. Located in New York, the new agency was responsible for the organisation of radical activity in the area, as an intermediary office for the Latin American Secretariat and liaison office for Comintern front organisations, such as the Anti-Imperialist League, the most active in the area. Geographically, the Caribbean Bureau extended the traditional boundaries for the region, which now comprehended the Spanish-speaking as well as the British and French territories. The unprecedented, geographical distribution, in turn, responded to the circumstances at that moment, which supposedly evinced the region's revolutionary potential. The winds of change in the political climate in Mexico, where many of the top Latin American Communists lived in exile, also forced the leadership to move the centre of radical operations from Mexico to New York. Centralisation of organisation and financial support, now in the hands of the CPUSA via its Colonial Department, was probably yet another consideration. Finally, the establishment of the Caribbean Bureau also forced a restructuring of the European Communist power structures in relation to their respective domains in the Caribbean, since now activity and, most importantly, finances, for race-related activity would be managed from New York's CPUSA quarters, and not from the traditional Comintern enclave in Hamburg, or the French and British Communist Parties.

Once settled in New York, the Caribbean Bureau defined several distinct areas of activity according to their particular conditions. The first one was Central America, where Augusto Sandino's anti-imperialist struggle was seen as a springboard for other revolts in nearby territories. The second comprised Venezuela and Cuba, then under unpopular dictatorial regimes. Another was the Lesser Antilles under British and French rule, in which racism and the plantations' unchecked exploitation of workers were the main issues. Although traditionally within the jurisdiction of other international Communist enclaves such as the British and French Communist Parties, the inclusion of the racial issue in these localities' radical agenda had opened the way to CPUSA intrusion, in view of its role as overseer of the struggle against race discrimination in the American region. Finally, there were support zones close to the main centres of action, including Puerto Rico, the Dominican Republic and Panama, as well as Colombia.[30] A small circle of CPUSA leaders shared the administration of the Bureau's operations with several exiled Cuban and Venezuelan leaders.[31] Due to the Latin American leaders' prior experience with anti-imperialist work in the Caribbean Basin and with the LADLA network of local Communists, anti-imperialism still served as a common denominator for activity in the region. In turn, the element of self-determination which also defined the Communists' race agenda facilitated the fusion of the Spanish Caribbean with its neighbouring British and French regional enclaves.

In view of the novel structure, the Bureau began by assessing the territory already charted, and restoring contact with local groups and leaders of the regional radical network the LADLA had previously organised from Mexico. Surreptitiously, the group also meant to reorganise the main Communist enclaves in the region under militant directives and strict centralisation, eliminating any 'bourgeois' vestiges in local leadership and policies. Out of all of these functions, collecting data seemed to be the most important activity during the first year, as it provided the necessary material to establish work plans and agenda priorities. Throughout 1931, meetings mostly consisted of continuous reports from either visiting instructors or local leaders.[32] Members of the Colonial Department also offered presentations on local conditions in the Bureau's newly acquired territories or the local activities of different radical associations in the city's Latin American community.[33] While some accounts underscored potential terrains of action in recently integrated zones such as Jamaica, and those long since left inactive, like Puerto Rico, others left little doubt of the internal disarray in some of the network's traditional outposts like Cuba and Colombia.

Data collecting also focused on race, in response to the Bureau's new mandate of consolidating the expanded Caribbean field of activity. However, the panorama was far from encouraging. In Colombia, for example, where 90 per cent of the population along its Pacific coastline and its coal mines were black, conditions and access were so difficult as to make it almost impossible to reach the area: 'They live there like in Africa, with huts off the ground ... The heat there is terrible. A white man cannot live there unless he is used to tropical climates.' Difficulties in travelling through the rugged terrain was another consideration, along with the strict regulations regarding access. 'For instance', the agent reporting pointed out, 'I could not venture in that territory ... It must be one that is [unintelligible] who travels across the mountains, under the pretense that he is going to work.' The only contact they had established in the area was limited to a few workers who occasionally went down to the nearest small town, Buena Vista, 'where we have a little group'.[34] Between 1933 and 1934, Bureau reports listed additional black communities in the Spanish-speaking Caribbean Basin, such as the one in Costa Rica's Puerto Limón, with a population of 22,000 black workers, mostly foreign.[35] In other places, however, the potential revolutionary force of race was lost. In Haiti, for instance, where the majority of the population was of African descent, the local Communist group's report basically left out most of them while heralding the activation of a 'projected agrarian-anti-imperialist revolution'. According to a Bureau letter to its leadership, they had not even mentioned 'one single word about the blacks, although their national problem will also play a role in the revolution'.[36]

Inconsistencies between the demographic realities regarding colour and race as a policy priority was also noted in the case of Cuba. The original appraisal of the situation included a strong critic in view of the party's serious 'failures in Negro work'. 'One could say', the reporter pointed out, 'that there is no such thing as the Negro question in Cuba.' The appraisal also analysed conditions in comparison to the situation in the United States:

About 24 per cent of the population are colored [sic]. With such a high percentage you can see that the Negro question is not the same kind of a question as in the United States. It is a question of persecution and oppression, but it is a Negro question in a different respect ... They do not lynch Negroes there, but with a superficial condition of equality they are more exploited than the other workers.[37]

According to the Bureau's assessment, black workers were imported into Cuba to work in the sugar plantations, where they were treated as 'virtual slaves'. But even in the case of Cuban nationals, inequality and lack of opportunities still prevailed: 'The Negroes are less organized, they hold no leading positions in the government ... [They can] be motormen, but never conductors. So this equality is only on the surface. It is a mistake that this question has not been recognized by the Party.'[38]

But despite such insight on the potential revolutionary component of race in the region, hardly anything changed throughout the next four years within the Spanish Caribbean Communist microcosm. Local Communist organisations did very little to integrate black workers into their groups or to actively engage in activity with them. Even in the most intense radical period during the 1933 revolutionary wave, letters to the Cuban central committee depicted the organisation of black workers as 'excessively weak' given the 'current situation'.[39] Acts recorded serious weaknesses during the year's strike movements where blacks played a role: '[the] slogan of self-determination for blacks has been proclaimed in a mechanical way. Regions where the communists are fighting for self-determination, that is, where [blacks] are the majority of the population, are not specified.'[40] Leaders in New York did not seem altogether sure of just how efficient the local Communist vanguard had been with respect to a policy of joint action either: 'The union of white and black workers (natives, Jamaican, and Haitian) ... is also under scrutiny.'[41] All in all, the integration of several young black cadres into party work, including Lázaro Peña, the celebrated future leader of Cuba's *Confederación de Trabajadores Cubanos*, was perhaps the most significant result in the period's race front in Cuba.

Racialising the Caribbean Basin: the Caribbean Bureau and the Communist race agenda

Throughout the first half of the 1930s, the Comintern's Caribbean Bureau focused on a radical yet generic propaganda that strived to project a sense of unity among workers and peasants, beyond nationality, gender, race and local conditions, exploiting what the Communists understood to be a revolutionary crisis in the making within the zone. The Comintern's internationalist concept of a workers' world without boundaries also played a part in creating a panoramic projection of a Caribbean struggle for freedom and justice in unison. According to this design, the anti-imperialist forces in Nicaragua, for example, now struggled in tandem with those who opposed the Juan Vicente Gómez dictatorship in Venezuela and the Gerardo Machado regime in Cuba. Even when so far apart, and despite their national particularities, these anti-imperialist legions and the movements to end the 'white terror' of the dictatorial regimes in Venezuela and Cuba also joined those who opposed the lynching of blacks in the Southern states of the US or the death sentences for the two anarchist workers, Nicolo Sacco and Bartolomeo Vanzetti, and simultaneously marched alongside those who opposed racial discrimination against black workers in Jamaica and Trinidad or indigenous plantation workers in El Salvador.[42]

In view of the multicultural and multilingual consolidated territory of activity the Bureau now had to tackle, unity was also underscored as a message when addressing communication strategies. While language traditionally segregated Caribbean territories, now it served to represent the many voices of one and the same common struggle. The Bureau spearheaded the use of a language of inclusion that would take into consideration cultural, linguistic and racial differences. Directives not only called for a 'clear and simple language' when addressing regional political and social issues in the Communist press, but insisted on including ethnic and racial groups traditionally ignored even by radical opposition groups.[43] In recruiting campaigns, the agency acknowledged the importance of these demographic elements, along with that of women workers, in view of their significant presence in the area.[44] In the case of important celebrations such as anti-imperialist demonstrations, instructions also pointed out that 'special manifestos for Indians and Blacks – in their own languages – are of great importance'.[45]

The Bureau's agenda also articulated the process of consolidation of organisation and activity that the new agency personified. Instructions called for a rhetorical fusion of 'the struggle against yankee imperialism and complete national independence of the countries of the Caribbean', adding the racial issue into the formula. Guidelines pointed out that the anticolonial movement was also 'a struggle against white supremacy of yankee imperialism against discrimination'. Within this formula, 'yankee imperialism' in the Caribbean almost imperceptibly blended with notions of 'lynching yankees' in the United States, while the struggle against unemployment and salary cuts simultaneously merged with the striving for 'complete equality' not only for blacks, but for women workers, and young workers as well. While in the United States and Europe, Communist ideology singled out capitalism as the enemy, 'yankee imperialism' meant to identify a variety of categories of exploitation in the Caribbean. The racial differentiation of 'white' versus 'black' also blurred national boundaries, particularly in the case of the differences between US and British imperialism, which in turn made it easier to identify the two as one and the same sort of evil.[46]

Instructions to Communist groups and parties in the region also enforced a particular attention to the racial element during special campaigns and celebrations. For the 1933 May 1st celebration, for example, the Bureau instructed local parties 'to uphold slogans and grievances of the indigenous populations and nationally oppressed Blacks, and spread the maxim of self-determination for these nationalities'.[47] That same year, plans for regional demonstrations in support of the Scottsboro case in the United States underscored the need 'to engage Blacks and indigenous people, broadcasting special slogans against discrimination and in support of absolute equality for the nationally oppressed peoples'.[48] The ideological and class issues were set aside, perhaps in view of the local populations' weak response to Communist propaganda. For the May 1st celebrations one year later, the Bureau recommended the parties to apply 'a united front in the base tactic' as one of the main tasks for Communists, 'without distinction of political affinities, sex, age, colour'.[49]

Despite the apparent facade of unity, however, the Bureau's agenda manifested a segregated concept of the area in view of its multicultural complexity and traditional geographical divisions established centuries before. Work in the region depended on whether activity would be carried out in the Spanish-speaking Caribbean or in the British or French areas. Administrative jurisdiction created another element of segregation, since different offices handled activity according to territory or specific work performed. For example, the Bureau established a special, separate subcommittee 'to further elaborate the C[ommunist] I[nternational's] plan among the black masses of the West Indies, especially in Jamaica and Trinidad'.[50] There was also the case of segregating terminology that stemmed from customary denominations inherited from Latin American culture, especially Spanish Caribbean lexical forms, since the Bureau's main leaders were Cuban and Venezuelan nationals. For example, while the Spanish-speaking Communists from the Spanish Greater Antilles were usually classified in documents by their nationality, i.e. Cuban or Puerto Rican, a separate term – *'antillanos'* – identified members from the other islands.[51] Hardly regarded as offensive or racially demeaning, the idiom traditionally meant to differentiate nationals from the non-Spanish-speaking Caribbean islands as a separate group in view of language and nationality, although the racial connotation could also apply. In other instances, instructions in Spanish used a distinctly racial denomination, *'Antillas de población negra* [Antilles of black population]', to identify the British and French Caribbean islands.[52]

In addition, the fact that the CPUSA strived to demonstrate its zeal in putting into action Comintern directives concerning race ironically also perpetuated segregation, since colour was underscored to confirm progress in the fulfilment of instructions. As a result, the discourse used to convey achievement on the race issue could sometimes create a somewhat showcase or 'token' effect with regards to the Communist network's scarce black leaders or workers, who were championed for their apparent 'special' status. Success was hyped even in the case of black non-Communist 'allies' at a time when Comintern 'Third Period' policies shunned this sort of cooperation in most other spheres or regions: 'At the head of the Confederation [the Cuban trade union conglomerate] was a general secretary, a Negro – Pelar [Pilar] Herrero. I was very glad to know that he was a non-Party worker, a Negro, a Negro from the Harbour Workers.'[53] In other cases, eagerness in implementing central directives on race did not translate well as a local black revolutionary imaginary. The muddled boundaries between racial struggle and revolution were a source of concern, as in the case of Cuba's Oriente region, where a number of strikes led by radical black workers signalled a potentially unsavoury crisis for the Communists: 'In view of the lack of popularity [of the slogan of self-determination for oppressed nationalities], it is often misinterpreted as [a way of] forcing self-determination, which, in the case of Cuba, has caused confusion among the black masses regarding the Communist Party line in this respect.'[54]

The Bureau's recurring complaints regarding the ineffective handling and disappointing results related to the race issue indicated other manifestations of segregation. For one, difficulties in communication between the central leadership in New York and the Caribbean periphery seems to have contributed to lack of information. In other cases, Caribbean interpretations of policies may have been very different to those in the United States, given the disparity in experiences, as the misreading of black self-determination in the Cuban context suggests. In turn, miscommunication and misinterpretation could also conceal another sort of segregation: local opposition to centralised policy. In July 1932, the Bureau instructed the central committee of the Cuban party to include in its immediate agenda 'the formulation of a program of demands for blacks, posing the question of equal rights and self-determination', and setting aside columns in its organ *El Comunista* for a discussion of the matter.[55] Several months later, however, Bureau acts frustratingly noted the local party's extreme delay in submitting a report on the subject, which was probably a tactic intended to snub central directives or cover up a job not carried out.[56] Acts also recorded the 'omission' of information, as in the case of the Cuban party's silence on their apparent mishandling of the self-determination issue in Oriente, one of the leading radical black regions.[57]

While the Caribbean Bureau's agenda includes slight indications of some cooperation between Spanish-speaking Caribbean Communist enclaves and the CPUSA's Colonial and Negro Departments, the scope and results of this interaction seem to have been minimal, according to the Comintern documents themselves. Archival materials, for instance, do not confirm a regular interaction of leaders. Out of more than one thousand Comintern agents and Communist 'fellow travellers' identified in Lazar and Victor Jeifets' biographical *magna opera, America Latina en la Internacional Comunista*, James W. Ford stands out as the only black leader involved in the region during the period.[58] Educated under a strict theoretical, militant curriculum in the Lenin International School, Ford masterminded the establishment of the International Trade Union Committee of Negro Workers (ITUCNW) for the Profintern in 1928, which served as the operational platform for a militant fragmentation and Stalinist takeover of the Pan-Africanist movement.[59] As Profintern rep for Latin America in 1930, Ford's experience and savvy probably proved valuable at a time when the Profintern was busy taking over control of local radical networks previously under its nemesis' jurisdiction, International Red Aid. His presence in Havana during the funeral of a leading 'old guard' Cuban Communist, Rubén Martínez Villena, several months after the Cuban Revolution of 1933, and right in the middle of an internal reshuffle of the local party leadership, may have been another not-so-serendipitous coincidence.

James W. Ford's presence in Cuba following the Cuban Revolution of 1933 may have also been connected with a Communist plan to establish a stronghold for race-related activity on the island, given the revolutionary effervescence among blacks there at the time. Despite the Bureau's reports on the local party's failures, Cuba had become the showcase for the Communists' race agenda in the United States as well, at the time of active propaganda in support of the Scottsboro trials.[60] During the 1933 revolutionary period, the southern region of Camaguey had become the centre of a serious radical wave among black workers in the sugar mills, while black unemployed workers had also been active in urban hubs like Havana. By early 1934, the League for the Defense of Negro Rights established a Cuban affiliate managed by the local party and the leaders of the Cuban trade union conglomerate, the *Confederación Nacional de Obreros Cubanos*, now a Communist stronghold. The party's basic task was to bring black workers into the trade unions, in order to take over 'the management of the Blacks liberation movement'.[61]

Results, however, were neither impressive nor promising. In May 1934, the Bureau acts recorded a report given by 'Comrade Frank', most probably Frank Griffen, member of the International Labour Defence, who had visited Cuba as part of a mainland delegation during its recent revolutionary period.[62] According to the Bureau records, Griffen had also acted as instructor for the agency. His presence had 'revealed in all its seriousness, the enormous weaknesses and failures of the *D[efensa] O[brera] I[nternacional]* (International Labour Defence)' in every field of activity, i.e. trade unions, the peasantry, and the black masses.[63] At the time, William Patterson, the ILD lawyer for the Scottsboro case, who apparently led the ILD's Cuban affiliate, had also arrived on the island.[64] While newspapers and propaganda hailed the work of Patterson and the now legal local ILD office, Griffen's report criticised its lack of a strong response 'to the decisions repeatedly adopted to improve the work ... [among the black masses]'.[65] The phrase 'in the practice' meant perhaps to underscore the difference between what was reported in the press and what was actually happening inside the ILD. The stress on 'decisions repeatedly adopted' most likely referred to Bureau directives that the ILD had chosen to disregard recurrently. The report also pointed out the local ILD's 'lack of understanding and underestimation of the black problem', most ironic given the fact that the majority of the agency's members were probably black themselves.[66]

Concluding remarks

The Red and Black history offers many examples of how lofty imaginaries became successful realities and powerful icons of identity and self-worth. It also affords insight as to how ideals of racial equality and justice not always succeeded in overcoming the discrimination and segregation that had traditionally tinted relationships among different races. However, the experience of the Caribbean Bureau points in yet another direction: when it came to implementing a Communist race policy, at least in the Caribbean Basin, race was only the tip of the iceberg. Racial discrimination, white chauvinism and racist stereotypes, no doubt, contributed to difficulties in communication and efficient activity within the Comintern's Caribbean radical network. But a number of factors unrelated to race and, for the most, overlooked when assessing the red/black dynamic, were actually at play.

Much like in the case of racial tensions in general, segregation served as the common denominator for the intricate dynamic that represented the Comintern's race project. But even if apparently bound by racial considerations, the sort of divisions that impeded the success of the Comintern's race agenda in the Americas originated from a much more complicated arrangement of circumstances. For example, geography and cultural elements that had defined and divided the region for centuries, such as the different imperial masters' own national background and language, would be a fundamental point of departure for the articulation of diversity and difference in the region. Relations between different races in the Caribbean, and traditional cultural values and bearing towards other races, must also be considered. Despite the resonance of Great Britain's 'black legend' propaganda alleging the Spaniards' cruel nature, the assortment of racial tonalities in the Spanish Caribbean as opposed to other islands' clear-cut racial demarcations clearly evinced a much more lenient attitude towards colour.[67] In addition, a population's own sense of racial identity would be another factor, particularly in the Spanish islands given the diversity of its racial palette in comparison to a stricter racial binary in the British or the French West Indies at the time. Such elements served as a first layer of 'attitudinal' and cultural segregation that could hinder the consolidation of the Caribbean into a racially homogenous territory for the Comintern's race project.

Another stratum of segregation was the internal administrative structure of radical operations in the area, since different Communist hubs had been in control during the first decade of Comintern activity in the Americas. Connections with an enclave in one of the Communist 'metropolises', such as Mexico or New York, followed geographical demarcations already established since colonial times. For example, British West Indies workers' movements throughout the 1920s were under the jurisdiction of the Communist Party of Great Britain, although work in the British Caribbean domain was practically inexistent.[68] In the Spanish Caribbean, Mexican, Cuban and Venezuelan Communists managed a radical network that extended to Colombian and Venezuelan costal territories in the southern continent through the LADLA. Needless to say, the merging of these separate regional networks under CPUSA jurisdiction as a result of the establishment of the Caribbean Bureau did not automatically eliminate the distance between these groups' agendas, interests and *modus operandi*. In any case, the forced fusion led to conflicts and even more separation given the potential rivalries among leaders and their particular visions concerning the implementation of policy.[69]

The local groups' own negative attitudes towards the imposition of a centralised structure, leadership and plan generated another layer of separation, this time between centre and periphery, and among the periphery's diverse enclaves. Although not necessarily related to a racial bias, such friction could affect the effective implementation of a race agenda. Deeper levels of conflict and tension, such as the internal ideological battles and rivalries, or who or what agency would control the agenda and, therefore, the funds to carry out activity, should also be taken into consideration. In the final analysis, the success or failure of the Caribbean Bureau's race project, and the Comintern's race policy in the Americas for that matter, may have depended on circumstances and conditions that had very little to do with racial discrimination or the traditional malaise of the black/white binary still used to interpret race-related issues today.

Competition for control at upper levels of the Comintern administrative edifice, particularly between the Profintern and International Red Aid (commonly known by its Russian acronym MOPR), opened the way to yet another layer of segregation, as the Profintern's takeover in the region eliminated the traditional power structure connected to the MOPR-sponsored

Anti-Imperialist League of the Americas. Local groups' reaction to the centralised race policy funnelled through the Caribbean Bureau may have been a reaction to bureaucratic intervention and not against the directives related to race. Documents confirm that segregation also existed in the management of activity, since several agencies shared jurisdiction, including the Caribbean Bureau, the CPUSA's Colonial Department, and the International Labour Defence.

Finally, the potential impact of other factors outside the realm of race should also be considered. Caribbean Bureau directives on the race issue may have had a local scope, but their essence was international. In fact, the Bureau's call for a 'struggle for the self-determination' of racial minorities as 'oppressed nationalities' may have actually responded to a Soviet mandate dictated from Moscow in view of Soviet internal considerations. Prior to serving as head of the Secretariat of Latin America, G. Sinani had been one of the chief political organisers in Turkestan and other areas of Central Asia during the years following the Russian Revolution. Sinani's coordination of the campaign for the formal policy of 'self-determination' of the non-Russian minorities had helped to secure Bolshevik control over those territories.[70] In 1922, he became the director of Moscow's Institute of Oriental Studies which later evolved into the Communist University of the Toilers of the East (KUTV), where Asian and African Communists were trained. His experience in the East helped him develop a perspective on issues related to imperialism, which he applied to the Caribbean situation. His connection to the KUTV may help explain why many Caribbean Communists studied there during the Bureau's administrative term. He may have also been responsible for organising the visit to Central Asia of the US black delegation which Langston Hughes wrote about.[71]

The Caribbean Bureau's race agenda, while well-intended and sharp in motive and strategy, had to rely on very complex organisational, social and cultural realities. Its imposition of a unified agenda related to race in the Caribbean Basin was bound to fail in view of the combination of aspects that divided the region beyond the race issue, along with the internal dynamics of an eclectic and culturally diverse network, and the Soviets' own goals. For the most part, Communist propaganda in the Spanish Caribbean did not manage to establish a strong cultural connection between ideology and race. The understanding of race itself, for example, was culturally and socially too complex to contribute to a clearly polarised racial dichotomy of a demonised white 'them' and a victimised black 'us'. In addition, the realities of such a diverse geographical territory resulted in contradictory interpretations of the supposedly unified directives. For example, although a struggle for racial justice was encouraged 'in theory', independent revolutionary action for black 'self-determination', as in Cuba's Oriente region, had to be curtailed in view of its autonomous nature. In some cases, both black and white populations tended to understand racial differences in relation to national identity, a geographic otherness identified as 'foreign', which added to the intricacies of communication and interaction.

In general, vestiges of a Comintern race policy remained as formulaic radical paradigms and slogans, rather than powerful components of the region's revolutionary tradition. While anti-imperialism remained the most outstanding icon of radical politics, especially in the Spanish Caribbean, Communists did not pursue an overt or distinct policy related to race. Segregation as a common denominator for relations among radical enclaves in the region's multiple Caribbeans also persisted, as did diverse notions of identity related to racial nuances. The region's other numerous layers of segregation, including the local white and black populations' own racial misapprehensions, were, in the final analysis, the most powerful factor hampering the success of the Caribbean Bureau's 'racialising' policy of its domain.

Notes

1 The author would like to express her appreciation to her research assistant Carmen Orive de la Rosa, PhD candidate of the History Department at the University of Puerto Rico, for her work on this project.

2 Throughout the chapter, the term 'black' is used, since most of the people involved were Afro-Caribbean or of African descent, and not African Americans. The choice of this sort of racial terminology is, thus, meant to ensure historical accuracy in view of the geographical complexities involved, and is in no way intended to injure racial sensibilities. Unless when quoted directly from the sources with an initial capital, the word is used with a small 'b'.

3 The formidable list includes: Paul Gilroy, *The Black Atlantic: Modernity and Double Consciousness* (Cambridge, MA: Harvard University Press, 1993); Mark Solomon, *The Cry Was Unity: Communists and African-Americans, 1917–1936* (Jackson, MS: University of Mississippi Press, 1998); Robin D.G. Kelley, *The Hammer and the Hoe: Alabama Communists During the Great Depression* (Chapel Hill, NC: University of North Carolina Press, 1990); James Smethurst, *Popular Fronts: Chicago and African-American Cultural Politics, 1935–1946* (DeKalb: University of Illinois Press, 1999); Cedric J. Robinson, *Black Marxism: The Making of the Black Radical Tradition* (Chapel Hill, NC: University of North Carolina Press, 2000); William J. Maxwell, *New Negro, Old Left: African-American Writing and Communism Between the Wars* (New York: Columbia University Press, 1999).

4 Barry Carr, 'Identity, Class, and Nation: Black Immigrants Workers, Cuban Communism, and the Sugar Insurgency, 1925–1934', *The Hispanic American Historical Review*, 78:1 (1998), 83–116. From the same author, see also:

'Mill Occupations and Soviets: The Mobilisation of Sugar Workers in Cuba, 1917–1933', *Journal of Latin American Studies*, 28:1 (1996), 129–158. For another excellent contribution to the subject, see: Jacob A. Zumoff, 'Black Caribbean Labor Radicalism in Panama, 1914–1921', *Journal of Social History*, 47:2 (2013), 429–457.

5 Jason Parker, 'Capital of the Caribbean: The African American–West Indian "Harlem Nexus" and the Transnational Drive for Black Freedom, 1940–1948', *Journal of African American History*, 89:2 (2004), 98–117; Carole Boyce Davies, *Left of Karl Marx: The Political Life of Black Communist Claudia Jones* (Durham, NC: Duke University Press, 2008); Winston James, *Holding Aloft the Banner of Ethiopia: Caribbean Radicalism in Early Twentieth-Century America* (New York: Verso, 1999).

6 Gary Edward Holcomb, *Claude McKay, Code Name Sasha: Queer Black Marxism and Harlem Rennaissance* (Gainsville, FL: University Press of Florida, 2009); Paul Buhle, *Tim Hector: A Caribbean Radical's Story* (Oxford, MS: University Press of Mississippi, 2006).

7 Minkah Makalani, *In the Cause of Freedom: Radical Black Internationalism from Harlem to London, 1917–1939* (Chapel Hill, NC: University of North Carolina Press, 2011); Michael Goebel, *Anti-imperial Metropolis: Interwar Paris and the Seeds of Third World Nationalism* (Cambridge: Cambridge University Press, 2015).

8 Margaret Steven, *Red International and Black Caribbean: Communists in New York, Mexico and the West Indies, 1919–1939* (New York: Pluto Press, 2019). The book's serious historiographical and methodological deficiencies make it, unfortunately, a most unreliable source. See the review on Margaret Steven's book, *Red International and Black Caribbean*, by Sandra Pujals in *Caribbean Studies*, 46:2 (2018), 225–229.

9 Kate A. Baldwin, *Beyond the Color Line: Reading Encounters Between Black and Red, 1922–1963* (Durham, NC: Duke University Press, 2002), 1–24.

10 See: John Barber, 'Stalin's Letter to *Proletarskaia revolyutsiya*', *Soviet Studies*, 28:1 (1976), 21–41.

11 Jan Plamper, 'Avoiding Ambiguity: Soviet Censorship Practices in the 1930s', *Russian Review*, 60:4 (2001), 526–544.

12 See, for example, Mark Naison's outstanding, methodical study on Communists' Harlem hub throughout several decades: *Communists in Harlem During the Depression* (DeKalb: University of Illinois Press, [1983] 2005).

13 Letitia Guran, 'Insurgent Hughes: Negotiating Multiple Narratives Digitally', *MELUS*, 42:4 (2017), 144. The author suggests that, unlike the lighter and freer original writings of his experience in the Soviet Union in the 1930s, Hughes's re-edited version during the McCarthy era included biased comments on Stalinist repressive attitudes that could help Hughes to distance himself from his political past. However, she does not question the authenticity of the original 1934 version, which may have actually been politically revamped by the Soviet Communist Party's *agit-prop* officials.

14 Baldwin, *Beyond the Color Line*, 54.

15 V.L. Jeifets and L.S. Jeifets, 'Krasnyi karandash sudby: Dve zhizni Georgiia Borisovicha Skalova', *Latinskaia Amerika*, 4 (1998), 84–92.

16 Manuel Caballero, *Latin America and the Comintern, 1919–1945* (Cambridge: Cambridge University Press, 1986), 31–33. From around 1930, the *instruktor* represented the most visible element of the Stalinist, militant takeover within the Comintern regional and local Communist spheres. He served a somewhat diplomatic task of assessing whether or not the parties were following the instructions of the Latin American Secretariat and the Caribbean Bureau and reporting it to the higher authorities. He also observed that local leaders enforced a strict theoretical line and that members who opposed the directives were duly reprimanded.

17 Stalinist policies in regard to Central Asia, beyond limited ideological confines, is a very recent subject of inquiry. See: Botakoz Kassymbekova, 'Understanding Stalinism in, from and of Central Asia: Beyond Failure, Peripherality and Otherness', *Central Asian Survey*, 36:1 (2017), 1–18. The whole issue of the journal focuses on a variety of issues regarding the subject, under the title 'Stalinism and Central Asia: Actors, Projects and Governance'.

18 Oscar Berland, 'The Emergence of the Communist Perspective on the "Negro Question" in America, 1919–1931: Part I', *Science and Society*, 63:4 (1999–2000), 411–432.

19 See, for example, Earl Browder's comments in his article 'For National Liberation of the Negroes! War Against White Chauvinism', *The Communist: A Magazine of the Theory and Practice of Marxism-Leninism*, 11:4 (1932), 295–309; Jacob A. Zumoff, 'The American Communist Party and the "Negro Question" from the Founding of the Party to the Fourth Congress of the Communist International', *Journal for the Study of Radicalism*, 6:2 (2012), 53–89.

20 Oscar Berland, 'The Emergence of the Communist Perspective on the "Negro Question" in America, 1919–1931: Part II', *Science and Society*, 64:2 (2000), 194–217.

21 *Ibid.*, 209.

22 *Ibid.*, 207–209. Yokinen, the club's janitor, had supposedly verbally mistreated three black members, manifesting his disapproval of desegregating the establishment's bath facilities. A 'people's court' trial organised by the Communists forced him to recant and apologise, before having him expelled.

23 Browder, 'For National Liberation of the Negroes!', 297.

24 Rossiiskii Gosudarstvenyi Arkhiv Sotsial'no-Politicheskoi Istorii (RGASPI), *fond (f.)* 500, *opis (o.)* 1, *delo (d.)* 5, *list (l.)* 56.

25 RGASPI, *f.* 500, *o.* 1, *d.* 5, *l.* 56.

26 *Ibid.*, *l.* 57.

27 *Ibid.*, *ll.* 57–58.

28 Robert J. Alexander, *International Labor Organizations and Organized Labor in Latin America and the Caribbean* (Santa Barbara, CA: Greenwood Publishing Group, 2009), 24–25.

29 RGASPI, *f.* 500, *o.* 1, *dd.* 1–3, '*Acta de la reunión del BC*', 1931.

30 RGASPI, *f.* 500, *o.* 1, *d.* 10, *l.* 15, Acts for the meeting on 16 February 1933.

31 RGASPI, *f. 500, o. 1, dd.* 1–3, Acts for the meetings, 1931.
32 For example, between March and June 1931, the work plan listed fifteen weekly meetings in which several reports were presented: RGASPI, *f. 500, o. 1, d. 3, l. 5.*
33 RGASPI, *f. 500, o. 1, d. 3, l. 5.*
34 RGASPI, *f. 500, o. 1, d. 5, ll.* 42–43.
35 RGASPI, *f. 500, o. 1, d. 11, l.* 30, '*Informe sobre Costa Rica*', 30 June 1933.
36 RGASPI, *f. 500, o. 1, d. 14, l.* 31, '*Carta del Buró del Caribe*', 19 July 1934.
37 RGASPI, *f. 500, o. 1, d. 5, l.* 40, 'Report of Comrade Juan'.
38 RGASPI, *f. 500, o. 1, d. 5, l.* 40, 'Report of Comrade Juan'.
39 RGASPI, *f. 500, o. 1, d. 11, l.* 43, '*Actas de la reunión del BC*', 11 August 1933.
40 RGASPI, *f. 500, o. 1, d. 11, l.* 22, '*Actas de la reunión del BC*', 29 May 1933.
41 RGASPI, *f. 500, o. 1, d. 11, l.* 10, '*Actas de la reunión del BC*', 2 March 1933.
42 See, for example, the guidelines for the Sacco and Vanzetti anniversary demonstrations: RGASPI, *f. 500, o. 1, d. 4, l.* 14, '*Carta de directivas*, 11 de junio, 1931*'. See also the Communist publications of the period, *El Comunista*, *El Machete* and *La Correspondencia Sudamericana*, for this sort of integrated vision connecting the workers' movements throughout Latin America, the Caribbean and the United States.
43 RGASPI, *f. 500, o. 1, d. 2, ll.* 31, 38, Letters from the Secretariat of Latin America to the Caribbean Bureau of the Comintern for 20 June 1931 and 27 July 1931.
44 RGASPI, *f. 500, o. 1, d. 2, l.* 35, Letter from the Secretariat of Latin America to the Caribbean Bureau of the Comintern of 29 June 1931; *d. 3, l.* 26, '*Plan de trabajo, julio a diciembre, 1931*'; *d. 4, l.* 15, '*Carta de directivas*', 11 June 1931.
45 RGASPI, *f. 500, o. 1, d. 4, l.* 15, '*Carta de directivas*', 10 June 1931. In the case of the manifestos directed to black workers, the language would most likely be English, since the population they were dealing with were usually migrant workers from the British West Indies.
46 RGASPI, *f. 500, o. 1, d. 4, ll.* 14–15.
47 RGASPI, *f. 500, o. 1, d. 12, l.* 19.
48 RGASPI, *f. 500, o. 1, d. 13, l.* 26.
49 RGASPI, *f. 500, o. 1, d. 16, l.* 22.
50 RGASPI, *f. 500, o. 1, d. 3, l.* 1.
51 RGASPI, *f. 500, o. 1, d. 3, l.* 7.
52 RGASPI, *f. 500, o. 1, d. 3, l.* 51, '*Memorándum de la discusión sobre el informe del trabajo del Buro (suplemento del acta de reunión, 31 de diciembre, 1931)*'.
53 RGASPI, *f. 500, o. 1, d. 5, l.* 34, 'Report of Comrade Juan to the Caribbean Secretariat, May 1931'.
54 RGASPI, *f. 500, o. 1, d. 18, l.* 10, '*Esquema sobre algunos problemas del movimiento revolucionario del Caribe relacionados con la discusión para el Séptimo Congreso de la I.C.*', 27 February 1935.
55 RGASPI, *f. 500, o. 1, d. 8, l.* 20, '*Actas de la reunión del BC*', 19 July 1932.
56 RGASPI, *f. 500, o. 1, d. 8, l.* 29, '*Actas de la reunión del BC*', 22 October 1932.
57 RGASPI, *f. 500, o. 1, d. 15, l.* 33, '*Actas de la reunión del BC*', 10 October 1934.
58 Lazar Jeifets and Victor Jeifets (eds), *América Latina en la Internacional*

Comunista, 1919–1943 (Santiago de Chile: Ariadna Ediciones, 2015), 219. While the 2004 edition of the biographical dictionary included approximately 800 people, the third edition of 2015 contributes sketches of almost twice that number of people, both native and foreign, in the Latin American network. Practically all of the data for the dictionary derives from the Comintern archives.

59 Holger Weiss, 'Framing Black Communist Labour Union Activism in the Atlantic World: James W. Ford and the Establishment of the International Trade Union Committee of Negro Workers, 1928–1931', *International Review of Social History*, 64:2 (2019), 249–278.

60 Gerald Horne, *Race to Revolution: The US and Cuba During Slavery and Jim Crow* (New York: Monthly Review Press, 2014), 204–231.

61 RGASPI, *f. 500, o. 1, d. 15, l.* 3, '*Acta de la reunión del BC*', 17 March 1934.

62 Horne, *Race to Revolution*, 224.

63 RGASPI, *f. 500, o. 1, d. 15, l.* 16, '*Informe sobre el trabajo del Secretariado del Caribe presentado por el compañero Frank en la reunión del BC*', 16 May 1934.

64 Horne, *Race to Revolution*, 219. For a discussion on Patterson in Cuba, see Horne, *Race to Revolution*, 219–220.

65 RGASPI, *f. 500, o. 1, d. 15, l.* 16, '*Informe sobre el trabajo del Secretariado del Caribe presentado por el compañero Frank en la reunión del BC*', 16 May 1934.

66 *Ibid.*

67 See, for example, the case of Puerto Rico in the nineteenth century in: María del Carmen Baerga, *Negociaciones de sangre: dinámicas racializantes en el Puerto Rico decimonónico* (Madrid: Iberoamericana Vervuert, 2015).

68 Marika Sherwood, 'The Comintern, the CPGB, Colonies and Black Britons, 1920–1938', *Science and Society*, 60:2 (1996), 137–163.

69 The CPUSA had already attempted to establish control of the LADLA from its Mexican, Cuban and Venezuelan leaders. The attempted takeover resulted in fierce arguments and disputes between the native Communists and the US reps, such as Bertram Wolfe and 'Manuel Gómez' (Charles Phillips). See: Daniel Kersffeld, 'Tensiones y conflictos en los orígenes del comunismo latinoamericano: las secciones de la Liga Antiimperiallista de las Américas', *EIAL*, 18:2 (2007).

70 On Sinani (G. Skalov), see: Jeifets and Jeifets, *América Latina en la Internacional Comunista*, 582–584; Jeifets and Jeifets, 'Krasnyi karandash sudby', 84–92.

71 Baldwin, *Beyond the Color Line*, 86–148.

8

The Left Book Club and its associates: the transnational circulation of socialist ideas in an Atlantic network

Matheus Cardoso-da-Silva

In 1937 the New Era Fellowship was established in South Africa which, together with the Lenin Club, founded in the early 1930s, formed the basis of the Workers Party of South Africa. Linked to Trotskyism, both groups would join the African National Congress, providing the party with numerous members of its intellectual cadres. A year later, in 1938, the Current Affairs Group was created in Southern Rhodesia, the same year in which the Left Book Club in Jamaica (LBCJ) appeared. These literary circles, which at the same time functioned as intellectual networks, acted as centres of diffusion of Marxist, anti-imperialist and anti-colonial ideas.

As a common feature, in addition to disseminating the debates of the international left at strategic points in the British Empire or in its zones of influence in Africa and the Caribbean, all these literary circles and local intellectuals had the direct influence of the Left Book Club (LBC), founded in late 1935 in London, running until the beginning of 1948.

During the years of its operation, the LBC founded more than 1,500 local sections spread across Britain. In addition to book publishing, the LBC distributed the monthly *Left News* magazine, which had 128 issues, published between 1935 and 1947.[1] The tripod of magazine publishing, book publishing and popular education enabled the LBC to amplify its network between the main groups of the British left in the 1930s. The LBC Collection catalogue, from the University of Sheffield,[2] indicates the publication of 255 titles over the years of its operation, made available exclusively to its subscribers and in special editions open to non-members.[3] The LBC's project in London also motivated the creation of other clubs under the same bases within the British Empire. The University of Warwick archives account for the founding of international sections in fifteen countries, including Australia, Canada, China, South Africa, India, Norway, Belgium, France, Palestine, Chile and Southern Rhodesia.[4] *Left News* magazine as well gives accounts periodically about the 'overseas groups' and its operations for the readers and club subscribers – showing that the magazine has an operational function as a promoter of the club activities both inside and outside England.[5]

The Left Book Club's transnational performance has favoured the expansion of existing exchange and circulation of ideas within national or regional contexts between areas of influence of the British Empire – regions in which themes of common interest could circulate, such as the struggles for independence, nationalism, anti-imperialist and anti-colonial ideas, debates on racism, etc.[6]

These transnational networks formed a 'two-way street' of circulation of ideas, from the socialist reading of these questions by the intellectuals gathered around the Left Book Club and its various international sections. From London to the colonies, the international action of the LBC helped, for example, to transform the cause of the Spanish Civil War – another theme that mobilised the apparatus of the LBC and the intellectuals around it – on a transnational theme.[7]

Conversely, from the colonies to Europe, these networks, amplified by the seams provided by the LBC, helped to transform national causes and struggles in international issues, such as the independence of India; the problem of Jewish settlements in British Palestine before the definitive creation of the State of Israel; the national anti-colonial struggle in the British colonies in Africa and the Caribbean, and so on.

Even though it functions independently, articulating debates and connecting intellectuals from existing regional networks, I understand that it was during the years of the LBC that such networks took on global proportions. Here, in my view, two factors are preponderant: on the one hand, the strength of the British economy (even undermined by the war years) and, on the other hand, the influence of the English language and of the intellectuals gravitating around London – many of them immigrants, some non-Europeans – which facilitated the diffusion of these debates and ideas in their local contexts.[8]

All literary groups and circles influenced by the club abroad were located at strategic points in the British Empire or in its zones of influence in Asia, Africa, the Caribbean and Oceania. In addition to functioning as centres for the diffusion of Marxist, anti-imperialist and anti-colonial ideas, to a large extent shaping local nationalisms, they acted as centres of congregation and education.[9]

My focus in this chapter, however, is restricted to the LBC relations with some of these sections located in Africa and the Caribbean forming, together with Europe, a triangular space of Atlantic circulation of ideas. My interest in these particular groups is justified on the one hand by the importance of the relations between the national liberation movements in Africa and the Caribbean, linked together by the Pan-Africanist and Communist movements, as well, on the other hand, by the importance of the debates that these movements generated among British intellectuals about the themes of imperialism, colonialism and racism.[10]

The Red and the Black Atlantic:
the spread of the Russian Revolution and the connections
between Europe, Africa and the Caribbean

Towards the connections of the book trade network built by the transnational activity of London's Left Book Club in both regions, they were connected deeply previously by the impact of the Russian Revolution in the Black Atlantic. The impact of the October revolution of 1917 in Africa, for example, was greater in contexts where the anti-colonial movement and the working class were better developed, such as Egypt – whose workers and anti-colonial movements reached another level of organisation after 1919 and in 1921, when the Socialist Party was founded and in 1922, when the Egyptian Communist Party was founded; and in South Africa, where foreign workers – many Indians, Europeans and Africans from other countries – played a central role in the circulation of new ideas among local workers, among them Marxism, brought with European workers, or anti-colonial ideas, largely brought with the Indians.[11]

The strength of this labour movement favoured the founding of transnational organisations based on socialist ideas, such as the International Socialist League, founded in 1915 – that is, prior to the Russian Revolution itself – and the Industrial Workers of Africa in South Africa. With the international repercussions of the wave of 1917, the transition from this militant movement towards Communism was not difficult, with the founding of the Communist Party of South Africa (CPSA) in 1921. It is seen then that the context of the Communist movements would also favour the organisation of a broader cultural movement where groups of intellectuals such as the Current Affairs Group or the New Era Fellowship, also largely influenced by the international debates promoted by the Communists, could organise.

Jamaica, in the same way, represents a symptomatic case in the international diffusion of anti-colonial thought, through the Pan-Africanist movement and the figure of Marcus Garvey. 'Garveyism', as Garvey's Pan-Africanist movement became known, emerged with the founding of the Universal Negro Improvement Association (UNIA) in Jamaica in 1914. The UNIA was refounded in New York in 1916 in a period of African-American cultural effervescence which also gave rise to a number of organisations, such as the African Blood Brotherhood, and which culminated in the so-called 'Harlem Renaissance' of the 1920s, and an increase in the influence of black movements in Africa, Europe and other parts of the World such as Brazil.[12]

The Left Book Club and its role in Africa

The Left Book Club acted in Africa in this context through established intellectual networks by the repercussion of the Russian Revolution on the continent. This is the case, for example, of the Current Affairs Group, the arm of the LBC in what was then Southern Rhodesia. The group was founded in 1938 under the direct influence of Victor Gollancz, editor-in-chief of the club and its main mentor, to support the Republican cause of the Spanish Civil War. Along with the South African Communist newspaper the *Guardian*, the Current Affairs Group was responsible for disseminating socialist ideas among the black population. However, disagreements over the role of the Communist Party of South Africa in forming a Southern Rhodesia Communist Party (which carried ideas of national liberation with it) led local members to create a more organised group under the nickname of the 'Left Club', of which the British writer Doris Lessing was secretary.[13]

In South Africa, the local LBC section was linked to the intellectual circle around the CPSA and had sections in six of the country's largest cities: Johannesburg, Pretoria, Cape Town, Durban, Port Elizabeth and East London.[14]

In these cities, an alternative Communist press was formed which served, in part, as a basis for disseminating both the ideas generated by the CPSA as well as by the African National Congress (founded in 1928). Within this circuit, the Non-European United Front (NEUF) was created in 1943, an alliance between Africans, Indians and other ethnic minorities, aimed at strengthening the struggle for racial equality and labour rights in South Africa, responsible for the movement of many of the anti-imperialist, anti-racist and nationalist ideas produced in this alternative press.

Some scholars had suggested the development of an alternative literate culture that tried to spread radical ideas among the black population, which would be crushed by the apartheid regime after 1948. Among its main disseminators were the Lenin Club (an amalgam of several smaller groups, linked to the CPSA and later independent of the Communists); Spartacus Club and the New Era Fellowship (founded in 1937), linked to the NEUF; and the oldest, the Teachers League of South Africa, formed in 1913, all in Cape Town.[15]

The Lenin Club, for example, organised Sunday schools for children and public lessons. The Spartacus Club and the October Club promoted their own reading networks. They all distributed the books edited by the Left Book Club. Among the most widely read were Jack London's *The Iron Heel* (published in the US in 1908 but distributed by the LBC in Britain) and Edgar Snow's *Red Star Over China*, published by the LBC in London in 1937.[16]

That 'subterranean' diffusion of this type of literature, considered subversive by the South African state and by the colonial authorities, helped to educate a generation that would later head the front line of the struggle against the apartheid regime, at a time when access of the black population to the public libraries was already restricted by the segregationist policies the state.

In a broader perspective, it is possible to note then the existence of a network of regional circulation of ideas and political projects in the extreme south of the African continent, independent of the relations with the Europeans, corresponding to a process of construction of an autochthon black identity that, by itself, took on transnational contours.[17] It was in this network, linked to the organisations of the international left, but acting in an autonomous way, debating local issues, that the Left Book Club was able to find an audience eager for the material it distributed.

In the same way, the participation of the LBC among these already existing networks in the extreme south of the African continent draws attention to some of its racial dynamics. The formation of an autochthonous black printed culture in South Africa dates from the end of the nineteenth and beginning of the twentieth century, linked to the emergence of a local black intelligentsia, with the founding of newspapers and publishers, and the South African Native Press Association in 1904 (renamed the South African Press Association in 1938 – which also served the then Southern Rhodesia). However, until the end of the Anglo-Boer War (1899–1902), circulation of printed matter was restricted to white settlers. As a result, the South African publishing market not only demonstrated a restriction of the readership to access to printed material produced by blacks, but also an attachment to certain ethnic connections in the circulation of such material. In large cities such as Cape Town or Johannesburg, for example, the coexistence of an ethnic print of Jewish, Dutch or Indian origin – many of them being published in Yiddish, Dutch and English – contrasted with an indigenous black press in Xhosa, Zulu and other local dialects.[18]

It is possible to estimate, then, that the presence of the Left Book Club in the middle of these alternative circuits of the South African press, notably among socialist circles, propelled by the founding of Communist Party of South Africa, also represented part of the local disputes by the reading public, who often also took a view based on ethnic lines, a symbol of the very formation of South African nationality.[19]

The Left Book Club and its role in the Caribbean

The Caribbean was another region in which the LBC acted, helped by the British Empire being a global space of circulation, and in which it played an important role among local intellectuals and the organisation of an anti-colonial discourse. Especially in Jamaica, there are references to these regional networks, which among them mention the founding of the Left Book Club by a local white historian, Richard Hart, who was also part of the LBC in London.[20] Hart had previous integrated other writers' clubs in Kingston, among them the Readers and Writer's Club, founded by Frank Mill and Una Marson.

As well as a trade union leader, Richard Hart was one of the first Marxists in the English-speaking West Indies.[21] He participated directly in strike and insurrectionary movements both within Jamaica and in the British Caribbean region in the 1930s and 1940s, and was also one of the leading Jamaican historians. Some of his books were fundamental to the founding of local historiography in the 1950s and 1960s, which throughout the process of decolonisation helped elucidate the relations of colonial domination to the economic, social and political development of Jamaica and the British Caribbean.[22]

Hart himself documented the operation model of the Left Book Club in Jamaica. In his work *Towards Decolonisation: Political, Labour and Economic Developments in Jamaica, 1938–1945* (1999), Hart gave an account of two circulars that show the activities of the LBCJ: one, dated 4 September 1939, described an International Symposium organised by the LBCJ which was attended by local intellectuals; another was a debate on the book *Tory MP* by 'Simon Haxey',[23] led by Ansell Hart, Richard Hart's father. The event also featured a presentation by W.A. McBean entitled 'Why I am a Communist' and a discussion of Joseph Stalin's book, *Marxism and the Colonial Question*, conducted by Henry Fowler.[24]

In the two circulars, in addition to the debates, the discussion of two books published by the LBC in London was announced for 12 March 1940: Edgar Snow's *Red Star Over China*, and Leonard Woolf's *Barbarians at the Gate*, which had been 'book of the month' in England in 1939. Interestingly, on the same day, there was a discussion on the history of the Indian National Congress, 'led by Dr H.T. Persaud or by I.N. Fyzullah [sic]'.[25]

It is important to clarify that the founding moment of the LBCJ was of extreme importance for local labour history, since in 1938 a general strike by Jamaican workers was attributed, by the British intelligence organs, to the Communist influence in the island.[26] The strike was part of a wave of strikes in the British Caribbean colonies between 1934 and 1939. The event in Jamaica in particular had great repercussions between the Pan-Africanist movement and the international Communist movement, being commented on by the activist George Padmore, in an article from 1938, 'Labour Unrest in Jamaica'.[27] In addition to critically publicising the strike wave that swept across the British Caribbean – which he also did in small notes published in the weekly newspapers, such as the *Daily Herald*, which Padmore later quoted himself – the 1938 article served to inform the local public, especially that linked to Pan-African circles and the London left, about the plight of the Jamaican population squeezed between an economy strangled by monoculture and the interests of large agro-exporting multinationals that monopolised local production, and a colonial administration whose purpose was to maintain social order and the local operating system. To a large extent, Padmore's portrayal of Jamaican strikes served to interconnect the economic and social situation that spread to the other British colonies throughout the 1930s.

Gollancz had shown a very close interest in documenting the waves of strikes in the West Indies, through William Arthur Lewis's *Labour in the West Indies: The Birth of a Workers' Movement*, the first report/analysis of strikes in the Caribbean in the 1930s, originally published in 1939, and jointly edited by Victor Gollancz and the Fabian Society.[28]

William Arthur Lewis (1915–91) was born on the Caribbean island of Saint Lucia, then a British colony, but settled in London, where he earned a degree and then a doctorate (1940) in Economics from the London School of Economics. He was a professor at the LSE until 1948, and then a professor at the University of Manchester until 1957 – the same year that Ghana declared independence. Its first government invited Lewis to become the country's first economic adviser, and he coordinated the first Five-Year Plan for Ghana's economic development (1959–63). In 1959, back in the Caribbean, Lewis was appointed vice chancellor of the University of the West Indies, and in 1963 he was knighted for his contributions to economics. In the same year, Lewis was appointed professor at Princeton University, where he remained until his retirement in 1983. In 1979, Lewis was the first black scholar to be awarded the Nobel Prize for Economics, jointly with Theodore Schultz, then a professor at the University of Chicago.

Lewis's original text was divided into three main parts: a) an analysis of the social situation of the West Indies; b) an analysis of the birth of the Caribbean Labour Movement in the different British Caribbean islands in the 1930s; and c) the chapter entitled 'What Can Be Done', focusing on economic and political issues. The original publication was accompanied by an appendix to the resolutions of the First Labour Congress of the West Indies in 1938 and an excerpt from the Moyne Commission in Barbados.

The narrative that Lewis presents leads the reader to follow the initial movements that led to the formation of the first unions in the British colonies in the Caribbean islands in the main areas where unemployment was concentrated, such as in the fields of oil exploration, water supply, etc. The formation of these first unions, following the first mass strikes that spread to the colonies after 1934, showed the beginning of the participation of the Caribbean working class in local politics. These early unions, according to Lewis, also served to secure the first forms of local labour legislation, guaranteeing, for example, a basic minimum wage for farm workers. These movements led to the formation of the Caribbean Labour Congress in 1945, the first major congress to unify the labour movements scattered throughout the British colonies in the Caribbean, which helped win historical achievements such as universal suffrage for those over 18 years of age, dismemberment of plantations and the creation of peasant cooperatives, nationalisation of sugar factories and public services, the creation of a social security system, health insurance and support for the unemployed, and reform of labour legislation.

As an economist, Lewis made several recommendations, such as revising the prices of exported products through state control of production; a national funding programme to counterbalance British colonial taxes; the development of local industry; redistribution of properties as a way to remedy the delays caused by colonisation; increase of wages, and the implementation of specific legislation for industrial production.

The repercussions of colonialism and imperialism through the publications of the Left Book Club

Among the 255 books published by the LBC during its years of operation, about twenty-four of them dealt directly with colonialism, imperialism and racism in the colonies. Among these titles we can find: Rajani Palme Dutt's *India Today* (1940); H.N. Brailsford's *Subject India* (1943); Santha Rama Rau's *Home to India* (1945); Bhabani Bhattacharya's *So Many Hungers* (1947), etc.

In addition to these, the LBC also published other books that had imperialism as their main theme, like John Burger's *The Black Man's Burden* (1943); A.G. Russell's *Colour, Race and Empire* (1944); Alexander Campbell's *Empire in Africa* (1944) and *It's Your Empire* (1945). This theme also added a significant amount of articles to the club's official magazine, *Left News*.

As a comparison with another subject that aroused the attention of the LBC, books aimed at the repercussions of the Spanish Civil War published by the LBC between 1937 and the 1940s, added a total of thirteen titles. In addition to the books, *Left News* magazine also extended the debates about the events in Spain, publishing two special issues dedicated to the subject in 1937 and 1938.[29]

British historiography has been debating for many years how issues of nationalism in the colonies have helped to question the idea of British 'exceptionalism', which led to the colonial project of the nineteenth century. Debates on the liberation of the colonies took shape among the British left in the 1940s, while the struggle against fascism in Europe was booming, changing British intellectuals' reading of the empire. And as is clear from my reading, the Left Book Club played a central role in this process by spreading reflections on imperialism and colonialism, giving meaning to the politicisation of these intellectuals, and anticipating by a decade and a half the New Left's anti-colonial debates,[30] as for example in the readings from people such as Stuart Hall, Perry Anderson and Eric Hobsbawm.[31]

It's also important to note that the triggers of the British left's reflections on the 'national question' of the colonies were the debates over India's independence. The constant presence of members of the Indian National Congress, Gandhi's visits to London, Jawaharlal Nehru's contacts with the British left, kept India on the daily agenda in the British press, making independence of its main colony a major 'internal' issue for the British during the years before the Second World War until the completion of the Indian independence process in 1947.

Contact between London LBC members and the Indian national movement, for example, was big enough to arouse the interest of the Foreign Office and Scotland Yard to the point that the two bodies produced consistent documentary material on the LBC's activities in and outside England, including lists of books released by the LBC that should be banned;[32] the relationship of intellectuals gathered around the LBC with the Indian national movement;[33] and the participation of Indians in rallies and meetings organised by the LBC in London.[34] This helped to structure a censor network to filter the circulation of LBC-produced material between colonies.[35]

The influence of Communist internationalism and all its cultural apparatus in the diffusion of anti-colonial struggles in the main European centres and in the USA is undeniable. This is an example of the connections created by international bodies such as the International Union of Revolutionary Writers (IURW), founded in Moscow in 1925, and its *Journal of International Literature*, which allowed local black writers – who would later become a reference for the diffusion of African anti-colonial struggles in the Anglophone countries as well as local racism – have their circulation facilitated by these transnational networks created by the Communists and socialists.

This is, for example, the case of Langston Hughes, the prominent African-American poet, who published key books on the Italian invasion of Ethiopia in 1935 (*Ballad of Ethiopia* and *Broadcast on Ethiopia*), whose first public appearance in England was sponsored by the Left Book Club in 1938.[36]

This cultural internationalism created by transnational Communist networks helped not only the diffusion of the thinking of intellectuals like Hughes, but opened the way for the translation of non-Anglophone English-language authors from problems first presented in other languages (such as radical anti- and post-colonial thinking of non-Anglophone colonies). Books such as the *Negro* anthology, edited by Nancy Cunard in 1934, which collected years of research material on the African diasporas, could be disseminated in the USA and England in editions promoted by these Communist networks, in magazines such as *New Masses* and *Partisan Review*, both in New York, and LBC's *Left News*. In addition to interest in Cunard's work, there was interest in the work of non-European authors, such as Cuban writer Nicolás Guillén or Haitian writer Jacques Romain, and Europeans such as the Spanish poet Federico García Lorca, whose murder early in the Spanish Civil War helped to internationalise the cause of the struggle in defence of the Second Republic.[37]

In this sense, another aspect to which the transnational networks created by the global circulation of the material produced by the LBC draw attention is the construction of interracial networks of articulation between intellectuals, connected by the themes of anti-imperialism, anti-racism and anti-colonialism. And such connections have occurred both in the Black Atlantic circuit and globally by connecting Indian intellectuals with these debates. It makes sense then to think of the interracial articulation between European white intellectuals, such as the LBC editors in London – Gollancz, Strachey and Laski – or peripheral white intellectuals such as the Jamaican Richard Hart, and black, peripheral or metropolitan intellectuals, such as William Arthur Lewis or even Langston Hughes, who circled between the US and London through networks sewn by the LBC.

Conclusion

The project around the founding of the LBC in London, by Victor Gollancz, John Strachey and Harold Laski, was born as a direct response to the context of the Popular Front in Great Britain. This is clear not only from the range of issues the LBC published – and the ideological diversity of its authors – but would also be stated publicly and in tacit terms in the editorials of its official magazine, *Left News*. In these terms, the role of the LBC would be to widely promote the ideas of the left, and to educate the British working class for a socialist political project. This would also justify the end of the Left Book Club in 1948, three years after Labour's victory in the 1945 general elections.[38] The LBC was often recognised as the largest political organisation in membership of that period in Great Britain, bringing together a wide range of people on the Labour left, and including African and Caribbean immigrants, Indians, expatriates from Eastern Europe and other parts of the world, allowing the club, both within and through their networks outside England, to negotiate with different groups on the left, balancing their rivalries.[39] This would also be reflected in the extent of its overseas activities.

On the other hand, as I argue above, the transnational relations created by the LBC around the globe, as well as integrating these circuits created by Communist networks, especially the Black Atlantic during the interwar period, connected British intellectuals to various international causes, such as the struggle for independence of the colonies in Africa, the Caribbean and Asia.

By the same process, non-European intellectuals who circulated in the LBC networks gained prominence in the debates in England on such subjects, such as the intellectuals of Indian, African and Caribbean origin, whose preponderance also increases within the British left, and of the CPGB itself, like Rajani Palme Dutt, general secretary of the CPGB between 1939 and 1941, who actively participated in the activities promoted by the LBC.

The Left Book Club is important not only for the debates within the British Popular Front in the period between the two world wars – for example, to publicise the effects of the Spanish Civil War – but also for its role in educating a generation on the themes of anti-colonialism and anti-imperialism. Even before the end of the Second World War, the LBC was debating the decline of the British Empire and the independence of its colonies, imagining the same destination as India's for the colonies in the Black Atlantic. And it also gave voice, through its books and its magazine, to the nascent debate on the situation of the British colonies in Africa, the Caribbean and Asia, even for intellectuals coming from these peripheral contexts.

Notes

1 The collection belonging to the University of Sheffield brings together many of *Left News*' microfilm editions. In it are numbers 15 (1937) and 21 to 128

(1938 to 1947); the first fourteen numbers are missing. I am grateful for all the help I had in my research, conducted in the first half of 2015, from the staff of the Special Collections of the Western Bank Library of the University of Sheffield, especially its archivist Chris Loftus.

2 Available online at www.sheffield.ac.uk/library/special/leftbook [accessed 12 February 2021].

3 Until the outbreak of the Second World War, subscribers were offered two monthly titles: the normal one, and the so-called 'book of the month', a special edition for members which cost two shillings and sixpence per unit. After 1939, when Britain faced the rationing of paper which lasted until the end of the war, the LBC made a unique title available. Both the structure of the Left Book Club, as well as its catalogue and its circle of intellectuals, was analysed in my doctoral thesis, defended in October 2016, in the Department of History, University of São Paulo. That research was conducted under the supervision of Professor Sara Albieri, and was granted a national scholarship from CAPES (Conselho de Aperfeiçoamento de Pessoal de Nível Superior), and a visiting fellow PDSE (Programa de Doutorado-Sanduíche no Exterior) scholarship, held in the first semester of 2015, with Royal Holloway, University of London, under the supervision of Professor Gregory Claeys. Before that, I had also evaluated the role of the LBC in the formation of the British left in the years of the Popular Front in my Master's dissertation, also defended in the University of São Paulo in 2010, under an FAPESP (Fundação de Amparo à Pesquisa do Estado de São Paulo) scholarship. Available online at: www.teses.usp.br/teses/disponiveis/8/8138/tde-19082016–140420/pt-br.php [accessed 12 February 2021].

4 All the information concerned with this is available in the Victor Gollancz Papers (VGP), Modern Records Centre, University of Warwick.

5 'Overseas Groups', *Left News*, 21 (January 1938), 661.

6 See, for example, the letter from Arthur Key (from the Middle East Press Service, London) to Gollancz, dated 11 June 1945, asking about the possibility of developing Left Book Club circulation in Egypt and Palestine through contact with Robert Schindler, editor of the Middle East Press for Cairo. (MSS.157/3/LB/1/2, VGP).

7 On this, see my latest article, Matheus Cardoso-da-Silva, 'Ecos da Guerra Civil espanhola na Grã-Bretanha através das publicações do *Left Book Club*', *Topoi (Rio J.)* 18:36 (2017), 608–638.

8 I have based this argument on research that has demonstrated the role of migrant communities from the colonial regions in expanding debates in the British public sphere – thus influencing the debates of the local left – during the period between the two world wars. As a reference see, for example, the works of Hakim Adi, *The History of African and Caribbean Communities in Britain* (London: Wayland, 2007); Hakim Adi, *West Africans in Britain: Nationalism, Pan-Africanism and Communism, 1900–1960* (London: Lawrence & Wishart, 1998); Louis James, 'The Caribbean Artists Movement' in Bill Schwarz (ed.), *West Indian Intellectuals in Britain* (Manchester: Manchester University Press, 2003), 209–227; Leslie James and Daniel Whittall, 'Ambiguity and Imprint:

British Racial Logics, Colonial Commissions of Inquiry, and the Creolization of Britain in the 1930s and 1940s', *Callaloo*, 39:1 (2016), 166–184.

9 See, for example, the letter from Father R. Conesa (MSS.157/3/LB/1/13, VGP), St Xavier College Librarian, Mumbai, India, 25 October 1945, on the signature of the *Left News* magazine, briefly commenting on the interest in the issues discussed in the magazine and the publicity it could reach on the college site with 2,500 students. Similarly, the request of Feroze S. Wadia in a letter dated 7 January 1946, requesting bulk copies of *Left News* to be sent to Bombay, in exchange for free publicity for the magazine there. (MSS.157/3/LB/1/15, VGP).

10 For the importance of the Left Book Club in educating a generation of British left-wing intellectuals during the Second World War, see Perry Anderson, *Arguments within English Marxism* (London: New Left Books, 1980); 'An opportunity to fight fascism': Interview about Jack Jones on *Today*, BBC Radio 4, 25 April 2009: http://news.bbc.co.uk/today/hi/today/newsid_8018000/8018004.stm [accessed 12 February 2021].

11 One of the leading scholars arguing the connection between the rise of national movements in the Black Atlantic during the colonial period within the Pan-Africanist and Communist movement is Hakim Adi. See, as an example, his latest book: *Pan-Africanism: A History* (London: Bloomsbury, 2018).

12 For the reception of Marcus Garvey and Garveyism in Brazil, see for example: Petrônio Domingues, 'O "Moisés dos Pretos": Marcus Garvey no Brasil', *Novos estud. CEBRAP* [online], 36:3 (2017), 129–150: www.scielo.br/pdf/nec/v36n3/1980-5403-nec-36-03-129.pdf [accessed 12 February 2021].

13 Sue Onslow, *Cold War in Southern Africa: White Power, Black Liberation* (London: Routledge, 2009), 86.

14 Les Switzer (ed.), *South Africa's Alternative Press: Voices of Protest and Resistance, 1880–1960* (Cambridge: Cambridge University Press, 1997).

15 There are references to so-called 'alternative' groups in South Africa in Switzer, *South Africa's Alternative Press*, especially in the chapter 'Inkululeko: Organ of the Communist Party of South Africa, 1939–1950' by Elizabeth Ceiriog Jones.

16 Elizabeth Ceiriog Jones, 'Inkululeko: Organ of the Communist Party of South Africa, 1939–1950' in Les Switzer (ed.), *South Africa's Alternative Press: Voices of Protest and Resistance, 1880–1960* (Cambridge: Cambridge University Press, 1997).

17 As pointed out, for example, by Leslie James, 'Transatlantic Passages: Black Identity Construction in West African and West Indian Newspapers, 1935–1950' in Derek R. Peterson, Emma Hunter and Stephanie Newell (eds), *African Print Cultures: Newspapers and their Publics in the Twentieth Century* (Michigan: Michigan University Press, 2016), 49–75. And for a broader view, see Paul Gilroy, *The Black Atlantic: Modernity and Double Consciousness* (Cambridge, MA: Harvard University Press, 1993).

18 This was the case, for example, of the *Abantu-Batho* newspaper, founded in Johannesburg in October 1912 and lasting until 1931, by Pixley ka Isaka Seme. The newspaper became the first official vehicle of the newly created

South African Native National Congress (SANNC), later renamed the African National Congress. *Abantu-Batho* was published in English, SeSotho, Zulu, Xhosa and SeTswana in order to have the widest possible reach among the local black audience, with the aim of making SANNC a national organisation. On the theme of building a local press that served as the intellectual arm of the autochthonous movements in South Africa, see Les Switzer and Mohamed Adhikari (eds), *South Africa's Resistance Press: Alternative Voices in the Last Generation Under Apartheid* (Athens, OH: Ohio University Press, 2000).

19 It is interesting to note the various criticisms of *Abantu-Batho*, including the South African Communists who, encouraged by the International Socialist League and its newspaper the *International*, even accused the paper of being under the influence of the Native Affairs Department and representative interests of the capitalist press. In the same way, *Abantu-Batho* was attacked by those who criticised the influence of the CPSA within the SANNC. In both cases, the creation of alternative newspapers to contest the readership of *Abantu-Batho* was articulated. On this, see Switzer and Adhikari, *South Africa's Resistance Press*.

20 Documents relating to Richard Hart's trajectory are located at the National Library of Jamaica, Kingston, at the University of the West Indies, and there is a large amount of microfilmed material at the Institute of Commonwealth Studies, University of London, Richard Hart papers, ICS122 (1937–1964). Catalogue available at: http://archives.ulrls.lon.ac.uk/Details/archive/110025177 [accessed 12 February 2021].

21 Hart's personal trajectory as a trade union leader can also help elucidate the foundations of the LBCJ. He was a member of the main pre-union organisation in Jamaica, the Labour Committee, founded in 1938 by Norman Manley and William Bustamante – two other names that made up the circles that would have originated the LBCJ. On the Labour Committee, Hart was responsible for composing a model trade union constitution. In 1939, he was secretary of the Trade Union Advisory Committee to the OECD, which would later become the Trade Union Council. Between 1942 and 1948, he was president of the Jamaica Government Railway Employees Union, and from 1949 to 1953, vice president of the Trade Union Congress of Jamaica. In regional terms, Hart served as assistant secretary of the Caribbean Labour Congress from its formation in 1945, and as its secretary general from 1946 to 1953. This shows Hart's strong connection with the Jamaican labour movement and the circles to which he belonged.

22 Among these titles are *The Origins and Development of the People of Jamaica* (1952); *Slaves who Abolished Slavery: Black Rebellions* (1980); *The End of Empire: Transition to Independence in Jamaica and Other Caribbean Region Colonies* (2006).

23 'Simon Haxey' was the pseudonym of Arthur Henry Ashford Wynn (1910–2001), a British civil servant, social researcher and Soviet spy, recruited during his years as a student at Oxford University, and his wife Margaret (Peggy) (1913–2010).

24 Richard A. Hart, *Towards Decolonisation: Political, Labour and Economic Developments in Jamaica, 1938–1945* (Kingston: University of West Indies Press, 1999), 37.

25 *Ibid.*

26 I have found arguments in this sense in the West Indies papers, which contain letters exchanged between Sir Edward Brandis Denham, a British colonial administrator who worked as governor of Gambia (1928–30), British Guiana (1930–35) and Jamaica (1935–38), and Sir Cosmo Parkinson, Undersecretary of State for the British Colonies between 1940 and 1942. This documentation can be found in the folder CO 318/427/13 – Document 71149/37, West Indies papers (relating to correspondence with British colonies of the West Indies), The National Archives, Kew, England.

27 George Padmore, 'Labour Unrest in Jamaica', *International African Opinion*, 1:1 (1938): www.marxists.org/archive/padmore/1938/unrest-jamaica.htm [accessed 12 February 2021].

28 William Arthur Lewis, *Labour in the West Indies: The Birth of a Workers' Movement* (London: New Beacon Books, 1978). See also W.A. Lewis, 'The Birth of the Trade Union Movement in the English-Speaking Caribbean Area', *Social and Economic Studies*, 48:3 (1999), 173–196.

29 'Second Spain number', *Left News*, 21 (January, 1938).

30 Obviously I do not intend to suggest here a homogeneity of thought and political programmes for the British New Left, according to the different origins of its members. From 1956 onwards, two groups would give rise to the New Left in the United Kingdom: one centred around *New Reasoner* magazine, and the other around the *Universities and Left Review* magazine. The second group was mainly composed of young Oxford students of immigrant origin, many from the Caribbean, gathered around the Cole Group (from the well-known seminars of veteran socialist and Oxford professor G.D.H. Cole, himself an effusive contributor to the Left Book Club), who were much more tied to colonial issues, on account of their own origins, than the previous generation, made up of veterans of the Popular Front and the anti-fascist struggle, and coalesced around the *New Reasoner*. Yet these same veterans, many of whom were former members of the Historian's Group of the Communist Party of Great Britain, led by Dona Torr, already presented a distinct view of Marxism in relation to the party's orthodoxy and the sectarian leadership of Rajani Palme Dutt – another emeritus member of the LBC. They were already sufficiently sensitive to the problems surrounding colonialism and imperialism at the time of the Suez Crisis in 1956 to understand the weight of a Franco-British imperialist intervention in Egypt during that period of the Cold War. In this sense, Khrushchev's revelations at the Twentieth Congress of the Communist Party of the Soviet Union on 25 February 1956, about the Soviet invasion of Hungary and the Franco-British intervention in Egypt, would melt away the basis for founding a group whose aim was to present a renewed socialist project, far from the Soviet orthodox interpretation of Marxism. This would also involve discussing the process of decolonisation and formation of the new independent states in Africa, Asia and

the Caribbean, or even the situation of Latin America during the Cold War (for example, incorporating Brazilian intellectuals in these debates from 1964, when the sociologist Octavio Ianni published his first article in the *New Left Review*: 'Political Process and Economic Development in Brazil, Part 1', *New Left Review*, 1:25 (1964). On the origins of the New Left and the influence of the decolonial debate, see Stuart Hall, 'Life and Times of the First New Left', *New Left Review*, 61 (2010).

31 As, for example, the numerous articles in the *New Left Review* in the early 1960s on Cuba; or articles on the decadence of European colonialism in Africa, such as Perry Anderson, 'Portugal and the End of Ultra-Colonialism, Part I', *New Left Review*, 1:15 (1962); Roger Murray, 'Colonial Congo', *New Left Review*, 1:17 (1962); or Roger Murray and Tom Wengraf, 'The Algerian Revolution, Part 1', *New Left Review*, 1:22 (1963).

32 CO 273/633/1, 'Left Book Club, London: prohibition of publications', 1937, The National Archives, Kew.

33 IOR/L/PJ/12/504: Folder 1025/36, 'The Left Book Club: reports on members, activities and Indian interests' (Dec 1936–Feb 1938)', The National Archives, Kew.

34 HO 144/21529, 'Disturbs: Reports on the activities of the "Left Book Club"' 1936–1941, The National Archives, Kew.

35 See, as an example of the letters addressed to Sir Edward Denham in Jamaica, one dated 7 October 1937, Folder CO 318/427/13 – Document 71149/37, West Indies papers (related to correspondence with the British colonies of the West Indies), The National Archives, Kew. Sir Cosmo Parkinson speaks of the impossibility of prohibiting the sending of books from the Phoenix Book Club to the colonies due to the lack of a specific law for this in the UK. However, he says that the Royal Mail Office could retain the correspondence in which its origin was marked in the letters. He also says he has no news that the books edited by the Phoenix Book Club were related to the Left Book Club – apparently unaware that the Phoenix Book Club was the LBC's main international distributor. In the latest document in folder CO 318/427/13, there is a cutting from the Jamaican newspaper with news of the LBC's refusal to accept Manley as a member, dated 20 July 1937. The Phoenix Book Club was the LBC agent in Jamaica, as the clipping makes clear.

36 See Edward Smethurst, *The New Red Negro: The Literary Left and African American Poetry, 1930–1946* (Oxford: Oxford University Press, 1999), 41.

37 *Ibid.*, 42.

38 On this, see the response of Victor Gollancz's secretary (MSS.157/3/LB/2/6.i) of 21 November 1956 to Roy Hill's letter (MSS.157/3/LB/2/5 of 20 November 1956), requesting details about the history of the organisation of the LBC for a book on the subject (VGP).

39 As early as 1938 (that is, just three years after its foundation), the LBC reached 57,000 members, announced in its official publication, *Left News* magazine, serving as an umbrella for many intellectuals and their cultural activities in the British Popular Front. These figures indicate that the LBC was Britain's largest

political organisation at the time, as classified in Scotland Yard's report of 17 January 1938. (Folder HO 144/21529, Home Office Papers, The National Archives, Kew.) The growth of the LBC in the 1930s, inside and outside England, was of concern to British state bodies such as the Home Office, Foreign Office and Scotland Yard, who followed the LBC's activities step by step, especially before the outbreak of the Second World War.

III

Africa, the Soviet Union and the Cold War

9

The beginning of the Cold War in the Gold Coast?

Marika Sherwood

Why did the Cold War begin in the Gold Coast (today's Ghana) in 1948?[1] As I recount in great detail in my book *Kwame Nkrumah and the Dawn of the Cold War: The West African National Secretariat (1945–48)*, it was because the 'Western' imperialist, capitalist powers wanted to stop, or at least control, the struggle for independence. But, as the Second World War had just ended, it would not have looked good to fight a 'real' war against the *independistas*, whether they were called that, or 'nationalists'. Africans were trying to work out how to unite with each other. Unity, they argued, would not only be crucial for real independence, but also for the creation of a new Africa, a united Africa. So their threat to the Western powers was huge.

Who were the *independistas* in the UK when the Second World War ended? As I think it was Kwame Nkrumah who was the prime target of the British government, this chapter will examine what he faced when he arrived in the UK. Kwame Nkrumah left the Gold Coast to study at universities in the USA in 1935. There he met/corresponded/worked with activists such as Ralph Bunche, C.L.R. James and the Council on African Affairs. With other African students he set up the African Students Association (ASA), which united them; their main task was to educate Americans, especially African Americans, about the realities of life in Africa and the continent's complex history and cultures.[2] There are no papers on the ASA in the files of the Communist Party of the USA (CPUSA), but Nkrumah wrote to Claudia Jones, secretary for the Women's Commission of the CPUSA and editor of its journal *Spotlight*, on 27 October 1942: he thanked her for her 'courage, inspiration and aid'. We don't know if this 'aid' was to Nkrumah himself, or the ASA, but the letter certainly indicates that Nkrumah was 'acquainted' with the CPUSA. Did this cease in 1942? Or had Claudia Jones given some very special aid in 1942?

It is also important to note that, for Nkrumah, the level of racial discrimination in the USA was his introduction to the glories of the Western world.

USA: the Communist Party and 'negroes'

So what was the CPUSA's attitude to 'negroes', as they were then called? Formed in 1919, its very first programme included a 'paragraph on the political, economic and racial oppression of the negroes and promised to carry on appropriate agitation'.[3] (It is important to point out that the CPUSA called for 'agitation', which the Communist Party of Great Britain (CPGB) certainly did not.) 'Negroes' began to go to Moscow to attend universities in 1923.

Not all the CPUSA's policies appealed to African Americans – more joined the National Association for the Advancement of Colored People (NAACP) and Marcus Garvey's Universal Negro Improvement Association (UNIA). But membership increased when the CPUSA set up an International Labour Defence Committee (ILD), which led the fight against the conviction of eight of the nine young Black men who were accused of raping two White women on a train in 1931 – the Scottsboro campaign. (The boy aged 12 was not convicted.) The ILD succeeded. But membership cascaded down when it was revealed that the USSR supported Italy's invasion of Ethiopia by providing it with 'military supplies'.[4]

The CPUSA attempted to weed out all forms of racism within its own membership and became the most active defender of Blacks' civil rights. Trinidad-born George Padmore, who had joined the party in the USA, was sent to Moscow in 1929; he was appointed head of the Negro Bureau of the Red International of Labour Unions (Profintern) and worked in Moscow and then in Hamburg. He resigned in 1933 and then settled in London in 1935. He was less than happy with the CPUSA and the CPGB, reporting that 'it is a pity that white Communists in Britain and America are not entirely free from racial prejudices'.[5] Nevertheless, many African-American writers – Langston Hughes, Richard Wright, Ralph Ellison, Chester Himes – joined the party. The ILD was shut down in 1947.

The highest proportion of 'Negro' members of the CPUSA were from Harlem, where the party was very active in supporting and campaigning with those opposed to the many forms of racial discrimination affecting them. The CPUSA wanted 'the Harlem [branch] to be thoroughly interracial, with blacks and whites sharing a common social and cultural life as well as participating in joint struggle ... Tendencies toward racial and ethnic separation had to be combatted'.[6]

The US government felt it had to deal with this Communist incursion. In 1938 it established the House Un-American Activities Committee and two years later passed the Smith Act 'which described as subversive any organization accused of advocating violent overthrow of the existing government ...

officially this was directed against Nazi organizations ... Actually, however, it could be twisted to apply to the Communist Party'.[7] Among those who were accused of such subversion was singer and actor Paul Robeson: in 1950, his passport was confiscated and his performances were stopped. Trinidad-born Claudia Jones was jailed many times and eventually deported to the UK in December 1950.[8]

Nkrumah's reason for migrating to the UK was to continue his studies there. However, he soon became so involved with 'Black' issues that he abandoned academia. What were Nkrumah, the Black organisations and activists, and the *independistas* facing in Britain in 1945? As Britain was the imperial power they were combating, a detailed examination is necessary.

The UK: Labour Party victory 1945

In Britain there was some hope among the many campaigners that the new Labour government, elected in July 1945, would grant independence to the colonies. They were quickly disillusioned. Joe Appiah, who had represented the West African Students' Union (WASU) at the 1945 Pan-African Congress and became president of the union, reports that

> independence for my country came under Tory rule and not under the rule of our 'best friends' – the so-called 'socialist believers' in human dignity – Labour! I count this as one of the greatest betrayals of friends by friends in all history ... In early January 1946 [Deputy Prime Minister] Morrison happily announced, 'We are great friends of the jolly old Empire and are going to stick to it.' On 21st Feb 1946 [Foreign Secretary] Bevin bellowed in Parliament: 'I am not prepared to sacrifice the British Empire because I know that if the British Empire fell it would mean the standard of life of our own constituents would fall considerably.'[9]

Arthur Creech Jones, then Under Secretary of State for the Colonies, stated in an article published in 1945 that the Labour Party's colonial policy included the 'building of self-government ... too often we have been slow in helping the apprenticeships and in training in the art of government'. 'The development of social services' was also included, as was the 'creation of public spirit, the idea of service'. Andrew Cohen, the head of the Africa department of the Colonial Office, argued in 1947 that in West Africa 'internal self-government is unlikely to be achieved in much less than a generation'. Almost simultaneously Creech Jones, now Secretary of State for the Colonies, argued that 'Kenya will not be independent in my lifetime'.[10]

So was there anyone in the UK the *independistas* could turn to for support? There was some support from a few members of Parliament such as Fenner Brockway, but there was not much they could do, given that even a supposed 'left-winger' like Bevin was imperialist.

UK: Fabian Society's Colonial Bureau

What about the Fabian Society? After all, it had a Colonial Bureau, which was headed by Creech Jones until his appointment as Under Secretary. In its report for 1944–45 the Society stated that 'it is now a commonplace for persons and organisations in all the colonies to communicate their problems to the Bureau'. The attitude of the Fabian Colonial Bureau (FCB) was clearly expressed by Rita Hinden, its secretary, regarding a speaker at its conference 'Relations between British and Colonial Peoples', in April 1946:

> When Mr Nkrumah said 'we want absolute independence' it left me absolutely cold. Why? ... British socialists are not so concerned with ideals like independence and self-government, but with the idea of social justice.[11]

In 1991 I got in touch with Marjorie Nicholson, who was the FCB's Assistant Secretary at that time. She had attended one of the West African National Secretariat's (WANS) inaugural meetings, and had, of course, been at the FCB's 1946 conference. In a telephone conversation on 27 January 1992, of which I took notes, she told me that she thought Padmore had made a mistake in recommending Nkrumah as a speaker. 'Nkrumah thought like a communist ... Didn't matter whether he was a CP member ... what distinguished him was his fascist tendencies ... At Clacton he came across as a communist ... No good to us, I told Rita.'

UK: the Communist Party and 'coloured people' and the colonies

What about the British Communist Party? According to George Padmore, the Communist Parties in the colonial powers in Europe 'sadly neglected anti-imperialist work since their formation ... So in 1920 [1919] the USSR formed the Comintern to take over this work'.[12] The aim was to spread information about Communist policies and philosophies through propaganda, through education, through journals. The journals, of course including the *Negro Worker*, were banned in all colonies, and any arriving were confiscated.

The Comintern espoused the liberation of colonies and charged the parties in the 'Mother Countries' to support independence movements and to recruit 'colonials' at home and in the 'métropoles'. From 1928, Communist Parties were also instructed to eradicate racist attitudes and practices within them. The Communist Party of Great Britain generally ignored these directives: no work was done in the colonies except a little in India and regarding the discriminations faced by Indian seamen on British merchant ships. The issue of racism within the CPGB was completely ignored.[13]

So did the British Communist Party deal with colonialism, with racism at all? Its Colonial Bureau was set up in 1925, headed by Clemens Palme Dutt. It became involved mainly with issues regarding India. People of Indian and African origin/descent in the UK and the racism they faced were ignored, except the conditions faced by Indian seamen.[14] One example of this lack of interest is revealed in the biography of Clemens's brother Rajani, by John Callaghan. There is no mention of Africa or the 'West Indies' in this book on the editor of the CPGB's newspaper the *Daily Worker*! Rajani Palme Dutt was also the CP's vice-chairman and headed the CPGB's International Section, and is acknowledged as an important 'theoretician'.[15]

Did the Colonial Information Bureau replace the Colonial Bureau? It published a fortnightly (duplicated) *Colonial Information Bulletin* beginning in 1937. This was replaced by the printed monthly *Inside the Empire* in 1940, a mere four small pages priced at 'twopence'; and then by *Inside the Empire Quarterly* in 1945. (This reduction in the frequency of publication appears to me to indicate a lack of sales.) In the copies I've seen, the focus is usually on India, with a few mentions of Africa and the 'West Indies'. The *Quarterly* is priced at sixpence; pages are now bound. I have only seen two copies: the issue for April 1945 (vol. 4, no. 1) contains an article 'Nigerian Labour on the move' by T.A. Bankole, the president of the Nigerian TUC, then in London to attend the World Federation of Trade Unions meeting. The *Editorial Comment* includes the 'Nigerian Constitution' and the 'Arab League'; there are two articles on India. In the July issue (vol. 4, no. 2) the *Editorial Notes* are on Burma, 'Middle East recriminations' and Lord Wavell's 'proposal' regarding the Viceroy's Council in India. The articles are on 'The colonies and San Francisco' by Dr K.S. Shelvankar; 'Jews and Arabs in Palestine' by L. Zaidman and 'The future of Ceylon' by P. Keuneman. According to historian Kevin Morgan, 'when an export ban was imposed on Communist periodicals mid-1940, [the circulation of 2000] was insufficient to sustain publication, so at the end of the 1940s it was discontinued'.[16]

The back pages list the editorial board: Ben Bradley, Michael Carritt, H. Palmer and K. Shelvankar – all CPGB members. This seems to indicate that there were no 'Black' members deemed acceptable for such positions. Was racial discrimination ever discussed in these papers?

Among the CPGB pamphlets I found listed/collected/copied there are some on colonial issues, but the first and only one I could find published before the 1960s on the situation 'coloured' people faced in the UK is *No Colour Bar for Britain* by Phil Bolsover, published in 1955.

In 1938 the CPGB issued a statement 'Peace and the Colonial Question' and a 'Charter of Rights for Colonial People', which included universal suffrage, free education and trade union rights. At its fifteenth congress, also in 1938, the CPGB stated that it had 'not departed from its fundamental demand with regard to the colonies', which, it reaffirmed, 'is the right to complete independence'.[17]

At its 1943 congress the CPGB 'condemned the government's repressive actions in India, and pledged solidarity with colonial peoples'.[18] Naturally the CPGB hoped that it would be able to establish some form of collaboration with the Labour Party when it was elected in 1945. As the USSR had been Britain's ally in the Second World War, we should not be surprised that two Communists were elected to Parliament in 1945. But disillusionment soon set in.[19]

Perhaps inspired by the Labour Party's colonialism, the CPGB called an Empire Communist Conference in 1947. In the official report of the conference, in 'Political Report', and 'Reply to Discussion', Rajani Palme Dutt wrote that the 'basic principle of communist policy was the right of self-determination of all peoples ... The present policy of British imperialism is characterised by its alliance with American imperialism.' But 'self-determination' was not for all: he demanded 'immediate independence for India, Burma and Ceylon' and some 'Middle Eastern' colonies. But in the African territories 'there is no developed national movement able to base itself on and speak for the people. The essential first step forward must be the establishment of full democratic and civil rights so as to facilitate the advance of popular organisations as the basis of advance to full freedom.'[20]

The twenty-eight delegates represented both the colonies and the self-governing dominions. In the official report the speeches of these representatives are fully reported and most include portraits. However, the only report on 'East and West Africa and the West Indies' is at the end; it is noted as 'Supplementary Report', and there is no portrait of the speaker. This was Desmond Buckle, a member of the CP's Colonial Committee.[21] He was the only African member.

Neither Desmond Buckle nor Richard Hart are listed on the 'Who's who among the conference delegates'. Hart, a lawyer, trade union activist, Marxist and one of the founders of Jamaica's People's Nationalist Party, represented Jamaica at the conference. He was very critical of the omission of 'current demands by the West African colonies', and the demands by the Caribbean colonies 'for a federation' and an 'Executive Council responsible to the elected legislatures'.

The final Declaration stated that 'the democratic right of self-determination of all peoples is the cardinal principle of communist policy ... It was necessary to grapple with the actual problems, recognising the steps forward needed in each particular territory, particularly those where no political movements yet existed.'[22] The Declaration also included: 'We condemn the denial of elementary rights and liberties, the widespread practices of racial and colour discrimination in Africa and other British Empire territories.'[23] So 'coloured' people in Britain were not suffering from these discriminations and lack of rights in the UK, the 'mother country'!

Was it as a follow-up to the conference that the CPGB began to publish a monthly *Africa Newsletter* in 1947? From 1950 till 1954, it was edited by Desmond Buckle! Hakim Adi argues that,

> disillusioned by the Labour government's stand towards the colonies, many increasingly gravitated towards the CPGB. In 1947 the party's Africa committee (a sub-committee of the Internal Department's international affairs committee) began the publication of the monthly *Africa Newsletter*, which by 1951 had sold nearly 700 copies, half in Britain and nearly a third in Africa. It ceased publication in 1954.[24]

Historian Stephen Howe reports somewhat differently:

> The CPGB's influence among Africans in Britain in the post-war years, though difficult to assess with any precision, seems to have become weaker in the post-war years than in the 1930s ... Whilst the party ran an African Committee from 1950 onwards, rather few of its members seem at any time actually to have been Africans. The party's two major colonial conferences, in 1947 and 1954, were notable for their lack of African representation.[25]

I also could not find any evidence of an increase in Black membership at this time: Barbadians Peter Blackman[26] and Arnold Ward;[27] Ghanaian Desmond Buckle; Chris Braithwaite (aka 'Jones');[28] and British-born Len Johnson from Manchester had all joined before 1945.[29] Of course, it is quite possible that local branches had Black members.

Blackman, Buckle, Ward and Braithwaite knew each other well, as Mr Blackman repeatedly told me in our many conversations beginning in 1998. No, he would not tell me anything about the Communist Party, except that 'the Party didn't *see* us. In all the years I worked with Bradley I never even had a drink with him!'[30] In the surveillance files released on Blackman, MI5 reports that he 'quarrelled with the CPGB on the ground that they regarded Colonial activity merely as a side-line'.[31]

For me, the attitudes and ignorance of the CPGB and its members and historians are also revealed by Noreen Branson in her book, *History of the Communist Party of Great Britain, 1941–51*: 'Civil liberties remained a crucial issue in all colonial countries'.[32] Surely it was not 'civil liberties', but economic and political independence that was a 'crucial issue' in the colonies!

That the Communist Party had been making 'little headway in Africa' is reported in a 1950 UK government report, 'Communist Influence in the African Continent', produced by the Foreign Office, the Colonial Office, the War Office and the Commonwealth Relations Office. The report notes the attempts by the CPGB to circulate its *Africa Newsletter*, and that in 'British West Africa communism is non-existent'. It is important to note here that there was a discussion by the report's authors with a representative of the US State Department, who was given a copy of the report.[33]

UK: Kwame Nkrumah

Kwame Nkrumah arrived in the UK in 1945, intending to further his academic qualifications. But the introduction to George Padmore led to his being totally consumed by political activism.[34] He was appointed Regional Organiser of the Pan-African Congress to be held in Manchester in October 1945. This was attended by about 200 people, the majority from Africa, and included many trade unionists. Among those Nkrumah met at the Congress were Jomo Kenyatta, Hastings Banda, Obafemi Awolowo and Jaja Wachuku.[35] In his *Autobiography* Nkrumah argues that 'the delegates who attended were practical men of action ... The Congress' ideology became African nationalism – a revolt by African nationalism against colonialism, racialism and imperialism in Africa – and it adopted Marxist socialism as its philosophy.'[36]

In the official report on the Congress, Nkrumah is listed as representing the International African Service Bureau and that he was appointed as the secretary of the new Publicity Committee. While in Manchester Nkrumah stayed with Wilf Charles, a colleague of Len Johnson at the Moss Side CP.[37]

The Congress' Declaration ended with the words 'Colonial and Subject People of the world, Unite'. The 'Congress unanimously supports the members of the West African delegations in declaring: *That complete and absolute Independence for the Peoples of West Africa is the only solution to the existing problems*' (this last sentence is in bold in the original).[38]

Nkrumah naturally joined the West African Students' Union, and was appointed its vice president in 1946. According to WASU's historian, Hakim Adi, post-war 'WASU continued to maintain its contacts with the CPGB', which in 1948 decided to intensify 'the drive to develop cadres among African students in Britain'. At WASU's annual conference in July 1948 the students were addressed by leading CPGB member, Emile Burns.

Adi advises that 'it is not clear how many West Africans actually joined he CPGB at this time ... Certainly many were close supporters'.[39]

To attempt to achieve at least West African unity, Kwame Nkrumah, along with Joe Appiah, who had attended the Congress, went to Paris to interest activists there. A conference in London followed at which the West African National Secretariat (WANS) was formed. Their aim was to 'push forward the struggle for West African National Unity and Absolute Independence'. Kwame Nkrumah was appointed secretary. Other officials were I.T.A. Wallace-Johnson, Kojo Botsio, G. Ashie Nikoi, Bankole Awoonor-Renner, an acknowledged Communist, and Bankole Akpata who joined the CPGB in 1948.[40] The first step would be to hold a conference not only of the 'intelligentsia', but of workers, trade unionists and farmers.

To achieve this, WANS published a monthly journal, *The New African*, which included articles by the Francophone members. Only six issues were published; the paper 'collapsed owing to lack of funds'. WANS also published Bankole Awoonor-Renner's small booklet, *West African Soviet Union*. The printer for both was R.E. Taylor & Sons; this is not a printer noted on any of the CPGB pamphlets on my shelves. So did neither receive any help from the CPGB?[41]

Naturally, contact was made with as many organisations and activists in West Africa as possible. Nnamdi Azikiwe from Nigeria was very supportive, as was I.T.A. Wallace-Johnson, who had returned to Sierra Leone. Local newspapers published many supportive articles – whether any were published in the French colonies I do not know.

Nkrumah also travelled around the UK, not only to seek support for WANS but as a member of the Coloured Workers' Association (CWA), campaigning against the many forms of racial discrimination in the UK. He reports that he made 'fairly regular visits to Liverpool, Manchester and Cardiff'; in the 'East End of London, the meanest kind of African mud hut would have been a palace compared to the slums'.[42] The CWA had been formed by Ernest Marke, probably in 1944 or 1945:

> coloured men came to the Club ... Some students came as well ... meetings every Sunday at Coloured Colonial Social Club ... Ghanaians introduced Nkrumah to me as a "brilliant boy, just back from America" ... Nkrumah travelled for me ... It was a political education association, to talk freedom ... All Nkrumah wanted was to free the Gold Coast and the whole of Africa ... There was no recruitment by the Communist Party among Blacks ... I was only a sympathiser ... We were British during the war, but not afterwards ...

In his recollection of the 1945 Congress, published in 1995, Mr Marke recalls that Nkrumah's speech was 'exhilarating ... I was not surprised at his speech; he had spoken once or twice at my meetings in London'. Nkrumah and Fenner Brockway were among the speakers at the CWA's first annual meeting, as reported in the *West African Pilot* on 19 December 1947. Mr Marke did not attend as he was ill. The CWA was taken over by G.V. Matthews.[43]

Given what he saw in the UK, his experiences with the Fabian Colonial Bureau and the attitudes of the just-elected Labour Party, and his experiences of the work of the CPUSA, it is not surprising that Nkrumah got in touch with the Communist Party in the UK. This is fully reported in the files released by MI5 – 'Military Intelligence'. These files begin with MI5 reports on Nkrumah from 1947; it is clear that material began to be collected on him and on WANS, also by the Police Special Branch beginning in 1945.[44] So Nkrumah and WANS were under surveillance from the time of his arrival in the UK.

There are extracts from Nkrumah's intercepted letters, mainly about WANS, and to the CPGB. From summaries of his telephone conversations with Maud Rogerson of the Africa Committee we learn that he had asked for some financial support, but she told him on 7 June 1947 that 'she hadn't got much money'. She tries and again does not succeed in raising funds, or for getting volunteers to do secretarial work for WANS. All phone calls to the CPGB were listened to, so we know Nkrumah spoke with Rogerson a number of times and met two or three times with Michael Carritt of the Colonial Committee.

The report on the phone conversation between Nkrumah and Rogerson on 21 June 1947 includes: 'she would read his manuscript and made an appointment with him for next Tuesday'. The report on the call on 22 September 1947 includes: 'He asks if she has gone through that thing yet. She says she is in the middle of it now. She will pass it on to Dutt when she has finished and hopes that it will be published.' Is it possible that this refers to Nkrumah's book, *Towards Colonial Freedom*, published in 1947? It had been printed by Farleigh Press, which was owned by the CPGB. In this, Nkrumah seeks support for:

1) complete and absolute independence from the control of any foreign government;
2) freedom from political tyranny and democratic freedom;
3) freedom from poverty and economic exploitation and the improvement of social and economic conditions

PEOPLES OF THE COLONIES, UNITE.[45]

Summarised information on Nkrumah and WANS begins to be sent to the Commissioner of Police in Accra regularly; some information is also sent to the Security Liaison Officer in Nairobi and to the police in Gambia.

Nkrumah attended the short course on Marxism taught by Emile Burns for students from the colonies.[46] But learning about Marxism is not the same as being a Communist!

The Gold Coast

After some persuasion by his colleagues, Nkrumah accepted the offer of the secretaryship of the newly formed United Gold Coast Convention (UGCC) in 1947. Together with Kojo Botsio, he left for home in November of that year. Their ship left from Liverpool. Nkrumah reports in his *Autobiography* that 'at Liverpool I unexpectedly encountered difficulties with the authorities at the docks, for, unknown to me, the police had collected quite a file of information about my political activities in London. They were not at all happy about my presence at Communist meetings.'[47]

The 1948 'riots' in the Gold Coast were attributed by the government to Communist activism. MI5, which was in collaboration with the CIA, set up offices there and in Nigeria. I have seen no reports of their work.

What is particularly relevant here is that Nkrumah and the other five officials of the UGCC were arrested after the 'riots' in the Gold Coast in early 1948. As many had been killed a commission was set up to investigate. The UGCC was exonerated. Nkrumah not surprisingly recounts in his *Autobiography* that the Watson Commission's report on him states that 'he appears while in Britain to have had some Communist affiliations and to have become imbued with Communist ideology ... Nkrumah has not departed one jot from his avowed aim for a Union of West African Soviet Socialist Republics'. Nkrumah notes that 'the inclusion of the word 'Soviet' by the authorities was entirely a product of their imagination ... They thought the introduction of the word 'Soviet' in itself was all that was needed to imply the threat of Communism in its most extreme form to the Gold Coast and to Africa as a whole.'[48] I agree. A Colonial Office official argued that 'monitoring was not sufficient ... The battle against Communism is not a battle against ring-leaders, but a battle against ideas.' Committees were set up in the colonies to analyse the continuously gathered intelligence and decide on actions to be taken. Broadcasting services were extended as was the British Council, both of course spreading pro-British information – i.e. propaganda. Press controls were introduced at different times in all colonies. The number of scholarships to British universities – and to the USA – were increased. And, as I account in my book, various attempts to influence the press were begun.[49]

The Foreign Office set up a 'propaganda' section, the Information Research Department, much of whose work was 'the moulding of opinion

on colonial matters in America ... and disseminating material to UN delegations in New York ... in addition to British embassies and consulates the
world over'.[50]

My research certainly indicates that Frank Furedi's conclusion that
'Cold War propaganda was a weapon that sought to discredit any legitimate nationalist impulse by reinterpreting it as a communist conspiracy' is
correct.[51] This is absolutely crucial to our understanding of what the struggle for independence actually involved, what those *independistas* actually
faced.

Why was the USA involved?

Post-war, the UK was hugely indebted to the USA. In October 1941
President Roosevelt had approved US$1 billion in 'Lend-Lease' aid to
Britain; as the war progressed Britain received much more. In December
1945 the USA terminated the Lend-Lease. So the country was in debt and
with almost no source of income.[52] It could not export much as it had been
badly bombed, and as its manufacturing had been converted to wartime
use. So the only possible exports were colonial produce. This meant the
colonies and their produce were more important than ever.

Much of Europe was in the same situation, so the colonies were probably
more important than ever to their 'owners'. The colonial masters needed
not only to retain control but to ensure that all 'foreign' purchasers paid
high taxes and higher prices. Foreigners were prevented from acquiring or
controlling any mines, productive fields, etc. This system, usually referred to
as 'Imperial Preference', *had* to be retained. The USA, which had been classified as 'foreign', wanted its own direct access to all the colonial produce.

However, as the USA also wanted to ensure that the USSR could not
spread right across Europe (or into the colonies), it had to achieve some sort
of European integration. In his originally unpublished manuscript, Allen
Dulles, who had served on the OSS (Office of Strategic Service – i.e. 'intelligence') till it was terminated in 1945, and was then placed on the committee
formulating its replacement, wrote that 'if Western Europe does not receive
substantial aid ... they are likely to be reduced to the status of impotent
minions of Russian communism'. So the USA stopped supporting demands
by colonials for 'self-determination' and devised what came to be known
as the Marshall Plan to support and unify Western Europe. According to
Dulles, 'without preaching or dictating, we can continue to show that the
free enterprise system is the most efficient and productive system in the
world ... The Plan has become a policy to contain the advance of Russia
westward in Europe.' Beginning in 1948, $15 billion was advanced to help

rebuild Europe, but 'some Marshall Plan aid was to be used in the colonies'.[53] Abbot Low Moffat of the State Department gives a very clear outline of how Plan money was to be used there: to increase production of raw materials. And, of course, much of what the West bought with Plan money was from the USA. The CIA was much involved in the Plan, for example in manipulations of elections in Italy to ensure Communists were outvoted.[54]

The colonial masters and the USA

As I summarise in Chapter 8 of my book, there were many conferences between the colonial masters to discuss what needed to be done in their colonies. And with the USA. There were sometimes conflicting interests among them. And America also had to contend with the growth of the civil rights struggles: open opposition to the *independistas* was impossible. So how could they be united? Very easily, by labelling all *independistas*, all activists in the colonies, as Communist. After all, the expansion of the USSR had to be stopped.[55]

Was this the *beginning* of the Cold War in at least the Gold Coast, or in all of Britain's colonies in Africa? And in all colonies in Africa? But: did the USSR plan to expand into Africa? Did it have any influence there? None of the books I have read recount any plans for such an expansion, or even for influence there, until well into the 1950s. So the war was against the *independistas* to ensure that control could be retained.

Notes

1 In terms of terminology, in this chapter I have followed the terminology that was current at the time being discussed.
2 Marika Sherwood, *Kwame Nkrumah: The Years Abroad 1935–1947* (Legon: Freedom Publications 1996), chapter 5, and Marika Sherwood, 'The African Students Association of America and Canada, 1941–1945', *Lagos Historical Review*, 14 (2015).
3 William A. Nolan, *Communism Versus the Negro* (Chicago, IL: Henry Regnery Co., 1951), 25.
4 Nolan, *Communism Versus the Negro*, 135; J. Calvitt Clarke, *Alliance of the Colored Peoples: Ethiopia and Japan Before World War II* (Oxford: James Currey, 2011), 62–77.
5 George Padmore, *Pan-Africanism or Communism?: The Coming Struggle for Africa* (London: Dennis Dobson, 1956), 315. The latest book on Padmore is: Leslie James, *George Padmore and Decolonization from Below* (Basingstoke: Palgrave Macmillan, 2015).

6 Mark Naison, *Communists in Harlem during the Depression* (New York: Grove Press, 1983), 47.

7 Taken from the very interesting biography by Nikolai Mostovets, *Henry Winston: Profile of a US Communist* (Moscow: Progress Publishers, 1983), 29.

8 On Claudia, see for example Marika Sherwood, *Claudia Jones: A Life in Exile* (London: Lawrence & Wishart, 1999).

9 Joe Appiah, *The Autobiography of an African Patriot* (Accra: Asempa Publishers, 1996), 162–163; I checked – it is in *Hansard*, 21/2/1946, vol. 419, col. 1365.

10 A. Creech Jones, 'Labour and the Colonies', *African Affairs*, 44:176 (1945), 111, 115; Paul Keleman, 'Modernising Colonialism: The British Labour Movement and Africa', *Journal of Imperial and Commonwealth History*, 34:2 (2006), 223–244; quotes are from 225.

11 Robert Clough, *Labour: A Party fit for Imperialism* (London: Larkin Publications, 1992), 99.

12 See chapter 16, 'Communism and Black Nationalism', in George Padmore, *Pan-Africanism or Communism* (London: Dobson Books, 1956), 289–379. Probably in order to ensure the support of the new allies needed after the Nazis invaded the USSR, the Comintern was dissolved in 1943.

13 John Callaghan, 'Colonies, Racism, the CPGB and the Comintern in the Inter-War Years', *Science and Society*, 61:4 (1997), 98, 513–525, and John Callaghan, 'The Communists and the Colonies: Anti-Imperialism Between the Wars' in Geoff Andrews, Nina Fishman and Kevin Morgan (eds), *Opening the Books: Essays on the Social and Cultural History of the British Communist Party* (London: Lawrence & Wishart, 1995), 4–22; Hakim Adi, 'West Africans and the Communist Party in the 1950s' in Geoff Andrews, Nina Fishman and Kevin Morgan (eds), *Opening the Books: Essays on the Social and Cultural History of the British Communist Party* (London: Lawrence & Wishart, 1995), 176–194; Marika Sherwood, 'The Comintern, the CPGB, Colonies and Black Britons, 1920–1938', *Science and Society*, 60:2 (1996), 137–163. See also Evan Smith, 'National Liberation for Whom? The Postcolonial Question, the Communist Party of Great Britain, and the Party's African and Caribbean Membership', *International Review of Social History*, 61:2 (2016), 283–315, and Holger Weiss, *CoWoPa – Comintern Working Papers*: www.yumpu.com/en/document/view/21666209/cowopa-comintern-working-paper-20–2010-abo-akademi [accessed 12 February 2021]. On lascars, see e.g. Marika Sherwood, 'Race, Nationality and Employment among Lascar Seamen 1660 to 1945', *New Community, A Journal of Research and Policy on Ethnic Relations*, 17:2 (1991), 229–244.

14 The CP's interest in India is, of course, indicated by two Indians – the Palme Dutt brothers – holding senior positions in the party. For some of the CPGB's interest in India, see The National Archives (TNA): HO45/25574 865000 'CPGB 1941–43'.

15 Marika Sherwood, 'Lascar Struggles against Discrimination in Britain 1923–1945: The Work of N.J. Upadhyaya and Surat Alley', *The Mariner's Mirror*, 90:4 (2004), and Sherwood, 'Race, Nationality and Employment among Lascar Seamen'; John Callaghan, *Rajani Palme Dutt: A Study in British*

Stalinism (London: Lawrence & Wishart, 1993); Pervaiz Nazir, *The Life and Work of Rajani Palme Dutt* (London: GLC Race Equality Unit, n.d.).

16 Kevin Morgan, *Against Fascism and War: Ruptures and Continuities in British Communist Politics, 1935–41* (Manchester: Manchester University Press, 1989), 187.

17 Hakim Adi, *Pan-Africanism and Communism: The Communist International, Africa and the Diaspora 1919–1939* (Trenton: Africa World Press, 2013), 287.

18 Noreen Branson, *History of the Communist Party of Great Britain, 1941–51* (London: Lawrence & Wishart, 1997), 23–24.

19 See for example Stephen Howe, *Anticolonialism in British Politics: The Left and the End of Empire 1918–1964* (Oxford: Clarendon Press, 1993), chapter 4.

20 R. Palme Dutt, 'Political Report to Conference' and 'Reply to Discussion' in *We Speak of Freedom* (London: CPGB, 1947), 4–30.

21 Buckle travelled very widely, collecting information as a journalist, and attending meetings, conferences, etc. in many parts of the world. From my limited conversations with a few Black activists of those days, he was well known to them. See Hakim Adi, 'Forgotten Comrade? Desmond Buckle: An African Communist in Britain', *Science and Society*, 70:1 (2001), 22–46.

22 Howe, *Anticolonialism in British Politics*, 165–166, n. 18, quoting from Richard Hart's 'notes'; Branson, *History of the Communist Party of Great Britain*, 145. See also Richard Hart, *Towards Decolonisation: Political, Labour and Economic Development in Jamaica 1938–45* (Kingston: Canoe Press, 1999); Hart – of European descent – makes clear that there were some Marxists in the Caribbean, but no Communists. See also Ken Post, *Strike the Iron: A Colony at War: Jamaica 1939–1945* (New Jersey: Humanities Press, 1981), vol. 2.

23 *We Speak of Freedom*, 90, n. 19.

24 Adi, 'West Africans and the Communist Party in the 1950s', 180, n. 12. Seven hundred does not seem a very large number of copies to me.

25 Howe, *Anticolonialism in British Politics*, 190, n. 18. On pages 161–164, Howe explores the problems/issues faced by the CPGB after the war.

26 There are no biographies of Peter Blackman, except for my entry on him for the *Oxford Dictionary of National Biography*; see his recently published poems: Peter Blackman, *Footprints* (Middlesbrough: Smokestack Books, 2013).

27 Arnold Ward was the founder of the Negro Welfare Association in 1931. The association worked with the CPGB and campaigned, with other organisations, on many issues, e.g. racial discrimination, the treatment of colonial seamen, Scottsboro, etc., and held social evenings. See Adi, *Pan-Africanism and Communism*, chapter 7, and Edward Thomas Wilson, *Russia and Black Africa before World War II* (New York: Holmes & Meier, 1974), 239–240. The level of police surveillance of such activists is indicated by the Metropolitan Police report in 1935 on a 'counter demonstration to Mosley by the London District CPGB at West Ham Town Hall': 'the following extremists were seen by Special Branch in vicinity of Hall – Chris Jones, Arnold Ward' (TNA: MEPO 2/3080). That Ward was a member is from Barbara Bush, *Imperialism, Race and Resistance* (London: Routledge, 1999), 221.

232 *Africa, the Soviet Union and the Cold War*

28 See Christian Høgsbjerg, 'Mariner, Renegade and Castaway: Chris Braithwaite, Seamen's Organiser and Pan-Africanist', *Race & Class*, 53:2 (2011), 36–57, and Christian Høgsbjerg, *Mariner, Renegade and Castaway: Chris Braithwaite: Seamen's Organiser, Socialist and Militant Pan-Africanist* (London: Socialist History Society/Redwords, 2014). Historian Stephen Howe thought that Buckle was a 'White man' (Howe, *Anticolonialism in British Politics*, 164, n. 18).

29 Johnson was apparently the main (or only?) speaker at a conference, 'What about the Colonies?', organised by the Moss Side branch of the CP held on 31 March 1946 (flyer in the files on Johnson held at the Working Class Movement Library in Salford). He had attended the 1945 Pan-African Congress. See Michael Herbert, *Never Counted Out! The Story of Len Johnson, Manchester's Black Boxing Hero and Communist* (Manchester: Dropped Aitches Press, 1992). It has not been possible to discover whether Gold Coast-born Bankole Awoonor-Renner had joined the CPGB. In the 1920s he studied in Moscow and the USA, where he joined the CP. There are MI5 files on him – KV2/1840–41 – but some of the very few released pages are unreadable. See also Holger Weiss, 'The Making of an African Bolshevik: Bankole Awoonor Renner in Moscow, 1925–1928', *Ghana Studies*, 9 (2009), 177–220.

30 I visited Mr Blackman many times after we met in 1991. He taught me so much, and was so patient with me. Occasionally he permitted me to take some notes; the quote is from a meeting on 22 February 1991. From 1940, Ben Bradley was secretary of the Colonial Information Bureau and published its *Bulletin* and then *Inside the Empire*.

31 TNA: KV2/1838, report 28/6/1941. There are three 'volumes' in this file, reporting on Blackman from 1937 till 1949. Many pages have been withheld. I have not seen KV2/1839, covering the years 1950–54 – opened in 2006. See also Sherwood, 'The Comintern, the CPGB, Colonies and Black Britons' and Adi, *Pan-Africanism and Communism*, chapter 7.

32 Noreen Branson, *History of the Communist Party of Great Britain, 1941–51* (Lawrence & Wishart, 1997), 145.

33 TNA: CO537/5263, 'Communist Influence in the African Continent', 1950.

34 Sherwood, *Kwame Nkrumah: The Years Abroad*, chapters 8–10; Kwame Nkrumah, *The Autobiography of Kwame Nkrumah* (Edinburgh: Thomas Nelson, 1957), chapter 5.

35 Kenyatta and Banda led their countries into independence; Awolowo was Leader of Government Business in the colony of Nigeria from 1951 to 1959, and leader of the opposition in the newly elected House of Representatives until he was imprisoned in 1962; Wachuku was a government minister in the just-independent Nigeria 1960–66.

36 Nkrumah, *The Autobiography of Kwame Nkrumah*, 53, n. 32.

37 Herbert, *Never Counted Out!*, 86, n. 27.

38 Hakim Adi and Marika Sherwood, *The 1945 Manchester Pan-African Congress Revisited* (London: New Beacon Books, 1995), 56, 103. See also, for example, Padmore, *Pan-Africanism or Communism?*, 154–170; Nkrumah, *The*

Autobiography of Kwame Nkrumah, 52–54; Howe, *Anticolonialism in British Politics*, 188–190.

39 Hakim Adi, *West Africans in Britain 1900–1960* (London: Lawrence & Wishart, 1998), 143.

40 Nkrumah, *The Autobiography of Kwame Nkrumah*, 55, n. 32. Letterhead on letter to W.E.B. Du Bois, 4/1/1946, Du Bois Papers, reel 59. On Awoonor-Renner, see Holger Weiss, 'Kweku Bankole Awoonor Renner, Anglophone West African intellectuals and the Comintern connection: a tentative outline – Part 2', Comintern Working Paper (2007); Marika Sherwood, 'Bankole Awoonor Renner', *Dictionary of African Biography* (Oxford: Oxford University Press, 2011).

41 Nkrumah, *The Autobiography of Kwame Nkrumah*, 57, n. 32.

42 *Ibid.*, 58–59, n. 32.

43 Adi and Sherwood, *The 1945 Manchester Pan-African Congress Revisited*, 38, n. 36; Ernest Marke, *In Troubled Water: Memoirs of My Seventy Years in England* (London: Karia Press, 1986), 136; notes from my conversations with Mr Marke, in February and March 1991.

44 TNA: KV2/1847, 1848, 1849m, 1850, 1851. The files begin with a letter dated 31 December 1942, from the 'Security Division of British Security Co-Ordination, USA'; 'Subject: Suspect Individual'; 'Source: US Second Service Command'; heading: 'Nwia Kosi Nkrumah'. It asks if there is any information on him. The file then jumps to an October 1945 brief note on the Manchester Congress, and gives '60 Burghley Road', where Nkrumah was living, as the address of 'K.O. Larbi, barrister-at-law'. (What an example of inefficiency!) Next is a 17 June 1947 report on WANS. This makes clear just how much has been withheld.

45 Kwame Nkrumah, *Towards Colonial Freedom* (London: Heinemann, 1962), 43. Nkrumah notes on the cover that 'this booklet is exactly as it was written originally, that is, twenty years ago'.

46 Sherwood, *Kwame Nkrumah: The Years Abroad*, 185, n. 1. Christian Høgsbjerg, 'An Interview with Joan Bellamy', *Leeds African Studies Bulletin*, 79 (2017–18), 148.

47 Nkrumah, *The Autobiography of Kwame Nkrumah*, 63, n. 32.

48 Nkrumah, *The Autobiography of Kwame Nkrumah*, 86–87, n. 32.

49 Marika Sherwood, *Kwame Nkrumah and the Dawn of the Cold War: The West African National Secretariat (1945–48)* (London: Pluto Press, 2019; Accra: Sub-Saharan Publishers, 2020), chapter 6. That the USA did the same is briefly mentioned in Larry Hancock and Stuart Wesler, *Shadow Warfare* (Berkeley: Counterpoint Press, 2014), 240.

50 Susan Carruthers, 'A Red Under Every Bed?: Anti-Communist Propaganda and Britain's Response to Colonial Insurgency', *Contemporary Records*, 9:2 (1995), 294–318; quotes are from 297, 298.

51 Frank Furedi, *Colonial Wars and the Politics of Third World Nationalism* (London: I.B. Tauris, 1994), 103.

52 According to the *Guardian* on 5 May 2006, 'the Treasury confirmed that the last payment of £45m will be made by the end of this year'. See Alan P. Dobson,

Anglo-American Relations in the Twentieth Century (London: Routledge, 1995), chapter 4.

53 Allen W. Dulles, *The Marshall Plan* (Oxford: Berg Publishers, 1993), 97, 101, 121; Peter Duignan and L.H. Gann, *The United States and Africa* (Cambridge: Cambridge University Press, 1984), 285 (on aid to colonies); Melvyn P. Leffler, 'The United States and the Strategic Dimensions of the Marshall Plan', *Diplomatic History*, 12:3 (1988), 277–306.

54 Abbot Low Moffat, 'The Marshall Plan and British Africa', *African Affairs*, 49:197 (1950), 302–308; Jan Carew, *Labour under the Marshall Plan* (Manchester: Manchester University Press, 1987), 10; Sallie Pisani, *The CIA and the Marshall Plan* (Lawrence, KS: University Press of Kansas, 1991), 67.

55 Sherwood, *Kwame Nkrumah and the Dawn of the Cold War*, chapter 8, n. 47.

10

Decolonisation and the Cold War:
African student elites in the USSR, 1955–64

Harold D. Weaver

This chapter undertakes a historical study of sub-Saharan Africa's education needs and the ways the Soviet Union responded to these needs, in particular the new, experimental, controversial Patrice Lumumba University. The years between 1955 and 1964 represent a critical period in the emergence of nationalism and unprecedented uprisings against European colonial powers. It marked the beginnings of a new age in Africa – a time to cast aside the vestiges of colonial dominance, together with its political, economic and cultural strangleholds. Importantly, as the period that represented a shift from dependence to self-determination, it was crucial for Africans to develop requisite expertise and skills to play new and expedient roles. The USSR, as leader of the socialist power bloc, represented an alternative model to Western ideas and practices on racial advancement, especially in the field of education. The radical political and economic ideas and the disparate educational models they presented to African scholars and leaders were cautiously embraced by some, and eagerly adopted by others.

This chapter will examine the developmental needs of African countries in this crucial decade. It will interrogate the recruitment, selection and sponsorship methods of the Soviets, and how they constructed a more appealing alternative to African advancement. By giving significant attention to the Patrice Lumumba Friendship University for the Peoples of Africa, Asia and Latin America, this chapter will discuss the ways an education in Moscow impacted Africans cognitively and affectively.

African priorities:
mental emancipation and the fight against white supremacy

In order to properly assess the effectiveness of Soviet training programmes for Africa and Africans, it is important to understand the rapid evolution of events on the continent in the post-Second World War period. To facilitate the evolution from colonialism to independence, some African leaders sought to confront its legacies. For them, education and indigenous human resource development were the instruments with which Africans could emancipate themselves and build strong and working nations.

During the years 1955–64, two outstanding phenomena emerged out of the experience of African nationalists. First was the changing status of their own countries from colonial dependencies to constitutionally sovereign states.[1] In 1955, there were only three nominally independent states in sub-Saharan Africa; by 1964, twenty-nine territories had achieved constitutional independence. Second was the reaction 'against the inferiority of status as members of a particular race'.[2] During this period there was a realisation that certain foreign procedures, concepts and techniques – oriented toward the metropole – were out of place in the African context. Other foreign adaptations were suitable, but rejected by African political leaders because of the perceived conflict between African objectives and values and foreign adoption. It was a period that Harvard political scientist Rupert Emerson called 'the rise of self-assertion',[3] including the keeping, adding or discarding of those practices that the populace, through its political leaders, saw fit. This was the politics and psychology of formal independence: the right to create the type of political, economic, cultural and educational systems that the African leadership wanted.[4] Nevertheless, Africa's leaders had to contend with the legacies of colonialism and the attendant impediments that came from being formerly governed subjects.

Colonial legacies

Legacies left by the departing European powers played prominent roles in the African ideological and behavioural responses to colonialism.[5] In the British colonial environment, little social contact existed between Africans and Europeans. In contrast, the French colonial administration intended to mould the Africans into 'good Frenchmen'. They encouraged the kinds of relationships that would cause an educated African to imitate all aspects of French culture, including education, dress and language.[6] Africans in British colonies, as Wallerstein's paraphrase of Nigerian Nobel Laureate, Wole Soyinka, indicates, 'did not need to invent the concept of négritude, for they had been practicing it all their lives'.[7] The adoption of a cultural-racial concept of pan-negrism (négritude) by African intellectuals in French colonies in Africa and the Caribbean revealed their disillusionment and discontent with the French colonial facade of 'assimilation'.[8] They were never truly considered and treated as Frenchmen. They were Black Frenchmen or French Africans or African Frenchmen. Similarly, the psychology of African nationalism in response to Belgian colonialism can be seen in portions of the speech by Prime Minister Patrice Lumumba at the Congolese independence ceremonies:

> We have known the mockery, the insults, the blows submitted to us morning, noon and night because we were 'nègres' ... We have known the law was never the same, whether dealing with a White or a Negro; that it was accommodating for the one, cruel and inhuman to the other ... We have known that in the cities, there were magnificent houses for the Whites and crumbling hovels for the Negroes, that a Negro was not admitted to movie theaters or restaurants, that he was not allowed to enter so-called 'European' stores, that when the Negro travelled, it was on the lowest level of a boat, at the feet of the White man in his deluxe cabin.[9]

What became clear was that white supremacy needed to be overhauled. It needed to be overcome as the key component of true and total liberation. Nationalism and anti-racism were synonymous, and their link was explicitly recognised by various African nationalists. Ndabaningi Sithole, founder of the Zimbabwean African National Union (ZANU), for example, specifically listed African nationalism in his colonised country as a response to white supremacy:

> There is a sense in which 'white supremacy' may be regarded as having been largely responsible for the effective cross-fertilization of African nationalism. Without the existence of this racially based doctrine of 'white supremacy', which adversely affected the African peoples, it is probable that the African peoples would not have sensed so quickly the 'consciousness of kind' which boomeranged on the colonial powers and the white settlers.[10]

One-time Ghanaian Prime Minister, Professor K.A. Busia, while in exile, was quoted: 'the fact that African nationalism is, in the first place, a demand for racial equality is its most conspicuous attribute'.[11] His political opponent, president and founder of modern Ghana, Kwame Nkrumah, observed that 'the Europeans relegated us to the position of inferiors'.[12] Because of this, African nationalists stressed the need for 'mental emancipation'.[13] Albert Memmi,[14] Frantz Fanon,[15] O. Mannoni,[16] Paulo Freire and Richard Wright[17] are among those who have written perceptively about the psychology of colonialism, including its racial aspects from the victim's vantage point. Hence, African decolonisers recognised that this new chapter in African history required not only political and economic emancipation but cultural and educational liberation as well. It was imperative to decolonise culture and history as presented in colonial texts in order to prompt that mental emancipation that was such a necessary prerequisite to true freedom. Decolonising both research and training was seen as a means of moving towards mental emancipation.

Afro-centric research

This stage in Africa's evolving history required a release from colonial restraints that went beyond political and economic dominance. Political leaders and scholars began discussing the necessary link between scholarship and political independence. Memmi, Fanon, Nkrumah and Freire were among those observers, who reminded us that colonial education in Africa was politically motivated and was used as a means to de-Africanise the continent's population.[18] Present in education, including colonial research, was the 'actual negation of every authentic representation of national peoples – their history, their culture, and their language ... (and) culture belonged (only) to the colonizers'.[19] African leaders recognised the importance of revitalising African research and studies to counter the demeaning influence of colonial education.

Harvard University's two prominent Africanists, Rupert Emerson and Martin Kilson, discussed the relationship between modern African nationalism and the need for an objective study of Africa's past. They argued that this search was necessary in order to counter the long-perpetuated view that Africa was a dark continent, and its people were little more than primitive 'tribesmen' before the arrival of the white man who endowed them with light, learning and civilisation. They pointed out that this racialised thinking was further influenced in the nineteenth century by the espousals of Darwin:

> If Africa had no culture worthy of taking its place among the other cultures of mankind, and had no history other than that of barbarism and slavery, then it was inevitable that the awakening of this inferior black race be seen only as a growing awareness of what Europe had to offer, and its advance measured only in terms of development along the lines laid down by the white man.[20]

African scholars and heads of state and government, including Jomo Kenyatta, Nnamdi Azikiwe and Leopold Senghor, all agreed that a rebirth of the history of Africa's peoples had to be acknowledged and, indeed, was mandatory. President Kwame Nkrumah put it most succinctly when addressing the opening session of the First International Conference of Africanists, in Accra, 1962; he stated that, for centuries, Africa was the receptacle into which flowed European culture, language, ideas and ideologies. To the rest of the world, Africa's past was unimportant. He also suggested that the surge of nationalism among Africans, and their growing interest in their roots, was viewed with considerable alarm by the colonisers:

> If Africa's history is interpreted in terms of the interests of European merchandise and capital, missionaries and administrators, it is no wonder that African

nationalism is regarded as a perversion and colonialism as a virtue ... In rediscovering, and revitalizing our culture and spiritual heritage and values, African Studies must help to redirect this new endeavour.[21]

The eminent Nigerian historian Kenneth Onwuka Dike was among those African scholars who linked African nationalism with scientific knowledge of the past. He stated that 'every nation builds its future on its past; (and) the African must not only instinctively have faith in his own existence, but must also satisfy himself by scientific inquiry that it exists'.[22]

Nigerian historian J.F. Ade Ajayi also shared Dike's view. He argued that every African political leader had to cast off the shackles of inferiority imposed by colonial regimes, and painstakingly search back into the history and culture in order to successfully engage in the nationalist struggle. He states that the African:

> needs an ideological answer to imperialism. He must believe in the future of Africa, and to do so convincingly, he must base his belief on a confident assessment of the achievements of the African in the past ... If he has any growing feelings of doubt about the future, he would demand less than self-government. Apart from his own personal emancipation, in order to succeed in the nationalist struggle, he would also need to restore the self-confidence of his followers ... Like the missionary seeking mass conversion, the nationalist leader realizes that he cannot reach the people effectively except in the language, the symbols, the culture, they understand. That is why the nationalist struggle and the organization of the nationalist party becomes an important exercise in national education and a major step in the building up of national unity and a common political loyalty.[23]

Afro-centric schooling

On their ascension to constitutional independence in the late 1950s and early 1960s, African nationalists began a review of the colonial legacy and exploration of the status of education in the post-colonial period. An examination of the nature of schooling will give us some idea of why it was imperative for African students to take advantage of study-abroad programmes offered by other nations in order to acquire the skills and knowledge needed for independence. Among the existing characteristics that required changes in order to aid decolonisation and development were the following: 1) an orientation towards Europe, both in content and in language of instruction; 2) a focus on humanistic studies; 3) a neglect of schooling opportunities for girls; and, 4) a shortage and underutilisation of facilities in higher education.

Several generalisations can be made about the education system inherited from the colonial government. Perhaps most important is that its major objective was to benefit the European coloniser, not the colonised African. In other words, the aim was to ensure Africa's continued dependency on Europe. American economist Martin Carnoy describes this relationship:

> The European powers used education to effect change, but only those changes that solidified their influence and control over the peoples of ... Africa. Although the policy was not altogether successful, it did manage to bring these areas into conditions of economic and cultural dependency which few have overcome with political autonomy.[24]

Considering the fact that the structures and models of education built by colonial governments were incapable of sustaining the needs of newly independent African nations, the Soviets built alternative programmes that Africa's scholars, nationalists and elites embraced.

Patrice Lumumba University: a new, experimental higher education institution in Moscow for newly independent African states

In order to help newly independent sub-Saharan African countries overcome deficiencies in human resources, Soviet authorities established an experimental, post-secondary training centre. This centre, called the Patrice Lumumba Friendship University for the Peoples of Africa, Asia and Latin America, was expected by Soviet officials to become instrumental in the struggle for African and other Third World decolonisation and independence. The initial statement announcing the Friendship University indicated Soviet governmental intentions. During his first visit to the Third World – Indonesia – in February 1960, the Soviet head of government and party, Nikita Khrushchev, indicated why the new university was needed:

> [To] give aid to colonial and neo-colonial Third-World countries in the training of their national cadres of engineers, agricultural specialists, doctors, teachers, economists, and specialists in other branches of knowledge, the Soviet Government has decided to set up in Moscow a university of the friendship of peoples.[25]

A significant factor about the university was the attention given to recruiting 'talented young people coming from poor families'.[26] In his speech, Khrushchev recognised some of the problems many Africans themselves considered as limiting Africa's progress and development. Prominent of all was that little attention was paid to technology and the applied sciences in higher education in Africa. This prompted the creation of Lumumba University in Moscow. What resulted was a university with a 'basic skills' faculty – for those needing language, subject-matter, and skills-and-attitude preparation for academic rigours – and six other faculties: Medicine; Engineering; Agriculture; History and Philosophy; Economics and Law; and Mathematics, Physics and the Natural Sciences. A University Council, its Board of Trustees, comprised the three founding organisations: the Central Committee of Trade Unions, the Soviet Afro-Asian Solidarity Committee and the Union of Soviet Societies for Friendship with Foreign Countries. Additional units represented in governance were the Soviet Ministry of Higher and Specialised Secondary Education, the Soviet Committee of Youth Organisations, the Rector and Pro-Rectors and elected representatives of faculty and students.

Friendship University v. other Soviet universities

In what ways did the Friendship University differ from other universities in the Soviet Union? Soviet higher education curricula were aimed at meeting the needs of a Soviet society. Industry was highly specialised; technology, demonstrated by the launching of Sputnik 1 in 1957, was internationally competitive. Agriculture, under Khrushchev's new programmes, became increasingly mechanised. Among the differences between the Friendship University and other institutions of higher education in the USSR was its recruitment, selection and sponsorship process; its governance; its curriculum; and the degrees awarded. Friendship University students differed from foreign students at other Soviet universities in that many did not meet formal admission requirements. Unlike many Soviet students, whose governments revered the relationship between theory and practice, African students were likely to have interrupted their schooling for work. However, in many cases, the schooling halt was compulsory, because of a shortage of placements in African secondary schools or because of economic poverty. This interruption did not measure the intellectual abilities or skills of African students; rather it revealed constraining aspects of the African colonial context. These factors accounted for a lack of academic preparation for higher education on the part of some African students.

Whereas bilateral agreements or home-government sponsorship sent many foreign students to the USSR for university training, Friendship University students were often dissidents or, at least, did not adhere to the favour of their own governments. Hence, many were in Moscow independent of the political machinery in their respective countries. Other foreign students in the USSR, especially from the USA and Europe, were selected with at least tacit approval of their governments. Khrushchev predicted this variety during his initial announcement when he stated that though 'the majority of [foreign] students have been sent by government organs ... [the Friendship University should be a place that would] train both those who are sent by government organs and those who express their personal wish to study at the university'.[27] University students who were already in the USSR came from Western industrialised countries. They also came from the socialist European, Asian and Caribbean countries, and from other Third World countries. They were being trained at the traditional Soviet universities. However, as was initially announced, Lumumba Friendship University was founded primarily for the benefit of Third World countries, with Soviet students complementing the enrolment. There was at least one African-American student, MaryLouise Patterson, whose parents had been active in Communist Party USA (CPUSA) activities, who was studying and completing her medical studies at Lumumba University.

Another unique aspect of the university was that, though students did not necessarily have a post-secondary school degree, they received a Master of Science degree at graduation. In addition, foreign students at Lumumba University, except for that minority majoring in social and human sciences, did not have to follow required courses in political economy, scientific socialism, Marxism–Leninism and the history of the Communist Party of the Soviet Union (CPSU) as did students at other Soviet universities. Furthermore, there was no compulsory physical education, and on-the-job training at the Friendship University was about half that of other Soviet universities. Hence, in comparison with the others, the Lumumba curriculum was able to lop one year off the time spent in the post-preparatory faculty.

Recruitment, selection and sponsorship: how did African students get to the USSR?

The Soviets used a variety of personnel and organisations to publicise and recruit for the university. At the World Festival of Youth and Students in Helsinki in 1962, I observed the recruitment campaign as aggressive, relying heavily on Third World students themselves, who often worked together in congenial teams. Minimal bureaucracy, a focus on subjects obviously geared to meet African human resource needs, and an emphasis on opportunities for training in fields which Africans were not receiving at home or in the West were among the characteristics of recruiting efforts. The Pro-Rector for Admissions, Professor Yerzin, travelled throughout Africa and Asia to recruit high-quality students. Soviet consulates and embassies in Asia, Africa and Latin America were also used for the dissemination of information and the reception of applications. They actively involved the home offices of international organisations, including the World Federation of Democratic Youth in Budapest, and the International Union of Students in Prague,[28] in recruiting students.[29] Once accepted, the students were guests of the Soviet government, which took care of all expenses. Tuition and medical care were free for all – citizen and non-citizen. In addition to stipends of 90 roubles per month, the African student, on arrival in Moscow, received about three hundred roubles to purchase winter clothes.[30] The 90 roubles included board money, but costs at the school cafeterias did not exceed several roubles per month. During the summer months, students were given an additional sum of 150 roubles and often a free stay at one of the rest homes on the Black Sea.

Students from Africa were at the Friendship University under varying sponsorship. Some, like many from South Africa, went under scholarships offered directly by the USSR. Usually those students were studying without permission of their home governments and required clandestine travel, which after students surfaced in the USSR, they would then write home to indicate their location.[31] Another group was under United Nations programmes, both in trust territories and in non-self-governing areas, in which the Soviet Union participated. Under a third sponsorship were those students with scholarships subsidised by home governments or dominant political parties. A fourth sponsorship was non-governmental international organisations with close ties to the USSR, as, for example, the International Union of Students in Prague. The percentage of students who did not have permission from their home governments was small. In fact, in the early days of the university, some students, especially those from countries still under colonial rule, had to do as the early revolutionaries trained at Moscow's Lenin International School: 'Most of the students who attended … traveled on false passports, under assumed names, and reached the Soviet Union via indirect routes.'[32] In a few cases, students of visiting delegations were actually offered scholarships on the spot and stayed on to study in the USSR.

The early days of the university, especially before the achievement of constitutional independence by individual African countries, were marked by a lack of coordination in the recruitment-selection process. East, South and Central Africans, for example, had to make their way to Cairo, where John Kalle,[33] a Ugandan later killed in an IL-18 flight on the way to Gary Powers's showpiece U-2 trial, made the necessary preliminary arrangements and secured their air passage to the USSR or, as the case might be, to another socialist country in Europe. Students from countries with 'moderate' regimes, without Soviet embassies and consulates, got Soviet visas in 'radical' countries[34] or in those countries with diplomatic relations with the USSR. This meant that many students left Africa without the knowledge and permission of their home governments. Take the spectacular example of a young Kenyan student so highly motivated to becoming a doctor that he actually walked from Nairobi to Cairo over a two-year period, assured that if he reached Cairo he would be able to study free of charge in a socialist country. In his case, he was assigned to a medical school in Poland. His story continued to be a happy one. He married a Polish classmate, raised a family of two successful film-makers and television creators, and later returned to Kenya with her, where they both became immersed in the Kenyan health service.

By the end of the Khrushchev era, October 1964, a significant shift occurred away from the fragmented, uncoordinated recruitment-selection process to a more centralised, coordinated process (by government agency or dominant political party) in keeping with the national human resource or political needs of African countries. The signing of the OAU [Organisation of African Unity] Charter, in May 1963, helped to ensure this by encouraging inter-African cooperation and discouraging subversive attempts from other African countries.[35] Meanwhile, the university had given the African continent a jump-start in trained personnel in medicine and other subjects needed in the first decade of decolonising, post-independent sub-Saharan Africa.

Adopting newly structured curricula to rethink Africa's industrialisation and development

Before looking at the cognitive curricula, let us briefly respond to the question: what were the affective experiences of African students when they arrived in Moscow? They found that they were given preferential treatment by a system that insisted that they succeed and a population that generally warmly welcomed them. Like the earlier African-American sojourning artists Langston Hughes and Paul Robeson ('for the first time, I walk in full human dignity') in the 1930s, the sub-Saharan African students of the 1950s and 1960s tended to find a warm, hospitable reception from faculty, fellow students and the general population. But it was the warm, passionate sexual relations that I witnessed between African males and Soviet females that was especially empowering for many African males, while at the same time antagonistic to some of their Soviet male counterparts. And then there were drunken Soviet men and women who were heard to curse Chairman Khrushchev for bringing in favoured foreigners, who, they said, were taking valuable resources away from Soviet students and other citizens. These were the exceptions, and not the rule, as mainstream Western media and scholarship reported to us.

At the university, first-year Preparatory Faculty instructors often came to the African students' dorms to give them one-on-one tutorials to help with the Russian language. African students also received language lessons from Russian students with whom they shared dormitory rooms.

The aims and organisation of the curriculum

The university's Board of Trustees (University Council) spelled out six major aims, the first of which was related to the curriculum:

> To train highly-qualified engineers, specialists in agriculture, doctors, teachers, economists, jurists and other specialists familiar with the latest developments in science and technology, and with the practical aspects of the subjects, who are educated in a spirit of humanism and friendship of nations.[36]

To implement those objectives, the university was organised into one general, preparatory faculty and six subject-area faculties, based on clusters of academic disciplines and specialisms: 1) Engineering; 2) Physics, Mathematics, Chemistry and Biology; 3) Economics and International Law; 4) Philology and History; 5) Medicine; and 6) Agriculture. A graphic breakdown of African students by faculty, for the final year of our study, 1963–64, follows:

Table 10.1 Approximate enrolment by faculty, Lumumba Friendship University, 1963–64[a]

Faculty	Approximate number
Engineering	500
Medicine	100
Physics, Mathematics, Chemistry, Biology	200
Agriculture	100
Philology and History	125
Economics and International Law	400
Total, less Preparatory Faculty	1,425
Preparatory	900
Grand total	2,325

[a] Press conference of the Rector, Lumumba Friendship University, Moscow, 3 December 1964. Also see J. Webbnik, *African Students*, 11. The Rector gave the total number as 2,582, but gave the breakdown by faculty as stated above. I cannot account for the discrepancy between the total in the chart – 2,325 – and the total figure he gave – 2,582 – except that the Rector indicated that his figures were *approximate*.

The transitional period: Preparatory Faculty of 'basic skills'

Prior to undertaking study in their regular and specialised fields, African students were exposed to an innovative educational experiment in the vanguard of special programmes that were also surfacing in the USA: SEEK (Search for Education, Elevation and Knowledge Program at the City University of New York), the Transitional Year, the Urban University, among others. The Preparatory Faculty served a transitional function for those neither linguistically nor academically prepared for the regular Soviet university curriculum. Because of their Russian-language deficiency, the students had to spend at least one year in the faculty. The specific length was determined by achievements during the first year. The authorised range was between one and three years as initially set by the university. The length of study, curriculum and student–teacher relations clearly were based on student needs as perceived by the administrators and teachers. All students spent the first three months in intensive training in the Russian language, especially on vocabulary related to their intended specialism. Then, language training was combined with secondary school mathematics (with emphasis on algebra), physical geography and the political history of the world as related to one's own continent. African students in world political history, for example, dealt with Africa's historical resistance to Europe. In addition, the preparatory course was expected to provide:

1. Study skills – discipline. Complicated by the fact that studying was to be done in a new and totally different language, e.g. with word endings in verb conjugations and adjectival and noun declensions in Russian that were not present in many languages.
2. Intensified capsule of secondary – and, in some cases, primary school – education, which was necessary for successful college study and often not accessible in Africa.
3. Acclimatisation to Soviet society – including the social system (with folkways, mores and codes of behaviour peculiar to the Soviet state and system). In the absence of a formal orientation programme, an ongoing, informal orientation occurred.[37]

Considering the limited technological training in African secondary schools, students coming from the continent were faced with a severe limitation in their competition with Soviet students. In the eight-year schools of Soviet pre-university education, science subjects took up an average of some 35 per cent of the formal class time[38] and increased to fifteen hours per week in the last year of secondary school.[39] African students, on the other hand, with few exceptions, had an entirely humanistic primary- and secondary-school education, and in most cases only minimal training in mathematics and the natural sciences.[40]

Natural resources: Geology Department

The Lumumba University curriculum reflected the priority of Soviet political, research and training personnel for African control of its natural resources. The Geology Department of the Faculty of Engineering prominently epitomised this priority. Students of Geology were among approximately 1,725 students studying in the regular faculties at the university during the 1963–64 academic year. Significantly, around 1,200 – or 70 per cent of all Friendship University students – were majoring in the natural, physical or medical sciences. The percentage of Africans in Medicine, Engineering, Physics, Chemistry, Biology and Agriculture was at least 75 per cent, and possibly higher.[41] All Engineering students were required to make a preliminary decision during their first year about a concentration. Options were 1) Geology, 2) Civil Engineering or 3) Mechanical Engineering. It was the Geology majors who received training in the prospecting, extracting and utilisation of natural resources. At the end of a four-year course, a successful Geology major left with a Master's degree in Mining Engineering.

Certain subjects were required of Geology majors during their course of study in the natural and mathematical sciences: the organisation and economics of mining operations, crystallography and mineralogy, petrography, heat engineering, hydraulics and hydrodynamics, the strength of materials, theoretical mechanics, physics, higher mathematics and chemistry. The luxury of selecting a major within the department was not deferred until the junior year, as it was then in the USA, but had to be decided during the freshman year. Students also had to make a further decision on specialisation within Geology itself in the first year. The options were 1) the mining of solid minerals, 2) oil and gas extraction or 3) geological prospecting and surveying.

The curriculum of mining solid minerals included other specialised courses such as the supply of electricity to mining operations, ore concentration, projecting mining enterprises and the technology of mechanisation of underground and open-pit mining. Those choosing to major in oil and gas extraction took the following courses to fulfil degree requirements: the geology of oil and gas deposits, the planning of oil and gas fields, oil and gas production equipment, the processing and chemistry of oil and gas, the technology and mechanisation of oil and gas transportation, the technology and technique of drilling, and the geology and geophysics of oil and gas extraction. Required courses in the area of geological prospecting and surveying included engineering geology, mineralogy and crystallography, petrography, structural geology and geological mapping, and analytical, physical and colloidal chemistry. Training was not limited to the classroom.

Practical work was gained through work in mines and oil fields, in laboratories and on geological expeditions. The training they received culminated in the production of a research paper that documented the findings from the student's research project on their country.

We turn to examine the relationship between the curriculum in Geology, on the one hand, and African realities, on the other, as pinpointed by the Soviet political leadership and senior Soviet Africanist researchers. Key Soviet political leaders expressed the need to diffuse technological skills in mineral extraction. In his well-publicised speech to the fifteenth session of the United Nations General Assembly on 18 September 1959, Premier Khrushchev noted his government's concern about the exploitation of Third World resources by Western interests:

> The peoples of many of these countries have won political independence, but they are still cruelly exploited by foreigners economically. *Their oil and other natural resources are being plundered.* They are being taken out of their countries for almost nothing in return, even while they yield huge profits to the foreign exploiters.[42] (emphasis mine)

Prior to this 1959 speech, Khrushchev and his government, through its Permanent Delegate, had used the United Nations as a forum to communicate its concern about the manifest influence of the West in African mineral exploitation. The Soviet representative at the UN had earlier accused Western prospectors, under the guise of United Nations-sponsored surveys, of prospecting to aid private Western businesses at the expense of the countries for which the prospecting was carried out. In addition to the General Assembly, Soviet delegates also used the Trusteeship Council as a forum to expose the administering powers' economic policies and practices in the trust territories: Cameroon (British and French), Togo (British and French), Southwest Africa (Namibia) (South Africa),[43] Somalia (British and French), Tanganyika (British) and Rwanda-Burundi (Belgium). The European trust administrators – Belgium, France and the United Kingdom – were specifically accused of allowing foreign, private companies, with official licenses, to prospect and exploit the mineral resources of Africa.

The reasons given for the Soviet criticism concerned the division of Africa at the Congress of Berlin (1884–85) that began the territorial scramble for Africa and resulted in European colonialism and territorial occupation. The colonial practice was not to consult with the local population nor to secure their consent on such vital matters.[44] This meant that even after African political or constitutional independence, the European governments would still maintain and retain significant economic influence, through natural resources, and thus inhibit self-determination and eventual autonomy. This is a classic example of neo-colonialism, that phenomenon of outside

Figure 10.1 Soviet anti-apartheid poster, 'Africa' *c.* 1960. On the clothing of the colonisers being dumped are the words 'apartheid' and 'racism'

economic control, of remote control, after independence, which insured continued cultural and political dominance from the outside.

Soviet scholars also reiterated in their published works the same charges made by their diplomats in international political forums. The widely respected academician Professor I.I. Potekhin, the founding Director of Moscow's Africa Institute, accused Western prospectors of intentionally underestimating the mineral potential of African countries.[45] The results of such distortions were twofold. One was that it misled African political and economic decision-makers into underestimating their own resources available for economic development. The other was that the nations received smaller remunerations for their raw materials than those to which they were entitled. One specific example reported by Potekhin was Guinea-Conakry: whereas French specialists had estimated iron ore reserves to be between 2.5 and 3.5 billion tons, 'Soviet geologists, who visited Guinea, following only a preliminary study, estimated iron ore reserves at 20 to 30 billion tons'[46] or up to ten times what the French experts had estimated. What effect did Potekhin feel that the development of mining and other industries had on African leadership coping with post-independence problems? To what extent was his writing prescriptive? He opined:

> The main condition for the conquest of economic independence, and for the creation of a harmoniously developed economy, is the development of industry. The slogan of industrialization is one of the most popular slogans in contemporary Africa. But the economically weak states of Africa do not at present have the strength for a creation of large-scale enterprises of the various *metallurgical* or machine-building industries. Therefore, industrialization is beginning with the enlargement of a *mining industry*, the building of hydro-electric stations, and enterprises of light industry plants for the processing of agricultural products.[47] (emphasis mine)

Did the Lumumba University curriculum respond to the industrialisation and development needs of African states? Yes. The university gave high priority to diffusing technological data to African students through the natural, physical and medical sciences. Students were free to select, or were coerced into selecting, the sciences in at least 70 per cent of cases,[48] a sharp contrast to the small number of African students who were majoring in the natural and physical sciences in Western countries and in sharp contrast to reports in USA scholarly literature and public media.

Conclusion

Limited national higher education facilities for males and females made it necessary for sub-Saharan Africans to utilise transnational opportunities in order to obtain rapid indigenisation (Africanisation) of human resources. Among those countries intervening was the USSR, with a variety of formal and non-formal education and training programmes inside and outside the country. The Soviet programmes in this critical decade of African decolonisation, 1955–64, demonstrated creative and pragmatic innovation 1) in programme development dedicated to African needs and priorities, with curricula focusing on technology, health and natural and physical sciences, including Geology; 2) in non-traditional admissions procedures, often for non-traditional students, in recruitment, selection and sponsorship; and 3) in providing an environment for mental emancipation and empowerment of future African elites. In relationship to sub-Saharan African needs and priorities, African students found Soviet education programmes, including those at Patrice Lumumba Friendship University for the Peoples of Africa, Asia and Latin America, to be useful in facilitating African industrialisation, development, conscientisation and democratisation through the indigenisation (Africanisation) of human resources.

Notes

1 For the ingredients involved in a transfer of bureaucratic power, see David Apter, *Ghana in Transition* (New York: Anthenum, 1963). I am grateful for the assistance of Gbemisola Abiola, Michelle Gibbs, Anne S. Nash, Rachel Lee Rubin and Mark Solomon in the preparation of this chapter.

2 Margery Perham, in Kenneth Kirkwood (ed.), *African Affairs 1*, St Anthony's Papers 10 (London: Chatto & Windus, 1961).

3 Rupert Emerson, *From Empire to Nation: The Rise to Self-Assertion of Asian and African Peoples* (Cambridge, MA: Harvard University Press, 1960).

4 L. Gray Cowan, 'The Current Political Status and Significance of Africa South of the Sahara', *The Journal of Negro Education*, 30:3 (1961), 92.

5 Rupert Emerson, 'Crucial Problems Involved in Nation-Building in Africa', *The Journal of Negro Education*, 30:3 (1961), 193.

6 Frantz Fanon, *The Wretched of the Earth* (New York: Grove Press, 1963).

7 Immanuel Wallerstein, *Africa: The Politics of Independence* (New York: Vintage Books, 1961).

8 Victor C. Ferkiss, *Africa's Search for Identity* (New York: George Braziller, 1969), 157.

9 Patrice Lumumba quoted in Hans Kohn and Wallace Sokolsky (eds), *African Nationalism in the Twentieth Century* (Princeton, NJ: Van Nostrand, 1965), 119.

10 Ndabaningi Sithole, *African Nationalism* (New York: Oxford University Press, 1968).

11 K.A. Busia, *The Challenge of Africa*, as quoted in Kohn and Sokolsky, *African Nationalism in the Twentieth Century*, 13.

12 Kwame Nkrumah, *Axioms of Kwame Nkrumah* (London: Nelson, 1967), 24.

13 See Nnandi Azikiwe, *Renascent Africa* (London: Cass, 1968 reprint).

14 Albert Memmi, *The Colonized and the Colonizer* (Boston, MA: Beacon Hill Press, 1960).

15 Fanon, *The Wretched of the Earth* and Frantz Fanon, *Black Skins, White Masks* (New York: Grove Press, 1967).

16 O. Mannoni, *Prospero and Caliban* (New York: Praeger, 1964).

17 Richard Wright, 'The Psychological Reactions of Oppressed Peoples', in Richard Wright, *White Man, Listen!* (New York: Doubleday, 1957).

18 Paulo Freire, *The Pedagogy of the Oppressed* (New York: Herder and Herder, 1970), 13.

19 Freire, *The Pedagogy of the Oppressed*, 14.
20 Rupert Emerson and Martin Kilson (eds), *The Political Awakening of Africa* (Englewood Cliffs, NJ: Prentice-Hall, 1965).
21 President Kwame Nkrumah, Address to the First International Congress of Africanists, University of Ghana, Legon, 12 December 1962. Quoted in Emerson and Kilson, *The Political Awakening of Africa*, 25–26.
22 K.O. Dike, 'History and African Nationalism', *Proceedings of the First Annual Conference of the West African Institute of Social and Economic Research* (Ibadan: Ibadan University College, 1952, reprinted 1957), 31.
23 J.F.A. Ajayi, 'The Place of African History and Culture in the Process of Nation-Building in Africa South of the Sahara (1960)' in Immanuel Wallerstein (ed.), *Social Change: The Colonial Situation* (New York: John Wiley and Sons, 1966), 612.
24 Martin Carnoy, *Education as Cultural Imperialism* (New York: David McKay Co., 1974), 82.
25 Seymour Michael Rosen, *The Peoples' Friendship University in the USSR* (Washington, DC: US Department of Health, Education, and Welfare, 1962), 4, quoting from a text carried by Radio Moscow, 22 February 1960.
26 *Ibid*.
27 *Ibid*.
28 *Ibid*. Headed for some years by an Iraqi youth leader, Razik, whom I last saw at a May 1969 meeting of experts in higher education, sponsored in Paris by UNESCO; surprisingly, no Africans were among the educational administrators participating.
29 Seymour Rosen, *The Peoples' Friendship University in the USSR*, 6–7.
30 Sources for this material include personal interviews and a University-issued booklet entitled 'Rules of Enrollment to the Peoples' Friendship University named after Patrice Lumumba for the 1963–1964 Academic Year' (Moscow: Peoples' Friendship University, n.d. [probable date 1963]), 1.
31 Edward A. Raymond, 'Education of Foreigners in the Soviet Union' (advance paper for the 66th Annual Meeting of the American Political Science Association, Los Angeles, California, 8–12 September, 1970), 7.
32 *Ibid*.
33 Interview with John Kalle, United Nations, New York, October 1959.
34 'Radical' in this sense refers to the self-proclaimed socialist governments in Ghana, Guinea, Mali and the United Arab Republic.
35 It is clear that this was not totally implemented, but it did tend to lessen tensions, at least temporarily, between certain neighbouring countries. Ghana, for example, stopped processing travel documents for Nigerian youth desiring to study in the Soviet Union.
36 *1964 Spravochnik (Catalogue: Peoples' Friendship University Named After Patrice Lumumba)* (Moscow: Peoples' Friendship University, 1964), 4. The other five objectives were (1) to carry out urgent scientific research work, including designs, technologies and cultures of Asian, African and Latin American countries, which would enable them to develop their national economies;

(2) to produce high-quality textbooks and educational and graphic aids in Russian and foreign languages for students of the University or other educational establishments; (3) to train scientific teaching staff for work in the University and in higher educational establishments abroad; (4) to popularise scientific disciplines; and (5) to cooperate on the basis of mutual help on questions of educational and scientific research, with higher educational scientific establishments, scientific societies, governmental establishments, social organisations and enterprises of the Soviet Union and abroad by means of exchange of information and participation in national, regional and international meetings and conferences.

37 Called 'Personal Adjustment' at some American universities.
38 Nigel Grant, *Soviet Education* (Baltimore, MD: Penguin, 1964), 39.
39 *Ibid.*, 38.
40 K.M. Panikkar, *The Afro-Asian States and their Problems* (London: G. Allen and Unwin Ltd., 1959) and Ken Post, *The New States of West Africa* (Baltimore, MD: Penguin Books, 1964) are among those writers dealing with the subject.
41 Press conference for foreign correspondents accredited by USSR Ministry of Foreign Affairs, by the Rector of Lumumba University, at the University, Moscow, December 1963.
42 Hassan Mirreh, *Soviet Foreign Policy in Sub-Saharan Africa* (Ann Arbor, MI: University Microfilms, 1962), 50–51. I am grateful for my numerous interactions with Hassan in the Colombia University Library, New York City, in the early 1960s. Over time, we shared many similar views about the USSR, the Cold War and Soviet relations with Africans and African countries. I drew heavily on his knowledge of the United Nations and the importance of the UN for Soviet education assistance to Africa and Africans.
43 *Ibid.*
44 *Ibid.*
45 I.I. Potekhin, *A Soviet Primer on Africa* (Washington, DC: US Joint Publication Research Service, 1962), 308.
46 *Ibid.*
47 *Ibid.*, 184–185.
48 A student's major field of concentration was often a joint decision, involving the student's success in the preparatory studies, his or her personal preference, African national human resource needs and the availability of Soviet training resources.

11

'Peoples' Friendship' in the Cold War: the Patrice Lumumba Peoples' Friendship University

Rachel Lee Rubin

The Patrice Lumumba Peoples' Friendship University[1] was founded in Moscow 1960 with the stated objective of providing higher education for the developing world. It was named for Lumumba immediately following his 1961 assassination. (Indeed, after his death there were a striking number of Soviet acknowledgements of Lumumba's contributions, from postage stamps to posters, from songs to biographies, and so on.) The university repeatedly articulated these goals in publicity materials, on-campus exhibitions and self-published books. An efficient example comes from a 1975 book about the university, which opens with a statement of goals:

> Университет основан в соответствии с ленинской политикой оказания бескорыстной помощи народам стран добивающихся подъема национальной экономики и культуры, и в связи с пожеланиями прогрессивных общественных и правительственных кругов многих стран Азии, Африки, и Латинской Америки и предложениями ряда советских общественных организаций.[2]

> [*The university was founded in accordance with the Leninist policy of providing objective assistance to the peoples of countries striving for a boom in the national economy and culture, and in connection with the wishes of progressive public and government circles in many countries of Asia, Africa, and Latin America and proposals of a number of Soviet public organisations.*][3]

The establishment of the university followed on the heels of (and sometimes played a role in) several important global movements; in addition to Lumumba's death, a historical exploration of the university must take into account the collapse of European overseas empires, the geopolitical fallout from the Second World War, the decolonisation movements of what was then known as the 'Third World', Arab–Israeli conflicts, and Cold War rhetorical battles in the United States and the Soviet Union. Indeed, to understand the many functions of the university, it is necessary to contextualise its founding, activities and reception in terms of the Cold War, in particular how African countries were pulled in as both the United States and the Soviet Union came to realise that expanding their influence in the Third

World would increase their military and diplomatic power. Thus, Africa came to host numerous proxy wars. This is particularly true of South Africa; the role of which it played in Cold War politics is efficiently captured – and made literal – by Steven Mufson's noting that there were two rival gangs in South Africa in the 1950s, called 'Russians' and 'Americans'.[4] Overall, South Africa is a particularly relevant example: in the South African Border War (1966–90), the two sides were supported by the United States (which supported the apartheid regime) and the Soviet Union (which supported the South West Africa People's Organization (SWAPO). This dynamic was visible across colonial and post-colonial Africa. It manifests in the career of Patrice Lumumba: after the Congo was denied aid by the United States and other Western countries, it received aid from the Soviet Union. Other African countries also turned to the Soviet Union for aid – first in establishing independence, and then, such as Ethiopia, facing both economic and military challenges. And numerous African countries sent representatives to the World Festival of Youth and Students, the 7th of which was held in Moscow in 1957 and the 12th in 1985, which was presented there as a manifestation of international solidarity (in 1985 the slogan of the festival was 'For anti-imperialist solidarity, peace and friendship') but in the West as Soviet propaganda (for example, a 1965 newspaper story in Sikeston, Missouri's *Daily Standard* notes that Communists 'got a lot of "propaganda mileage"' out of stories about the festival).[5]

It is also important to note that the founding of the university closely followed significant gatherings of post-colonial and colonial nations with the aim of self-definition, establishing relationships with other African countries. A gathering that received a great deal of attention is the 1955 Afro-Asian Bandung Conference, the aim of which was to 'celebrate the demise of formal colonialism, and pledge themselves to some measure of joint struggle against the forces of imperialism'.[6] While mainstream newspapers in the United States noted that the conference 'produced advance jitters at the Department of State', it was celebrated in African-American newspapers; for instance, in *Freedom*, a column by Paul Robeson (who co-founded the publication with Louis Burnham) states in the headline that 'the Afro-Asian Conference Represents a Turning Point in World Affairs'.[7]

Entering international discourse on the heels of the Bandung Conference, Lumumba University offers a useful lens for a fascinating set of international relations. Named for a prominent symbol of independent Africa, it gathered future leaders from various (mostly newly independent) African, Asian and Central American countries. For many Africans – especially those from former British colonies, which did not invite its former colonials to its own educational institutions until much later – Lumumba University was one of the only avenues for post-secondary education, along with the

United States' historically black colleges and universities. For instance, in 1999, Nelson Mandela (at a banquet in Russia) commented that 'Hundreds of young South Africans found here the education they were denied in their own homeland.' Notably, he also spoke positively about how '[m]any of our cadres found the military training that turned them into skilled combatants for freedom and justice.'[8]

Both of Mandela's comments are very useful here, because they capture the most prominent ways the university functioned in international conversations. Globally, many people praised it for providing higher education and training to Africans, Asians and Latin Americans. Simultaneously, others accused it of not actually being a university but instead being a training ground for terrorists (and all too often included anti-colonial and liberation movements in this framework). This chapter, then, seeks to introduce Lumumba University's operation as a concrete nexus of interaction among the various African, Asian and Latin American countries whose students travelled there; the Soviet Union as host and 'instructor'; and the interventionist global vision of the United States and its allies. I have several related scholarly goals: to expand on Atlantic Studies' valuable but limited impulse to consider global economies of money, statehood, politics and culture; to indicate how Lumumba University was marshalled in international ideological battles (and indeed, is still marshalled); and to trace the global paths of Lumumba University's graduates and rehabilitate their stories.

One of the most useful sources for this chapter has been interviews with many of the university's graduates from different African countries, for several reasons: first, of course, is that their perspectives frequently challenge what is assumed about the university – in the United States in particular. Indeed, what I have seen about the experience of African students at the university is rather sweeping and does not include individual stories. But it is just as significant how these interviewees stitch their experience at the university into the post-colonial development of their own countries. To convey these insights, I extensively quote several alumni at the end of this chapter.

A major aspect of the university's concrete international role is the way historical narratives were quickly deployed after Lumumba's death to discredit the basic activity of alliance-building that was presented from the very beginning as core to the university's mission. In the US, it became a Cold War article of faith that lasted well past the dissolution of the USSR that Lumumba University was organised around military training for a dangerous band of rogues. US interests focused in a sustained way on the university and its global impact – a focus that included discourse, policy and action. Central here is the question of how disparate rhetorical forces battled over the meaning of Lumumba University's historical example for contemporary political and cultural battles.

Very quickly after the university began operating, observers in the US began to refer to it as a site of Communist indoctrination and, increasingly, a training ground for terrorists; its symbolic connection with Patrice Lumumba was frequently presented as evidence of this. In 1963, for example, journalist and author Dan Kurzman wrote about Lumumba University in his dramatically – and condescendingly – titled *Subversion of the Innocents: Patterns of Communist Penetration in Africa, the Middle East, and Asia.*[9] The following year, *Time* ran an article that began by scoffing, 'Four years after his death, a lot of people talk as though Patrice Emery Lumumba were still the Congo', and moved on to list Patrice Lumumba Peoples' Friendship University as an example of 'terrorists' and 'agitators' who are 'invoking Lumumba's name' with its 'rhythm of jungle drums.'[10] In 1978, the recently disgraced President Richard Nixon wrote that 'Malcontents from all over the world are trained ... at the appropriately-named Patrice Lumumba Friendship University in Moscow – in the arts of kidnapping, assassination, sabotage, bomb-making, and insurrection, and then sent off to ply their trade.'[11] Similarly, in a collection of essays edited by Benjamin Netanyahu in 1980, Brian Crozier wrote:

> The National Liberation entrants are initially offered academic courses through the Patrice Lumumba People's [sic] Friendship University in Moscow, and those selected for terrorist training are later dispersed to one or other of the camps ... In one stream or another, the trainees come from Latin America, Africa, the Arab world, the Middle East, Western Europe, South-East Asia and Australia. Subjects taught include: agitation and propaganda, target practice and bomb-making, sabotage, street-fighting and assaults on buildings, and assassination techniques.[12]

This line of reasoning permeated a wide range of sources – newspapers, governmental documents, cultural representations, online commentary, and so on – and continued very close to the fall of the USSR. Indeed, even after the break-up of the Soviet Union (which had a dramatic shaping effect on the university, as I will address below) it would still be referred to as having been a terrorist training camp. For example, a 2013 textbook (of which multiple editions came out), *Understanding Terrorism: Challenges, Perspectives, and Issues*, uses Lumumba University as a case study under the subheading: 'Understanding State-Sponsored Terrorism: State Patronage and Assistance.' The university, this textbook asserts, demonstrates that 'the state sponsorship of terrorism is not always a straightforward act'.[13]

The naming of Lumumba University immediately received some positive mention in the Black media. For instance, in 1961, *Jet* reported that Ghana's

Church of Africa had declared Lumumba a saint following his assassination, noting that other posthumous honours included that 'Moscow's Friendship University was renamed Patrice Lumumba Friendship University.'[14] In addition to the importance of naming the university after Lumumba, which received a great deal of worldwide attention that was both condemning and congratulatory, it's worth noting that the street on which the university is located – Miklukho-Maklaya – is the name of a Russian explorer (1846–88) who opposed the 'blackbirding' slave trade in Australia and colonialism. He was also one of the first to refute the idea that different races were different species.

As Nelson Mandela commented, for many students Lumumba University was one of the only avenues for post-secondary education available. Since many of these countries had very low literacy rates in the 1960s, graduates of the university went back to occupy top positions in their countries. Demonstrating the metonymic importance of the university, some of the same graduates who are touted in the university's publicity material as prominent alumni are listed in US Department of State and Defense documents as proof that the university's purpose was to increase Soviet influence.

The first cohort included students from fifty different countries. Since its founding, Lumumba University counts among its graduates former president of Namibia, Hifikepunye Pohamba; South African Minister of Social Development, Lindiwe Zulu; Professor Sumo Kupee, chair of the Senate Ways and Means committee of Liberia; former president of the Central African Republic, Michel Djotodia; Pretidev Ramdawon, CEO of a laser medicinal clinic in Mauritius; Andrew Kawani, history professor at the University of Zimbabwe; and Porfirio Lobo Sosa, former president of Honduras, as well as many other prominent figures in a range of fields. Following the worldwide attention paid to the death of Nelson Mandela, the project has emerged as even more relevant, as several ANC leaders were educated there.

In the 1980s, the CIA launched a programme titled 'Moscow's Third World Education Programs: An Investment in Political Influence' (a report on which has been released now, albeit in a 'sanitised' version). The report states: 'A review of the overall program ... suggests that Moscow's motive for initiating and funding educational programs for foreign students remains political ... In Bolivia, Ecuador, and Guyana, graduates of the Soviet program have attained ministerial positions.'[15]

In the United States, the person most frequently invoked as having studied at Lumumba University is Ilich Ramírez Sánchez, better known as Carlos the Jackal, even though he was expelled for 'bad behavior'[16] and being a 'poor student'.[17] The US response to Lumumba University has been brought into the twenty-first century: during the 2016 presidential campaign in the

United States, Republican candidate Ben Carson insisted that Mahmoud Abbas and Ruhollah Khomeini studied there together, along with Vladimir Putin. Similarly, the university's name crops up in discussions of Lee Harvey Oswald, convicted of assassinating President John F. Kennedy.

Commentary about Lumumba University permeated many rhetorical locations in the United States. There are a striking number of United States governmental documents that take up the university. In 1981, for instance, the United States Department of State issued a special report titled 'Cuba's Renewed Support for Violence in Latin America'. The report states that Cuban subversion was backed by a substantial secret intelligence and training apparatus, modern military forces, and a large and sophisticated propaganda network. The overall claim here is that Cuba would not be able to carry out its extensive and far-flung operations (including secret training camps) without the help of the Soviet Union. Lumumba University is identified as part of that support. The report adds that this Soviet support allowed Cuba to intervene in Africa as well as the Caribbean, pointing to its support for anti-colonialism in Angola in the 1970s, for instance. In exchange for Soviet support, Cuba 'champions the "natural alliance" between the Soviet bloc and the Third World in the nonaligned movement'.[18] The report also claims that sports activities are actually recruiting fronts. Similarly, a list of graduates are referred to as 'Moscow's Spokesmen in the Third World' by the CIA in 'Moscow's Third World Educational Programs'. This interpretation found its way into the popular press as well: for instance, a 1967 newspaper article titled 'Weapons: Controversial CIA Programs Defended' notes, 'According to Western intelligence sources, the university is operated directly by senior staff officers of the main Soviet intelligence organization', and goes on to state that former students at Lumumba University are now to be found in government positions in various African countries, and that Western intelligence officers are aware that the students remain in active collaboration with their mentors in Moscow.[19]

The United States' fear of Lumumba University as a site of Soviet indoctrination was not limited to governmental documents – or, for that matter, political conservatives: Richard Rorty of the University of Virginia, in a 1987 response piece in *Political Theory* in which he calls himself a 'liberal' (which is also how he was generally known), writes: 'Granted that a lot of American intervention in the Third World has been for the sake of protecting investments (or supporting oligarchs who hired the right Washington lobbyists), it remains quite likely that Third World governments manned by graduates of Patrice Lumumba University will end up as the same kind of ruthless oligarchies that we find in contemporary Rumania and Vietnam – with the same forcible suppression of reform from below.'[20]

On the more local stage, during the 1960s, 1970s and into the 1980s, there were hundreds of United States newspaper articles, including from small cities and towns, that expressed anxiety about Lumumba University and world politics, frequently in a racialised form. A horrifying example was in the Shreveport *Times* – and a number of other small newspapers from across the country, including the San Bernadino County *Sun*, the Dixon *Evening Telegraph*, the Scranton *Tribune* and the Wilmington *Morning News*, among others – which published a piece that claimed that the students at Lumumba University are chosen 'on the pattern of Hitler's Brown Shirts' (9 March 1965). The piece states that after the Second World War, Moscow collected SS officers and had them teach their strategies to Soviets and Lumumba students. 'Once home', the article explains, 'these students move in their anti-American and other demonstrations like baboons'.[21]

By the 1980s, there was an interesting move in American newspapers from fretting over anti-colonialism in Africa, which had mostly been accepted and even begun to be hailed, to fretting over Central America. A 1983 article in the Toledo *Blade*, for instance, states about Soviet involvement: 'One area of particular concern is Central America and the Caribbean.'[22] At this time, the strongest fear around Soviet influence via Patrice Lumumba Friendship University became focused on the Fidel Castro-headed government of Cuba.

And Western fear of Lumumba University was not limited to governmental documents and newspaper articles. It found its way into fiction, such as *El Manto* (1998) by Richard Earl Hansen (a retired US Air Force pilot), which begins with the declamation that 'In the late Eighties, Thousands [sic] of immigrants trampled our Mexican border to illegally enter the United States.'[23] He notes that Nicaragua under the Communist Sandinistas was one of the prominent sources of this emigration to the United States. But the main focus is the assembling on the US border of thousands of 'Latinos' – who are being managed by the Comandantes ('ruling Nicaraguans') and their Cuban and Soviet sponsors as a 'massive weaponless invasion' to create enough havoc that the US doesn't notice Communist expansion in Central America – showing that Lumumba had become a cliché in the United States. The university is identified early on in this book as being informally known as 'Revolution U', with graduates whose mission was to 'fan out and form cadres in Costa Rica, El Salvador, Honduras, Guatemala, Panama, and some of the Caribbean island nations' using their technical skills as cover. Hansen notes a couple of times that a character's 'terrorist training' had taken place at Lumumba University.

Indeed, the fear trickled into places like a book review of Salman Rushdie's first non-fiction book, *Jaguar Smile*, which he wrote after a visit to Nicaragua in 1986. The review frets:

The Nicaraguan revolution of 1979 must surely go down as one of the best-marketed efforts of its kind in history. When the dictator Anastasio Somoza fled the country on July 17, after an explicit US decision to withdraw support from his family's forty-six-year-old regime, domestic and international opinion anointed a small – about 500-member – Marxist-Leninist grouping, the Sandinista National Liberation Front (FSLN), as the principal legitimate political force in the country. Only five years earlier, the Sandinistas had been regarded as a minor terrorist fringe element, founded by a graduate of Moscow's Patrice Lumumba University, Carlos Fonseca, and peopled by cadres trained in Cuba, the Eastern bloc, and sundry PLO training camps.[24]

This line of reasoning continued very close to the fall of the Soviet Union. In 1987, United States Senator Bob Graham wrote a newspaper column stating that 'the Soviet Union and its Eastern Bloc satellites offered about 14,000 full university and graduate scholarships to students in the Caribbean Basin. Most of those students studied in the Soviet Union. Many attend Patrice Lumumba University in Moscow. Thousands more get free vocational training in Cuba. In that same year, the United States awarded fewer than 1,000 scholarships.' Graham refers to the dedication of poor Dominicans and Haitians who received American scholarships to private industry, calling them 'ambassadors for our way of life.' He notes how many students from the Caribbean Basin are annually offered scholarships to Lumumba, arguing that 'we can regain the advantage in regional relations' and that 'our professors and bankers and business people understand' what is facing poor Caribbean students.[25]

As there was such a great deal of anti-Lumumba writing around the world, a fascinating way to confront this is to contextualise in terms of what the author is trying to convince the reader of on a larger scale. Paul Kengor, for instance, in his 2012 book *The Communist* – which is about African-American and Communist poet, journalist and activist Frank Marshall Davis's connection to Barack Obama – still mentions Lumumba as 'the favored school of William Patterson', (p. 232) another African-American Communist, and 'a grooming school for third world revolutionaries' that schooled 'some of the world's leading terrorists' (p. 117).[26] He also goes out of his way to focus on the anti-Zionism of the university, its graduates and the USSR. But the overall priority of his book is to attack Obama with as many historical strategies as possible, and Lumumba University serves this purpose well.

Fear of Lumumba University found its way into tourist guides. It found its way into cartoons. And it found its way into television shows. A very illustrative clip is found in 'The Gladiators', an episode of *The New Avengers*, a British spy series from 1976–77, in which the main characters discuss their fear of a Russian:

John Steed: You're jittery.

Chuck Peters: On account of Karl Sminsky. You got me thinking. So I ran a special check on him.

John Steed: And?

Chuck Peters: He was in Siberia. And before that, he attended the Patrice Lumumba University, in Moscow. They don't teach the classics there, Steed.

John Steed: Oh, yes they do. Modern classics. Guerrilla warfare, terrorism, how to kill, maim, destroy ... but never how to live in peace! So Karl Sminsky majored there.[27]

It's important to recognise that when it comes to television shows, it is rare that scriptwriters will include references that very few people would get.

In my interviews with Lumumba alumni (which I will address in detail below), I have asked if they were aware of the accusations being levelled against the university in the United States. Some were amused; some were incredulous; some already knew. But the most striking reaction came from a South African, Zwelakhe Mankazana, who went straight to Lumumba from an exile camp outside the country – in other words, he could not return home because of his activities with the African National Congress. The story of his revolutionary work was very moving, including that while he was in exile he heard that his mother had died. Several years later, he found out that she hadn't – but she had to put out the news that she died so that she wouldn't be killed. When I asked him if he knew the stories about Lumumba University, he answered, 'Yes, I heard those stories. When I got there, and it turned out not to be true, I was disappointed!' This was a fascinating comment – because, as is well known, the ANC tried to remain non-violent – and this principle, admirable as it was, did not work because, of course, the colonialists did not respond to non-violence. As Nelson Mandela's funeral demonstrated, ANC revolutionaries are currently mostly seen as heroes in the United States, which creates a fascinating historical tension with the fact that, as Mandela pointed out and my own interviews confirm, so many of them were educated in the USSR.

It also must be taken into consideration that Soviets also located the university in terms of its face-off with the United States. For instance, a relatively recent post-Soviet Russian book about the university still opens with the claim that the earliest victims of colonialism were Native Americans:

Открывая новые земли, европейцы тут же, едва ли не автоматически, объявляли их своими колониями. Поцле открытия в 1492 г. X. Колумбом Америки иммено этот котинент и его народы в первуюю очередь оказались жертвами колонизации.[28]

[*Discovering new lands, the Europeans immediately, almost automatically, declared them their colonies. After the discovery in 1492 by C. Columbus of America, this continent and its peoples were the first to become victims of colonization.*]

In a similar anti-colonialist assertion, the next page of the pamphlet includes a photograph of African children triumphantly climbing on a knocked-over statue of a white coloniser. (Which country this is from is not revealed here.) With a similar desire to push back against claims that Lumumba University's founding, and then training and educating, were motivated by the Soviet Union's desire to spread its power and control to other continents, a 1963 Soviet English-language pamphlet titled *Two*

Figure 11.1 Pamphlet cover, 'Two Universities: Lumumba Friendship University and Moscow State University' (London: Novosti Press Agency, 1963)

Universities (it is half about Lumumba University and half about Moscow State University) directly addresses – and denies – whether the university is 'educating communist propagandists'.[29]

But despite various Soviet attempts to connect the United States to colonialism (in the short, post-Soviet publication mentioned above, and in many other locations as well, including the USSR's prominent political poster art), the raising of anti-colonialism as relevant to the university's mission is certainly not limited to Soviet voices. A good example of this, because it muddies the Soviet–American binary the university (mostly) presents, is the statement made by American musician, actor, athlete and activist Paul Robeson – who is visible in many places all over campus, including posters in dormitories. Describing Robeson's trip to Lumumba, the university-published pamphlet quotes him as follows:

> Миллионы и миллионы людей гордятся великим сыном Африки Патрисом Лумумбой. Великий Университет дружбы народов его имени – историческое учреждение![30]

> [*Millions and millions of people are proud of the great son of Africa, Patrice Lumumba. The Great University of Friendship of the Nations named after him is a historical institution!*]

This pamphlet expresses confidence that a considerable number of Asian, African and Latin American youth understand the true nature of this 'anti-university' propaganda, rhetorically noting the significance of the fact that in spite of all inventions and fabrications, 50,000 applications were received for 500 vacancies at Lumumba University in the first year. And, strikingly, United States Communist and African-American activist William Patterson proposed that Lumumba admit African Americans, because, he argued, they are 'internally colonized.' This argument was not accepted, although the idea of 'internal colonisation' has begun to get more attention.

In order to understand the role Lumumba University played in the world, in addition to responses from the *outside*, it is valuable to trace the paths of students who studied there – to see where they came from, what they experienced – both negative and positive – and what they did after returning from the university. Napoleon Abdulai, from Tamale in north Ghana, usefully stitched his impulse to attend Lumumba into post-colonial African politics. He told me that when he first heard about the university, he was a student activist. Because of the purported dangers of his activism, he was convinced to *leave* the country foremost. 'As far back as 1978', he told me, 'I met Ghana's foreign minister (Colonel Roger Felli) who called me into his office and told me in plain language that if I continued what I was doing, I would not live long.' I interrupted Abdulai to ask, 'What were you doing then that made him say that?' and he explained:

Figure 11.2 Pamphlet cover, 'We are from Friendship University'
(Moscow: Progress Publishers, 1966)

We had a military dictatorship then, and the military dictatorship did not want our country to return to a multi-party system. What they wanted was a combination of the military and civilians forming a party and then ruling. By their logic, that would prevent coups, and counter-coups, and the country would be on the road to development. We members of the National Union of Ghana Students were against it. Completely. We were calling for multi-party democracy. This is *long* before people came to talk about multi-partyism. It was as far back as 1978. So, the foreign minister, he said he knew all the things I had been doing, and then made mention of some of my friends, their names. And he proposed that if the government had scholarships, I should leave on one of them. I came and told my friends, 'No. This is going to divide our front.' I didn't take it. But not long after that came 1979, and that regime was overturned. We continued our struggle for democracy in Ghana. We supported one of the radicals – John F. Hansen who had earlier co-founded the People's Revolutionary Party in Ghana – but 1979 was a very difficult year for the country. The new rulers executed about 6 or 8 military officers for corruption. The student leadership was at the vanguard. I was told I was given one scholarship. That's how I finally found myself in Lumumba University.

On the student body at Lumumba, Abdulai commented:

People came and studied and went. I have not seen anyone from Lumumba University so far who has led an armed violence in the country that they originated from. The problem was that the university opened the eyes of the students. For example, if you take the law of the sea. In discussing the law or in studying the law of the seas you realize that you have to take into account maritime disputes. Demarcations of bodies both coastal and in the immediate sea. Very few African countries, I would say virtually no African country, had a university where this issue would have been talked about.

Abdulai is currently Ghana's ambassador to Cuba.

Gideon Shoo is from what is now Tanzania and is currently in his sixties. He described being a very successful high school student of physics, chemistry and biology. But after doing required national service for a year in 1977, he told me, 'My service in the army left a mark. I came out a changed person. I wanted a revolution – NOW.' Although he was admitted to medical school, he became a journalist, and was sent to cover the Moscow Olympics in 1980. When he came back, he told me, he found an announcement that there were scholarships available to study international journalism at Lumumba University. 'And I thought, "Let me just apply".' He said, 'Going to Lumumba was like, "This is it. I am going to a place to set me up to make changes in society."'

According to Shoo, international journalism was a new programme of study at Lumumba when he arrived; while there were more than 150 students from his country, about 95 per cent were doing applied sciences and there were only two in the new journalism programme. 'We needed to know that journalism mattered', he told me passionately. When I asked him about Lumumba University's relationship to international solidarity, anti-colonialism, he replied:

One good thing about Lumumba is that was a big family of oppressed people from different backgrounds. All of them oppressed, but differently ... if it was not for Lumumba University, they would not have had higher education. [At Lumumba University] I met for the first time guys from Cambodia. And they tell you these stories about what really happened, how their parents were killed, you know, you get all these nightmares. How is it possible to understand that? I had a roommate from Morocco, and a Russian. The three of us. My Russian roommate could not understand that you could live in a house without running water ... and I remember him telling me, 'Stop those anecdotes! ['Anecdote' is the Russian word for joke.] Someone walks 5 kilometres for water.' But for most of the students, he said, they felt, 'We are all alike! Only it is happening in different locations! But it's the same oppression! The perpetrator is the same ... the owner of the factory, you know? The land-grabber? The international drug dealer? This is real!

I asked Shoo what it was like being a non-white person in Moscow, and he told me it was fine, that he didn't feel different at the time, but acknowledges that he does hear about racial discrimination now. But not everyone I've interviewed answered that question the same way. In some cases, it was clearly just novelty: one person told me about taking a summer job in a rural area, and a small boy asking him if his face was dirty. But several alumni I interviewed – even those who described their time at Lumumba as thrilling and useful – expressed disappointment that the government did not intervene more in this matter. For instance, when I asked a Ghanaian OB-GYN doctor, Jehu Komla-Appiah, about facing stigma as an African in the Soviet Union, he told me, 'The discrimination, the stigma is still there. I would say that I've lived though the stigma all my life. Stigma of coming from Africa to Russia was there. Returning from Russia to Ghana, the stigma of studying in the East and coming to Ghana was also bad, because everything in the East was bad. My current work, I work in abortion and other issues, the stigma is always there. I'm someone who has lived through all things, so I'm OK with the stigma.'

Elizabeth Magambo, of Dar es Salaam, Tanzania, also conveyed that she confronted racialised stigma at Lumumba University, where she studied international law from 1970–75. (She was 69 years old when I interviewed her.) Magambo had learned about Lumumba from other people studying there, who convinced her to study there instead of at an American university, where she was planning to go. She told me:

> Russian is not an easy language, but Lumumba University had 'miraculous teaching, because we go there in August, and by November are expected to start classes in Russian. After three months, they gave an exam – an interview. Then you chose your department. They asked what I was interested in, I said economics. They said no, how about history. If they had said Tanzanian history, that would have been different! Somehow, my answer about economics did not satisfy the teacher. That was what I was interested in, because I was working in a bank. The teacher in charge of law said, do you object if I take you into law? I said no.

When I asked Magambo to describe her sense of the student body at Lumumba University, she replied, 'There were students from all over the world. We were different, but we were all friendly to each other. One significant thing I learned was that if you speak English, everybody looks at you, like "Why are you speaking a colonial language?" Everybody! So English was taboo. Because of that, we hardly spoke English.' I asked Magambo to describe the relationship of Lumumba University to international solidarity regarding anti-colonialism. She replied that Lumumba was very anti-colonial. 'We all spoke of it as a bad thing', she told me. When I asked her if being at Lumumba was, for many students she knew, the only chance for higher education, she replied, 'Yes. I think everyone thought it was a good chance for education.'

But Magambo's answers got more complicated when I asked her what it was like being an African in the USSR. At first she found it 'difficult to say'. 'Because', she went on:

> if you speak of racism, there were elements of racism everywhere, but it wasn't so obvious. The Russians were hardly speaking to us, especially the boys. The girls – I had a Russian roommate – didn't express racism. The university worked to control this. But more broadly – I don't know if it was racism or ignorance. I used to regard it as ignorance, because – well, here's an example. If you are going out, you go to the metro, and you are just walking down the stairs, or up the stairs, on an escalator, they might say, 'Gasp! In your place, do the baboons use escalators?' and we say, 'Baboons???!!' And they say, 'We are told you are like baboons!' So we were always being told Africans are like baboons. Especially children, the small ones. They would cry out, 'Mama, mama, baboons!' And they would come and touch your skin, and say, 'You are dusty!' We used to regard this as ignorance. But it was not that simple, because Nigerians, especially, pushed back at use of 'baboons', and would fight. If police came, they would kick the African while saying something good – 'Don't fight! Don't attack the foreigner! He is our friend! They are our friends!' By words, he is defending you. By acts, he is hurting you.

Locating African studies in various international conflicts, Magambo revealed, went far beyond some students' fury at being called 'baboons' (which, as I have noted, happened in the US press as well). Teachers in Russia would say 'Western countries' rather than 'America', Magambo noted, 'because most of us had been colonized by Western countries (not America) so we used to know Western countries more. But it was still clear that the Cold War was between Russia and the US.'

While a student at Lumumba University, Magambo visited several Western countries – so I asked her to compare them to Soviet Union.

> I preferred staying in Russia rather than the West. Racism in the West is much more direct: they don't like you because you are black. Russians didn't show it directly like that. And when Russians called you 'baboons', I still think they did it because they were ignorant. They actually thought you were baboons. But the West – oh, my god. We used to [go there in the summer and] work in factories. And the person next to you would just *step* on you with their shoe and then go on as if nothing has happened. And then he steps on you again.

That actually happened! And in the UK we used to work with Irish people. And *they* were being segregated like Africans. But if you find you are working there – they like you, you are together. They are also being segregated. Just the same as Africans! To the British, they are no different.

After graduating from Lumumba University, Magambo returned to Moscow often for work-related meetings.

A particularly fascinating example of a Lumumba University graduate is Kofi Mawuli Klu, because he went from Ghana to study at Lumumba University, and from there became an activist in London (he is the founder of a Pan-African community advocacy organisation). So when he talked about any one of those three places, he tended to compare it, or stitch it into a relationship with, the other two. He told me:

> The Lumumba story itself gives you a graphic example of Africa being caught up in the Cold War, the tragedies that ensued. It spread all over the place that Lumumba was a place where terrorists were trained … but I think Lumumba prided itself very much on being the place where young people from all over the world were offered opportunity alongside your professional studies to engage with the history and knowledge of resistance of the peoples of Africa, Asia and Americas. And I think maybe political lessons we liked came more from our peers even more than from the classroom.

Klu told me that:

> Personally I was so adamant about criticizing what I thought were non-socialist things I encountered in the Soviet Union, I was quite uncompromising in class on some of these things. And there were three types of teachers. There were teachers who were indifferent and would say 'Come on, let's move on and talk about something else.' And there were also teachers who were adamantly opposed to any of these criticisms. There were also teachers who, without actively encouraging those criticisms, allowed us to say what we wanted to say while we had to say those things. I remember one of my teachers who had a standard answer any time I went on this rant of criticism. He said, 'Okay, okay, okay. You know something. I'm waiting for the day you will have a chance to build socialism in Africa. And I will be so thankful if you can do it better than us.'

Overall, Klu told me:

> To be honest, being an African in Moscow was one of the most thrilling experiences in my life. Because I had never lived in such a huge city before. And I could go almost everywhere. And I still say the most fascinating thing about the Soviet Union, and Moscow in particular, was walking on the streets of Moscow and not seeing any individual person's name on any shop, any factory, any building. And I used to envy Soviet people so much because they could claim that everything belonged to them … I had an aunt here [in London]

Figure 11.3 Photograph of African student learning Russian folk dance

so I used to come here for summer holidays. And I just hated the sight of all these big shops and buildings with the names of individuals inscribed on them. So that was one thing that thrilled me about the Soviet Union. It was there, in that country, people could say this is ours. It reminded me to a certain extent of my village … Then when I came to live here the contrast was so, so stark. In this country, from the fact of how really dirty this place is compared with the Soviet Union at the time to the fact that resources are so unequally distributed. The kind of racism I've encountered in this place was unthinkable in the Soviet Union. The denial of fundamental human rights in terms of the right to work.

The university still exists, though after the Soviet Union broke up Lumumba's name was removed and the proportion of local to foreign students flipped from 80 per cent non-Russian to 80 per cent Russian. But the university's publicity materials are still quite assertive about the anti-colonialist role the university played, and the university itself is still decorated with gifts from

African students, photographs and a statue of Lumumba, and photographs of visitors from various countries (including Angela Davis, Pablo Neruda, Fidel Castro, Alphonse Massamba-Débat, Thor Heyerdahl and, more recently, Hugo Chávez). The university's operation as a concrete nexus of interaction among the various Latin American, African and Asian countries whose students travelled there, the Soviet Union as host and 'instructor', and the active global vision of the United States and its global allies remains instructive. Equally as important, it operated as a *rhetorical* nexus of interaction, and interrupted a bifurcated vision of the Cold War. The university is still marshalled retrospectively in international ideological battles – with 'terrorist training' replacing 'communist indoctrination' and 'neoliberalism' replacing 'imperialism' – while still raising familiar historical assertions. This continued function is powerful confirmation of the significant role the Patrice Lumumba Peoples' Friendship University played as an educational institution and as a multifaceted ideological formation.

Notes

1 For many reasons, including the different ordering of words in English and Russian, the university's name is written in English in several different ways. In this chapter, I will be mainly using 'Lumumba University'.

2 В.С. Амитров, редактор, *Университет дружбы народов имени Патриса Лумумбы в 1975* г (Москва: Университет дружбы народов имени Патриса Лумумбы, 1975), 3. [V.S. Amitrov (ed.), *University of Peoples' Friendship named for Patrice Lumumba in 1975* (Moscow: University of Peoples' Friendship named for Patrice Lumumba, 1975).]

3 All translations in this chapter are by the author.

4 Steven Mufson, *Fighting Years: Black Resistance and the Struggle for a New South Africa* (Boston: Beacon Press, 1990), 36.

5 'Youth's Idealism Misused by Communism', *Daily Standard* (Sikeston, MO), 10 September 1968, 2.

6 Vijay Prashad, *The Darker Nations: A People's History of the Third World* (New York: The New Press, 2008), 32.

7 Forrest Davis, 'Chiang Asks: How Many Divisions Has Eden?' *Cincinnati Inquirer*, 29 April 1955, 4. Paul Robeson, 'Greetings to Bandung: Afro-Asian Conference Represents a Turning Point in World Affairs', *Freedom*, 5:4 (1955), 1. Robeson would end up visiting the University, and photographs of him remain hung in several of the University buildings.

8 *Address by President Nelson Mandela at a Banquet in Russia*: www.mandela. gov.za/mandela_speeches/1999/990429_russia.htm [accessed 10 February 2021].

9 Dan Kurzman, *Subversion of the Innocents: Patterns of Communist Infiltration in Africa, the Middle East, and Asia* (New York: Random House, 1963).

10 'The Congo: Lumumba Jumbo', *Time*, 25 December 1964, 21.

11 Richard Nixon, *The Real War* (New York: Touchstone, 1980), 37.

12 Brian Crozier, 'Soviet Support for International Terrorism' [1981] in Benjamin Netanyahu (ed.), *International Terrorism: Challenge and Response* (New Brunswick and Oxford: Transaction Publishers, 1989), 68.

13 Gus Martin, *Understanding Terrorism: Challenges, Perspective, and Issues*, Volume 4 (Los Angeles: Sage, 2013), 96.

14 'Ghana Church Proclaims Lumumba As a Saint', *Jet*, 9 March 1961, 13.

15 'Moscow's Third World Educational Programs: An Investment in Political Influence', CIA Historical Review Program [Released as Sanitized], 1999, iii.

16 Noémie Bisserbe, 'Carlos the Jackal Faces New French Trial', *Wall Street Journal*, 7 November 2011: www.wsj.com/articles/SB1000142405297020462 1904577018310576209878 [accessed 10 February 2021].

17 'Factfile on Illich Ramirez-Sanchez, aka Carlos the Jackal', *Irish Times*, 24 December 1997: www.irishtimes.com/news/factfile-on-illich-ramirez-sanchez-aka-carlos-the-jackal-1.140461 [accessed 10 February 2021].

18 US Department of State, 'Cuba's Renewed Support for Violence in Latin America', Special Report No. 90 (Washington, DC: Bureau of Public Affairs, US Department of State, 14 December 1981), 5. Presented by the Department of State, 11 December 1981.

19 'Weapons: Controversial CIA Programs Defended', *Austin American*, 6 March 1967, 1, 6.

20 Richard Rorty, 'Thugs and Theorists: A Reply to Bernstein', *Political Theory*, 15:4 (1987), 566.

21 Henry J. Taylor, 'Moscow "Demonstrators" Are Trained Agents', *Shreveport Times*, 9 March 1965, 10.

22 Jack Anderson, 'Soviets Far Ahead in Education', *Daily News-Journal* (Murphreesboro, TN), 2 May 1983, 4.

23 Richard E. Hanson, *El Manto* [The Mantle] (Bloomington, IN: 1st Books Library, 1998), n.p.

24 George Russell, '*The Jaguar Smile*, by Salman Rushdie', *Commentary*, April 1987: www.commentarymagazine.com/articles/the-jaguar-smile-by-salman-rushdie/ [accessed 10 February 2021].

25 Bob Graham, 'US Needs to Invest in Caribbean's Future', *Orlando Sentinel*, 22 February 1987, H-4.

26 Paul Kengor, *The Communist: Frank Marshall Davis: The Untold Story of Barack Obama's Mentor* (New York: Threshold Editions, 2012), 232, 117.

27 'The Gladiators', *The New Avengers* TV series, 25 November 1977.

28 В.Н. Никитин, Университет дружбы: краткий очерк полувековой истории (Москва: Российский Университет дружбы народов, 2010), 3. [V.N. Nikitin, *Friendship University: A Short History of a Half-Century* (Moscow: Russian University of Peoples' Friendship, 2010).]

29 'Two Universities: An Account of the Life at Work of Lumumba Friendship University and Moscow State University (Soviet Booklet No. 110)', compiled by Novosti Press Agency (APN) (London: Novosti Press Agency, 1963).

30 Никитин, Университет дружбы, 15. [Nikitin, *Friendship University*, 15.]

Afterword: A Black journey of Red hope

Maxim Matusevich

How fitting it is that the first chapter in this important new volume focuses on a political and personal odyssey of Claude McKay, one of the preeminent bards of the Harlem Renaissance and the person who 'discovered' Soviet Russia for black America. McKay's own journey from his euphoric 1922–23 trip to Petrograd and Moscow to an eventual disillusionment with Soviet Communism captured the hopes, the tensions and the maddening complexities of the encounter between the Black and the Red. McKay embarked on his 'magic pilgrimage' to Soviet Russia just five short years after the Great October Socialist Revolution had 'shaken the world' and captured the imagination of many of its downtrodden.

To understand the wide resonance of the revolutionary events in Russia, one has to consider the nature of their appeal for the masses of the oppressed and dispossessed by a combined pressure of Western industrial capitalism and its attendant imperialist expansion. In the age of colonialism and institutionalised and ideological racism, when the ideas of Social Darwinism reigned supreme across the West and its colonial empires, the emancipatory and unambiguously anti-racist message of the 1917 Bolshevik uprising in Petrograd could not be lost on at least some of the victims of racism and colonialism. But it was not just the rhetoric coming out of the halls of the Communist International (Comintern) in Moscow that excited the imagination of the West's second- and third-class citizens and subjects of colour. During the 1920s and 1930s, a journey by a non-white person from colonial Africa or Jim Crow America to the land of the Soviets entailed a dizzying transition – from daily humiliations to an apparent equality and even redemption. A number of these black travellers experienced their sojourn in the early Soviet Union as akin to a religious awakening. Claude McKay, for example, reminisced about feeling redeemed as 'an African, and black' on his arrival in Soviet Russia. 'I was', he wrote, 'like a black icon in the flesh ... Yes, that was exactly what it was. I was like a black icon.'[1]

When it came to an enthusiastic acceptance of the Soviet experiment of creating the ultimate just society, Claude McKay was hardly an outlier.

The great pan-Africanist W.E.B. Du Bois travelled in the Soviet Union in 1926 and returned to the United States convinced that he had caught a glimpse of the future. 'I stand in astonishment and wonder', he gushed forth in a *Crisis* editorial, 'at the revelation of Russia that has come to me. I may be partially deceived and half-informed. But if what I have seen with my eyes and heard with my ears in Russia is Bolshevism, I am a Bolshevik.'[2] In 1932–33, the poet Langston Hughes also embarked on a journey throughout the Soviet Union. Initially conceived as a joint film venture with the Soviets to make a propaganda movie about American racism, the trip eventually evolved into a multifaceted encounter between the Soviet Union and a motley crew of young black Americans. Their responses to the country varied, ranging from the enthusiastic to the sceptical, the latter likely the reflection of their personal circumstances. Langston Hughes left the most detailed and wide-ranging account of the voyage that took him from Moscow to the beaches of Crimea to the cotton fields of Central Asia. Just like McKay and Du Bois before him, Hughes responded to his Soviet odyssey with a mixture of awe and hope. He was less concerned with the postulates of Marxism-Leninism then with the promise of a society where racial inequality and prejudice had been declared taboo.[3] In fact, for a number of black Americans and Africans, the attractiveness of Communist ideology rested exactly on the anti-racist and anti-imperialist rhetoric of the Bolsheviks. In 1917, in a faraway Russia, a new political regime stated unequivocally its commitment to the dismantling of the international system of colonial dependency and racial inequality. The power of this message could not be lost on those who historically occupied the lowest ranks of Western societies. And that message was received during the heyday of colonialism and at the height of the Jim Crow. As one NAACP official pointedly observed at the time, 'The greatest pro-Communist influence among Negroes in the United States is the lyncher, the Ku Klux Klan member, the Black Shirt, the Caucasian Crusader and others who indulge in lynching, disfranchisement, segregation and denial of economic and industrial opportunity [to black people].'[4]

In some ways, this early appeal of the Bolsheviks' colour-blind internationalism, so exhaustively reflected in the extensive coverage it received in the black press in the United States and elsewhere, as well as captured in the experiences of numerous black travellers in the Soviet Union during the two pre-war decades, would set the stage for a relationship marked by mutual fascination, real and imagined alliances, but also numerous misconceptions and, occasionally, frustrations. The evidence of the sincerity of the early Soviet commitments to anti-racism is overwhelming and can be found in the Comintern archives, in the memoir literature and travelogues, and even in the FBI files of those suspected of pro-Soviet sympathies. Historian Meredith Roman noted the centrality of anti-racism not only to the official Soviet ideology at the time, but also to the ideal of a 'new Soviet man' – a new type of socialist human being, whose historical agency is predicated on the rejection of the prejudices of the past.[5] Soviet identity (at least as imagined by the founders of the Soviet state) was to be forged in a direct and performative opposition to Western racism.

When analysing the impact of the Russian Revolution on the fates of non-white populations around the world and the global conversation about racism, one inevitably confronts the ambiguities of Russia's history, culture and national identity. The Great October Socialist Revolution occurred in a country that had never been assured of its own belonging in the West. Historically, Russian intelligentsia and even members of Russia's pre-revolutionary aristocracy questioned their connection to the European story, and on occasion these debates grew in intensity and even bitterness. Russia's disputed identity – whether or not Russia actually belongs in the West, whether or not Russians are European or even properly 'white' – has remained an issue of contention that has continued to divide the society well into the post-Soviet era. A number of scholars have noted a certain common-ality of fate and historical experience between Russia and black America that placed Russia outside the standard European narratives of colonialism or institutionalised anti-black racism.[6] Obviously, the Russians had to contend with their own history of enslavement (not abolished until 1861) and their own colonial project that saw the expansion of the Russian Empire into Central Asia and all the way to the Pacific. But, as many Russian politicians and cultural figures are keen on pointing out even now, the country never colonised any part of Africa, never participated in the trans-Atlantic slave trade or the brutal regimes of extraction established by European colonisers throughout the continent. Some recent research also suggests that at least some late-imperial Russian ethnographers and explorers eschewed the crude notions of Social Darwinism and its attendant racial hierarchies so common among their Western contemporaries.[7] Some circumstantial evidence of this peculiarly Russian *Sonderweg* can be found in a broad support that the strug-gle against American slavery enjoyed among the educated Russian public or in the fact that even before the October revolution Russia had received a trickle of black refugees from American racism.[8] Interestingly, Claude McKay zeroed in on this unusual for the times racial egalitarianism and insisted that it may have had less to do with Bolshevism than with a culture that had evolved outside the history of white-on-black racism. Indeed, by his own account, while in Russia, McKay found as much warmth and hospitality in the company of 'bourgeois persons' and former aristocrats as he did among the factory workers and proletarian students who feted and celebrated him.[9]

One of the challenges of assessing the impact of the Red October on the personal histories and imagination of black intellectuals, visionaries and radicals lies in the tension between the Marxist-Leninist interpretation of history (including the histories of non-white communities) and the political and cultural movements that shaped the history of black liberation. The Soviet Union's example presented an inspiration, but also a challenge and, to some, a distraction. It is this complexity, which included both the appropriation and the contestation of the Soviet message of Marxist-Leninist internationalism by black intellectuals and activists, that needs to be addressed in any substantive account of the Russian Revolution's impact on the Black Atlantic. Russia and the Soviet Union would come to loom large in the political and intellectual biographies of such Black Atlantic pilgrims as Claude McKay, Langston Hughes, W.E.B. Du Bois, Paul Robeson, George Padmore, Jomo Kenyatta, Harry Haywood, William Patterson, Louise Thompson, Claudia Jones, Angela Davis and numerous lesser known figures. It is the diversity of this group that is truly remarkable and indicative of the broad allure of the Soviet promise. For each Comintern-affiliated, card-carrying Communist (for example, Harry Haywood or William Patterson) there were others – whose connection to the Red October was more aspirational than ideological. The rich memoir literature and archival research make it abundantly clear that the early Soviet Union offered some very tangible emotional and professional incentives to the black refugees from European colonialism and Jim Crowism. At the height of the Great Depression, black arrivals in the USSR could often count on a fairly well-compensated job and enhanced social status. Some of them, especially those affiliated with the Comintern, assumed political clout and even entered the inner sanctum of Soviet power.[10]

The extent to which the Soviet Union either inspired or disappointed its contemporary black observers depended on their personal political leanings and experiences, on the fluctuation of economic cycles of global capitalism, on the changing domestic policies (including socio-economic reforms) in the United States and other parts of West, on the shifting international situation, and, ultimately, on the evolving nature of Soviet society and the Soviet state. The early Soviet Union had no trouble showcasing its impeccable internationalist credentials and did so eagerly, especially through the Comintern and its affiliates and by organising such massive public protest campaigns as the vociferous efforts on behalf of the Scottsboro defendants. But the Soviet Union also evolved – by the late 1930s it had begun to act less like a sponsor of the revolutionary change worldwide and more as a nation-state. Joseph Stalin, having triumphed over his rivals (especially Leon Trotsky), seemed to be content with a less ambitious and more inward-looking project – the construction of socialism 'in a single country'.[11] The newly found isolationism and such earlier hare-brained schemes as the proposed establishment of a black nation in the American South (the so-called 'Black Belt thesis', first sounded at the Sixth Comintern Congress in 1928) tended to alarm or even antagonise some of the early enthusiastic Soviet supporters, including the flamboyant polymath Lovett Fort-Whiteman, whose disagreements with Stalin would lead to an untimely and tragic death in the Gulag.[12] Another prominent dissenter, George Padmore, fared much better by way of a well-timed departure from the Soviet Union. Padmore's intellectual and political journey from Communism to Pan-Africanism was well documented in his autobiography; it exposed a prominent point of contention between the class-based internationalism of Marxism-Leninism and the powerful thrust towards global black solidarity.[13] The tension will never quite dissipate and will leave its mark on the relations between the Soviet Union and independent African states. It will also reveal itself in the ambivalence with which Moscow would look at both the civil rights and black nationalist movements in the United States during the second half of the twentieth century. Initially, the arrival of the Second World War further contributed to the cooling off of the 'Red–Black' romance. In the run-up to the war, the Soviets acted pragmatically – as befits a nation-state, concerned less with the future of the internationalist utopia than with its own survival. While loudly decrying the Italian invasion of Ethiopia in 1935–36, Moscow, in fact, simultaneously entered into a series of trade agreements with the Italian fascists. Even more significantly, in August 1939, the Soviet Union signed a non-aggression pact with Nazi Germany and thus damaged its otherwise well-deserved reputation as an anti-racist crusader. For many of the Soviet Union's sympathisers among the black community, the unexpected alliance between the world's most dedicated anti-racist power and the most openly racist regime on earth was nothing short of a 'great betrayal'.[14] In a symbolic reversal, Claude McKay – the very person, who had served as the first bridge between black America and Soviet Russia – would eventually shed his Communist sympathies in favour of conservative Catholicism.[15]

Obviously, the disillusionment was far from universal. The Soviet Union's heroic struggle against Nazism that followed the Nazi invasion of the USSR in 1941, partially put to rest any lingering doubts about Soviet anti-fascist credentials. By the end of the Second World War, Moscow could plausibly claim its newly gained superpower status and, once again, wield its international clout to better promote its national interests, while also ostensibly acting on behalf of its stated anti-racist and anti-colonial agenda. The arrival of the Cold War and the rising tensions between the Soviet Union and the West provided a backdrop to the accelerating process of Third World awakening and decolonisation. Even though Soviet engagements with Third World liberation movements, and particularly with black nationalism and Pan-Africanism, were far from straightforward, Moscow did position itself successfully (and credibly) as an ally of Third World independence and a foe of Western racism and segregation. It was the consistency of this anti-racist messaging through the voluminous propaganda output and the Soviet Union's diplomatic support for anti-colonial movements that eventually earned Moscow quite a bit of goodwill among the most dedicated critics of Western racism and colonialism. The famed actor and human rights campaigner Paul Robeson was among those who pinned their hopes for racial emancipation and the ultimate destruction of fascism squarely on the Soviet Union. Robeson's deep attachment to the Soviet Union reflected his dismay over the sad state of race relations in the United States, his frustration with US support for the anti-liberation wars, waged by various US allies across the decolonising Third World, and his apprehension about the resurgence of fascism. Other concerns, including worries over the fate of some of his close Soviet friends swept up in the Stalinist purges, remained secondary to this need to see in the Soviet Union the main bulwark against Western racism. At least outwardly, Robeson never wavered in his oft-stated affections for the USSR and its people. His loyalty to Moscow cost him his career in the West and, for a while, the freedom of travel; it also subjected him and some of his fans to death threats. In 1956, while his passport was still revoked by the US State Department, he bravely faced down the interrogators at the House Un-American Activities Committee (HUAC). And he refused to denounce Stalin, even after the revelations of the tyrant's crimes had been presented to the Twentieth Party Congress by the then Soviet leader, Nikita Khrushchev.[16] For Robeson, like for a number of his black contemporaries, the Soviet Union would remain the only place in the world where he 'felt not like a Negro but a human being'. In the Soviet Union, he insisted, 'for the first time in my life, I walk in full human dignity'.[17]

Some two decades later, another prominent black American human rights activist, Angela Davis, would follow in Paul Robeson's steps and develop a huge and passionate following in the Soviet Union. As opposed to Paul Robeson (who never admitted to a membership in the Communist Party), Angela Davis was indeed a proud and card-carrying Communist and an even bigger global celebrity than Robeson, due to her famous trial and the massive international campaign waged on her behalf by the socialist states. Similarly to Robeson, Angela Davis emphasised the centrality of the Soviet Union to the eventual success of the co-joined projects of anti-racism and anti-colonialism. Similarly to Robeson, she refused to criticise Moscow and its allies for their own human rights violations.[18] For Davis, just like for Robeson before her, Soviet flaws and missteps were not to distract from the overarching goal of racial and economic justice. 'Your solidarity campaign and the actions of the Soviet public in support of the movement of black Americans answer the spirit of internationalism', Davis stated on her triumphant arrival in Moscow in the aftermath of the dramatic 1972 acquittal.

'Without the support of the Soviet Union, it would be incomparably more difficult for us to wage the struggle for social progress.'[19]

In the political biographies of such prominent ideological anti-racists as Paul Robeson and Angela Davis we can recognise the long-lasting import of the Red October on the global struggles against racism and colonialism. Another global manifestation of the Soviet Union's engagement with these issues can be found in Moscow's reach-out efforts in Africa. Following the end of the Second World War, and on the heels of African decolonisation, Moscow began to pay closer attention to the continent that it had previously written off as the preserve of vested Western interests. In the early years of the Cold War, the Soviets, while constantly agitating against colonialism, usually took a somewhat dim view of Africa's prospects for a successful transition to self-governance and socialism. This wariness of Africa was born out of Stalin's general suspicion of political movements of ethnic or racial particularism, which Soviet propagandists routinely labelled as bourgeois. Soviet political commentators, whose commentary invariably reflected the official party line, remained largely unfriendly to both black nationalism and Pan-Africanism.[20] But this ideological rigidity would not survive Stalin's rule. Stalin's successor, Nikita Khrushchev, took a far more optimistic line when it came to the independent Africa's political emancipation and ties with the Soviet Union. On Khrushchev's watch, Moscow undertook several important initiatives aimed at promoting the academic study of Africa in the USSR. It sought to promote its own concept of modernisation in the rapidly decolonising Africa.[21] In part to better pursue these goals, it also founded a new university, specifically designed to cater to the needs of students from the developing world (Lumumba University) and began to offer generous educational scholarships to African students, who, by the beginning of the 1960s, had started to arrive in the country in significant numbers.[22]

It was the presence of this new contingent of non-white foreigners in the midst of the Soviet society (and not necessarily the state-sponsored celebrations of such black luminaries as Paul Robeson or Angela Davis) that likely had the most profound impact on the ways in which Soviet society interacted with blackness and the issues related to racial liberation. Thousands of African students enrolled at various educational institutions in the Soviet Union often proved to be more effective communicators and symbols of blackness and the struggle for racial equality than the most skilful of the Soviet propagandists. These young Africans not only partook of the Soviet largess, but also acted as inadvertent educators of their Soviet peers, whom they introduced to political ideologies and cultural sensibilities largely absent from the officially sanctioned discourses in the Soviet Union.[23] In a strange historical about-face, the very individuals who had been expected to draw inspiration and learn from the Soviet example began, on occasion, to function as the agents of change and modernity within an insular society.[24] The Black Atlantic that Paul Gilroy identified as a modernising force within the former colonial metropoles, found its way across the Iron Curtain, where its agents and messengers performed a similar function of modernisation and cultural and political subversion.[25]

And here lies one of the most remarkable features of the twentieth-century encounter between the emancipatory pathos and anti-racist visions of the Red October and the aspirations towards freedom and autonomy so powerfully articulated by the global citizens of the Black Atlantic. The Soviet Union undoubtedly served as an inspiration to many black intellectuals and radical anti-colonial activists pursuing racial liberation and independence. Yet the encounter was far from being a 'one-way street'. The Soviets were to learn that their own visions of modernity had to pass the tests of local particularisms, black nationalism, and Pan-Africanism. Conversely, for the globe-trotting activists, particularists, and cosmopolitans of the Black Atlantic, the Red October presented a model of emancipation and development, whose utility was to be explored, evaluated, tested, and, if necessary, challenged.

Notes

1 See Claude McKay, *A Long Way from Home* (New York: L. Furman, 1937), 132.
2 W.E.B. Du Bois, 'Russia, 1926', *Crisis*, 33:1 (November 1926), 8.
3 Langston Hughes, *I Wonder as I Wander: An Autobiographical Journey* (New York: Hill and Wang, 1964); Langston Hughes, *A Negro Looks at Soviet Central Asia* (Moscow: Co-operative Publishing Society of Foreign Workers, 1934).
4 'Lynchings Food for Soviets', *Chicago Defender*, 4 October 1930, 13.
5 See Meredith L. Roman, *Opposing Jim Crow: African Americans and the Soviet Indictment of US Racism, 1928–1937* (Lincoln, NE: University of Nebraska Press, 2012).
6 Dale Peterson, *Up from Bondage: The Literatures of Russian and African American Soul* (Durham, NC: Duke University Press, 2000).
7 See, for example, Nathaniel Knight, 'Geography, Race and the Malleability of Man: Karl von Baer and the Problem of Academic Particularism in the Russian Human Sciences', *Centaurus: An International Journal of the History of Science and its Cultural Aspects*, 59:1–2 (2017), 97–121.
8 John MacKay, *True Songs of Freedom: Uncle Tom's Cabin in Russian Culture and Society* (Madison, WI: University of Wisconsin Press, 2013); Vladimir Alexandrov, *The Black Russian* (New York: Grove Press, 2014).

9 Claude McKay, 'Soviet Russia and the Negro, Part 1', *Crisis*, 27:2 (1923), 61–65; Claude McKay, 'Soviet Russia and the Negro, Part 2', *Crisis*, 27:3 (1924), 114–118.

10 Harry Haywood, *Black Bolshevik: Autobiography of an Afro-American Communist* (Chicago, IL: Liberator Press, 1978); William L. Patterson, *The Man Who Cried Genocide: An Autobiography*, 1st edn (New York: International Publishers, 1971); Robert Robinson and Jonathan Slevin, *Black on Red: A Black American's 44 Years inside the Soviet Union* (Washington, DC: Acropolis Books, 1988); Maxim Matusevich, '"Harlem Globe-Trotters": Black Sojourners in Stalin's Soviet Union' in Jeffrey Ogbar (ed.), *Harlem Renaissance Revisited: Politics, Arts, and Letters* (Baltimore, MD: Johns Hopkins University Press, 2010), 211–44; Maxim Matusevich, 'Blackness the Color of Red: Negotiating Race at the US Legation in Riga, Latvia, 1922–33', *Journal of Contemporary History*, 52:4 (2017), 832–52.

11 J.V. Stalin, 'On the Final Victory of Socialism in the USSR', 18 January–12 February 1938, Marxist Internet Archive: www.marxists.org/reference/archive/stalin/works/1938/01/18.htm [accessed on 20 June 2020].

12 Harvey Klehr, John Earl Haynes and Kyrill M. Anderson (eds), 'Document 65: Death Certificate for Lovett Fort-Whiteman, 13 January 1939' in Harvey Klehr, John Earl Haynes and Kyrill M. Anderson (eds), *The Soviet World of American Communism* (New Haven, CT: Yale University Press, 1998), 225; Sean Guillory, 'The Reddest of the Blacks', SRB Podcast: https://srbpodcast.org/2019/05/21/the-reddest-of-the-blacks/ [accessed 21 May 2019]; Dick Reavis, 'The Life and Death of Lovett Fort-Whiteman, the Communist Party's First African American Member', *Jacobin*, 7 April 2020: https://jacobinmag.com/2020/4/lovett-fort-whiteman-black-communist-party [accessed 10 February 2021].

13 George Padmore, *Pan-Africanism or Communism?* (London: Dennis Dobson, 1956).

14 'Editorial: The Great Betrayal', *Crisis*, 46:10 (1939), 305.

15 Jean-Christophe Cloutier, 'Amiable with Big Teeth: The Case of Claude McKay's Last Novel', *Modernism/Modernity*, 20:3 (2013), 557–576.

16 Paul Robeson, 'Сердечный Привет Советскому Народу!' ['Heartfelt Greetings to the Soviet People'], *Pravda*, 1 January 1957.

17 Paul Robeson, quoted in Martin Bauml Duberman, *Paul Robeson* (New York: Alfred A. Knopf, 1988), 190.

18 Meredith L. Roman, 'Soviet "Renegades", Black Panthers, and Angela Davis: The Politics of Dissent in the Soviet Press, 1968–73', *Cold War History*, 18:4 (2018), 503–519.

19 'Angela Cites Red Backing of Blacks', *Chicago Defender*, 30 August 1972, 3.

20 A.B. Davidson (ed.), *The Formative Years of African Studies in Russia* (Moscow: RAN, 2003); Apollon Davidson and Irina Filatova, 'African History: A View from Behind the Kremlin Wall' in Maxim Matusevich (ed.), *Africa in Russia, Russia in Africa: Three Centuries of Encounters* (Trenton, NJ: Africa World Press, 2006), 111–131.

21 S.V. Mazov, *A Distant Front in the Cold War: The USSR in West Africa and the Congo, 1956–1964* (Washington, DC, Stanford, CA: Woodrow Wilson Center Press, Stanford University Press, 2010).

22 S.V. Mazov, 'Sozdanie Instituta Afriki [The Creation of the Africa Institute]', *Vostok*, 1 (1998), 80–88; S.V. Mazov, 'Afrikanskie Studenty v Moskve v God Afriki [African Students in Moscow in the Year of Africa]', *Vostok*, 3 (June 1999), 91–93.

23 Maxim Matusevich, 'Expanding the Boundaries of the Black Atlantic: African Students as Soviet Moderns', *Ab Imperio*, 2 (2012), 325–350.

24 Constantine Katsakioris, 'Burden or Allies?: Third World Students and Internationalist Duty through Soviet Eyes', *Kritika*, 18:3 (2017), 539–567; Rossen Djagalov and Christine Evans, 'Moscow, ca. 1960: Imagining a Soviet-Third-World Friendship' in Andreas Hilger (ed.), *Soviet Union and the Third World: USSR, State Socialism, and Anticolonialism during the Cold War* (Munich: Oldenborg Verlag, 2009), 83–107.

25 Matusevich, 'Expanding the Boundaries of the Black Atlantic'.

Index

CPSIA information can be obtained
at www.ICGtesting.com
Printed in the USA
JSHW062309140323
38937JS00003BA/27